*The Art of Fiction
in the Heart
of Dixie*

AN ANTHOLOGY
OF ALABAMA WRITERS

The Art of Fiction
in the Heart
of Dixie

EDITED BY
PHILIP D. BEIDLER

THE UNIVERSITY OF ALABAMA PRESS

Library of Congress Cataloging-in-Publication Data

The Art of Fiction in the Heart of Dixie

   1. American fiction—Alabama.   2. Short stories,
American—Alabama.   3. Alabama—Fiction.
I. Beidler, Philip D.
PS558.A5A57   1986   810'.8'09761   86-6919
ISBN 0-8173-0313-8
   0-8173-0314-6 (pbk)

To the people of Alabama

Contents

Contents

Acknowledgments

ONE of the many lessons this project has taught me is that Huck Finn was right: it is a lot of trouble "to make a book." Like Huck, I certainly knew that was so about writing a book. I now also know it is true about assembling and editing one. Fortunately, there were a lot of good people around to offer help, including several of the authors themselves. I am particularly grateful to Shirley Ann Grau, Cecil Dawkins, Elise Sanguinetti, and William Cobb, who personally helped me to secure permission to reprint their work. Thanks also to a research assistant, Kelly Dobyns, who was largely responsible for assembling and drafting out biographical sketches appended at the conclusion.

Two debts in particular extend far beyond a paragraph or a page. They are to my distinguished colleague, Dr. O. B. Emerson, who generously shared with me his rich and deep knowledge of Alabama literature, and to Malcolm M. MacDonald, Director of The University of Alabama Press, who has been an indefatigable guiding spirit for this project from start to finish. It will be, I hope, some small form of repayment to these two good men if this has turned out to be a book they can be proud of.

Grateful acknowledgment is also made to: The University of North Carolina Press, for Chapters IV and V from *Adventures of Captain Simon Suggs, Late of the Tallapoosa Volunteers* by Johnson Jones Hooper, with an Introduction by Manly Wade Wellman. © 1969 by The University of North Carolina Press. Reprinted by permission of the publisher; *Harper's* Magazine, for "'Lijah," by Edgar Valentine Smith, Copyright © 1924 by *Harper's* Magazine. All rights reserved. Reprinted from the August 1924 issue by special permission. Copyright © renewed by *Harper's* Magazine; Harold Ober Associates, for "Miss Ella," by Zelda Sayre Fitzgerald. Reprinted by permission of

Editor's Preface

THIS volume comprises works of fiction written about Alabama from the 1840s to the present by authors who either were native-born or have revealed some distinct affiliation with the state. Each is part of a vital legacy of culture. To read any selection is to feel one's self in the presence of nothing less than the whole of a world. Always there is the sense of knowing the piece in relation to the pattern, of coming into touch with a rich complex of association born at once of memory, experience, and collective imagining. In making various editorial decisions, it is this sense of relationship I have tried to keep in mind.

Detailed commentary on the various texts will be deferred to the introductory essays for the book's five sections. (Brief biographical sketches of individual authors appear at the conclusion.) Here I wish simply to add a brief outline of my rationale for selection and organization.

The book embraces a broad chronology. It begins with selections from various Southwestern Humorists of the mid-1800s and continues with writers of the Civil War era and the decades of Reconstruction. It then goes on to deal with the two generations of Alabama writers—the term "generation" is an approximate but serviceable one—who established themselves between the turn of the century and the 1960s, the first mainly in the 1920s and early 1930s, and the second from the mid-1930s onward. In a final section, there are some excerpts from recent publications by well-known authors of the contemporary era.

There has also been an attempt to include a mixture of selections written from various historical perspectives. While many of the stories or extracts are about people and events contemporary with the lives of their authors or the periods of their composition, others are conscious efforts to recover visions of a rich and colorful past. Taken together, they commit to our collective literary record a whole apparatus of culture—of value and belief, of custom, usage, tradition, and observance.

I have also tried to do justice to the complex possibilities of the Alabamian's sense of place. The settings of works in the volume have been chosen to include a wide variety of the identifiable regions of the state: the Black Belt, the hill country of the north and west, the Tennessee Valley, the fertile plains of the south and east. There is the wiregrass, the pine wood, the red clay border region, the coastal lowlands.

Most of all, I have tried to keep faith with the people. They are here, I hope, in at least some adequate measure of their variousness and complexity. The characters in these stories are white, black, red; they are rich and poor, urban and rural, genteel and rough-hewn; they are elect and unregenerate, humble and proud, pious and profane. They are the people of Alabama; and to them, this book is dedicated.

*The Art of Fiction
in the Heart
of Dixie*

Introduction

I. *The Old Southwest*

S OME other, more colorful titles for this section might include "Flush Times and Fast Characters," or, perhaps simply, "A Gallery of Rapscallions." The earliest Alabama fiction comes from the quarter century before the Civil War when the state, still bearing the stamp of its origins as a rumbustious frontier territory, lay at the center of the region we have now come to know as the Old Southwest. The distinguishing feature of life there is to this day captured entire in the credo of one of its most famous fictional inhabitants, Captain Simon Suggs. "It is good," Suggs warned, "to be shifty in a new country." Here was a time and place in which living by one's wits seems to have been not only a virtue but a necessity.

And live by all means they did, the denizens of the Old Southwest, if at times anxiously and even perilously, also joyously and fully. Early Alabama fiction carries the flavor of this life in all its earthy immediacy. We feel the hubbub and bustle in the dirt streets of Tuscaloosa during its days as a backwoods capital; we experience the hot, roiling tumult of the camp meeting; we breathe the crowded air of the inn and boarding house, full of wash and cookery and clamor. One meets lawyers, storekeepers, gamblers, drinkers, con-artists and their ill-fortuned victims. There are deft pretenders to wealth and social rank; legislators whose integrity is strictly cash-on-the-barrel-head; devotees of the practical joke, bending their talents endlessly toward new arts of exquisite complication.

Beyond its great value and entertainment and social documentary, however, early Alabama fiction can also lay claim to considerable literary importance. Indeed, as revealed by the selections here— several of them quite familiar to students of American thought and writing—it contains some of the most accomplished examples of perhaps the only truly indigenous fictional form American literature has produced, the genre called Southwestern Humor that cultural historians now see as standing at the origins of a native tradition of realism. It is a tradition that nurtured such diverse figures as Twain, Howells, and James, as well as inheritors such as Hemingway, Fitzgerald, Faulkner, and Gertrude Stein; and in the particular line of evolution extending through Twain and Faulkner, it has also produced that distinctive Southern strain evident in the work of such modern and contemporary figures as Flannery O'Connor, Truman Capote, William Styron, Carson McCullers, Eudora Welty, Harper Lee, and Barry Hannah.

The major forms and conventions of Southwestern Humor manifest themselves in early Alabama fiction in full relief. The chief characters are invariably in transit from one place to another or gathered at some place of local commerce or entertainment. In the familiar rhythm of the picaresque, they are on the road of life in all its gross, teeming plenitude. Like the classic hero of the genre, they learn quickly, again to quote Johnson J. Hooper's incorrigible Simon Suggs, "all the arts by which men 'get along' in the world."

The picaro becomes the confidence-man, his life itself an unending trail of linked chicaneries. Aboard a stagecoach to Tuscaloosa, Suggs, taken by a slippery applicant for a bank charter to be the "representative from Tallapoosa," decides to play the role and find out what, as usual, may be in it for him. In this case it is a bribe, investment capital that Suggs coolly pockets as part of his stake when he goes to do battle with the Faro machine. Shortly, however, the new scheme comes to naught. Simon matches wits with the "Tiger" and loses all. Still, no matter. Even as he is bankrupted at the tables, the Captain already busies himself with the attempt to profit from a new case of mistaken identity. Seizing on an overheard conversation, he assumes the role of a visiting tycoon pig-farmer and gulls that worthy's hapless nephew into supplying not only a new stake but also an immense oyster and champagne dinner for himself and all his roistering companions.

In Baldwin's "Samuel Hele, Esq.," there is another kind of con, its mark this time a Yankee schoolmistress. She, with all her meddlesome, moralistic, Northern ways, has proved "a bundle of prejudices—stiff, literal, positive, inquisitive, inquisitorial, and biliously pious. *Dooty,* as she called it, was a great word with her. Conscience was another." Clearly she must go, and it is the titular hero, the acid, dyspeptic town lawyer, who is dispatched by his unregenerate drinking companions to vanquish her from the precincts once and for all. This he does by painting himself and his fellows as a thieving, drinking, blaspheming, murdering rabble altogether beyond even the hope of redemption. On the delicate subject of slavery, he is particularly graphic. They torture and murder their blacks on a whim; they sell slave babies in baskets by the dozens; if they can't spare an occasional victim, for the sake of authority, to be hanged as an example, they paint an Indian and use him instead. In the case of more immediate matters, they also seem to have a similarly lurid history with Yankee schoolmistresses. As may be suspected, the lady is shortly put to rout, bag and baggage. Yet as with Ichabod Crane in the "Legend of Sleepy Hollow," which this story somewhat resembles, there is also a postscript that makes one finally wonder who has bested whom. Sam claims credit for a victory; but the school principal has complicating information. A good deal of money has changed hands as a consequence of the departure, much of which Miss Charity happily asserts she will put at interest and enjoy through a lifetime's worth of profit. As with Irving, then, so with Baldwin: the easygoing backwoods gentry has had its joke; meanwhile the progressive Yankee has made adversity a source of practical power. The story is desperately doublesided; and for Baldwin's South, especially, it would of course soon be re-imaged in an actual lesson of power which that old, laughing world itself would not survive.

In Barr's "The Widow Dudu," there is more inspired trickery in the form of a running contest between two leading lights of the provincial gentry. John Bealle, thanks to some elaborate prior misrepresentation by his friend John Smith of Mobile, spends a night of impromptu confinement in a country inn visited often by both men, harassed and exasperated by a train of petty tortures inflicted on him by the well-meaning widow and her industrious servants. They have been convinced, it turns out, during Smith's visit of two weeks earlier, that Bealle has become disposed to sudden fits of insanity. The fits are normally induced, Smith has told them, by contact with items such as coffee, milk, butter, eggs, cotton sheets, pillowcases, towels, "&c." Having now spent his night doing without down to the last "&c.," and having now found out the occasion of his travails, Bealle ends the story swearing revenge; and one does not doubt that he will get it. Here, one good prank is always worth another. In this world, one must always give at least as well as one gets. The most precious of all virtues, to cite Suggs one last time, is "mother wit," and life in the Old Southwest an endless education in how to use it.

Indeed, as is shown in Barr's story and in many other classics not included here—Hooper's "The Captain Attends a Camp Meeting," for instance, or Baldwin's "Ovid Bolus, Esq."—this kind of comic exercise, depending on its success, seems often in large part to have become the measure of its own justification. Profit or self-promotion notwithstanding, at issue in many cases seems mainly just the satisfaction of a creative and worthy joke well played. Here one senses, as in the works of other humorists such as George Washington Harris, Augustus Baldwin Longstreet, and Thomas Bangs Thorpe, as well as in those of later figures such as Artemus Ward, Josh Billings, Petroleum V. Nasby, and—the master—Mark Twain, that on a rough-and-tumble frontier, a good laugh may have been in itself one of the most precious of all achievements.

Fighting the "Tiger" and Other Speculations

Johnson Jones Hooper

I

SIMON STARTS FORTH TO FIGHT THE "TIGER," AND FALLS IN WITH
A CANDIDATE WHOM HE "DOES" TO A CRACKLIN'.

R EADER! didst ever encounter the Tiger?—not the bounding creature of the woods, with deadly fang and mutilating claw, that preys upon blood and muscle—but the stealthier and more ferocious animal which ranges amid "the busy haunts of men"— which feeds upon coin and bank-notes—whose spots, more attractive than those of its namesake of the forest, dazzle and lure, like the brilliantly varying hues of the charmer snake, the more intensely and irresistibly, the longer they are looked upon—the thing, in short, of pasteboard and ivory, mother-of-pearl and mahogany—THE FARO BANK!

Take a look at the elegant man dealing out the cards, from that *bijou* of a box, there. Observe with what graceful dexterity he manages all the appliances of his art! The cards seem to leap forth rather in obedience to his will, than to be pulled out by his fingers. As he throws them in alternate piles, note the whiteness and symmetry of his hand, the snowy spotlessness of the linen exposed by the turn-up of his coat-cuff, and the lustre of the gem upon his little finger. Now look in his face. Isn't he a handsome fellow—a man to make hearts feminine ache? And how singularly at variance with the exciting nature of his occupation, is the expression of his countenance! How placid! He has hundreds depending upon the turn of the next card, and yet his face is entirely calm, if you except a very slight twitching of the eye-lids, which are so nearly closed that the long lashes nearly intermingle. A pretty, gentlemanly Tiger-keeper, in sooth! He smiles now—mark the beauty of that large mouth, and the dazzling splendour of those teeth!—as he addresses the florid and flushed young man, there at the table, whose last dollar he has just swept from the board. "The bank is singularly fortunate to-night. Nothing but the best sort of luck could have saved it from the skilful combination with which you attacked. Ninety-nine times out of a hundred you would have broken it—I've had an escape." Spite of his ruinous losses, the poor devil is flattered by the compliment. Oh ass! of skull most impenetrable! To-day you are, or rather you were, on your way to college, with the first year's expenses—the close parings of the comforts of the old widow your mother, and the thin, blue-eyed girl your sister—in your pocket. This day twelvemonth, you will keep the scores of a gambling house and live upon the perquisites! See if you don't! The Tiger has cheated the professors, and you have cheated your family and—yourself!

Almost every man has his idiosyncrasy—his pet and peculiar opinion on some particular subject. Captain Simon Suggs has his; and he clings to it with a pertinacity that defies, alike the suggestions of reason, and the demonstrations of experience. Simon believes that he CAN WHIP THE TIGER, A FAIR FIGHT. He *has* always believed it; he *will* always believe it. The idea has obtained a lodgment in his cranium and peremptorily refuses to be ejected! It is the weak point—the *Achilles' heel,* as one might say—of his character. Remind him of the time, in Montgomery, when by a bite of this same Tiger, he lost his money and horse, and was compelled to trudge home afoot! ah, but *then,* he "hadn't got the hang of the game." Bring to his recollection how severely it scratched him in Girard!—oh, but "*that* fellow rung in a two-card box" upon him. Ask him if he did'nt drop a couple of hundreds at the Big Council? Certainly—but *then* he was "drinky and played careless;" and so on to the end.—Still he inflexibly believes he is to get the upper hand of the Tiger, some day when it is exceedingly fat, and wear its hide as a trophy! Still the invincible beast lacerates him instead! Such is the infatuation of Captain Suggs.

Acting under this delusion Simon determined, as soon as he obtained the money by the "land transaction" recorded in our last, to visit the city of Tuscaloosa, where the Legislature was to commence its session in a few days, with the double object of "weeding out" members, and making a grand demonstration against some bank. His "pile," to be sure, considering how extensive were the operations contemplated, was certainly small—inadequate. But as Simon remarked, upon setting out, "there is no telling which way luck or a half-broke steer will run." So perhaps the amount of his capital was really not a matter of any great consequence. He carried a hundred and fifty dollars with him; the results might not have been different, had he carried a thousand and fifty—who shall say?

The Captain—would that we could avoid the anachronism we commit every time we apply the military designation of Simon, in speaking of events which occurred anterior to the year of grace 1836;—however, let it go—the Captain left his horse at a farm-house near Montgomery, and took the mail-coach for the capital. The only other passenger was a gentleman who was about to visit the seat of government, with the intention of making himself a bank director, as speedily as possible. The individual assumed, and insisted on believing, that Simon was the member from Tallapoosa. This, of course Simon denied—but denied "in such a sort!"——

"I should be highly pleased, sir, if you could make it consistent with your views of the public good, to receive your support for that directorship, sir"—quoth the candidate.

"What keen people you candidates are, to find out folks," said Simon. "But mind, I haint said yet I was a member. I told wife when I started, I warn't goin' to tell nobod——hello! I liked to a ketcht myself—didn't I?" said Simon, winking pleasantly at the embryo director.

"Ah, you're a close, prudent fellow, I see," said the candidate; "I like prudence, sir, in public officers, sir! It's the bulwark, sir, to hang the anchor of the state upon, to speak nautically, sir. But as I was remarking, if duty to the state, to the country, and to the institution itself, would permit, I would be profoundly grate——."

"Yes"—interrupted Suggs—"prudence is the stob I fasten the grape-vine of *my* cunnoo to. I said I wouldn't tell it—nor I won't."

"The present directory, sir, or at least a portion of it, sir, does not display that zeal, sir, in the service of the public—that promptitude, sir, and that spirit of accommodation—which the community has a right to expect, sir. Though, perhaps, I oughtn't, on account of the delicacy of my position, to make invidious remarks, sir—and sir, I make it a point never to do so—still, I may be permitted to say, that should the legislature honor *me* with their confidence, sir, I shall— that is to say, sir, a very different state of affairs may be anticipated. The institution, sir, should command the whole of my intellectual energies and faculties, sir. The institution, sir——."

"To be sure! to be sure! I onderstand," said Simon. "The institution's what we're all after. As for the present directory, they're all a pack of d——d swell-heads. Afore I left Montgomery I went to one on 'em, and told him who I was, and let on that I wanted a few dollars to pay expenses down. He knowed, in course, I'd soon be gittin' four—— hello! I'm about to ketch myself agin!"—and Simon laughed, and winked at his companion.

"Four dollars *per diem,* besides mileage," said the candidate with a witching smile.

"Never mind about that, I say nothin' myself—other people can say what they please. Any how, that feller wouldn't let me have a dollar!"

"What ungentlemanly conduct!" remarked the financier, energetically."

"D——d if he would—not a dollar—without I'd pledge myself to support him. *That* sir, I scorned to do," continued Simon, half rising from his seat, and swelling with indignation; "so I told him I'd see him as deep in h–ll as a pigeon could fly in a fortnight, first————"

"A very proper reply, sir—a very spirited reply, sir—just such a one, sir, as a man of high moral principle, refined feelings, pure patrio————"

"Oh, I gin him thunder and lightnin' stewed down to a strong pison, I tell you. I cussed him up one side and down tother, twell thar warn't the bigness of your thumb nail, that warn't *properly* cussed. And in the windin' up, I told him I'd pay my stage fare as fur towards Tuskalusy as my money hilt out, and walk the rest of the way, I would—but I'll show him," added the captain with a savage frown.

"Magnanimous, sir! that was magnanimous! A great moral spectacle, sir! You cursing the director, sir—withering him up with virtuous indignation—threatening to walk eighty miles, sir, over very inferior roads, to discharge your public functions—he cowering, as doubtless he did, before the representative of the people! Yes, sir, it was a sublime moral spectacle, worthy of a comparison with any recorded specimens of Roman or Spartan magnanimity, sir. How nobly did it vindicate the purity of the representative character, sir!"

"Belikes it did"—said the Captain—"shouldn't be surprised. There *was* smartly of a row betwixt us, certin. We did'nt make quite as much noise as a panter and a pack of hounds, but we made *some*. When we blowd off, I judge he had the wust of it: he looked like he had, any how."

"No doubt of it, sir; no doubt at all, sir. And now, my dear sir, if you will permit me to indicate what would have been *my* deportment upon such an occasion, I trust I can make you comprehend the difference between the conduct of an insolent official, and that of the high-bred, gentlemanly, public functionary!"

Captain Suggs gesticulated his willingness to listen; felicitating himself the while, upon the fact that Mr. Smith, his county member, would not be along for several days. The chances were altogether favourable for making a "raise," without fear of *immediate* detection— which is all the Captain ever cared for. So he isn't taken red-handed, after-claps may go to the devil!

"Why, sir," resumed the candidate, after taking a sly peep at a printed list, to get the name of the member from Tallapoosa—"why, sir, if you had approached *me* as you did the individual of whom we have been speaking; I occupying—you understand, sir—the important fiscal station of bank director, and you the highly honorable official position which you do occupy, of representative of the respectable county of Talla—"

"Stop! I never said my name was Smith; nor I never set myself up for a legislatur man! You heerd me tell the driver when I got up, not to tell the people who I was and whar I was goin'!"

"Oh, *we* understand all that, my dear sir, perfectly—perfectly!" said the candidate, with a smile of humorous intelligence.—"There are many reasons why gentlemen of distinction should at times desire to travel without being known."

"*I'll* be d——d if thar ain't!" thought Captain Simon Suggs.

"But my dear sir, there are persons so skilled in human nature, so acute in their perceptions of worth and talent, that they detect at a glance those whom the people have honored. You can't pass us my dear sir!—ha! ha! Oh no! We recognize you at once! However, as I was going on to remark—had you approached me under the circumstances stated, I should have said to you—Colonel Smith, your election by the enlightened people of the important county you represent, is ample guaranty to *me,* that you are a gentleman of the nicest honor, and the most unimpeachable veracity, even if the fact were not conclusively attested by your personal appearance. The sum you need, my dear Colonel, for expenses, is of course too small to justify a discount. Will you oblige me by drawing for the requisite amount on my private funds?—that's what *I*, sir, should have said, sir, under the circumstances."

"By the Lord, stranger," remarked the Captain, seizing the candidate's hand and shaking it repeatedly with great warmth, to all appearance as completely overwhelmed with gratitude for the supposititious loan, as he could possibly have been had it been real—"by the Lord, that *would* a-been the way! I'd a'stuck to a feller that done *that* way, twell the cows come home—I'd cut the big vein of my neck before I'd *ever* desert sich a friend! I'd wade to my ears in blood, to fight by *that* man's side; d——d if I wouldn't."

"Perhaps," said the candidate, "it isn't too late *yet,* to offer you a trifling accommodation of the sort?"

"No, it aint too late at all," answered Simon with admirable *naiveté;* "I could take a twenty, to right smart advantage yet!"

The office-seeker's pocket book was out in a twinkling, and a bank note transferred therefrom to Suggs' vest pocket.

"Of course, without the slightest reference to this little transaction, my dear Colonel, I count on your help."

"Give us your hand," said Suggs between his sobs—for the disinterested generosity of his companion had moved him to weeping—and they shook hands with great cordiality.

"You'll use your influence with your senator and other friends?"

"Look me in the eye!" replied the Captain with an almost tragic air.

The candidate looked steadily, for two seconds, in Simon's tearful eye.

"You see *honesty* thar—don't you?"

"I do! I do!" said the candidate with emotion.

"That's sufficient, aint it?"

"Most amply sufficient—most amply sufficient, my dear Colonel"—and then they shook hands again, and took a drink from the tickler which the financier carried in his carpet bag.

Suggs and his new friend travelled the remainder of the way to Tuskaloosa, in excellent companionship, as it was reasonable they should. They told their tales, sang their songs, and drank their liquor like a jovial pair as they were—the candidate paying all scores wherever they halted. And so things went pleasantly with Simon until his meeting with the tiger, which ensued immediately upon his arrival, and whereof we defer a description to the succeeding chapter.

II

SIMON FIGHTS "THE TIGER" AND GETS WHIPPED—BUT COMES OUT
NOT MUCH THE "WORSE FOR WEAR."

As a matter of course, the first thing that engaged the attention of Captain Suggs upon his arrival in Tuskaloosa, was his proposed attack upon his enemy. Indeed, he scarcely allowed himself time to bolt, without mastication, the excellent supper served to him at Duffie's, ere he outsallied to engage the adversary. In the street, he suffered not himself to be beguiled into a moment's loitering, even by the strange sights which under other circumstances would certainly have enchained his attention. The windows of the great drug store cast forth their blaze of varied light in vain; the music of a fine amateur band preparing for a serenade, was no music for him; he paused not in front of the bookseller's, to inspect the prints, or the huge-lettered advertising cards. In short, so eager was he to give battle to the "Tiger," that the voice of the ring-master, as it came distinctly into the street from the circus—the sharp joke of the clown, and the perfectly-shadowed figures of "Dandy Jack" and the other performers, whisking rapidly round upon the canvass—failed to shake, in the slightest degree, the resolute determination of the courageous and indomitable Captain.

As he hurried along, however, with the long stride of the back-woods, hardly turning his head, and to all appearance, oblivious altogether of things external, he held occasional "confabs" with him-self in regard to the unusual objects which surrounded him—for Suggs is an observant man, and notes with much accuracy whatever comes before him, all the while a body would suppose him to be asleep, or in a "turkey dream" at least. On the present occasion his communings with himself commenced opposite the window of the drug-store,—"Well, thar's the most deffrunt sperrets in *that grocery* ever *I* seed! Thar's koniac, and old peach, and rectified, and lots I can't tell thar names! That light-yaller bottle tho', in the corner thar, that's Tenness*ee!* I'd know that *any whar!* And that tother bottle's rot-gut, ef I know myself—bit a drink, I reckon, as well's the rest! What a power o' likker they do keep in this here town; ef I warn't goin' to run agin the bank, I'd sample some of it, too, I reether expect. But it don't do for a man to sperrets much when he's pursuin' the beast—"

"H——ll and scissors! who ever seed the like of the books! Aint thar a pile! Do wonder what sort of a office them fellers in thar keeps, makes 'em want so many! They don't read 'em *all,* I judge! Well, mother-wit kin beat book-larnin, at *any* game! Thar's 'squire Had-enskelt up home, he's got two cart-loads of law books—tho' that's no tech to this feller's—and here's what knocked a fifty outen him once, at short cards, afore a right smart, active sheep could flop his tail *ary* time; and kin do it agin, whenever he gits over his shyness! Human natur' and the human family is *my* books, and I've never seed many but what I could hold my own with. Let me git one o' these book-larnt fellers over a bottle of "old corn," and a handful of the dokkyments, and I'm d——d apt to git what he knows, and in a ginral way gives *him* a wrinkle into the bargain! Books aint fitten for nothin' but jist to give to childen goin' to school, to keep 'em outen mischief. As old Jed'diah used to say, book-larnin spiles a man ef he's got mother-wit, and ef he aint got that, it don't do him no good—"

"Hello agin! Here's a sirkis, and ef I warnt in a hurry, right here I'd drop a quarter, providin' I couldn't fix it to slip in for nothin', which is always the cheapest in a ginral way!"

Thus ruminating, Simon at length reached CLARE'S. Passing into the bar-room, he stood a moment, looking around to ascertain the direction in which he should proceed to find the faro banks, which he had heard were nightly exhibited there. In a corner of the room he discovered a stair-way, above which was burning a lurid-red lamp. Waiting for no other indication, he strode up the stairs. At the landing-place above he found a door which was closed and locked, but light came through the key-hole, and the sharp rattling of dice and jingling of coin, spoke conclusively of the employment of the occupants of the room.

Simon knocked.

"Hello!" said somebody within.

"Hello yourself!" said the Captain.

"What do you want?" said the voice from the room.

"A game," was the Captain's laconic answer.

"What's the name?" again inquired the person within.

"Cash," said Simon.

"He'll do," said another person in the room; "let 'Cash' in."

The door was opened and Simon entered, half-blinded by the sudden burst of light which streamed from the chandeliers and lamps, and was reflected in every direction by the mirrors which almost walled the room. In the centre of the room was a small but unique "bar," the counter of which, except a small space occupied by a sliding door at which customers were served, was enclosed with burnished brass rods. Within this "magic circle" stood a pock-marked clerk, who vended to the company wines and liquors too costly to be imbibed by any but men of fortune or gamesters, who, alternately rich and penniless, indulge every appetite without stint while they have the means; eating viands and drinking wines one day, which a prince might not disdain, to fast entirely the next, or make a disgusting meal from the dirty counter of a miserable eating-house. Disposed at regular intervals around the room, were tables for the various games usually played; all of them thronged with eager "customers," and covered with heavy piles of doubloons, and dollars, and bank notes. Of these tables the "tiger" claimed three—for faro was predominant in those days, when a cell in the penitentiary was not the penalty for exhibiting it. Most of the persons in the room were well-dressed, and a large proportion members of the legislature. There was very little noise, no loud swearing, but very deep playing.

As Simon entered, he made his rustic bow, and in an easy, familiar way, saluted the company with

"Good evenin' gentle*men!*"

No one seemed inclined to acknowledge, on behalf of the company, their pleasure at seeing Captain Suggs. Indeed, nobody appeared to notice him at all after the first half second. The Captain, therefore, repeated his salutation:

"*I say,* GOOD EVENIN', gentle*men!*"

Notwithstanding the emphasis with which the words were re-spoken, there was only a slight laugh from some of the company, and the Captain began to feel a little awkward standing up before so many strangers. While he was hesitating whether to begin business at once by walking up to one of the faro tables and commencing the "fight," he overheard a young man standing a few feet from him, say to another,

"Jim, isn't that your uncle, General Witherspoon, who has been expected here for several days with a large drove of hogs?"

"By Jupiter," said the person addressed, "I believe it is; though I'm not certain, as I haven't seen him since I was a little fellow. But what makes *you* think it's him: you never saw him?"

"No, but he suits the description given of your uncle, very well— white hair, red eyes, wide mouth, and so forth. Does your uncle gamble?"

"They say he does; but my mother, who is his sister, knows hardly any more about him than the rest of the world. We've only seen him once in fifteen years. I'll de d——d," he added, looking steadfastly at Simon, "if that isn't he! He's as rich as mud, and a jovial old cock of a bachelor, so I must claim kin with him."

Simon could, of course, have no reasonable objection to being believed to be General Thomas Witherspoon, the rich hog drover from Kentucky. Not he! The idea pleased him excessively, and he determined if he was not respected as General Witherspoon for the remainder of that evening, it should be "somebody else's fault," not his! In a few minutes, indeed, it was whispered through the company, that the red-eyed man with white hair, was the wealthy field-officer who drove swine to increase his fortune, and in consequence of this, Simon thought he discovered a very considerable improvement in the way of politeness, on the part of all present. The bare suspicion that he was rich, was sufficient to induce deference and attention.

Sauntering up to a faro bank with the intention of betting, while his money should hold out, with the spirit and liberality which General Witherspoon would have displayed had be been personally present, he called for

"Twenty, five-dollar checks, and that pretty toloble d——d quick!"

The dealer handed him the red checks, and he piled them upon the "ten."

"Grind on!" said Simon.

A card or two was dealt, and the keeper, with a profound bow, handed Simon twenty more red checks.

"Deal away," said Simon, heaping the additional checks on the same card.

Again the cards flew from the little box, and again Simon won.

Several persons were now over-looking the game; and among the rest, the young man who was so happy as to be the nephew of General Witherspoon.

"The old codger has nerve; I'll be d——d if he hasn't," said one.

"And money too," said another, "from the way he bets."

"To be sure he has," said a third; "that's the rich hog drover from Kentucky."

By this time Simon had won seven hundred dollars. But the Captain was not at all disposed to discontinue. "Now!" he thought was the "golden moment" in which to press his luck; "now!" the hour of the "tiger's" doom, when he should be completely flayed.

"That brings the fat in great fleeks as big as my arm!" observed the Captain, as he won the fifth consecutive bet: "it's hooray, brother John, every fire a turkey! as the boy said. Here goes again!" and he staked his winnings and the original stake on the Jack.

"Gracious heavens! General, I wouldn't stake so much on a single card," said a young man who was inclined to boot-lick any body suspected of having money.

"*You* wouldn't, young man," said the Captain, turning round and facing him, "bekase *you* never tote a pile of that size."

The obtrusive individual shrunk back under this rebuke, and the crowd voted Simon not only a man of spunk, but a man of wit.

At this moment the Jack won, and the Captain was better off, by fifteen hundred dollars, than when he entered the saloon.

"That's better—jist the least grain in the world better—than drivin' hogs from Kaintucky and sellin' 'em at four cents a pound!" triumphantly remarked Suggs.

The nephew of General Witherspoon was now confident that Captain Suggs was his uncle. He accordingly pushed up to him with—

"Don't you know me, uncle?" at the same time extending his hand.

Captain Suggs drew himself up with as much dignity as he supposed the individual whom he personated would have assumed, and remarked that he did *not* know the young man then in his immediate presence.

"Don't know me, uncle. Why, I'm James Peyton, your sister's son. She has been expecting you for several days;" said the much-humbled nephew of the hog drover.

"All very well, Mr. Jeemes Peyton, but as this little world of ourn is tolloble d——d full of rascally impostors; and gentle*men* of my— that is to say—you see—persons that have got somethin', is apt to be tuk in, it stands a man in hand to be a leetle perticler. So jist answer me a strait forrard question or two," said the Captain, subjecting Mr. Peyton to a test, which if applied to himself, would have blown him sky-high. But Simon was determined to place his own identity as General Witherspoon above suspicion, by seeming to suspect something wrong about Mr. James Peyton.

"Oh," said several of the crowd, "every body knows he's the widow Peyton's son, and your nephew, of course."

"Wait for the wagin, gentle*men*," said Simon; "*every body* has give me several sons, which, as I aint married, I don't want, and" added he with a very facetious wink and smile, "I don't care about takin' a nephy on the same terms without he's giniwine."

"Oh, he's genuine," said several at once.

"Hold on, gentle*men;* this young man might want to borrow money of me—"

Mr. Peyton protested against any such supposition.

"Oh, well!" said the Captain, "*I* might want to borrow of *you,* and—"

Mr. Peyton signified his willingness to lend his uncle the last dollar in his pocket book.

"Very good! very good! but *I* happen to be a little *notion*y about sich matters. It aint every man I'd borrer from. Before I handle a man's money in the way of borrerin, in the fust place I must know him to be a gentleman; in the second place, he must be my friend; and in the third place, I must think he's both able and willin' to afford the accommodation"—and the Captain paused and looked around to receive the applause which he knew must be elicited by the magnanimity of the sentiment.

The applause *did* come; and the crowd thought while they gave it, how difficult and desirable a thing it would be, to lend money to General Thomas Witherspoon, the rich hog drover.

The Captain now resumed his examination of Mr. Peyton.

"What's your mother's fust name?" he asked.

"Sarah," said Mr. Peyton meekly.

"Right! so fur," said the Captain, with a smile of approval: "how many children has she?"

"Two: myself and brother Tom."

"Right again!" observed the Captain. "Tom, gentle*men,*" added he, turning to the crowd, and venturing a shrewd guess; "Tom, gentle*men,* was named arter *me.* Warn't he, sir?" said he to Mr. Peyton, sternly.

"He was, sir—his name is Thomas Witherspoon."

Captain Suggs bobbed his head at the company, as much as to say, "*I* knew it;" and the crowd in their own minds, decided that the *ci-devant* General Witherspoon was "a devilish sharp old cock"—and the crowd wasn't far out of the way.

Simon was not acting in this matter without an object. He intended to make a bold attempt to win a small fortune, and he thought it quite possible he should lose the money he had won; in which case it would be convenient to have the credit of General Witherspoon to operate upon.

"Gentle*men*," said he to the company, with whom he had become vastly popular; "your attention, *one* moment, ef you please!"

The company accorded him its most obsequious attention.

"Come here, Jeemes!"

Mr. James Peyton approached to within eighteen inches of his supposititious uncle, who raised his hands above the young man's head, in the most impressive manner.

"One and all, gentle*men*," said he, "I call on you to witness that I reckognize this here young man as my proper, giniwine nephy—my sister Sally's son; and wish him respected as sich. Jeemes, hug your old uncle!"

Young Mr. James Peyton and Captain Simon Suggs then embraced. Several of the bystanders laughed, but a large majority sympathized with the Captain. A few wept at the affecting sight, and one person expressed the opinion that nothing so soul-moving had ever before taken place in the city of Tuskaloosa. As for Simon, the tears rolled down his face, as naturally as if they had been called forth by real emotion, instead of being pumped up mechanically to give effect to the scene.

Captain Suggs now renewed the engagement with the tiger, which had been temporarily suspended that he might satisfy himself of the identity of James Peyton. But the "fickle goddess," jealous of his attention to the nephew of General Witherspoon, had deserted him in a pet.

"Thar goes a dozen d——d fine, fat hogs!" said the Captain, as the bank won a bet of two hundred dollars.

Suggs shifted about from card to card, but the bank won always! At last he thought it best to return to the "ten," upon which he bet five hundred dollars.

"Now, I'll wool you," said he.

"Next time!" said the dealer, as he threw the winning card upon his own pile.

"That makes my hogs squeal," said the Captain; and every body admired the fine wit and nerve of the hog drover.

In half an hour Suggs was "as flat as a flounder." Not a dollar remained of his winnings or his original stake. It was, therefore, time to "run his face," or rather, the "face" of General Witherspoon.

"Could a body bet a few mighty fine bacon hogs, agin money at this table?" he inquired.

The dealer would be happy to accommodate the General, upon his word of honor.

It was not long before Suggs had bet off a very considerable number of the very fine hogs in General Witherspoon's uncommonly fine drove. He began to feel, too, as if a meeting with the veritable drover might be very disagreeable. He began, therefore, to entertain serious notions of borrowing some money and leaving in the stage, that night, for Greensboro'. Honor demanded, however, that he should "settle" to the satisfaction of the dealer. He accordingly called

"Jeemes!"

Mr. Peyton responded very promptly to the call.

"Now," said Simon, "Jeemes, I'm a little behind to this gentleman here, and I'm obleeged to go to Greensboro' in to-night's stage, on account of seein' ef I can engage pork thar. Now ef *I* shouldn't be *here,* when my hogs *come in,* do *you,* Jeemes, take this gentleman to wherever the boys puts 'em up, and let him pick thirty of the finest in the drove. D'ye *hear,* Jeemes?"

James promised to attend to the delivery of the hogs.

"Is that satisfactory?" asked Simon.

"Perfectly," said the dealer; "let's take a drink."

Before the Captain went up to the bar to drink, he patted "Jeemes" upon the shoulder, and intimated that he desired to speak to him privately. Mr. Peyton was highly delighted at this mark of his rich uncle's confidence, and turned his head to see whether the company noted it. Having ascertained that they did, he accompanied his uncle to an unoccupied part of the saloon.

"Jeemes," said the Captain thoughtfully, "has your—mother bought—her—her—pork yet?"

James said she had not.

"Well, Jeemes, when my drove comes in, do you go down and pick her out ten of the best. Tell the boys to show you them new breed— the Berkshears."

Mr. Peyton made his grateful acknowledgements for his uncle's generosity, and they started back towards the crowd. Before they had advanced more than a couple of steps, however—

"Stop!" said Simon, "I'd like to a' forgot. Have you as much as a couple of hunderd by you, Jeemes, that I could use twell I git back from Greensboro'?"

Mr. Peyton was very sorry he hadn't more than fifty dollars about him. His uncle could take that, however—as he did forthwith—and he would "jump about" and get the balance in ten minutes.

"Don't do it, ef it's any trouble at all, Jeemes," said the Captain cunningly.

But Mr. James Peyton was determined that he would "raise the wind" for his uncle, let the "trouble" be what it might; and so energetic were his endeavours, that in a few moments he returned to the Captain and handed him the desired amount.

"Much obleeged to you, Jeemes; I'll remember you for this;" and no doubt the Captain has kept his word; for whenever he makes a promise which it costs nothing to perform, Captain Simon Suggs is the most punctual of men.

After Suggs had taken a glass of "sperrets" with his friend the dealer—whom he assured he considered the "smartest and cleverest" fellow out of Kentucky—he wished to retire. But just as he was leaving, it was suggested in his hearing, that an oyster supper would be no inappropriate way of testifying his joy at meeting his clever nephew and so many true-hearted friends.

"Ah, gentle*men,* the old hog drover's broke now, or he'd be proud to treat to something of the sort. They've knocked the leaf fat outen him to-night, in wads as big as mattock handles," observed Suggs, looking at the bar-keeper out of the corner of his left eye.

"Any thing this house affords is at the disposal of General Witherspoon," said the bar-keeper.

"Well! well!" said Simon, "you're all so clever, I must stand it I suppose, tho' I oughtn't to be so extravagant."

"Take the crowd, sir?"

"Certainly," said Simon.

"How much champagne, General?"

"I reckon we can make out with a couple of baskets," said the Captain, who was determined to sustain any reputation for liberality which General Witherspoon might, perchance, possess.

There was a considerable ringing of bells for a brief space, and then a door which Simon hadn't before seen, was thrown open, and the company ushered into a handsome supping apartment. Seated at the convivial board, the Captain outshone himself; and to this day, some of the *bon mots* which escaped him on that occasion, are remembered and repeated.

At length, after the proper quantity of champagne and oysters had been swallowed, the young man whom Simon had so signally rebuked early in the evening, rose and remarked that he had a sentiment to propose: "I give you, gentlemen," said he, "the health of General Witherspoon. Long may he live, and often may he visit our city and partake of its hospitalities!"

Thunders of applause followed this toast, and Suggs, as in duty bound, got up in his chair to respond.

"Gentle*men,*" said he "I'm devilish glad to see you all, and much obleeged to you, besides. You are the finest people I ever was amongst, and treat me a d——d sight better than they do at home"—which was a fact! "Hows'ever, I'm a poor hand to speak, but here's wishing of luck of you all"—and then wickedly seeming to blunder in his little speech—"and if I forgit you, I'll be d——d if you'll ever forgit me!"

Again there was a mixed noise of human voices, plates, knives and forks, glasses and wine bottles, and then the company agreed to disperse. "What a noble-hearted fellow!" exclaimed a dozen in a breath, as they were leaving.

As Simon and Peyton passed out, the bar-keeper handed the former a slip of paper, containing such items as—"twenty-seven dozen of oysters, twenty-seven dollars; two baskets of champagne, thirty-six dollars,"—making a grand total of sixty-three dollars.

The Captain, who "felt his wine," only hiccoughed, nodded at Peyton, and observed.

"Jeemes, you'll attend to this?"

"Jeemes" said he would, and the pair walked out and bent their way to the stage-office, where the Greensboro' coach was already drawn up. Simon wouldn't wake the hotel keeper to get his saddle-bags, because, as he said, he would probably return in a day or two.

"Jeemes," said he, as he held that individual's hand; "Jeemes, has your mother bought her pork yet?"

"No, sir," said Peyton, "you know you told me to take ten of your hogs for her—don't you recollect?"

"Don't do that," said Simon, sternly.

Peyton stood aghast! "Why sir?" he asked.

"Take TWENTY!" said the Captain, and wringing the hand he held, he bounced into the coach, which whirled away, leaving Mr. James Peyton on the pavement, in profound contemplation of the boundless generosity of his uncle, General Thomas Witherspoon of Kentucky!

Samuel Hele, Esq.

Joseph G. Baldwin

I CANNOT omit Sam from my gallery of daubs. I should feel a sense of incompleteness, grieving the conscience with a feeling of duty undischarged and opportunities neglected, such as Cave Burton would have felt had he risen from table with an oyster-pie untouched before him.

Of all the members of the bar, Sam cultivated most the faculty of directness. He could tolerate nothing less than its absence in others. He knew nothing of circumlocution. He had as soon been a tanner's horse, and walked all his life pulled by a pole and a string, around a box, in a twenty-foot ring, as to be mincing words, hinting and hesitating, and picking out soft expressions. He liked the most vigorous words; the working words of the language. He thought with remarkable clearness; knew exactly what he was going to say; meant exactly what he said; and said exactly what he meant. A sea-captain with his cargo insured, would as soon have made a "deviation" and forfeited the insurance, as Sam, especially when in pursuit of a new idea, would have wandered for a minute from his straight course. His sense was strong, discriminating, and relevant. Swift was not more English in his sturdy, peremptory handling of a subject, than Sam; nor more given to varnish and mollifying. He tore the feathers off a subject, as a wholesale cook at a restaurant does the plumage off a fowl, when the crowd are clamorously bawling for meat. Sam was well educated and well informed. But his memory had never taken on more matter than his mind assimilated. He had no use for any information that he could not work into his thought. He had a great contempt for all prejudices except his own, and was entirely uncramped by other people's opinions, or notions, or whims, or fancies, or desires. The faculty of veneration was not only wanting, but there was a hole where there ought to have been a bump. *Prestige* was a thing he didn't understand. *Family* he had no idea of, except as a means of procreation, and he would have respected a man as much or as little, if, improving on the modern spirit of progress, he had been hatched out in a retort by a chemical process, as if he had descended from the Plantagenets, with all the quarterings right, and no bar sinister. He had no respect for old things, and not much for old persons. Established institutions he looked into as familiarly as into a horse's mouth, and with about as much respect for their age. He would, if he could, have wiped out the Chancery system, or the whole body of the common law, "the perfection of human reason," as he would an ink blot dropped on the paper as he was draughting a bill to abolish them. He had no tenderness for the creeds or superstitions of others. A man, tender-toed on the matter of favorite hobbies, had better not be in Sam's neighborhood. If he cherished any mysteries and tendernesses of belief that the strong sunlight of common sense caused to blink in the eyes, Sam was no pleasant companion to commune with; for Sam would drag them from the twilight as he would an owl, into noonday, and laugh at the figure they cut in the sunshine. A delicately-toned spiritualist felt, when Sam was handling his brittle wares, as a fine lady would feel, on seeing a blacksmith with smutty fingers taking out of her box, her complexion, laces and finery.

Doctor Samuel Johnson objected to some one "that there was no salt in his talk;" he couldn't have said that of Sam's discourse. It not only contained salt, but salt-petre: for probably, as many vigorous, brimstone expressions proceeded from Sam's mouth, as from any body else's, the peculiar patron of brimstone fireworks only excepted.

The faculty of the *wonderful* did not hold a large place on Sam's cranium. He believed that every thing that was marvellous was a lie, unless he told it himself; and sometimes even then, he had his doubts. He only wondered on one subject; and that was, that there always happened to be about him such "a hell of a number of d——d fools;" and this wonder was constant, deriving new strength every day; and he wondered again at his inability to impress this comfortable truth upon the parties whom he so frequently, in every form and every where, and especially in their presence, sought to make realize its force and wisdom, by every variety of illustration; by all the eloquence of earnest conviction and solemn asseveration.

If Sam had a sovereign contempt for any one more than another, it was for Sir William Blackstone, whom he regarded as "something between a sneak and a puke," and for whose superstitious veneration of the common law he felt about the same sympathy that Gen. Jackson felt for Mr. Madison's squeamishness on the subject of blood and carnage, which the hero charged the statesman with not being able "to look on *with composure*"—(he might as well have said, pleasure).

Squire Sam was of a good family—a circumstance he a good deal resisted, as some infringement on his privileges. He would have preferred to have been born at large, without any particular maternity or paternity; it would have been less local and narrow, and more free and roomy, and cosmopolitan.

There had once been good living in the family. This is evident from the fact that Sam had the gout; which proof, indeed, except vague traditions, which Sam rejected as unworthy of a sensible man's belief, is the only evidence of this matter of domestic economy. Sam thought particularly hard of this; he considered it a monstrous outrage, that the only portion of the prosperous fortunes of his house which fell to his share, should have been a disease which had long survived the causes of it. As his teeth were set on edge, he thought it only fair he should have had a few of the grapes.

Sam's estimate of human nature was not extravagant. He was not an optimist. He had not much notion of human perfectibility. He was not apt to be carried away by his feelings into any very overcharged appreciation either of particular individuals or the general race. I never heard him say what he thought would eventually become of most of them; but it was very evident, from the tenor of his unstinted talk, what he thought *ought* to become of them, if transmundane affairs were regulated by principles of human justice.

The particular community in which the Squire had set up his shingle was not, even in the eyes of a more partial judgment than he was in the habit of exercising upon men, ever supposed to be colonized by the descendants of the good Samaritan; and if they continued perverse, and persevered in iniquity, it was not Sam's fault—he did *his* duty by them. He cursed them black and blue, by night and by day. He spared not. In these divertisements he exercised his faculties of description, prophecy and invective, largely. The humbugs suffered. Sam vastated them, as Swedenborg says they do with them in the other world, until he left little but a dark, unsavory void, in souls, supposed by their owners to be stored up, like a warehouse, with rich bales of heavenly merchandise. He pulled the dominos from their faces, and pelted the hollow masks over their heads lustily. These pursuits, laudable as they may be, are not, in the present constitution of village society, winning ways; and therefore I cannot truly say that Sam's popularity was universal; nor did it make up by intensity in particular directions, what it lacked of diffusion. Indeed, I may go so far as to say, that it was remarkable neither for surface nor depth.

It is a profound truth, that the wounds of vanity are galling to a resentful temper, and that few people feel much obliged to a man who, purely from a love of truth, convinces the public that they are fools or knaves; or who excites a doubt in themselves touching the right solution of this problem of mind and morals. Hence I may be allowed to doubt whether Sam's industry and zeal in these exercises of his talents—whatever effect they may have had on the community—essentially advanced this gentleman's personal or pecuniary fortunes. However, I am inclined to think that this result, so far from grieving, rather pleased the Squire. Having formed his own estimate of himself, he preferred that the estimate should stand, and not be shaken by a coincidence of opinion on the part of those whose judgments in favor of a thing he considered was pretty good *prima facie* evidence against it.

Sam's disposition to animadvert upon the community about him, found considerable aggravation in a state of ill health; inflaming his gout, and putting the acerbities and horrors of indigestion to the long account of other provocatives, of a less physical kind, to these displays. For a while, Sam dealt in individual instances; but this soon grew too tame and insipid for his growing appetite; for invective is like brandy—the longer it is indulged in, the larger and stronger must be the dose. Sam began to take them wholesale; and he poured volley after volley into the devoted village, until you would have thought it in a state of siege.

25

There had, a few days before, been a new importation from Yankeedom—not from its factory of calicoes, but from its factory of school-teachers. The article had been sent to order, from one of the interior villages of Connecticut. The Southern propensity of getting every thing from abroad, had extended to school-mistresses,—though the country had any number of excellent and qualified girls wishing such employment at home,—as if, as in the case of wines, the process of importing added to the value. It was soon discovered that this article was a bad investment, and would not suit the market. Miss Charity Woodey was almost too old a plant to be safely transplanted. What she had been in her youth could not be exactly known; but if she ever had any charms, their day had long gone by. I do not mean to flatter her when I say I think she was the ugliest woman I ever saw—and I have been in places where saying that would be saying a good deal. Her style of homeliness was peculiar only in this—that it embraced all other styles. It is a wonderful combination which makes a beautiful woman; but it was almost a miracle, by which every thing that gives or gilds beauty was withheld from her, and every thing that makes or aggravates deformity was given with lavish generosity. We suppose it to be a hard struggle when female vanity can say, hope, or think nothing in favor of its owner's personal appearance; but Miss Charity had got to this point: indeed, the power of human infatuation on this subject—for even *it* is not omnipotent—could not help her in this matter. She did not try to conceal it, but let the matter pass, as if it were a thing not worth the trouble of thinking about.

Miss Charity was one of those "strong-minded women of New England," who exchange all the tenderness of the feminine for an impotent attempt to attain the efficiency of the masculine nature; one of that fussy, obtrusive, meddling class, who, in trying to *double-sex* themselves, *unsex* themselves, losing all that is lovable in woman, and getting most of what is odious in man.

She was a bundle of prejudices—stiff, literal, positive, inquisitive, inquisitorial, and biliously pious. *Dooty*, as she called it, was a great word with her. Conscience was another. These were engaged in the police business of life, rather than the heart and the affections. Indeed, she considered the affections as weaknesses, and the morals a sort of drill exercise of minor duties, and observances, and cant phrases. She was as blue as an indigo bag. The starch, strait-laced community she came from, she thought the very tip of the ton; and the little coterie of masculine women and female men—with its senate of sewing societies, cent societies, and general congress of missionary and tract societies—the parliaments that rule the world. Lower Frothingham, and Deacon Windy, and old Parson Beachman, and all the young Beachmans, constituted, in her eyes, a sort of Puritanic See, before which she thought Rome was in a state of continual fear and flutter.

She had come out as a missionary of light to the children of the South, who dwell in the darkness of Heathenesse. It was not long— only two days—before she began to set every thing to rights. The whole academy was astir with her activity. The little girls, who had been petted by their fathers and mothers like doll-babies, were over-hauled like so much damaged goods by her busy fingers, and were put into the strait-jacket of her narrow and precise system of manners and morals, in a way the pretty darlings had never dreamed of before. *Her* way was the Median and Persian law that never changed, and to which every thing must bend. Every thing was wrong. Every thing must be put right. Her hands, eyes, and tongue were never idle for a moment, and in her microscopic sense of *doo*ty and conscience, the little peccadilloes of the school swelled to the dimensions of great crimes and misdemeanors.

It was soon apparent that she would have to leave, or the school be broken up. Like that great reformer Triptolemus Yellowby, she was not scant in delivering her enlightened sentiments upon the subject of matters and things about her, and on the subject of slavery in particular; and her sentiments on this subject were those of the enlightened coterie from which she came.

The very consideration with which, in the unbounded hospitality and courtesy to woman in the South-West, she was treated, only served to inflame her self-conceit, and to confirm her in her sense of what her *doo*ty called on her to do, for the benefit of the natives; especially to reforming things to the standard of New England insular habitudes.

A small party was given one evening, and she was invited. She came. There were some fifteen or twenty persons of both sexes there; among them our friend Sam, and a few of the young men of the place. The shocking fact must be related, that, on a sideboard in the back parlor was set out something cold, besides *solid* refreshments, to which the males who did not belong to the "Sons" paid their respects. A little knot of these were laughing and talking around Sam, who, as usual, was exerting himself for the entertainment of the auditors, and, this time, in good humor. Some remarks were made touching Miss Charity, for whose solitary state—she was sitting up in the corner by herself, stiff as steelyards—some commiseration was expressed; and it was proposed that Sam should entertain her for the evening. And it was suggested to Sam that he should try his best to get her off, by giving her such a description of the country as would have that effect. "Now," said one of them, "Sam, you've been snarling at every thing about you so long, suppose you just try your best this time, and let off all your surplus bile at once, and give us some peace. Just go up to her, and let her have it strong. Don't spare brush or blacking, but paint the whole community so black, that the Devil himself might sit for the picture." Sam took a glass, and tossing it off, wiped his mouth, after a slight sigh of satisfaction, and promised, with pious fervor, that, "by the blessing of Heaven, he would do his best."

One of the company went to Miss Charity, and, after speaking in the highest terms of Sam, as a New England man, and as one of the most intellectual, and reliable, and frank men in the country, and one, moreover, who had conceived a lively regard for her, asked leave to introduce him; which having been graciously given, Sam (having first refreshed himself with another potation) was in due form introduced.

Miss Woodey, naturally desirous of conciliating Squire Hele, opened the conversation with that gentleman, after the customary formalities, by saying something complimentary about the village. "And you say, madam," replied Sam, "that you have been incarcerated in this village for two weeks; and how, madam, have you endured it? Ah, madam, I am glad, on some accounts, to see you here. You came to reform: it was well. Such examples of female heroism are the poetry of human life. They are worth the martyrdom of producing them. I read an affecting account the other day of a similar kind—a mother going to Wetumpka, and becoming the inmate of a penitentiary for the melancholy satisfaction of waiting upon a convict son."

Miss Woodey.—"Why, Mr. Hele, how you talk! You are surely jesting."

Sam.—"Madam, there are some subjects too awfully serious for jest. A man had as well jest over the corruptions and fate of Sodom and Gomorrah—though, I confess, the existence of this place is calculated to excite a great deal of doubt of the destruction of those cities, and has, no doubt, placed a powerful weapon in the hands of infidelity throughout the immense region where the infamy of the place is known."

Miss W.—"Why, Mr. Hele, I have heard a very different account of the place. Indeed, only the other evening, I heard at a party several of the ladies say they never knew any village so free from gossip and scandal."

Sam.—"And so it is, madam. Men and women are free of that vice. I wish it were otherwise. It would be a sign of improvement,—as a man with fever when boils burst out on him,—an encouraging sign. Madam, the reason why there is no scandal here is, because there is not character enough to support it. Reputation is not appreciated. A man without character is as well off as a man with it. In the dark all are alike. You can't hurt a man here by saying any thing of him; for, say what you will, it is less than the truth, and less than he could afford to publish at the court-house door, and be applauded for it by the crowd. Besides, madam, every body is so busy with his own villany, that no one has time to publish his neighbor's."

Miss W.—"Really, Mr. Hele, you give a poor account of your neighbors. Are there no honest men among them?"

Sam.—"Why,—y–e–s—a few. The lawyers generally acknowledge, and, as far as circumstances allow, practise, in their *private* characters, the plainer rules of morals; but, really, they are so occupied in trying to carry out the villany of others, they deserve no credit for it; for they have no time to do any thing on private account. There is also *one* preacher, who, I believe, when not in liquor, recognizes a few of the rudiments of moral obligation. Indeed, some think he is not blamable for getting drunk, as he does it only in deference to the public sentiment. I express no opinion myself, for I think any man who has resided for ten years in these suburbs of hell, ought modestly to decline the expression of any opinion on any point of ethics for ever afterwards."

Miss W.—"But, Mr. Hele, if all this villany were going on, there would be some open evidence of it. I have not heard of a case of stealing since I've been here."

Sam.—"No, madam; and you wouldn't, unless a stranger came to town with something worth stealing; and perhaps not then; for it is so common a thing that it hardly excites remark. The natives never steal from each other—I grant them that. The reason is plain. There are certain acquisitions which, with a certain profession, are sacred. 'Honor among,' &c.—you know the proverb. Besides, the thief would be sure to be caught: 'Set a'—member of a certain class—you know *that* proverb, too. Moreover, all they have got they got, directly or indirectly, in that way—if getting a thing by purchase without equivalent, or taking it without leave is stealing, as any where else out of Christendom, except this debatable land between the lower regions and the outskirts of civilization, it is held to be. And to steal from one another would be repudiating the title by which every man holds property, and thus letting the common enemy, the true owner, in, whom all are interested in keeping out. Madam, if New York, Mobile, and New Orleans were to get their own, they might inclose the whole town, and label the walls "the lost and stolen office." When a Tennesseean comes to this place with a load of bacon, they consider him a prize, and divide out what he has as so much prize money. They talk of a Kentucky hog-drover first coming in in the fall, as an epicure speaks of the first shad of the season."

Miss W.—"The population seems to be intelligent and—"

Sam (with Johnsonian oracularity).—"*Seems*—true; but they are not. Whether the population first took to rascality, and that degraded their intellects, or whether they were fools, and took to it for want of sense, is a problem which I should like to be able to solve, if I could only find some one old enough to have known them when they first took to stealing, or when they first began playing the fool; but that time is beyond the oldest memory. I can better endure ten rascals than one fool; but I am forced to endure both in one. I see, in a recent work, a learned writer traces the genealogy of man to the monkey tribe. I believe that this is true of this population; for the characteristic marks of a low, apish cunning and stealing, betray the paternity: but so low are they in all better qualities, that, if their respectable old ancestor the rib-nosed baboon, should be called to see them, he would exclaim, with uplifted paws, 'Alas, how degenerate is my breed!' For they have left off all the good instincts of the beast, and improved only on his vices."

Miss W.—"I have heard something of violent crimes, murders, and so forth, in the South-West, but I have never heard this particular community worse spoken of—"

Sam.—"Madam, I acquit them of all crimes which require any boldness in the perpetration. As to assassination, it occurs only occasionally,—when a countryman is found drunk, or something of the sort; and even assaults and batteries are not common. These occur only in the family circle; such as a boy sometimes whipping his father when the old man is intoxicated, or a man whipping his wife when she is infirm of health: except these instances, I cannot say, with truth, that any charge of this kind can be substantiated. As to negroes—"

Miss W.—"Do tell me, Mr. Hele—how do they treat *them?* Is it as bad as they say? Do—do—they,—really, now—"

Hele.—"Miss W., this is a very delicate subject; and what I tell you must be regarded as entirely confidential. Upon this subject there is a secrecy—a chilling mystery of silence—cast, as over the horrors and dungeons of the inquisition. The way negroes are treated in this country would chill the soul of a New Holland cannibal. Why, madam, it was but the other day a case occurred over the river, on Col. Luke Gyves's plantation. Gyves had just bought a drove of negroes, and was marking them in his pen,—a slit in one ear and an underbit in the other was Luke's mark,—and a large mulatto fellow was standing at the bull-ring, where the overseer was just putting the number on his back with the branding-iron, when the nigger dog, seeing his struggles, caught him by the leg, and the negro, mad with the pain,—I don't think he did it intentionally,—seized the branding-irons, and put out the dog's—a favorite Cuba bloodhound—left eye. They took the negro down to the rack in the plantation dungeon-house, and, sending for the neighbors to come into the entertainment, made a Christmas frolic of the matter. They rammed a powder-horn down his throat, and lighting a slow match, went off to wait the result. When gone, Col. Gyves bet Gen. Sam Potter one hundred and fifty dollars that the blast would blow the top of the negro's head off; which it did. Gen. Sam refused to pay, and the case was brought into the Circuit Court. Our judge, who had read a good deal more of Hoyle than Coke, decided that the bet could not be recovered, because Luke bet on a certainty; but fined Sam a treat for the crowd for making such a foolish wager, and adjourned court over to the grocery to enjoy it."

Miss W.—"Why, Mr. Hele, it is a wonder to me that the fate of Sodom does not fall upon the country."

Sam.—"Why, madam, probably it would, if a single righteous man could be found to serve the notice. However, many think that its irredeemable wickedness has induced Heaven to withdraw the country from its jurisdiction, and remit it to its natural, and, at last, reversionary proprietors, the powers of hell. It subserves, probably, a useful end, to stand as a vivid illustration of the doctrine of total depravity."

Miss W.—"But, Mr. Hele,—do tell me,—do they *now* part the young children from their mothers—poor things?"

Sam.—"Why, no,—candidly,—they do *not* very much, now. The women are so sickly, from overwork and scant feeding and clothing, that the child is worth little for the vague chance of living. But when cotton was fifteen cents a pound, and it was cheaper to take away the child than to take up the mother's time in attending to it, they used to send them to town, of a Sunday, in big hamper baskets, for sale, by the dozen. The boy I have got in my office I got in that way—but he is the survivor of six, the rest dying in the process of raising. There was a great feud between the planters on this side of Sanotchie, and those on the other side, growing out of the treatment of negro children. Those who sold them off charged the other siders with inhumanity, in drowning theirs, like blind puppies, in the creek; which was resented a good deal at the time, and the accusers denounced as abolitionists. I did hear of one of them, Judge Duck Swinger, feeding his nigger dogs on the young varmints, as he called them; but I don't believe the story, it having no better foundation than current report, public belief, and general assertion."

Miss W. (sighing).—"Oh, Mr. Hele! are they not afraid the negroes will rise on them?"

Sam.—"Why, y–e–s, they do occasionally, and murder a few families,—especially in the thick settlements,—but less than they did before the patrol got up a subscription among the planters to contribute a negro or two apiece, every month or so, to be publicly hung, or burned, for the sake of example. And, to illustrate the character of the population, let me just tell you how Capt. Sam Hanson did at the last hanging. Instead of throwing in one of his own negroes, as an honest ruffian would have done, he threw in yellow Tom, a free negro; another threw in an estate negro, and reported him dead in the inventory; while Squire Bill Measly painted an Indian black and threw him in, and hung him for one of his Pocahontas negroes, as he called some of his halfbreed stock."

Miss W.—"Mr. Hele! what is to become of the rising generation—the poor children—I do feel so much for them—with such examples?"

Sam.—"Madam, they are past praying for—there is one consolation. Let what will become of them, they will get less than their deserts. Why, madam, such precocious villany as theirs the world has never seen before: they make their own fathers ashamed of even *their* attainments and proficiency in mendacity; they had good teaching, though. Why, Miss Woodey, a father here never thinks well of a child until the boy cheats him at cards: then he pats him on the head, and says, 'Well done, Tommy, here's a V.; go, buck it off on a horse-race next Sunday, and we'll go snooks—and, come, settle fair, and no cheating around the board.' The children here at twelve years have progressed in villany beyond the point at which men get, in other countries, after a life of industrious rascality. They spent their rainy Sundays, last fall, in making a catechism of oaths and profanity for the Indians, whose dialect was wanting in those accomplishments of Anglo-Saxon literature. There is not a scoundrel among them that is not ripe for the gallows at fourteen. At five years of age, they follow their fathers around to the dram-shops, and get drunk on the heel-taps."

Miss W.—"The persons about here don't look as if they were drunk."

Sam.—"Why, madam, it is refreshing to hear you talk in that way. No, they are *not* drunk. I wish they were. It would be an astonishing improvement, if dissipation would only recede to that point at which men get drunk. But they have passed that point, long ago. I should as soon expect to see a demijohn stagger as one of them. Besides, the liquor is all watered, and it would require more than a man could hold to make him drunk: but the grocery keeper defends himself on the ground, that it is only two parts water, and he never gets paid for more than a third he sells. But I never speak of these small things; for, in such a godless generation, venial crimes stand in the light of flaming virtues. Indeed, we always feel relieved when we see one of them dead drunk, for then we feel assured he is not stealing."

Miss W.—"But, Mr. Hele, is there personal danger to be apprehended—by a woman?—now—for instance—expressing herself freely?"

Sam.—"No, madam, not if she carries her pistols, as they generally do *now*, when they go out. They are usually insulted, and sometimes mobbed. They mobbed a Yankee school-mistress here, some time ago, for saying something against slavery; but I believe they only tarred and feathered her, and rode her on a rail for a few squares. Indeed, I heard some of the boys at the grocery, the other night, talk of trying the same experiment on another; but *who* it was, I did not hear them say."

Here Sam made his bow and departed, and, over a plate of oysters and a glass of hot stuff, reported progress to the meeting whose committee he was, but declined leave to sit again.

The next morning's mail-stage contained two trunks and four bandboxes, and a Yankee school-mistress, ticketed on the Northern line; and, in the hurry of departure, a letter, addressed to Mrs. Harriet S——, was found, containing some interesting memoranda and statistics on the subject of slavery and its practical workings, which I should never thought of again had I not seen something like them in a very popular fiction, or rather book of fictions, in which the slave-holders are handled with something less than feminine delicacy and something more than masculine unfairness.

[Sam takes the credit of sending Miss Charity off, but Dr. B., the principal, negatives this: he says he had to give her three hundred dollars and pay her expenses back to get rid of her; and that she received it, saying she intended to return home and live at ease, the balance of her life, on the interest of the money.]

John Bealle's Accident—or, How the Widow Dudu Treated Insanity

John Gorman Barr

Friendship is constant in all other things,
Save in the office and affairs of—SPORT

SHAKSPERE IMPROVED.

IN the domain of Momus, all things are considered fair, as in love and war. Such, at least, was the private opinion, publicly illustrated, of John Bealle and his friend, John Smith—a brace of inveterate wags, residing in the sister States of Alabama and Mississippi, whose "constant care" seemed to be, maugre their intimate friendly relations, the merciless exercise of each other in that species of fun, 'yclept practical joking. The friendship of these gentlemen—compared with which that of Orestes and Pylades, or Damon and Pythias, was a mild form of the disease—was of long standing; of such antiquity, indeed, that it might be said (if it was not for the fact that one of the party has not *yet* joined the "noble army of *martyrs*," meaning married men, and therefore might take it in high dudgeon) to have dated back to that remote period "whereof the memory of (young) men runneth not to the contrary." Suffice it to say, that their intimacy had never been broken, and that it deserved to be classed among the institutions known as "time-honored." That these amicable relations were preserved through a series of years and a multiplicity of mad pranks, was mainly attributable to the circumstance, perhaps, that in their joking vocation, they were very equally matched, and that the game was generally "diamond cut diamond." Victory perched as often on the standard of one as on the other; if John, of Mobile, was for the nonce "under the hack," he set to work as energetically as he did in the mines of California, and labored, until, from the depths of his invention, he dug up something *"precious"* with which to pay off old scores, and turn the laugh upon his friend— well satisfied, as indeed would most men have been, TO GET EVEN with so adroit a manager of a hoax as the inimitable John, of Beallesville.

It happened that in the last jocose rencontre between the individuals above named, that the entire Smith family, and its numerous connexion, had been, in the representative person of John, of Mobile, incontinently *sold,* "lock, stock and barrel." Such a misfortune, occurring as it did on the eve of his departure from the city of Tuskaloosa, in whose bracing and health-restoring atmosphere he had been sojourning during the sultry August month, to the lively village of Beallesville, in Mississippi, was really intolerable, for the reason, that want of time prevented his resort to the *lex talionis* in order to relieve himself, and, there being few objects along the road to divert the mind of the traveller, he must, perforce, as he jogged along his lonely way, be chewing the cud of "sweet or bitter fancy," according as, in the slang of the politicians, his "antecedents" might have been exceptionable or otherwise. That our traveller's reflections were not of the most pleasant description, might have been inferred from the sourness of his countenance, and the undeserved applications of the spur to the spirited animal he rode; and a fair clew to the nature of his mental occupation might have been had in the following words, which fell with indescribable emphasis and earnestness from his lips:

"If I don't get *even* with him, durn MY BUTTONS!!!"

Having given audible expression to his resolution, and clenched it with *round* security, our traveller seemed to think that he had done all that manhood could require at his hands at present; and banishing from his mind the late disturbing cares, he jogged on merrily, alternately humming the air of some lately imported *schottisch,* singing an affecting description of his leave-taking with his "OWN MARY ANN," and winding up, gaily, by making the woods resound with the music and comforting philosophy of, "TRUST TO LUCK."

Night coming on apace, our musical way-farer drew rein in front of a commodious looking dwelling by the roadside, and alighting, sought and obtained permission to pass the night. On entering the piazza, the new-comer was politely saluted by the lady of the house— a matronly looking woman, somewhat past the meridian of life, of healthy, boxom appearance, dressed neatly in plain attire, with a rather comely set of features. In her general air and bearing, he who runs might have read, "I am monarch of all I survey."

"Warm and dusty travelling, sir," she said; "have you ridden far to-day?"

"Not very," was the response, "I only came from Tuskaloosa."

"Indeed," rejoined the hostess, "may be you live in Tuskaloosa?"

"No, madam," he replied, "I live now in Mobile, but am travelling through the country, and am, at present, making my way to the plantation of my friend, John Bealle, in the neighborhood of Beallesville, in Mississippi. Do you know how far it is to Beallesville?"

After giving the distance, and informing the traveller that she was well acquainted with Col. Bealle—that the Colonel always stopped and staid all night at her house in passing that road—showering, meanwhile, sundry encomiums on the good qualities and amiable traits of the aforesaid Colonel, she launched out as follows:

"Sakes alive! That Mobile is an awful place. I wouldn't live there for all the money on earth. How can you live there? Its worse than some of them places Scriptur tells about. I hate it; I despise it. Nothing would do my old man, Nimrod Dudu, about twelve year ago, but he must get on a steamboat and go down to sell our little cotton in the everlastin' pestiferous hole. Well, he come back after so long a time, but he was no more the same man than I am the same man; so altered that nobody hardly knew him. From that day he naturally pined away, and pined away, until, about a month after he got home, his whiskey begun to disagree with him, and he turned in and died. Do you know what I think was the matter with him?"

Breathless and excited, she paused, and keeping her eye fixed searchingly on the face of the guest, she leaned forward, and in a high stage-hiss, whispered, pausing between each word—

"I—THINK—HE—WAS—PISONED!!!"

Waiting a moment to allow her auditor an opportunity of recovering from the shock which the astounding intelligence concerning the death of her Nimrod was expected to produce, she opened again with a revelation which she fully calculated would remove all scepticism in the mind of her listener, as it had in her own mind, unquestionably added "confirmation strong as proof of holy writ," to the correctness of her surmises—pronouncing each word separately and in a whisper, and with startling emphasis—

"And—Col. Bealle—thinks—so—too!!!"

"When, madam,'" asked our traveller, working himself up to the old lady's high fever-heat, and showing an intense anxiety in his manner, "when did Col. Bealle say he thought so?"

"Only about six months ago," replied the widow. "Though I 'spicioned that Nimrod never come by his death fairly, I kept my 'spicions to myself for eleven long year, till I got so full of 'm that I think I should have *busted* if I hadn't told somebody. But you look like a gentleman, and being that you are a friend of the Colonel's, I'll tell you how I come to tell him. It was six months ago last Monday that the Colonel came along this road, and put up here, as he always does, to stay the night. After supper he took a seat, right where you are now sitting, and looking me straight in the eyes, with the most searching and 'sinuating looks I ever saw, says he to me, says he, 'Widow'—I declare to gracious Mister, my heart jumped right spang up in my mouth as he spoke—'Widow,' says he, 'what is the matter? you look out o' sorts. Tell me what pesters you.' And then, Mister, if you could only have seen how he rolled round his eyes and held his breath as he went on to say—'Widow Dudu, you've got something on your mind; tell it; don't let concealment, like a *worrum* in a rosebud, eat up your damaged face.' Mercy me! I never shall forget them words—the curiousest I ever heard. I just felt that the Colonel read it all from my looks, so I made a clean breast of it, and told him plump out my 'spicions about Nimrod's death. When I was done the Colonel set a little while, looked sorter dumb-flustered, then kinder puckered up his mouth, whistled a tune, and then looking savigrously riled, he said to me, says he—'Widow, you're right; I think he must have been *pisoned;* I've heard of men being *pisoned* in Mobile before. It's a dangerous place; I always go there in fear and trembling; and the worst of it is, you can't find out who does the *pisoning.* I thought I was pisoned once myself, at Holt's, but it wore off. I sorter think a man gets *pisoned* generally who goes there, and no particular person does it. Nor do I know what sort of "pison" they use; if they used *minerals,* it could be found out if the man had been dead fifty year; but if they used *vegetables,* it couldn't be found out a minute and a half after he's dead. But I'll tell you what I'll do, widow; the next time I go to Mobile, I'll inquire around and see what I can pick up about the way they pison them off there, and let you know; for I'm sure it would be a great comfort and consolation for you to learn what killed your poor husband.' Now warn't this kind of him, Mister? O, he is the best naturedest, the best heartedest man I ever saw!"

"Madam," solemnly responded the guest, "I agree with you entirely in your estimate of my friend, Colonel Bealle's character; there is not a higher souled, nobler hearted, or more generous-spirited man in the universe, and that is the reason his misfortune is so much lamented."

"Misfortune?" eagerly inquired the widow, "has any misfortune befallen Col. Bealle?"

"I am surprised," replied the traveller, assuming deep seriousness, "that you have not heard of it. It occurred near seven months ago; whilst riding in a carriage in Mobile, the horses took fright, ran away, smashed up the vehicle, and poor John's head struck with such violence against the curb-stone, that it addled his brain to the extent that he has been *crazy,* off and on ever since."

"Saints look down!" exclaimed the widow, with much feeling. "Oh, that rotten place, Mobile! Them it don't pison, it knocks out their brains with curb-stones! Mercy on us, I shall never find out now whether it was *vegetables* or *min'rals* killed my poor husband. How long ago did you say it was since the accident happened? Seven months? Man alive, the Colonel was crazy then when he was here last, and rolled his eyes about so awfully. Oh, what a risk I run—all the white person in the house—all night with a crazy man, and the niggers sleep as sound as mill-stones! The Lord make us thankful! Does he ever try to kill anybody?"

"Never," was the reply, "except when the paroxysm is upon him; then he requires to be restrained by force; then he is really dangerous. As a general thing, he is mild, good-natured, and quiet; it is only when something occurs to excite him that he gets into these destructive rages; but his friends know what brings them on, and being careful to avoid them, he goes along his business, and behaves with such good sense that an acquaintance who had never heard of his misfortune would never suspect that he was crazy."

"And pray, sir," inquired the widow, with eager interest, "what are the things that throw him into the rages and convulsions?"

"There are only a few things," replied the romancer, "that produce this unhappy effect upon him. The taste of coffee, the sight of milk, or butter, or eggs, or fried chicken, or cotton in any shape, coming in contact with his skin, as sheets, towels, pillow-cases, &c. These things bring on a convulsion immediately, which lasts about two hours, and then he becomes perfectly quiet and tractable, and seems, after it is all over, to have no recollection of the fearful paroxysm through which he has passed. Still, there is one other thing that excites him more ungovernably than any I have yet mentioned, and that is, being *told he is crazy*. With the information I have given you, if you will be upon your guard, and give your servants suitable directions, you may, in case Col. Bealle, in passing here next week, should stop to stay all night, have a tolerable comfortable time with him. But you must be careful, and remember the coffee, the milk, the butter, the eggs and the cotton sheets, pillow-cases, towels, &c."

"Careful!" exclaimed the widow, now fearfully excited; "I'll take my affidavy that I will be careful that neither he nor any other crazy man sets foot in my house. But what does the poor man eat, and on what does he sleep?"

"He is allowed nothing but the plainest and coarsest diet," was the ready reply; "corn bread, and bacon and water; as to sleeping, when linen sheets cannot be had, blankets are substituted, which are disagreeable enough this warm weather; but what can't be cured must be endured."

"Well, I am really sorry for him," broke forth the true woman's heart in the widow's bosom. "I am as sorry for him as if he had been of my own kith and kin. But it's no use for him to come here, and be wanting to stay all night; it would be the everlastin' death of me!"

"Madam," said the traveller, evincing much feeling, "I trust you will pardon me for saying that I think you are very wrong, for threatening to turn away from your house an old friend like Col. Bealle, whose misfortune should rather excite your commiseration and kind offices, than provoke ill-usage and harsh treatment."

"Well," said the widow, relenting, and showing, by her manner, that the appeal had not been made in vain, "I should certainly not be so unfeeling as to turn an old friend away from my house; but, the Lord be praised! I hope he may not come."

The conversation had just reached this point, when, supper being announced, our imaginative Mobile friend did ample justice to the excellent fare under which the table groaned. Indeed, the widow Dudu's house was famed, far and near, for all those substantial comforts, both in the eating and the sleeping departments, which are so highly prized by that class of persons who delight to "take their ease at their inn."

The next morning, before our traveller set out, he took pains to refresh his hostess' memory concerning the forbidden things which brought the paroxysms on his friend, duly impressing her with the fact that his friend became most outrageous and ungovernable when told that he was crazy, and that he would deny his insanity most vehemently.

Thus having accomplished, to his entire satisfaction, his mission—everybody has a mission, now-a-days, or wants one—our ingenious romancer suddenly found himself in the exact situation, so graphically described by the historian John Phœnix, of our ancestors, at the fourth and last charge of the British, at the battle of Bunker's Hill; viz.: like them, he recollected that he had urgent and pressing business at home, that demanded his immediate presence; and, acting on this opportune remembrance, it is said, and there are many who believe the story to be true, that grass did not grow under his horse's hoofs between the widow Dudu's and the city of Mobile.

In less than a week after the occurrences above related took place, and whilst they were still fresh in the memory of the widow, as well as every servant about the premises, John Bealle drove up to her gate, and springing quickly from his buggy—for John does everything in a hurry, especially if it is a generous act he intends to perform—he bounded with a light step, and his usual joyous manner, over the intermediate space between the gate and the house, and, in an instant afterwards, before the old lady, who was standing in the piazza when he passed the gate, had time to satisfy herself fully as to his personal identity, he was wringing her hand, and greeting her in the most friendly and familiar style. If her defunct Nimrod, in all his grave-clothes' ghastliness, had suddenly popped upon her, and gone through the same mode of salutation, it is highly probable that she would not have shown a greater degree of trepidation and amazement. Partially recovering herself after a manifest effort, she begun to greet her visitor in return, but it only ended in a faint and half-hysterical "How-de-do, Col. Bealle?"

"Never better in my life as to health," quickly responded the hilarious and open-hearted Colonel, whose confidence in the kind feelings the widow had ever manifested towards him, prevented him from observing anything unusual in her manner, "but as to hunger, I am more ravenous than a whole regiment of Russian wolves. I have travelled all day without breaking my fast, and have a villanously-destructive feeling about me, when I think of your dairy, larder and hen-house."

"O Lord, look down and have mercy on us all!" in trembling accents petitioned the widow.

"Have you any fresh butter-milk in the house?" the newly arrived went on to inquire, without seeming to have noticed her fervant ejaculation, "I feel as if I could drink a full pitcher of my favorite beverage, butter-milk, before I take it from my mouth. But what's in the wind now? what are you staring at?"

"Gracious Redeemer, protect me now!" piously supplicated the affrighted woman, who thinking she already saw indications of an approaching paroxyism, fully believed that her time had come.

"Gracious what?" hurriedly exclaimed the lover of butter-milk, sorely puzzled to divine the meaning of her pious supplications, and now, for the first time, directing his attention to her wild and unnatural appearance, "I am no bugaboo or monster that you should be standing and gazing at with your eyes sticking out of your head, but a tired and dusty traveller, who at present, more than to be stared at, desires a basin and water, soap and *towel*."

"Heavenly Parent! what will become of me?" saying which the old lady darted with the speed of light past the guest, who, just as he had finished speaking, was making his way along the piazza to the end, where water and washing facilities were to be had, and seizing the neat white *cotton* towel, which hung in its accustomed place, disappeared with it before the traveller had time to comprehend what she was doing.

"Well," said he, soliloquizing, "that was a rare shine—a queer kick, indeed! O, I understand now; some one had wiped their dirty hands on that towel, and she has taken it away with a view of getting a clean one. Still, there was no necessity for being in such a devil of a hurry about it. But women are curious creatures, and the old lady is the tidiest, neatest house-keeper in the country, and I verily believe that anything like uncleanliness about her house, her table, her cooking, her furniture or bedding, would drive her raving distracted. And how wonderfully pious she has become; something's wrong."

Having finished his ablutions, and whilst waiting for the towel to be replaced, (which, by-the-by, was *not* replaced), his attention was attracted to the manœuvres of a couple of the stoutest and most able-bodied of the negroes belonging to the widow, who, from their motions, seemed to desire to enter the piazza, and yet hesitated, from some cause, to do so.

"Toney," said the Colonel, addressing one of the negroes, and thinking some information might be drawn from him which would throw light on the eccentric behavior of their mistress, "has anything happened to your mistress?"

"*Sa?*" grunted the negro, the picture of idiotic fright and stupidity.

"Has anything, out of the common run, occurred to your mistress?" reiterated the Colonel.

"*Sa?*" burst forth from both negroes at once, and both seemingly stricken with terror.

"You black rascals," said the questioner warming up a little, "if you don't stop staring at me, and find the use of your tongues, I'll cut both your heads off."

"O Lord!" burst in a groan of agony from their lips at once.

"Well," said the Colonel, *sotto voce,* and as if addressing himself, "this is getting rather interesting. I believe that both mistress and negroes are afflicted with the same pious disease."

Returning to the charge once more, our enterprising friend said, addressing the two negroes, "Has a camp-meeting been held about here lately?"

"Yes, massa Colonel, yes, sir," both the darkies replied in the same breath.

"Did many get religion?" inquired he.

"Lord bress you, massar," said Toney, recovering somewhat the power of speech, "most everybody went up an' took a chance. Ole Missus tried two days, and then she *come through a-taring.*"

"Yes, yes," said the heretofore puzzled Colonel, thinking aloud; "I understand the case now, I think. If these camp-meetings do a great deal of good, they, sometimes, likewise do much injury. The old lady has gone there—got religion, and got half-crazy in the bargain—and now cuts her piety so thick, that she must interlard her common conversation with it, and 'hence the milk in the cocoa-nut.' "

Having, at length, satisfactorily settled, in his own mind, the cause of the eccentric behavior of his old friend, Mrs. Dudu, and experiencing lively hints from an appetite which had grown, prospectively, "upon what it fed on"—for if the widow excelled in anything, it was in her suppers—our traveler was not slow in obeying the summons to the table, which he had never failed to find loaded with the choicest and most savory esculents that the season and country afforded. His surprise may well be conceived of—description is powerless to paint it—when, taking a seat at the table, and looking around, he discovered nothing for his meal but *corn bread* and *bacon*. And no Isaac, in olden or modern times—no Israelite, in or out of Christendom, ever turned up his nose at this homely dish, with more ineffable scorn and contempt, than did our hungry Mississippian on the present occasion. Throwing himself back in his chair, he inquired of one of the two "big, buck negroes" in attendance—neither of whom, be it known, were the regular dining-room servants of the house, but who, for reasons best known to the widow, had been especially detailed for the present service—as follows:

"Where is your mistress?"

"Gone to bed, massa."

"Gone to the d—— Hem! Have you nothing else to eat but what I see before me?"

"No, massa."

"What's in that pitcher?"

"Water, massa."

"Have you got any milk?"

"No, massa."

"Bring me some coffee."

"Ain't none, massa."

"Any butter?"

"No, massa."

And so on to the end of the catalogue of forbidden articles. The astounded traveler, as if doubting his own identity, turned sharply on Toney and catechised thus:

"Do you know who I am?"

"Oh, yes, massa."

"Then I wish you would tell me, for, hang me, if I don't begin to distrust who I am. Who am I?"

"You am massa John Bealle, sar."

"And what's your name, imp of darkness?"

"Toney, sar."

"And what's your mistress' name?"

"Widow Dudu, sar."

The last three questions and answers did the business for the Widow, who had stolen noiselessly from her chamber, and was a breathless listener at the dining-room door. An angel of light could not have more fully impressed her with a belief of the insanity of her guest. Nor did she wait to hear any more, but, hastening rapidly back to her bedroom, closed and double-bolted the door behind her, and ensconsed herself between a couple of feather-beds, which, considering the thermometer stood 98° in the shade, was quite a *snug* berth, when she addressed herself to sleep,

"That balm of hurt minds, great Nature's second course!" as the sleep-murdering Macbeth so aptly terms it.

The Colonel, who knew nothing of this eave-dropping, or of the dose he had unwittingly administered to the lady of the house, sat silently at the table, after the conversation above related occurred, with a countenance indicative of trouble and perplexity, and with a vast deal of "speculation in his eyes."

At length, spurred by an appetite that knew no distinction in dishes, he overcame his repugnance to the coarse diet before him, and, in spite of early prejudices and hasty first impressions, made a tolerably hearty meal on corn-bread, bacon,—and limpid water!

After which, complaining of fatigue, he was escorted by the brace of stalwart "ebonies," who kept in close attendance, to a bed-room in the second story. Here, dismissing his sable servitors and closing the door, he proceeded leisurely, meanwhile, "wrapped in sombre and harassing thought," to divest himself of his outward habiliments, when, turning to the bed into which he was about to spring, he discovered a *bed,* it is true, but nothing on it, save blankets and pillows without *slips.* Inwardly cursing the servants for their negligence in not putting on a spread and sheets on the bed, or cases on the pillows, and fully resolved to "blow up" all hands about their carelessness in the morning, he went to the door and endeavored to open it, intending to call for the indispensible bed-clothing. After tugging away violently, for some time, he found that his labor was in vain; that the door remained firmly closed, resisting his utmost strength. He next fell to kicking and thumping the door to burst it open, but *that* door was not to be burst open by kicks and thumps. All other resources failing, he called aloud:—

"Somebody come here!" No answer.

"Fire!" "Murder!" "Water!" "Man overboard!" "Woman drowning!" "Steamboat blown up!" "Cars run off!" "Hello!" "The Devil!!"

No answer.

"Toney!" shouted the exasperated prisoner, at the top of his voice, "Open the door, or I'll set fire to the house!"

" 'Spec if you does, you be fus' one burn up," answered the individual addressed, from the other side of the door.

"What's this door fastened for on the outside? Undo it, you infernal scoundrel, or I'll break it down and cut your head off."

"Massa Colonel, you better be still. Ole missus have door fastened, and say you mus'nt come out till mornin'."

After many bootless surges against the door, and repeated fruitless attempts to get further replies from the black sentinel outside, our traveller, exhausted, took a seat on the side of the bed, and began to ponder seriously on his situation. The more he pondered on the matter, the farther he was from arriving at a satisfactory conclusion. The current of his thoughts was about in this wise:—

"If they intended to murder me and rob me, so much pains would not have been taken to put me on my guard. But to be safe, I'll take out my pistols and have them handy; yet I know I shall have no need for them. And how extravagantly ludicrous and ridiculous the whole thing looks. If it wasn't that the old lady is one of the most sober-sided and conscientious of women, I should largely suspect that there was some infernal hoax about the whole matter; but such a conjecture is the sheerest nonsense. * * * * I have it; the old woman is deucedly superstitious, and I heard some time ago that the spiritual-rappers had been along this way. Yes, yes, it's as clear as mud—she's a *medium!* ha! ha! ha! and has had a revelation about me that has scared her wits away. What a fool I was not to see into the thing before! What is this world a coming to?"

It is unnecessary to pursue any further the Colonel's speculations. Suffice it, that lying down on the bed, intending to continue his investigations into the mysterious affair, he was so worn out by the fatigues of the day as to be overcome by sleep, and never waked until broad daylight next morning, when he was roused by knocks at the door, and the announcement that "breakfast was ready."

Hastily dressing himself, and performing his ablutions in his room, from whence the widow had failed to remove the *cotton* towel, he descended to the breakfast room, as eager for something to eat, as he was to get an explanation of the enigmatical proceedings of the past evening. Saluting the mistress of the house, as she sat, stiff as whalebone and buckram, at the head of the table, guarded by her two herculean servitors, and looking as if she had valorously made up her mind to "face the music," he took a seat at the table, a hasty glance at which told him that his breakfast was to be a "piece of the same cloth," as his supper, (i.e.) that it consisted of no other viands than corn-bread, bacon and water.

"Mrs. Dudu," said the Colonel, looking calmly at her, and speaking in a mild tone of voice, "do you believe in the Bible?"

"I thank my God that I do," nervously responded the widow, not at all relishing the unorthodox insinuation conveyed by the question.

"Do you pretend to shape your conduct by its holy teachings?" pursued the querist.

"I endeavor, with divine assistance, to do so," was the devout response.

"Did you ever read the 19th chapter in LEVITICUS?" continued he.

"I reckon," said the old lady, stammering, "I reckon I have?"

"Do you remember the divine injunctions that chapter contains?"

"I don't know, exactly, as I do," answered the lady, troubled beyond measure, and not at all prepared for the "course of chaticism" through which she was being put.

"If you will be so good as to send for your Bible, I would like, before we begin our breakfast, to refresh your memory, by reading to you a portion of the 19th chapter of Leviticus," continued the catechist, in a serious and solemn tone.

The widow was both astounded and disconcerted by this proposition. By this, there is no intention to intimate that the Colonel's religious opinions were not of the most orthodox stamp, but a more intimate friend than the widow had ever claimed to be, might have been pardoned for being astounded or for mistrusting his own senses, had he heard the Sacred Volume called for, at breakfast, by the hero of our story. Of course the book was brought and placed before him, and after turning over the leaves awhile, he stopped and said:

"Mrs. Dudu, I read from the 33d and 34th verses, 19th chapter of Leviticus, the words:—

" 'And if a stranger sojourn with thee, thou shalt not vex him. But the stranger that dwelleth with you, he shall be unto you as one born among you, and thou shalt love him as thyself. I am the Lord thy God!'

"Now, madam, with this precept staring you in the face, what am I to think of the manner in which I was vexed, worried, locked up and made a prisoner of, in your house last night? You seem confounded, and well you may be."

"Indeed, Colonel," said the old lady, in much confusion, for that "scriptur argument" had opened all the avenues of her heart towards him, "I'm sure I did not mean to vex you or worry you. You know that my house, and everything in it, is at your service, for I haven't a friend in the world that I set more store by than I do you. But you know circumstances alters cases."

"They do, indeed, madam," replied the traveller, with some bitterness, "as I have had the pain and mortification of exemplifying in this house lately. I demand, madam, to be informed why you directed your servants to fasten the door of my room last night as soon as I entered it, keeping me a prisoner until this morning?"

"O, Lord," said the widow, fearing to make the disclosure that would bring on the "most ungovernable of the paroxysms," "I can't tell you;—it would be worse for us all if I told you. Besides, you won't believe it. Lord have mercy on me."

There were such unmistakable evidences of real distress pictured in her countenance, and betrayed in her general manner and bearing, that he forebore to press her after the peremptory fashion he had at first assumed, but adopting a more respectful tone, he said:

"Well, madam, I certainly shall not insist on an explanation, if it would be so very unpleasant to your feelings; though a man should be readily excused for speaking peremptorily, who has been unceremoniously fastened up in a room all night, and asks the reason. But let that pass. I presume there will be no harm in asking the cause of the scarcity of sheets, bed-spreads, and pillow-cases? Has the rise in the price of cotton suggested this economy?"

"Bless your soul, sir, I have the greatest abundance of sheets, spreads, and pillow-cases, and—and—but I must not tell you; it would make mischief; pray don't urge me," plead the distressed woman so beseechingly, as to disarm the gentleman from pursuing his inquiries further upon that point.

"Madam, your wishes shall be law," replied the gallant and good-natured Colonel, "since you request it, and think mischief would come of it, I shall not urge an explanation. Still you must excuse me for declaring your conduct is very strange and altogether unaccountable. I trust no mischief would ensue if you were to answer me as to whether the coons have swept your hen-house? that you have banished the chicken from your table; or that your hens have ceased to lay? that you have no eggs; or that your cows have gone dry? that you have no milk or butter;—and why is coffee interdicted on your table as a beverage?"

"Spare me, Colonel," piteously supplicated the widow; "God knows I would tell you if I dared; but I would be running the risk of my life to do so. I don't think Christian people should fly in the face of Providence. If you knew all you wouldn't blame me, or think hard of me, indeed, you wouldn't."

"This is decidedly interesting; nay, it borders on the romantic," said the oft-baffled guest; "I am at the end of my row. Madam, you are the most incomprehensible woman I ever saw—outside of a lunatic asylum. Every word you utter is ambiguous, every question a puzzle, every look an enigma, your whole conduct a riddle. And as I have but little fancy for or skill in the solution of mysteries, a mystery your conduct may remain until the crack of doom for me. I will trouble you to order my horse and buggy."

The natural vexation and anger which this speech indicated, and which it was impossible any longer to conceal or subdue, had the effect to precipitate matters and hasten the *denouement*.

"O, Colonel Bealle! Colonel Bealle!" exclaimed the poor woman, half distracted between contending emotions; fear of her life on one hand, in case she disclosed to him his dire misfortune, and the certain prospect of losing a highly-prized friend if she made no disclosure, "if you knew all and would believe it, you would regret this harshness to the longest day you live. But if I die for it, I will tell you. *Look, Toney! Be ready, Jim!* You—havn't—been—the—same—man—since—the AC-CI-DENT!!"

"Accident? what accident?" burst vehemently from the amazed Colonel.

"*The* accident! don't you recollect? Did they never tell you?" said the widow, carried away by an excitement which loosened her tongue and caused it, as Mr. Weller figuratively remarks, to "roll on like a barrow with veel greased," "when the horses got scared, and run away with the carriage, broke it all to splinters, and smashed your head agin the curb-stones, which brought on the misfortune."

"Misfortune!" echoed the Colonel, now completely bewildered. "What kind of misfortune? Speak, woman."

"Oh, Lord, sir, you havn't been the *same man* since the accident! For God's sake, don't kill me," supplicated she, thinking she had let the "cat out."

"I am not the same man?" ejaculated he, more and more astounded. "Saving your presence, madam, I'll be d——d if you are any longer the same woman! You've lost your mind! you are demented! you are stark, staving mad!"

"Lord have mercy on your soul!" yelled the widow, now wild and furious, "the boot's on the other leg; it's *you!* It's YOU!! you—are—CRAZY!!!"

"Ha! ha! ha! haw! haw! haw!" roared the Colonel, in a torrent of incontrollable laughter, as he threw up both hands high above his head, and would have followed suit with his heels, but for the table at which he was still sitting.

The cachinatory explosion was suddenly cut short by a very unexpected circumstance. No sooner were his hands fairly elevated above his head, than Toney and Jim, acting under orders from a higher authority, each seizing a hand, intending to hold it fast during the paroxysm, which both mistress and servants now believed was coming on. A respectable row, or rather a fierce struggle ensued, which lasted two and a half minutes; at the end of which time the remains and fragments might be thus noted: the table was upset and had fewer legs than tables are wont to have, broken china and crockery were scattered very impartially around the room, corn-bread and bacon "lay loose about," Mrs. Dudu had *vamosed*—the widow and her favorite tabby having made themselves scarce early in the action—the Colonel was sprawling on the floor, with Toney and Jim holding him down as *easy* as they could, and the *finale* enriched and enlivened by the furious barking and yelping of a couple of curs, who, though not put down in the bill as among the *"dramatis personœ,"* nevertheless performed a conspicuous part by way of musical accompaniment.

By dint of threats and promises to behave, our hero was, after a time, released and permitted to rise from the floor. Once more on his feet, it was "smartly mixed" in the Colonel's mind whether or not he shouldn't save the hangman a job and blow out the brains of his assailants on the spot, but the trembling and terror-stricken spectacle they presented disarmed him of his murderous intentions towards them. The next instant, seeking their mistress, he was resolved, at all hazards, to have an explanation of her conduct, and of the indignity with which she had caused her servants to treat him. Finding, at length, that she had locked herself up in a room, he rapped at the door, and in a firm and decided tone of voice, addressed her:

"Madam, this 'hide-and-seek' game won't do. I intend to have an explanation before I leave the house. Keep your door closed, if you choose, but an explanation I am determined to have, or I never will quit the premises."

"Mercy on me, Colonel," exclaimed the widow, from the interior of the room, in a smothered key, as coming from beneath a feather-bed, "I can't explain any more than I have already done. *You are crazy!* and, for the Lord's sake, don't murder me!"

"Madam," answered he, vehemently, "you are crazy yourself. I'll swear I am not crazy. Somebody has imposed upon you."

"I knew you would deny it," responded the voice from under the feather-bed; "but I'll swear to you that you *are* crazy."

"Who told you that I was crazy?" demanded our hero.

"A friend of yours," answered she from within, "who saw you when the horses ran away with the carriage in Mobile, and the accident occurred."

"What's his name?"

"He lives in Mobile, he said," she answered, "and his name, I think, is SMITH!—JOHN SMITH!!"

There were no more questions asked; there were no more answers from beneath the feather-beds; "the milk in the cocoa-nut" was most satisfactorily accounted for!

Springing into his buggy, which had been for some time in readiness, our indignant Mississippian drove rapidly away, muttering between his teeth as he went, "I'll show that crittur', John Smith, a *kinch* worth two of that!" and, as the Patlanders say, "Be jabers! he kept his word intirely."

Tuscaloosa, Alabama. OMEGA.

Introduction

II. *Alabama Baroque*

ALABAMA fiction in the second half of the nineteenth century plunges headlong into the thick, richly scented atmosphere of historical romance. Indeed, in the hands of its two most renowned practitioners, Caroline Lee Hentz and Augusta Evans Wilson—both of whom gained not just local, but national celebrity—the genre one might now call Alabama Baroque takes on an almost stifling, hothouse opulence. Plot compounds itself into stunning labors of complex implausibility: abductions, rescues, thwarted loves, chance meetings that make all the difference, near-misses that might, but do not. Character plays out in bejasmined variations on a number of familiar types: the old soldier-aristocrat, the sage educator, the young lawyer or physician, the wild youth, the delicate, yet steely maiden. Setting recurrently devolves to the ruined great house, the darkling pastoral landscape, the provincial seat of government or education, square and courthouse, college and church. Description is florid, heavy, insistently dramatic. Dialogue takes place—except when a part falls to vernacular characters such as faithful servants, village eccentrics, or scheming, upstart Yankees—in a single tenor of impassioned, operatic declamation.

Yet for good or ill, writing such as this once bespoke the dominant tastes of a genteel culture; accordingly, Hentz, in the years just before the Civil War, and Wilson, from the same period onward through the war and well into the new century, proved immensely popular with a wide following of readers, North and South.

In terms more distinctly literary, they may have fared less well. Although Nathaniel Hawthorne, too, called himself a "romancer," trying to unite the novelist's concern for "the probable and ordinary course of man's experience" with the larger "truth of the human heart," he nonetheless had writers such as Hentz and Wilson in mind when he castigated "the damned scribbling women" who seemed bent on turning the genre into an empty, frivolous parody of itself. And even more vehement on the subject of romance and what seemed its particular attractions for the Southern mind—its overblown characterizations of love, virtue, and honor, for example, not to mention its enshrinement of a warrior code of knightly heroism—would be Mark Twain. In *Huckleberry Finn,* before sending a steamboat to the Mississippi bottom, he is at pains to name it the "Walter Scott"; and one has to think he would have especially wished Civil War–era Southern practitioners aboard. Romance had ruined the South, he felt; and those that continued to honor its outworn forms were performing the literary equivalent of worship at an altar of death, raising up in popular consciousness shades of the very trumpery— chivalry, reactionary nostalgia, and all the other old notions of race, custom, class, and culture at large—that had brought about the society's tragic demise.

Still, the fact remains that the works of Hentz and Wilson do truly appear to have been what people in large numbers were reading; and as such, they must still continue to tell us a good deal about how both the writer and the reader regarded themselves in relation to Southern history and culture.

As regards the vast and generally monotonous body of Wilson's writing, it seems more or less just that the indictments of the baroque school have largely stood. Hentz, in contrast, at least in her most inventive work, might be worthy of significant reconsideration. The selection here is a case in point, taken from an 1856 collection entitled *The Banished Son; and Other Stories of the Heart.* To be sure, like the title story or many of its companions, "Wild Jack; or, the Stolen Child" may in the abstract seem an almost outrageous concoction of sentimental balderdash. The characters are close to a romance stock-company: the glorious child; the doting, genteel whites; the bereft mother, Dilsy (oddly anticipating the comparable figure in Faulkner's *The Sound and the Fury*); the wise, paternal university president; and finally Jack, the wild, gallant boy, at once hero and outlaw. Plot and theme collide in a curious mishmash of intention. The main scenario of abduction and recovery, the wonder-struck child swept away by the dashing rider, mixes uneasily with a paean to Southern civic virtue, as well as a defense of the provincial community for its "kindness and humanity to a lowly race whose feelings the Southron is too often accused of disregarding and trampling under foot." Yet after all the pious, overwrought Victorian sentimentalism, what one really remembers about the tale is its air of intense imaginative mystery. What is it, this odd spiritual attraction of Wild Jack for the child, or the child for the fleet, dark rider? It is something like the mystery, one feels, that so fascinated Washington Irving in the tales of Grimm and compelled his recasting of them upon the haunted landscapes of such earlier "provincial" American stories as "Rip Van Winkle" and "The Legend of Sleepy Hollow." Or perhaps, closer to home, it is that same pull of the native imagination toward its gothic nightside that had already come to dominate the literary sensibilities of Hentz's Southern contemporary, Edgar Allan Poe. There is ultimately something at work in "Wild Jack" that takes us beyond mere sentimental romance or provincial nostalgia; in the last years before the War Between the States, we find ourselves afoot in a lost world of forgotten mysteries that we can now know again through the shapes of deeply remembered collective myth.

The texture of Augusta Evans Wilson's Alabama Baroque fiction can be largely inferred on the basis of her exotic, overblown titles: *Inez, a Tale of the Alamo; Beulah; Infelice; Macaria; St. Elmo; 'Vashti.* The selection here is the first portion of a relatively late novel, *At the Mercy of Tiberius,* and is entitled, for purposes of this collection, "The Old General and the Lost Granddaughter." In many ways, it is again, like the Hentz selection, all too typical of the genre it represents: there has been the disputed marriage, and, as a consequence, the disobedient daughter banished to the grim, anonymous North; now the child of the ill-omened union returns to the aristocratic house of her mother's childhood. Soon will come the melodramatic complications: the murder of the Old General; the "photograph" of the death scene etched by lightning on a pane of windowglass; the intervention of the young lawyer in the granddaughter's defense. Even as one prepares to scoff, however, it is worth remembering that a great number of literate people once read this eagerly. Indeed, still now, for all its contrivances, trumped-up mysteries, and forced emotions, one senses in the tale a vivid strength of aspiration and energy. One feels that he or she too might have read on just to see if it all really was going to turn out as one suspected and, for the sake of a good ending, probably hoped.

The fiction of the third writer represented in this section, Samuel

Minturn Peck, will probably come as a surprise to some readers, since Peck during his career was much better known for the writing of poetry than of fictional narrative. As the quaint, almost demure tale included here suggests, it may be that the divided interest worked to the author's benefit, at least on the side of his fiction. It is as if he saved whatever Victorian grandiloquence he had in him for his verse and let the realistic, familiar, even homely subjects of his stories speak for themselves. For if, in "Pap's Mules," for instance, the mood is that of romance, it is in a form decidedly chastened and subdued. The vision of mighty conflict broods over the landscape; but the memory is not that of the glorious lost cause. The mood is unquestionably nostalgic, even close to elegiaic; but there is also a sense of realistic economy, a concern for working out the significance of the everyday and particular. War is a question here of saving what one can, of children fleeing Yankee invaders with their father's broken-down mules, so that in the wake of destruction, something of normal life can at least begin to go on again; it is a matter, in short, of simple people entertaining the simple hopes that sustain them in their common humanity.

Similarly, description in Peck, as compared to the fevered hyperbole of Hentz and Wilson, is muted, almost spare. Dialogue, if invested with a certain period sentimentality, suggests nonetheless a new faithfulness to the character of actual speech; this is likewise the case with dialect, which is often used here not for comedy or color, but in a serious attempt to suggest its own particular credibility as a form of fictional discourse. In sum, Peck's fiction reveals a distinct movement away from Victorian romance and toward the realism of the sort soon to be taken up by succeeding Alabama writers such as T. S. Stribling, Sara Haardt Mencken, Robert Gibbons, William March, and others. In modern realistic fiction, a true Alabama flowering was about to begin.

Wild Jack; or, The Stolen Child

Caroline Lee Hentz

I

"Think not the heart in ebon mould
To nature's softest touch is cold,
Or that the negro's skin contains
No bright or animated veins,
Where, though no blush its course betrays,
The blood in all its wildness plays."

"WE might call this Elliottville," said Mrs. Elliott to her husband, as they wandered about the grounds of the habitation which he had just rented, and which were beautiful in vernal bloom. "I have counted at least several houses in this single green enclosure."

"Each about as large as a humming bird's nest," answered her husband laughingly. "This white building, with green blinds and broad piazza, is our parlour. The one on the right, with low, slanting roof, containing three rooms, will accommodate us with a sitting room, dormitory, and refreshment room. Yonder, under the shade of the chestnut boughs, is my library, and study. Every building has its appropriate office; and dotting, as they do, this smooth green sward, have quite a novel and picturesque effect."

"What a singular taste the architect must have had!" said the lady. "These little cabins remind me of a watering place, and far down in that wild-looking glen, behind the buildings, I hear the murmur of a gushing spring. How charming! But there is a house quite remote from this cluster, embosomed in a grove of young oaks. It looks as if it might be a chapel, from its devout, sequestered appearance."

"You can convert it into one, if you please. But here comes our darling Bessy. She will revive here in this pure, sweet air. It is almost like living in the country."

A young black girl approached, bearing in her arms an infant of about nine months old. The child was exceedingly fair and delicate, and the clear blue of the heavens was painted on the mirror of its soft, smiling eyes. It was lovely, but wanted the rosy charm of health, the spring, the bound that belongs to vigorous infancy. The child seemed to have inherited from its mother, extreme delicacy of constitution, for Mrs. Elliott's cheek was pale as the white rose she had just gathered, and her figure was slender, even to fragility.

"Have you succeeded in your search?" she asked in a tremulous voice, of her husband, casting a tearful glance at little Bessy, who, now seated on the grass, by her sable attendant, looked round with a pleased and wondering expression.

"I have," he replied, "and think you will be perfectly satisfied. She is a young mulatto woman, of the name of Dilsy, with a little boy, about one year old. She is free, and lives by herself, taking in sewing and washing. Her husband is dead, and there seems to be no obstacle to her accepting the situation in our family you are anxious to have filled."

"I cannot bear the idea of her having a coloured nurse," said the mother, gazing anxiously on the sweet pale infant playing in the grass, "but I would make any sacrifice for our mutual health. I should like to see this woman."

"Yonder she comes now, leading her little boy," exclaimed Mr. Elliott, pointing towards the gate. "I told her to come immediately, thinking she would recommend herself better than I could do it for her."

"She has a very prepossessing countenance," said Mrs. Elliott, watching with interest the advancing figure of Dilsy. "I think I could trust her."

Dilsy walked slowly, accommodating her movements to those of her little boy, who waded through the long grass by her side, his black, woolly head popping up and down, with marvellous quickness, as if his journey were more upward than onward. Dilsy was tall and well formed, and moved with the native grace of an African. Her complexion was a clear golden brown, and, what was very remarkable in one of her colour, her lips had a tinge of redness which beautified her whole face. She wore a party-coloured handkerchief round her head, but her hair was visible below it, and the crispy wool of the African was straightened and burnished in her, into Indian glossiness and length. She had an indolent, reposing countenance, exceedingly pleasant and rather handsome. Though, as we have said, her own complexion had a bright golden tint, the child whom she led by the hand, was as black as ebony. The white of his eyes and the ivory of his teeth gleamed dazzlingly from the little shining, sable face they enlivened. His very short frock exhibited to the fullest advantage his round, glossy, and well proportioned limbs. As he came near, he broke from his mother's hand, and began to make somersets in the grass, with inconceivable rapidity, and to the delight of little Bessy, who clapped her waxen hands and laughed outright.

"Behave yourself, Jim!" said his mother; but he was too much engaged in his antics to heed her rebuke, and Mrs. Elliott told her to let the children amuse themselves, while she questioned her on the subject nearest her heart. Her own health, and that of her infant, were so feeble that the physician had urged upon her the necessity of transferring her child to another nurse, as the only means of restoring either. Mr. Elliott had been for some time in search of a proper person, when Dilsy was recommended, who seemed to possess every necessary qualification.

"We can give her the *chapel* for her room," said Mrs. Elliott; and Dilsy and little Jim took possession of the cabin, shaded by young oaks, and the little fragile Bessy soon derived health and strength from the veins of the handsome mulatto.

The only objection Mrs. Elliott could make to Dilsy was, that she seemed deficient in sensibility. She never lavished on Bessy any of those endearing caresses which negro nurses usually bestow on their masters' children, thus breaking down, as it were, the dark wall that separates the races from each other. She was kind and attentive to her charge, but as soon as she had fulfilled her duty, she would transfer it without any demonstration of affection to its other nurse, and occupy herself calmly with her accustomed work. Neither did she manifest any tenderness for her own child. She took great pride in dressing him neatly, and when the ladies, who visited Mrs. Elliott, noticed the boy, praising his intelligence and sprightliness, she would look pleased, but she was singularly undemonstrative; and it is not strange that Mrs. Elliott, whose heart was always gushing forth in the warmest expressions of love to her child, should think Dilsy cold and unfeeling.

"Do you love Jim?" asked she of her one day.

"Yes, mistress. To be sure I does. He's my own child, and I'm obliged to love him."

"But you are not very fond of children, are you?"

"I never cares about hugging and kissing 'em as some does. I thinks and feels though, and would do as much to keep harm from 'em, as anybody else."

This was a great deal for the quiet mulatto to say. She was that rare, and some believe fabulous character—a silent woman.

Spring, summer, and autumn glided away, and little Bessy frolicked with Jim about the beautiful green enclosure, the picture of rosy health, as she was of angel loveliness. Jim had grown wonderfully. He was stout, strong, and brave as a little lion, and as full of mischief and pranks as a monkey. He could jabber and dance for the entertainment of Mrs. Elliott's guests, and cut more capers for the amusement of Bessy than necromancer ever taught.

Dilsy's mission was ended, for Bessy, as the cooler season advanced, was gradually withdrawn from her nursing cares. Mrs. Elliott, however, who had become attached to her, in spite of her cool, unimpassioned manners, gave her permission to remain in the chapel (as she always called the shade-embosomed cabin), and continue her usual occupations.

There was a young man of about twenty, whose father resided somewhere in the vicinity, but who was seldom seen at home. Indeed, he seemed to live on horseback, dashing about on a wild, black horse, that no one could venture to ride but himself. His name was John Green, but he was known only by the appellation of Wild Jack. Wherever he went the sound of clattering hoofs preceded him—a cloud of dust followed. "Get out of the way—Wild Jack's coming," was the cry of the children in the street, as they scampered towards the fence. In short, he was the wild huntsman of the country, and as he passed along, like a swift dark cloud, a thrill of admiration was always excited by his matchless horsemanship. It was said he lived by gambling, for he was never seen to work, yet the glitter of silver sparkled through the meshes of his purse, and its clinking made constant music in the bar-room.

One evening, as Wild Jack was riding rather more slowly than usual along a back road that wound round the grounds of Mr. Elliott, he caught a glimpse of little Jim, perched on the top of the fence, laughing and clapping his hands, at the sight of the black steed, and its shining, flowing mane. Jack reined in his horse and rode directly up to the fence where the child was seated.

"Here, jump on to my saddle, and I'll teach you how to ride, you little black rascal," exclaimed the horseman, leaning forward, seizing the child by the arm and swinging him in front of himself, as if he had no more weight than a feather.

"Me feard," said the child, shrinking from the fierce, bright eyes of Jack, that ran up and down his plump little body, like live balls. It was strange for him to express fear.

"*You* afraid! why I took you for a man. I'll bring you back directly."

Away he flew, and little Jim forgot his terrors in the delight of motion, and the charm of novelty. Up hill and down hill they went, over fields and creeks, and it was not till the gray of evening began to darken the glow of sunset, that the little equestrian returned to the shades of the chapel. Dilsy stood at the fence calling her truant boy, whose absence she had just discovered.

"Here I be, mammy," cried little Jim in a tone of exultation, holding up a large paper of candy, with which the liberality of Wild Jack had supplied him.

"You've got the smartest little fellow here I ever saw," said Jack, giving the child a swing into his mother's arms. "I'm going to make a first-rate horseman of him. Don't you want to ride again, you young harlequin?"

"Yes," answered the delighted child, sucking a long stick of red candy, the seal of his friendly compact with the formidable Jack.

Dilsy was flattered by his notice of her child, and when, evening after evening, he disappeared with the flying horseman, she quietly awaited his return, without any misgivings or apprehensions. As for little Jim, he conceived a most extraordinary and passionate love for Wild Jack. For hours before his coming, he would mount the fence and strain his eyeballs and bend his ear, for the dusty cloud and clattering hoofs he so much loved to greet. Dilsy became more and more reconciled to his new passion, as it kept him still several hours on the top of the fence, instead of gamboling about in her way, as he formerly did.

Once Jim was gone longer than usual. It grew quite dark, and yet his little woolly head was not seen peeping in at the door, nor was his childish voice heard exclaiming as usual—

"Me come back, mammy."

Dilsy had worked hard during the day, and was sitting by a warm, bright, lightwood fire. It had been a clear frosty day, and the contrast of the cold, bracing atmosphere abroad, and the glowing heat within, disposed her to a kind of luxurious drowsiness. The negro sleeps as comfortably and sweetly in a split-bottomed chair, as on a downy bed, and Dilsy closed her weary eyes, and slept in happy unconsciousness of the prolonged absence of her child.

That night, before Mrs. Elliott retired to rest, she stood by the couch of her sleeping infant, gazing with a mother's joy and gratitude on its round, roseate cheek, and white, dimpled arms. She compared its present appearance of health and strength with its former waxen paleness and extreme fragility, and her heart swelled with emotions of thankfulness to Dilsy, who had been the instrument, in the hands of God, of her darling's restoration.

"Look at her," she cried, turning to her husband, while she shaded back the soft flaxen hair from Bessy's snowy forehead. "How sweet, how placid, how well she looks! That was a blessed day you brought Dilsy to me. Had it not been for her, I do not think Bessy could have survived the summer months. She really is a treasure. I feel as if I wanted to do something to prove my gratitude to her."

"Why, you are proving it all the time, my dear. Not a day passes that is not crowned by some act of loving kindness on your part, towards this clever mulatto. I am sure *her* lines have fallen in pleasant places. You make almost as great a pet of Jim as you do of Bessy. Is that fine dress for him?" pointing to a gay tunic of brilliant scarlet, trimmed rather fantastically with black.

"Yes. I long for the morrow to come, to see him dressed in this suit. The bright red will set off so well his jetty skin. I really think the boy is handsome—he is so black and shining and has such an intelligent, merry face. I always wondered his mother did not show more fondness for him—her only child, too. I do not think she has much sensibility, but a great deal of principle."

"All mothers are not as foolish as you are, my dear," said he with an affectionate smile; and Mrs. Elliott felt, though he called her foolish, he did not condemn her folly. She fell asleep with the vision of little Jim, arrayed in his scarlet clothes, dancing before her eyes.

She was awakened by a cry so loud, so thrilling, that it seemed as if something sharp was stabbing her ears. It broke on the silence of night with terrible distinctness, and sounded like the wail of a breaking heart.

"Good heavens!" exclaimed Mrs. Elliott, starting from her pillow, "what cry is that? It is in our own yard."

Mr. Elliott sprang from the bed and hastily dressing himself opened the door, letting in as he did so a whole flood of moonlight. Mrs. Elliott rose also, trembling with terror, and wrapping herself in a large woollen shawl, followed her husband into the piazza. The cry arose again more distinctly. It came nearer, and the words—

"My child! my child! They've stolen my child!" were audible amid shrieks of agony.

"It's Dilsy!" cried Mrs. Elliott. "Oh! husband, what is the matter? See her—running up and down the yard. Call her, for mercy's sake, and find what she means."

While she was speaking, Dilsy came rushing to the gate, looking like a distracted creature, with her hair loosely flying, tossing her arms wildly above her head.

"My child!" she shrieked. "Master—mistress—they've stole him. I never see him no more."

Here she wrung her hands, and, bursting afresh into an exceeding loud and bitter cry, was about to run off towards the street, when Mr. Elliott caught her by the arm and forced her into the house.

"Let go!" she cried frantically. "Wild Jack's got him—he never brought him back—he never will bring him back again."

The truth flashed upon Mr. Elliott's mind. He had seen Jim before sunset, mounted in front of the Wild Huntsman, and from Dilsy's broken exclamations, he learned how long he had been gone, how she had awakened out of a long, deep sleep, seated by the cabin's hearth, and how she remembered waiting there for her boy, and wondering that he did not come. She sought him and called him, till she was hoarse—sought him in every nook and corner of the cabin, shaking the bed clothes as if he were a needle or a pin, that could be hidden in their seams—then seizing a torch, forgetful of the moonlight, and swinging it above her head, rushed to the wood-pile, and hurled the sticks in the air, sometimes imagining the end of a blackened pine knot the head of her missing child. At length came the horrible conviction that he was stolen, carried off, to be sold to the slave-trader, and the cry which had banished the slumbers of Mrs. Elliott, was wrung from a mother's breaking heart.

All that kindness and sympathy could do, was done by Mrs. Elliott, to soothe and comfort the poor, half-distracted Dilsy. The household was roused, a warm fire kindled, and warm covering wrapped round her chilled and shivering limbs. But Dilsy refused to be comforted. The sensibility that had been sleeping in the bottom of her heart, gushed out in an overwhelming stream. Nor was it sorrow alone that stirred the before unsounded depths of her soul. The thirst of vengeance mingled with the yearnings of affection, and infused wormwood and gall into the flowing brine. She threw herself on the floor, and tore her long Indian tresses, calling on her Jim, her baby, her child, in the most piteous and heart-rending accents.

"I accused her of not *feeling*," thought Mrs. Elliott, wiping away her own fast falling tears. "Ah! how little we know of what is passing in the heart. Poor creature—what can I do to comfort her?"

"I will go over this moment and see the President," exclaimed Mr. Elliott. "The villain must be pursued and overtaken. Be quiet, Dilsy—you shall have your boy again—we'll see about it."

"God Almighty bless you, master—will you? God bless you—will you, master?" cried Dilsy, springing up from the floor and shaking back her dishevelled hair, her eyes glittering with excitement. "I thought nobody care for little negro—free, too. Oh, Lordy! Jimmy—little Jimmy! S'pose he come back again!"

Covering her face with her hands, she burst into an hysterical laugh, and picking up a white muslin apron of little Bessy's that had fallen upon the floor, began to wipe her eyes with it, without knowing what she was doing. In the mean time, Mr. Elliott, burning with indignation for the outrage on the poor mulatto, walked over, in the dead of night as it was, to the President's mansion, which was not far from his own. He was one of the Professors of the University, which was situated on the beautiful hill, near which he resided; and when the President was roused from his slumbers by the voice of Mr. Elliott, he naturally concluded that the students had been detected in some midnight depredation. He was a man of surpassing benevolence of character, united to a stern and inflexible sense of justice. He entered warmly into Mr. Elliott's plans for the recovery of the child, and proposed that emissaries should be despatched on the three roads, which led from the hill, in pursuit of the robber and his prey, promising to bear his part of the expense, and pledging himself for the other members of the faculty. Early the next morning, three men, hired by the President and professors, started in three different directions, for the purpose of tracking the human bloodhound.

It has been said that self-interest alone prompts the white man to be kind to the negro race—that he feeds, and clothes, and warms him, because he is his own property, and he himself would suffer, if his slave were neglected or wronged. This may be the case in some instances, but it certainly was not in this. Here was a poor, humble, unprotected mulatto, a free woman, with a free child. She enriched no one, she belonged to no one; her child was her own property, and its loss impoverished no one but herself. And yet, in defence of this woman's rights, for the recovery of her stolen boy, were enlisted the sympathies and influence of the dignified President of a celebrated University, and its intelligent and learned professors. Was this self-interest? No, it was divine philanthropy; it was the acknowledgment of that bond which unites the great brotherhood of mankind, and which is drawn closer and closer by misfortunes and wrongs. Dilsy and her child were of the lowly African race, and yet how many hearts were now throbbing in unison with hers; how many prayers were ascending to heaven for the recovery of her child!

II

"God help me, in my grievous need;
God help me, in my inward pain,
Which cannot ask for pity's meed;
Which has no license to complain;
Which must be borne, yet who can bear
Hours long, days long, a constant weight,
The yoke of absolute despair,
A suffering wholly desolate?"

Two weary days passed away, and no tidings of the lost child. The wild agony of the mother had settled down into a kind of stupor, the result of despair. Mrs. Elliott kept her in the house, and, by giving little Bessy entirely to her charge, tried to interest her feelings and divert her attention from her own sorrows. She did this in kindness, but perhaps it was an error in judgment, for the sight of the beautiful child, blooming in the security of home, reminded her only more vividly of her own wandering boy. She would sit for hours, gazing with a dull, vague look, on the little scarlet dress, so fancifully margined with jetty braid, hanging conspicuously on the wall.

"Some how or other, mistress," she said mournfully, "that looks just like Jim's shroud. To look at it long, it turns all over black."

"You will see little Jimmy wear it before long," replied Mrs. Elliott, kindly. "When so many are interested in his recovery, it is almost impossible that he should not be found."

"Oh, mistress, that black horse goes like the wind. Nobody could catch him. 'Taint like other horses. O dear! O Lord! how I wish I'd never let Jimmy get up with that awful man."

The second night one of the men returned, weary, and unsuccessful. He had perceived no trace of the fugitives, and, convinced they must have taken some other route, thought it best to return. The next morning the other two also came back, but without the child. One of them, however, imparted information of great interest. He had followed in the track of a young man, mounted on a fiery black horse, who had been seen at early dawn, riding along, with a little child before him. The description corresponded exactly to Wild Jack, and the man was sure of overtaking the robber, but he soon came where four roads met, and knew not which way to turn. In his perplexity, he suffered one of the superstitions of his childhood to guide him, and he directed his course to the rising sun. In the course of the day he heard of a slavetrader, who had passed that way with a large number of slaves, and among them was a little boy, of the age of Jim, who was represented, like him, to be black as polished ebony. There was no doubt that Wild Jack had had an understanding with the man, and sold to him the stolen child.

The emissary, who was not a bold man, thought not of contending with one of these desperate characters, but immediately turned his face homeward, to communicate the facts which had come to his knowledge.

Dark were the clouds that now gathered round the fate of little Jim. While the man was returning, *he* was borne still further from them, on a wild, unfrequented road, and perhaps even then he was transferred to some other master, who might be bearing him away on the wings of the morning.

Mr. Elliott sat with the President in his office, with an anxious and troubled countenance. While they were engaged in earnest conversation on the subject, the door opened, and Mr. Green, the father of Wild Jack, was announced.

He was a meek, sorrowful-looking man, with a stooping frame and downcast countenance. One might look in vain in his pale, dim eyes, thin cheeks, and melancholy mouth, for any resemblance to the bright, fierce, wicked face of Wild Jack.

There was something in his appearance that appealed irresistibly to the compassionate feelings of the gentlemen; and the President, moved by commiseration, as well as by habitual politeness, addressed him kindly, and offered him a seat, by the ample and blazing fire. But he would not be seated. He stood with his hat crushed between his knees, with an expression of conscious unworthiness, and the worn and crushed hat seemed a meet emblem of his crushed and grief-worn heart. The father of a wicked, law-defying son, whom he had in vain endeavoured to "train up in the way he should go," must feel abject and wretched.

"Are there any tidings of your son, sir?" asked the President, breaking the silence, which began to be irksome.

"I've heard of the lost child, sir," he replied meekly, "and I've come to tell you that if you'll stop the search after him, he shall be brought back day after to-morrow night. Yes, sir, I'll swear on the Bible, if you say so, that what I say is the truth."

The gentlemen looked at each other in surprise. They knew but little of Mr. Green, and, judging of him by the character of his son, as people are apt to do, imagined him to be a man with very dim perceptions of right and wrong. He was considered a poor man, owning a small farm and a few negroes, whose work he shared while he superintended their labours. Jack was his only son, whose birth and his mother's death were simultaneous events. Poor Jack! had he ever known a mother's restraining influence and tender watchfulness, his evil propensities would never have acquired their present rank and poisonous luxuriance.

"This is very strange," said the President, fixing his eyes sternly on his agitated and working features. "Am I to consider you an accomplice with your son in this felonious act?"

The poor man looked up to heaven with an humble, deprecating air, and the President felt something knocking against his heart, painfully and reproachfully. He had no son of his own, but he could comprehend what were a father's feelings, and he knew those of a man.

"I didn't come here to criminate or defend myself, sir; neither did I come to defend my son. It wouldn't do any good, if I did, for you all know him. I don't pretend to deny that he's carried off the child. I know if he's taken, his life will be forfeited. But I don't think he can be. He's got a way that nobody ever had before. I sometimes think an evil spirit is in him—but he is my son, for all that—all that I've got in the world. He's bone of my bone, and flesh of my flesh, given me by his mother, now in heaven. You can't catch Jack, but you can keep him from coming near me as long as I live. You will advertise him and set a price on his head, and it will be all right."

"To be sure, it will," interrupted the President emphatically, and Mr. Elliott's clear eye pronounced *amen.*

"You can do it," continued Mr. Green, "but with all that, it is very doubtful whether you ever see him or the boy either. But I promise you solemnly, gentlemen, if you'll all keep quiet and say nothing, that day after to morrow night, at about midnight, the child shall be in front of Mr. Porter's tavern. If he's not there, you may take *me,* put me in jail, and hang me in place of my son."

There was an air of such earnestness and sincerity about the man, combined with such profound melancholy, that they were both deeply impressed. They were beginning to be convinced of the hopelessness of pursuit, and were ready to listen to any proposition which reason might sanction and justice approve.

"If we put faith in your promises and suspend our present efforts," said the President, whose inflexible justice upbraided him for a too easy surrender of his judgment, "and your son should appear again in our midst, we cannot suffer so dangerous an individual to be at large. The law must claim its due."

"He never shall appear among you. He never again shall disturb the peace of this community. We will both seek a home remote from this, where, I trust, he will begin a new and better life."

"Well, then," said the President, looking at Mr. Elliott.

Mr. Elliott bowed his head in token of assent, and Mr. Green was assured that on the faith of his promise, they would suspend the pursuit and wait the coming of the child.

"I pray you," said Mr. Green in departing, "not to allow a crowd to collect round the tavern. Let the mother be there waiting, but say nothing to anybody else. If anything happens to keep the child, you will find me at my farm, ready to give myself into your hands, for imprisonment or death."

It is not strange that Dilsy should not believe the promise of Mr. Green, or that she should consider her boy as lost for ever. Two more long, weary days were to pass, before the appointed hour, in heart sickness and anguish. She could not sit still, but wandered like a restless ghost about the grounds, with little Bessy warmly clasped in her arms, who would fix her soft blue eyes in mute wonder on her dark, despairing countenance, and sometimes wipe away a large tear from the mulatto's cheek, with her snow-white, dimpled hand. She would stand at the gate, and look up and down the road, till her strained and dazzled glance could see nothing in the bright sunshine, but a painful glitter, obscure as darkness.

"You are wrong to give up to despair, Dilsy," said Mrs. Elliott, "when so much has been done for you. You've told me sometimes that you had no friends—that a poor, free mulatto couldn't have any. You see you are mistaken. If my Bessy was stolen away, there could not be more active measures taken to restore her to my arms. You must not be ungrateful, Dilsy."

"I don't mean to be, mistress—you're too good. I knows it—I feels it—but I can't talk. Ah, mistress, nobody would think of stealing your baby. Nobody would *buy* a white baby."

A flush passed over Mrs. Elliott's white cheek, as she replied—

"White children are sometimes stolen, as many a weeping mother can bear witness. But it is not often the case in this country. But, Dilsy, Mr. Elliott firmly believes Mr. Green's promise, and is sure that Jimmy will come back again. You should put trust in God, if not in man, for his promise never fails."

"I can't think of any promise to comfort me," said the poor mulatto.

"He suffers not a sparrow to fall to the ground without his knowledge, and He feedeth the young ravens when they cry."

"That *may* mean little Jimmy. He's black like the raven," said Dilsy, thoughtfully, "and he's got nobody to feed him now if God don't."

She brought the white muslin apron of Bessy's which she had moistened with tears on the night of Jimmy's abduction, and presented it, nicely washed and starched, to Mrs. Elliott.

"Beg pardon, mistress," said she. "I didn't know nothing of what I was doing, or I wouldn't have used it so."

"You have not hurt it, Dilsy. A mother's tears are sacred. Keep it, and when Jimmy comes back you must dress him in the scarlet tunic, and this pretty apron, and carry him round as a show-boy. They who sow in tears shall reap in joy, Dilsy."

As the night appointed for the child's restoration drew on, Mr. Elliott himself lost his sanguine hopes, and became anxious and restless. He feared that he had been duped by the elder Green, who had probably had recourse to a stratagem, to gain time for his son's escape from justice. He thought he would feel very foolish to wait half the night, as he intended to do, at the tavern, for the fulfilment of a solemn promise, and then find he had been baffled and deceived.

It would be better, perhaps, to let Dilsy go alone, for, should his doubts be confirmed, he could not bear to witness her grief and despair. Yet, when night came on, an irresistible impulse urged him to the spot, where a crowd was already assembled, and among them was the grave and reverend President. This gathering was "not in the bond," for secrecy had been enjoined, but Dilsy could not keep her own counsel. Her heart was too full not to overflow, and the curiosity of the whole neighbourhood was excited by the information.

The President was obliged to make a long harangue before he could induce the people to condense themselves within doors, so as not to frighten away the being, whoever it might be, whose mission it was to restore the stolen child. His words had the desired effect, and Dilsy was left alone in the piazza, counting each moment of the waning hours by the quick beatings of her throbbing heart. Mr. Elliott had lent her his large, warm cloak, to wrap around her, for the night air was cold and frosty. She did not feel it, however, so great was the tension of her mind. If she walked the length of the piazza once, she did hundreds of times, while the big tavern clock, that great auctioneer of time, kept ringing with its iron tongue, "going, going, gone." Yes! the hours were going, slowly, but surely. Ten, eleven—twelve was near at hand.

It was a clear, cloudless night. The moon shone with the pallid glory peculiar to a Southern wintry night, as sweetly and calmly as if there were no scenes of rapine and anguish passing beneath her holy beams. Large pine-fires were blazing in the chimneys, throwing a red glare upon the window panes, and lighting up, with more than noonday brightness, the promiscuous groups within. It was strange to see the majestic President and dignified professors in such company, especially at that unwonted hour. It must have been a strong motive to induce them to leave their families and homes during the silent watches of the night—to haunt a tavern, too—such sober, pious men, as they were: and this motive was the restitution of the wrongs of a poor mulatto, the restoration of a little negro boy. Verily, there is some humanity, some Christian benevolence, at the South, notwithstanding the strenuous efforts to prove the contrary.

Hark! the clock strikes twelve—that is the appointed hour. Yes! just at twelve, said the elder Green, the boy should be returned. The people rushed to the doors and windows, and would have passed into the street had they not been restrained by the commanding voice of the President.

Dilsy pressed forward, and winding one arm around a pillar of the piazza, for she felt suddenly very weak, leaned out into the moonbeams, that burnished with silver her golden-coloured forehead. All was still abroad; not an evergreen leaf quivered in the frosty atmosphere. The road was white and sandy, and had a ghost-like look, stretching on, long and winding, into the dark pine woods.

Dilsy stood panting against the pillar, when suddenly her eyes kindled with revengeful fire. "It was all a base sham; they never were going to bring him back; Master Elliott knew it all the time; they were all making a fool of her; there was no truth in white folks, not one of them." While these dark, vindictive thoughts, rolled through her mind, she heard the distant sound of something, she scarcely knew what. The soil was too sandy, along the road that ran along in front of the tavern, for hoofs to clatter, but still she knew that a horseman was approaching. A black speck seemed to be driven swiftly along over sandy waves; it grew larger and larger, came swifter and swifter, till the outlines of Wild Jack and his black horse were distinctly visible; and perched in front of him was a little child, as black as a starless midnight. Dilsy gave a sharp, loud shriek, and sprang, with one bound, down the steps. The people rushed after her with considerable vehemence. Whirling the child by one arm from the saddle to the ground, Wild Jack dashed his spurs into his horse's flanks, and went off with the speed of the whirlwind. One might as well think of overtaking the whirlwind, as this fierce, wild youth. A yell, loud as an Indian warwhoop, rent the silence, and some plunged into the sand, in a vain effort of pursuit.

"Oh! Jimmy, Jimmy!" exclaimed his mother, snatching up the shivering child, and folding him in her cloak—"is it you?"

"Yes, it's me, mammy," answered a little, weak voice. The mulatto burst into tears. Those little, feeble accents told a tale of suffering and privation.

"Bring him in, bring him in to the fire," cried many voices, and Dilsy, staggering like a drunken woman, made her way through the crowd in the door-way and sunk down on a seat near the fire.

Poor little Jimmy did indeed look as if he had endured sufferings, which he was too young to relate. His round fat cheeks were thin and hollow, and his bright eyes had a dim, strange, bewildered look, that it was painful to witness. The back part of his dress was all worn to tatters, and his woolly head was all bristling with burs and tangled with leaves. He was as cold as an icicle, and when brought near the hot blaze, he began to cry bitterly.

"Remove farther from the fire—it makes his numb limbs ache," said Mr. Elliott; "he must be warmed gradually."

Had Jimmy been a young prince, instead of an unowned negro child, he could not have been treated with more kindness and consideration. He had warm milk and nice warm buttered biscuit brought him to eat, and warm flannel rolled around him, till the painful, bewildered expression of his face changed to one of dreamy satisfaction. They began to question him, but all he could answer was—"Don't know." His dawning faculties seemed obscured by the fright and sufferings of the few past days. He soon fell asleep in his mother's arms, that soft cradle from which the poor little fellow had been so cruelly torn away.

Dilsy's softened heart was now overflowing with gratitude to the white friends who had exerted themselves so energetically in her cause. She was ashamed of her hard, vindictive feelings, and inwardly resolved never again to cherish them. She had a good deal of the Indian in her nature, as was indicated by her straight, shining hair. She was quick to resent and slow to forgive an injury, but the remembrance of blessings conferred was lasting as life.

Mrs. Elliott wept with joy, when her husband returned accompanied by the reunited mother and child, and then she wept with grief over his forlorn and altered appearance. Such a long and terrible journey on horseback, as he must have had with Wild Jack, was enough to kill an older child. Little Jimmy must have been made of tough materials, not to have been shaken and battered to pieces. His flesh was sore and bruised, and in many places his dusky skin was lacerated and worn off. But kind hands anointed him, and the wounds of a child's body are healed almost as soon as those of his heart. After a day's rest and nursing, he was bright enough to be arrayed in the dazzling scarlet suit and white muslin apron. The apron did not look quite in place, but Dilsy said she loved it better than anything she had, and she wouldn't have him leave it off for anything. Jimmy looked really quite magnificent in his royal-hued raiment, and as all the burs were picked out of his head, and his cheeks were already beginning to round themselves, "little Richard was himself again."

Dilsy carried him from house to house, in triumph, while a younger nurse *toted* the fair blue-eyed Bessy, who was only a satellite to the primary planet Jim, on this memorable occasion; Jimmy was emphatically the young Lion of the day, and great regret was expressed that he could not relate his adventures. At first, all he could say was, "I don't know." Now his invariable answer to every question was, "Wild Jack." That fierce, bright image was for ever darting across his little mind, and for a time it seemed doubtful whether any other would ever be imprinted there.

The ladies loaded him with presents, and if Dilsy had suffered much, she also rejoiced much, and in consequence *loved much*. She was certainly better and happier after this event than before. She had cherished the idea that nobody cared anything about her or hers. Even the kindness of Mrs. Elliott she thought selfish, because she was necessary to her child. Now, she acknowledged the existence of disinterested benevolence, and her heart warmed and expanded under its genial influence.

The history of Jim, during his days of absence, was never known. It was conjectured that Mr. Green had bought him back from the trader to whom his son had sold him, at the sacrifice of his little farm and possessions; for they were all sold, and the master departed to some unknown regions, probably accompanied by his reprobate son.

The wild equestrian was never again seen, flying along on his raven steed, after he had darkened for a moment the moonlight night we have described. Whether he has repented of his evil ways, or keeps rushing on the downward road that leads to death, we have never learned.

The following summer little Jim was playing blithely on the green by the side of the blue-eyed Bessy. He seemed to have forgotten Wild Jack; yet if a horse came galloping by, he would jump up and run to his mother, and bury his face in her lap.

There is no romance in the story of Jimmy, but there is truth, without any alloy of fiction. We have related it, as one of many instances of Southern kindness and humanity to a lowly race—whose feelings the Southron is too often accused of disregarding and trampling under foot.

The Old General and the Lost Granddaughter

Augusta Evans Wilson

"I DO not want a carriage. If the distance is only a mile and a half, I can easily walk. After leaving town, is there a straight road?"

"Straight as the crow flies, when you have passed the factory, and cemetery, and turned to the left. There is a little Branch running at the foot of the hill, and just across it, you will see the white palings, and the big gate with stone pillars, and two tremendous brass dogs on top, showing their teeth and ready to spring. There's no mistaking the place, because it is the only one left in the country that looks like the good old times before the war; and the Yankees would not have spared it, had it not been such comfortable bombproof headquarters for their officers. It's our show place now, and General Darrington keeps it up in better style, than any other estate I know."

"Thank you. I will find it."

Beryl walked away in the direction indicated, and the agent of the Railway Station, leaning against the door of the baggage room, looked with curious scrutiny after her.

"I should like to know who she is. No ordinary person, that is clear. Such a grand figure and walk, and such a steady look in her big solemn eyes, as if she saw straight through a person, clothes, flesh and all. Wonder what her business can be with the old General?"

From early childhood Beryl had listened so intently to her mother's glowing descriptions of the beauty and elegance of her old home "Elm Bluff," that she soon began to identify the land-marks along the road, after passing the cemetery, where so many generations of Darringtons slept in one corner, enclosed by a lofty iron railing; exclusive in death as in life; jealously guarded and locked from contact with the surrounding dwellers in "God's Acre."

The October day had begun quite cool and crisp, with a hint of frost in its dewy sparkle, but as though vanquished Summer had suddenly faced about, and charged furiously to cover her retreat, the South wind came heavily laden with hot vapor from equatorial oceanic caldrons; and now the afternoon sun, glowing in a cloudless sky, shed a yellowish glare that burned and tingled like the breath of a furnace; while along the horizon, a dim dull haze seemed blotting out the boundary of earth and sky.

A portion of the primeval pine forest having been preserved, the trees had attained gigantic height, thrusting their plumy heads heavenward, as their lower limbs died; and year after year the mellow brown carpet of reddish straw deepened, forming a soft safe nidus for the seeds, that sprang up and now gratefully embroidered it with masses of golden rod, starry white asters, and tall feathery spikes of some velvety purple bloom, which looked royal by the side of a cluster of belated evening primroses.

Pausing on the small but pretty rustic bridge, Beryl leaned against the interlacing cedar boughs twisted into a balustrade, and looked down at the winding stream, where the clear water showed amber hues, flecked with glinting foam bubbles, as it lapped and gurgled, eddied and sang, over its bed of yellow gravel. Unacquainted with "piney-woods' branches," she was charmed by the novel golden brown wavelets that frothed against the pillars of the bridge, and curled caressingly about the broad emerald fronds of luxuriant ferns, which hung Narcissus-like over their own graceful quivering images. Profound quiet brooded in the warm hazy air, burdened with balsamic odors; but once a pine burr full of rich nutty mast crashed down through dead twigs, bruising the satin petals of a primrose; and ever and anon the oboe notes of that shy, deep throated hermit of ravines—the russet, speckled-breasted lark—thrilled through the woods, like antiphonal echoes in some vast, cool, columned cloister.

The perfect tranquillity of the scene soothed the travel-weary woman, as though nestling so close to the great heart of nature, had stilled the fierce throbbing, and banished the gloomy forebodings of her own; and she walked on, through the iron gate, where the bronze mastiffs glared warningly from their granite pedestal—on into the large undulating park, which stretched away to meet the line of primitive pines. There was no straight avenue, but a broad smooth carriage road curved gently up a hill side, and on both margins of the gravelled way ancient elm trees stood at regular intervals, throwing their boughs across, to unite in lifting the superb groined arches, whose fine tracery of sinuous lines was here and there concealed by clustering mistletoe—and gray lichen masses—and ornamented with bosses of velvet moss; while the venerable columnar trunks were now and then wreathed with poison-oak vines, where red trumpet flowers insolently blared defiance to the waxen pearls of encroaching mistletoe.

On either side, the grounds were studded with native growth, as though protective forestry statutes had crossed the ocean with the colonists, and on this billowy sea of varied foliage Autumn had set her illuminated autograph, in the vivid scarlet of sumach and black gum, the delicate lemon of wild cherry—the deep ochre all sprinkled and splashed with intense crimson, of the giant oaks—the orange glow of ancestral hickory—and the golden glory of maples, on which the hectic fever of the dying year kindled gleams of fiery red;—over all, a gorgeous blazonry of riotous color, toned down by the silver gray shadows of mossy tree-trunks, and the rich, dark, restful green of polished magnolias.

Half a dozen fine Cotswold ewes browsed on the grass, and the small bell worn by a staid dowager tinkled musically, as she threw up her head and watched suspiciously the figure moving under the elm arches. Beneath the far reaching branches of a patriarchal cedar, a small herd of Jersey calves had grouped themselves, as if posing for Landseer or Rosa Bonheur; and one pretty fawn-colored weanling ran across the sward to meet the stranger, bleating a welcome and looking up, with unmistakable curiosity in its velvety, long lashed-eyes.

As the avenue gradually climbed the ascent, the outlines of the house became visible; a stately typical Southern mansion, like hundreds, which formerly opened hospitably their broad mahogany doors, and which alas! are becoming traditional to this generation— obsolete as the brave, chivalric, warm-hearted, open-handed, noble-souled, refined Southern gentlemen who built and owned them. No Mansard roof here, no pseudo "Queen Anne" hybrids, with lowering, top-heavy projections like scowling eyebrows over squinting eyes; neither mongrel Renaissance, nor feeble sickly imitation Elizabethan façades, and Tudor towers; none of the queer, composite, freakish impertinences of architectural style, which now-a-day do duty as the adventurous vanguard, the æsthetic vedettes "making strait the way," for the coming cohorts of Culture.

The house at "Elm Bluff" was built of brick, overcast with stucco painted in imitation of gray granite, and its foundation was only four feet high, resting upon a broad terrace of brick-work; the latter bounded by a graceful wooden balustrade, with pedestals for vases, on either side of the two stone steps leading down from the terrace to the carriage drive. The central halls in both stories, divided the space equally into four rooms on each side, and along the wide front, ran a lofty piazza supporting the roof, with white smooth round pillars; while the upper broad square windows, cedar-framed and deeply embrasured, looked down on the floor of the piazza, where so many generations of Darringtons had trundled hoops in child-hood—and promenaded as lovers in the silvery moonlight, listening to the ring doves cooing above them, from the columbary of the stucco Capitals. This spacious colonnade extended around the north-ern and eastern side of the house, but the western end had formerly been enclosed as a conservatory—which having been abolished, was finally succeeded by a comparatively modern iron veranda, with steps leading down to the terrace. In front of the building, between the elm avenue and the flower-bordered terrace, stood a row of very old poplar trees, tall as their forefathers in Lombardy, and to an iron staple driven into one of these, a handsome black horse was now fastened.

Standing with one foot on the terrace step, close to the marble vases where heliotropes swung their dainty lilac chalices against her shoulder, and scarlet geraniums stared unabashed, Beryl's gaze wandered from the lovely park and ancient trees, to the unbroken façade of the gray old house; and as, in painful contrast she recalled the bare bleak garret room where a beloved invalid held want and death at bay, a sudden mist clouded her vision, and almost audibly she murmured: "My poor mother! Now, I can realize the bitterness of your suffering; now I understand the intensity of your yearning to come back; the terrible home-sickness, which only heaven can cure."

What is presentiment? The swaying of the veil of futurity, under the straining hands of our guardian angels? Is it the faint shadow, the solemn rustle of their hovering wings, as like mother birds they spread protecting plumes between blind fledglings, and descending ruin? Will theosophy ever explain and augment prescience?

"It may be—
The thoughts that visit us, we know not whence,
Sudden as inspiration, are the whispers
Of disembodied spirits, speaking to us
As friends, who wait outside a prison wall,
Through the barred windows speak to those within."

With difficulty Beryl resisted an inexplicable impulse to turn and flee; but the drawn word of duty pointed ahead.

Striking her hands together, as if thereby crushing her reluctance to enter, she waited a moment, with closed eyes, while her lips moved in silent prayer; then ascending the terrace, she crossed the stone pavement, walked up the steps and slowly advanced to the threshold. The dark mahogany door was so glossy, that she dimly saw her own image on its polished panels, as she lifted and let fall the heavy silver knocker, in the middle of an oval silver plate, around the edges of which were raised the square letters of the name "Darrington." The clanging sound startled a peacock, strutting among the verbena beds, and his shrill scream was answered by the deep hoarse bark of some invisible dog; then the heavy door swung open, and a gray-headed negro man, who wore a white linen apron over his black clothes, and held a waiter in one hand, stood before her.

"I wish to see Mr. Darrington."

"I reckon you mean Gin'l Darrington, don't you? Mr. Darrington, Marse Prince Darrington, is in Yurope."

"I mean Mr. Luke Darrington, the owner of this place."

"Jess so; Gin'l Luke Darrington. Well, you can't see him."

"Why not? I must see him, and I shall stay here until I do."

" 'Cause he is busy with his lie-yer, fixin' of some papers; and when he tells me not to let nobody else in I'de ruther set down in a yaller jacket's nest than to turn the door knob, after he done shut it. Better leave your name and call agin."

"No, I will wait until he is at leisure. I presume my sitting on the steps here will not be a violation of your orders."

"To be shore not. But them steps are harder than the stool of repentance, and you had better walk in the drawing-room, and rest yourself. There's pictures, and lots and piles of things there, you can pass away the time looking at."

He waved his waiter toward a long dim apartment, on the left side of the hall.

"Thank you, I prefer to sit here."

She seated herself on the top of the stone steps, and taking off her straw hat, fanned her heated brow, where the rich waving hair clung in damp masses.

"What name, miss, must I give, when the lie-yer finishes his bizness?"

"Say that a stranger wishes to see him about an important matter."

"It is mighty oncertain how long he will tarry; for lie-yers live by talking; turning of words upside down, and wrong side outards, and reading words backards, and whitewashing black things, and smutting of white ones. Marse Lennox Dunbar (he is our lie-yer now, since his pa took paralsis) he is a powerful wrastler with justice. They do say down yonder, at the Court House, that when he gets done with a witness, and turns him aloose, the poor creetur is so flustrated in his mind, that he don't know his own name, or when he was born, or where he was born, or whether he ever was born at all."

Curiosity to discover the nature of the stranger's errand had stimulated the old man's garrulity, but receiving no reply, he finally retreated, leaving the front door open. By the aid of a disfiguring scar on his furrowed cheek, Beryl recognized him as the brave, faithful, family coachman Abednego (abbreviated to "Bedney")—who had once saved her mother's life at the risk of his own. Mrs. Brentano had often related to her children, an episode in her childhood, when having gone to play with her dolls in the loft of the stable, she fell asleep on the hay; and two hours later, Bedney remembering that he had heard her singing there to her dolls, rushed into the burning building, groped through the stifling smoke of the loft, and seizing the sleeping child, threw her out upon a pile of straw. When he attempted to jump after her, a falling rafter struck him to the earth, and left an honorable scar in attestation of his heroism.

Had she yielded to the promptings of her heart, the stranger would gladly have shaken hands with him, and thanked him, in the name of those early years, when her mother's childish feet made music on the wide mahogany railed stairs, that wound from the lower hall to the one above; but the fear of being denied an audience, deterred her from disclosing her name.

Educated in the belief that the utterance of the abhorred name of Brentano, within the precincts of "Elm Bluff," would produce an effect very similar to the ringing of some Tamil Pariah's bell, before the door of a Brahman temple, Beryl wisely kept silent; and soon forgot her forebodings, in the contemplation of the supreme loveliness of the prospect before her.

The elevation was sufficient to command an extended view of the surrounding country, and of the river, which crossed by the railroad bridge north of the town, curved sharply to the east, whence she could trace its course as it gradually wound southward, and disappeared behind the house; where at the foot of a steep bluff, a pretty boat and bath house nestled under ancient willow trees. At her feet the foliage of the park stretched like some brilliant carpet, before whose gorgeous tints, *ustáds* of Karman would have stood in despair; and beyond the sea-green, undulating line of pine forest, she saw the steeple of a church, with its gilt vane burning in the sunshine, and the red brick dome of the *ante bellum* Courthouse.

Time seemed to have fallen asleep, on that hot, still afternoon, and Beryl was aroused from her reverie, by the sound of hearty laughter in the apartment, opposite the drawing-room—followed by the tones of a man's voice:

"Thank you, General. That is my destination this afternoon, and I shall certainly expect you to dance at my wedding."

Quick, firm steps rang on the oil-cloth-covered floor of the hall, and Beryl rose and turned toward the door.

With a cigar in one hand, hat and riding-whip in the other, the attorney stepped out on the colonnade, and pausing involuntarily, at sight of the stranger, they looked at each other. A man, perhaps more, certainly not less than thirty years old, of powerful and impressive *physique;* very tall, athletic, sinewy, without an ounce of superfluous flesh to encumber his movements, in the professional palæstra; with a large finely modeled head, whose crisp black hair closely cut, was (contrary to the prevailing fashion) parted neither in the middle, nor yet on the side, but brushed straight back from a square forehead, thereby enhancing the massiveness of its appearance.

Something in this swart, beardless face, with its brilliant inquisitorial dark blue eyes, handsome secretive mouth veiled by no mustache—and boldly assertive chin deeply cleft in the centre—affected Beryl very unpleasantly, as a perplexing disagreeable memory; an uncanny resemblance hovering just beyond the grasp of identification. A feeling of unaccountable repulsion made her shiver, and she breathed more freely, when he bowed slightly, and walked on toward his horse. Upon the attorney her extraordinary appearance produced a profound impression, and in his brief scrutiny, no detail of her face, figure or apparel escaped his keen probing gaze.

Glancing back as he untied his bridle rein, his unspoken comment was: "Superb woman; I wonder what brings her here? Evidently a stranger—with a purpose."

He sprang into the saddle, stooped his head to avoid the yellow poplar branches, and disappeared under the elm arches.

"Gin'l Darrington's compliments; and if your bizness is pressin' you will have to see him in his bed charmber, as he feels poorly to-day, and the Doctor won't let him out. Follow me. You see, ole Marster remembers the war by the game leg he got at Sharpsburg, and sometimes it lays him up."

The old servant lead Beryl through a long room, fitted up as library and armory, and pausing before an open door, waved her into the adjoining apartment. One swift glance showed her the heavy canopied bedstead in one corner, the arch-shaped glass door leading out upon the iron veranda; and at an oblong table in the middle of the floor, the figure of a man, who rose, taller and taller, until he seemed a giant, drawn to his full height, and resting for support on the hand that was pressed upon the table. Intensity or emotion arrested her breath, as she gazed at the silvered head, piercing black eyes, and spare wasted frame of the handsome man, who had always reigned as a brutal ogre in her imagination. The fire in his somewhat sunken eyes, seemed to bid defiance to the whiteness of the abundant hair, and of the heavy mustache which drooped over his lips; and every feature in his patrician face revealed not only a long line of blue-blooded ancestors, but the proud haughtiness which had been considered always as distinctively characteristic of the Darringtons, as their finely cut lips, thin nostrils, small feet and unusual height.

Unprepared for the apparition that confronted him, Luke Darrington bowed low, surveyed her intently; then pointed to a chair opposite his own.

"Walk in, Madam; or perhaps it may be Miss? Will you take a seat, and excuse the feebleness that forces me to receive visits in my bedroom?"

As he reseated himself, Beryl advanced and stood beside him, but for a moment she found it impossible to utter the words, rehearsed so frequently during her journey; and while she hesitated, he curiously inspected her face and form.

Her plain, but perfectly fitting bunting dress was of the color, popularly denominated "navy-blue," and the linen collar and cuffs were scarcely whiter than the round throat and wrists they encircled. The burnished auburn hair clinging in soft waves to her brow, was twisted into a heavy coil, which the long walk had shaken down, till it rested almost on her neck; and though her heart beat furiously, the pale calm face might have been marble, save for the scarlet lines of her beautiful mouth, and the steady glow of the dilated pupils in her great grey eyes.

"Pray be seated; and tell me to whom I am indebted for the pleasure of this visit?"

"I am merely the bearer of a letter which will explain itself, and my presence, in your house."

Mechanically he took the proffered letter, and with his eyes still lingering in admiration upon the classic outlines of her face and form, leaned back comfortably against the velvet lining of his arm-chair.

"Are you some exiled Goddess travelling incognito? If we lived in the 'piping days of Pan' I should flatter myself that 'Ox-eyed Juno' had honored me with a call, as a reward of my care of her favorite bird."

Receiving no reply, he glanced at the envelope in his hand, and as he read the address—"To my dear father, Gen'l Luke Darrington"—the smile on his face changed to a dark scowl, and he tossed the letter to the floor, as if it were a red-hot coal.

"Only one living being has the right to call me father—my son, Prince Darrington. I have repeatedly refused to hold any communication with the person who wrote that letter."

Beryl stooped to pick it up, and with a caressing touch, as though it were sentient, held it against her heart.

"Your daughter is dying; and this is her last appeal."

"I have no daughter. Twenty-three years ago my daughter buried herself in hopeless disgrace, and for her there can be no resurrection here. If she dreams that I am in my dotage, and may relent, she strangely forgets the nature of the blood she saw fit to cross with that of a beggarly foreign scrub. Go back and tell her, the old man is not yet senile and imbecile; and that the years have only hardened his heart. Tell her, I have almost learned to forget even how she looked."

His eyes showed a dull reddish fire, like those of some drowsy caged tiger, suddenly stirred into wrath, and a grayish pallor—the white-heat of the Darringtons—settled on his face.

Twice Beryl walked the length of the room, but each time the recollection of her mother's tearful suffering countenance, and the extremity of her need, drove her back to the arm-chair.

"If you knew that your daughter's life hung by a thread, would you deliberately take a pair of shears and cut it?"

He glared at her in silence, and leaning forward on the table, pushed roughly aside a salver, on which stood a decanter and two wine glasses.

"I am here to tell you a solemn truth; then my responsibility ends. Your daughter's life rests literally in your hands; for unless you consent to furnish the money to pay for a surgical operation, which may restore her health, she will certainly die. I am indulging in no exaggeration to extort alms. In this letter is the certificate of a distinguished physician, corroborating my statement. If you, the author of her being, prefer to hasten her death, then your choice of an awful revenge must be settled between your hardened conscience and your God."

"You are bold indeed, to beard me in my own house, and tell me to my face what no man would dare to utter."

His voice was an angry pant, and he struck his clinched hand on the table, with a force that made the glasses jingle, and the sherry dance in the decanter.

"Yes, you scarcely realize how much bravery this painful errand demands; but the tender love in a woman's heart nerves her to bear fiery ordeals, that vanquish a man's courage."

"Then you find that age has not drawn the fangs from the old crippled Darrington lion, nor clipped his claws?"

The sneer curved his white mustache, until she saw the outline of the narrow, bloodless under lip.

"That king of beasts scorns to redden his fangs, or flesh his claws, in the quivering body of his own offspring. Your metaphor is an insult to natural instincts."

She laid the letter once more before him, and looked down on him, with ill-concealed aversion.

"Who are you? By what right dare you intrude upon me?"

"I am merely a sorrowful, anxious, poverty-stricken woman, whose heart aches over her mother's sufferings, and who would never have endured the humiliation of this interview, except to deliver a letter in the hope of prolonging my mother's life."

"You do not mean that you are—my—"

"I am nothing to you, sir, but the bearer of a letter from your dying daughter."

"You cannot be the child of—of Ellice?"

After the long limbo of twenty-three years, the name burst from him, and with what a host of memories its echo peopled the room, where that erring daughter had formerly reigned queen of his heart.

"Yes, Ellice is my dear mother's name."

He stared at the majestic form, and at the faultless face looking so proudly down upon him, as from an inaccessible height; and she heard him draw his breath, with a labored hissing sound.

"But—I thought her child was a boy?"

"I am the youngest of two children."

"It is impossible that you are the daughter of that infernal, low-born, fiddling foreign vagabond who—"

"Hush! The dead are sacred!"

She threw up her hand, with an imperious gesture, not of deprecation, but interdict; and all the stony calm in her pale face, seemed shivered by a passionate gust, that made her eyes gleam like steel under an electric flash.

"I am the daughter of Ignace Brentano, and I love, and honor his memory, and his name. No drop of your Darrington blood runs in my veins; I love my dear mother—but I am my father's daughter—and I want no nobler heritage than his name. Upon you I have no shadow of claim, but I am here from dire necessity, at your mercy—a helpless, defenceless pleader in my mother's behalf—and as such, I appeal to the boasted Southern chivalry, upon which you pride yourself, for immunity from insult while I am under your roof. Since I stood no taller than your knee, my mother has striven to inculcate a belief in the nobility, refinement, and chivalric deference to womanhood, inherent in Southern gentlemen; and if it be not all a myth, I invoke its protection against abuse of my father. A stranger, but a lady, every inch, I demand the respect due from a gentleman."

For a moment they eyed each other, as gladiators awaiting the signal, then Gen'l Darrington sprang to his feet, and with a bow, stately and profound as if made to a duchess, replied:

"And in the name of Southern chivalry, I swear you shall receive it."

"Read your daughter's letter; give me your answer, and let us cut short an interview—which, if disagreeable to you, is almost unendurable to me."

Turning away, she began to walk slowly up and down the floor; and smothering an oath under his heavy mustache, the old man sank back in his chair, and opened the letter.

Pap's Mules

Samuel Minturn Peck

THE Widow Barbour stood on the edge of the throng which had gathered under the big oak in front of the corner store, and listened with growing consternation to the great news of the impending battle. Fortunately she had disposed of the contents of her basket before the arrival of the stage, or her butter and eggs would have remained unsold, so great was the excitement that convulsed the village. As the widow's rustic mind gradually apprehended the tale of the approaching carnage which threatened Oakville, her thoughts reverted to her home at Hickory Hollow, and an irresistible desire seized her to communicate the fearful tidings to the benighted denizens of that mountain hamlet. If there was to be a battle at Oakville, and blood was to flow in the streets, Nancy Barbour did not wish to see it, so she mounted old Sorrel and started at speed for home.

But it was far to Hickory Hollow, and with her heart beating time to Sorrel's cantering feet, Nancy soon recognized the impossibility of surviving four hours without telling the news to some one, so she resolved upon a diversion up Blackberry Lane for the purpose of terrifying the family of Susan Cline, a crony of hers, who had formerly dwelt at Hickory Hollow.

" 'Tain't likely Susan's heard the great news," murmured the widow as she galloped, "an' if I don't tell somebody soon I'll jes' bust."

The trees around John Cline's log cabin were in half leafage, although it was but April, and the foliage afforded considerable protection against the West Alabama sun. The tide of war was rapidly engulfing the doomed Confederacy, but there was no hint of conflict in Cline's dooryard. True, there was smoke, but it was not the sulphurous fumes of battle, smelling of burned powder and carnage, but the incense of peace curling gracefully from the fire about Susan Cline's soap-pot, and redolent of the spicy scent of pine knots and hickory boughs. The south wind at intervals blew the pungent smoke into the peach-trees that hung over the garden fence, and the bees that were rifling the pink blossoms rose with an indignant hum, to return to their toil when the gust had passed.

Susan stirred the steaming caldron meditatively with a long soap-stick. Sometimes she made a brief remark to guide the labors of her two daughters, Betsy and Judith, the first of whom bent over a wash-tub, while the other churned a turn of milk; sometimes she looked across the field to where her husband was ploughing with a pair of bay mules; or her glance fell tenderly upon Johnny, her little boy of ten, who made it his duty to keep the fire burning about the pot of soap.

A messenger of ill to this peaceful scene might well lament his errand. But no compunction visited Nancy Barbour's brain, as she galloped up the lane. With her brown skirt sailing in the wind and her sunbonnet flapping from side to side, the widow's appearance was well calculated to excite the anxious fear of the little group in the dooryard.

"Lan' sake! Nance, what's the matter?" exclaimed Susan, as Nancy drew rein at the gate. "Has anything happened to my kin at the Hollow?"

With a breathlessness, partly real, but largely assumed, Nancy shook her head negatively, and asked for a gourd of water, and it was not till after repeated solicitation that she proceeded to unfold her tale of terror. Time was precious, yet the widow could not deny herself the enjoyment of her friend's suspense.

"The day o' wrath's at han', Susan Cline," she finally began, "an' you pore critters are washin' clo'es, churnin' milk, an' bilin' soap!"

Susan threw a quick, questioning glance at Nancy as if she suspected her sanity.

"Nance, have yer come gallopin' up the lane jest to norate about Judgment Day?"

"No, Suse, I've come from Oakville; the Yankees are a-comin'; thar's goin' to be a battle thar, and blood's goin' to run in the streets."

"The Yankee Raiders a-comin' at last!" exclaimed Susan. "Are yer shore the news is true, Nance?"

"Yes, Suse; the news was brought by stage, and it's a sartin' fact. The mayor, the aldermen, and the one-armed and the one-legged soldiers have helt a meetin' under the big oak front of Brown's sto'.

The soldiers 'llow it's no use to put up a fight, for thar's no able-bodied men left to fight; but the mayor and t'others say it would be a dessgrace to surrender without a gun pinted or a lick struck. It was a great meetin', Suse. His honor stood on a barrel and made a grand speech."

Nancy paused to enjoy the sensation she was creating. Meanwhile, to brace her nerves, she took out a box of snuff from her flat bosom, and, inserting her brush, she mopped up a brown ball and put it between her thin lips.

"His honor's a fool, and the old soldiers are in the right," said Susan, gesticulating with her soap-stick. "Thar's been enough blood and tears shed in this pore country."

"Well," resumed Nancy, "his honor outtalked 'em and carried the people with him. I tell yer, Suse, thar's goin' to be a battle, shore. The mayor's organized a company, and named it the Oakville Home Guard, and appinted Abner Wilkins cap'n. And you know the old cannon on the bluff which used to be fired on the Fourth o' July, and ain't been fired in nigh on to four year? Well, they've drug it down to the bridge and loadened it with scrap iron. But thar's some folks agin' the cannon, sayin' she's too old and rusty to shoot; an' if she do shoot, nobody knows which end's a-goin' off."

A stronger gust shook the peach trees, driving out the bees, shattering the blossoms and flaking Judith's yellow hair with pink. After it there came a hush as if the wind had suddenly stopped and held its breath, like a frightened child. Then it fled furtively down the lane. One could trace its feet by little eddies of dust. Then came a bit of April cloud, no larger than one's hand, and floated under the noontide sun, casting a shadow over the little group.

Susan glanced at her frightened children, and a feeling of resentment toward the bearer of ill tidings who had alarmed them rose in her heart.

"We are much obliged to you, Nance, for comin' out of yer way to bring us bad news, but we're not beholden to you for namin' us pore critters jes' because we are washin' our clo'es and bilin' our soap. Livin' or dead, a body needs soap and clean clo'es. Furthermoah, if the Raiders be a-comin', we can't hender 'em."

Susan's affected calmness vexed Nancy, who vaguely felt herself defrauded. She had expected more of a panic.

"I'm powerful glad to see you so reesigned, Suse, for it's a Christian's duty. Howsomever, in Oakville they 'llowed the Raiders 'ud skin the county, and thar wouldn't be a four-legged critter left to milk or plough. What are you-uns goin' to do when yer mules is gone?"

"It would be a hard case to lose our mules, for they are our main support, Nance, but the ground's broke and planted, and we could make out to work it with a hoe."

Having parried Nancy's final effort to create dismay, Susan ordered her little flock back to their labors; and the widow, fearing to be forestalled as a messenger of ill to the dwellers on Little Creek, declined Susan's invitation to dinner, and giving Sorrel a blow with her switch, departed at a brisk pace for Hickory Hollow.

When Nancy's lank figure had disappeared down the lane, a sigh from his mother filled Johnny's face with gloom.

"Mammy, do yer reckin' the Yanks'll take pap's mules?" asked the little boy, anxiously.

"I don't know, son; they mought, and then agin they moughtn't. But go tell yer pap to come to the house, and take Tige with you; I'm feard he'll git scalted with this soap."

"Don't you be skeered, sonny," said Cline, as he saw a tear roll down the little boy's thin cheeks while he helped to ungear the mules.

"I ain't feard o' nothin', pap. But Mis' Barbour she 'llowed as how the Yanks 'ud sholy carry off our mules, and since I heard that word seems like I love Cindy and Beck more'n anything on the place. Tige he ain't nowhar now."

"Well, son, don't borry trouble; wait till the Raiders are here 'fore you take to grievin'."

Johnny was not comforted. He pulled down Cindy's head by her long ears and laid his cheek against the mule's muzzle.

"I tell yer, pap, I couldn't give up Beck and Cindy nohow. They've been here ever since I was born. I've rid 'em to the creek to drink. I've rid 'em to mill, and I've rid 'em ever'whar. Pap, Beck and Cindy ain't no young mules; both of 'em's seen their best days. They couldn't stand it to pull cannon and sich like, day and night. More'n that, them Yanks ain't usen' to mules, and don't know the ways o' mules. Now thar's Cindy, she'd jes' as soon kick a stranger as not, and she'd be shore to kick them Yanks, and they mought shoot her. I tell yer, pap, lesser'n two days thar'd be a dead Yank or a dead mule, and I'm a-feard it mought be Cindy."

"Do make haste and come to bed, Bet," said Judith, impatiently, that night in the small back bedroom where the children slept. "Mammy's shet me up, and shet me up the holen joren day since Mis' Barbour left, till I feel jest like a grain o' hot corn 'fore it pops."

"It's all your fault, Jude," replied Betsy, blowing out the tallow dip and lying down. "If you hadn't tuned up to cry I wouldn't 'a cried, and mam wouldn't 'a got mad."

"But jest think, Bet, maybe the Yanks'll come fore day, and thar's pap and mam gone to bed same as common. Seems like we-uns ought to be sittin' up singing hymes, or doin' some'h'n different to what we do every night."

"Lan' sake, Jude! I wouldn't sing a hyme in the dead o' night for nothin' you could give me."

"Wouldn't yer sing a hyme for that string o' yaller beads in Brown's sto'?"

"No! I wouldn't sing a lonesome hyme in the dead o' night for nothin' and nobody. It 'ud make me feel like we was a watchin' with a dead corpse."

Judith fell back, covered her head with the quilt, and exclaimed in half-smothered tones of horror: "Bet, if you say ary 'nother word about a dead corpse, I tell you pint blank, I'll holler jest as loud as I can."

After a moment's silence, Judith, half suffocated, uncovered her head and peered around the room, when, her eyes falling on the little trundle-bed in the corner where Johnny lay, she whispered:

"Sis, is Johnny asleep?"

"Yes, don't wake him," drawled Betsy, drowsily.

"I ain't goin' to wake him. If he was asleep I was goin' to say, s'posin'—" The girl paused suddenly as if overcome by the magnitude of the supposition.

"S'posin' what?" asked Betsy, turning in the bed with increased interest.

"S'posin'—s'posin' our Johnny was to run off with pap's mules unbeknownst down to Bearheaven swamp and save 'em from the Raiders?"

"Shucks! Johnny's too little," replied the prosaic Betsy, who straightway turned over and went to sleep; and Judith, deprived of a listener, soon followed her sister's example and was wrapped in slumber.

But the little tow-headed boy in the trundle-bed remained awake. His sisters had been mistaken in thinking him asleep. Still wide awake and with his eyes fixed upon the pencil of moonlight that slanted through the window, dimly illuminating the room, his childish imagination, fed upon the piny-woods superstitions, transformed the shaft of light into the apparition of a long white hand beckoning him to the world outside. But the fancy faded when he heard Judith's wild supposition, and his heart gave a great bound. It had not before occurred to him that he might save the mules which he loved so well and which he knew were so necessary to the support of the family. The idea, carelessly sown by Judith, grew in his little brain like a grain of mustard-seed. He knew Bearheaven swamp well, and he felt certain that he could run the mules off into its recesses and keep them there safe till the Raiders had left Oakville. He wondered that the plan had not occurred to him at once. As soon as his sisters were asleep he would start. While he lay quiet in bed thus maturing his scheme, the clock in his mother's room struck twelve, and the slow, regular breathing of his sisters told him that they were both in deep slumber.

Rising cautiously from the trundle-bed, and slipping on his clothes, he tiptoed to the window, caught the sill with both hands, gave a spring, wriggled through the opening, and dropped lightly to the ground.

Safe outside, the thought came to him that he must take something along to eat. The mules could graze on the young cane that grew abundantly in the swamp. Congratulating himself on the happy thought, he glided through the open hallway to the pine cupboard to see what it contained. In it was a yellow dish heaped with cold boiled bacon, collards, and corn-pone. On the next shelf was a cup of sorghum molasses and a pitcher of butter-milk.

Taking a cottonade bag from a nail and removing the garden-seed it held, he whispered to himself: "I can carry the bread and meat in this seed bag o' pap's; and I can make out to take them merlasses in a bottle. But these here collards that's wet and cold, this is the onliest way they can be carried," said he, filling his mouth with them, and giving voice to a suppressed laugh. "In the mornin' when mammy finds I'm gone, and the collards gone, too, she'll know I couldn't a-carried 'em no other way, and she'll be powerful glad I took a bite o' somethin' 'fore I lef'.'"

Carefully lifting the pitcher of buttermilk he took a drink, which seemed to go the wrong way.

"It's quare; when I think about leavin' mam I begin to choke."

Replacing the pitcher on the shelf, he turned his head.

"Jest listen at pap snorin'! He's clean forgot about them Yanks."

Here, with a scratch and a yawn, Tige rose from the floor and came forward wagging his tail.

"Tige, you must come, too, and he'p save pap's mules," said Johnny, patting the dog on the head. Tige licked the boy's hand and followed him to the stable.

When all was ready for the flight, mounted on Cindy and leading Beck, Johnny paused in the lane for a parting look at the little cabin. The full moon was still high in the heavens, and its rays, sifting through the half-grown foliage of the oaks, dappled the rough board roof of the cabin with the shadow of baby leaves, which flickered and danced as the night wind blew. The soft radiance fell also on the pink blossoming peach-trees, bleaching the dewy flowers till they were white and glistening. Whatever the moonbeams touched they beautified with silent peace.

Suddenly from the Oakville way came a mighty sound—boom—oom—oom—ooom—that shook the very ground, and rolled away to the wilds of Bearheaven swamp, and reverberated through the distant hills as far as Hickory Hollow.

Johnny delayed no longer. Followed by Tige, barking furiously, he was well on his way to the morasses of Bearheaven when the echoes died away. The inmates of the cabin were speedily frightened out of their slumbers.

"John, John! wake up, thar's the cannon! The Raiders are come to Oakville," said Susan, excitedly, and at the same moment two screams rang from the back room, and the girls bounded in. But it was not till the alarmed family had dressed themselves that Johnny was missed.

"Whar's the boy?" Susan exclaimed to the frightened girls. Their bewildered faces testifying to their ignorance of their brother's where-abouts, the anxious mother hastened to the door and called: "Johnny, Johnny! come to yer mam, sonny; she wants you."

Meanwhile from Oakville there came a confused sound of human voices and barking dogs, while many little lights began to appear, some of which were stationary, while others moved about like fireflies, appearing and disappearing as their rays were intercepted by inter-vening objects.

In the yard Susan met her husband returning from the stable.

"Johnny can't be found," she said, "and I'm a-feared he's taken Tige and gone to Oakville."

"The mules are gone, too," answered John.

"Then maybe the mules have broke out, and Johnny's gone to fetch 'em."

"No, Susan, the bridle and saddle are missin', too, and the gate's latched."

"Then," said the distressed mother, "Johnny's run off with the mules. He was standin' by when Nancy Barbour 'llowed the Raiders would carry 'em off. Yes, he's run the mules off to Hickory Hollow to save 'em; and, oh, John, he may be shot and killed on the road, like my other boy in Virginia, and I'll never see him agin!" and dropping into a chair, Susan Cline buried her face in her apron.

*   *   *

Oakville had fallen! But the old town had not surrendered without a blow, and municipal honor remained spotless. The city fathers felt a thrill of pride even in defeat.

Everything had gone off in style—even the old rusty cannon. The load of scrap-iron had passed out at the proper end, thus belying the predictions of the croakers. Yet, for some reason (perhaps from in-accuracy of aim, perhaps from the queer shapes of the projectiles—old nails, corkscrews, sardine-boxes, etc.) the greater part of the load was found next day sticking in the sides and rafters of the bridge.

Jack Green, old Brown's fifteen-year-old red-headed clerk, fired the cannon. Only one man was needed to man the gun, for there was not enough powder for a second load. Jack was a proud boy. As the man who fired the cannon on the night of the Raid, his fame in

Oakville would be eternal. It was not an ordinary cannon; Jack wished the fact kept in mind. It was a gun that half the town regarded as certain to bring death to the man who applied the match.

The old mayor was equally proud. What was a war governor beside a raid mayor! To repulse the enemy had been beyond his expectation; and when it was discovered at daylight that they were fifteen hundred strong, while the Home Guard were but fifty, his honor remarked to a friend that no braver defense was recorded in the pages of history.

When Susan rallied from the blow of Johnny's flight, the rigor of household discipline increased rather than diminished, and in spite of her discomposure, she busied herself with her usual duties, and set the girls each a large task of ironing.

"I know it'll be as it always is," said Judith, seizing the occasion of her mother's morning visit to the hen-house; "we'll be the last fambly the Raiders come to."

"Well, I don't know as anybody's pinin' for 'em," replied her sister.

"Bet, yer don't understand!" exclaimed Judith, fretfully, dropping her iron on the rest with a loud clink. "It's this way: I didn't want the Yanks to come, but since they are come, I don't want to be the last human bein' in Oak County to set eyes on 'em. I think it's a dessgrace to be the last about everything, and I don't want folks to be a-pityin' we-uns and sayin' the Yanks came to Oakville and went away, and them pore Clines in Blackberry Lane never seed a Yank."

Judith took up her iron again, but finding it had grown cold, she replaced it before the bright bed of embers in the fireplace, and lifting another, rubbed it on a roll of rags to free it of ashes. Meantime a loud cackling in the hen-house gave token that old Speckle and Susan were not of one mind in the matter of nest-building; and the din was much increased when the red rooster lifted his voice in sympathy with Speckle's domestic woes.

"Bet," said Judith, solemnly, after a long pause, "thar's some'h'n on my mind, and it's a-swellin' and a-swellin' like bread sponge. If I don't tell it soon, it'll choke me."

"Then you'd better tell it 'fore mam comes back," responded her phlegmatic sister.

Judith put down her iron.

"It's this, sis. Mam 'llows that Johnny's run the mules off to Hickory

Hollow, but that's not my b'lief. I 'llow Johnny's many miles from the Hollow. He'd never 'a' run off nohow if somebody hadn't a-put the notion in his head."

The girl's eyes grew misty, and her voice trembled. "Oh, sis, it's all my doin's. Johnny warn't asleep last night when I was s'posin'. He ain't gone to Hickory Hollow; he's down in Bearheaven swamp, an' if the Yanks find him and chase him, takin' him to be a man in the bresh and briers, he'll chance it to be shot 'fore he'd give up ary one o' them mules; an' if anything was to happen to our Johnny it would break my heart, it sholy would."

Judith gazed at her sister tearfully. The latter thought a moment.

"Oughtn't pap and mam to know it?"

"No; what's the use o' tellin' 'em? Pap won't leave us by our lone selves, and go look for Johnny; and mam would give me a tongue lashin' for puttin' notions in Johnny's head."

With this Judith walked to the window, and as she did so she gave a cry.

Approaching the cabin from Oakville was a squad of blue-coated cavalry. The thick dust rolling in dark billows around the knees of the horses, passed into a gray cloud which wrapped its sullen garments about the April breeze, and floated down the zigzag fence, stifling the fragrant breath of the sassafras blossoms, and blinding the startled blue eyes of the wild violets.

The troop was met at the gate by John, with Susan and the girls behind him. A brief dialogue ensued, in the course of which Cline answered truthfully the inquiries in regard to his stock, telling the story of Johnny's flight in the night with the mules, and his mother's consequent anxiety. But the account did not satisfy the officer in charge, and he ordered the stable to be searched. The search proving fruitless, he began to question Cline afresh, when Susan stepped forward: "My husband's given yer a true word, sir. We had two mules, but our little boy, our onliest boy—his brother was killed in Virginia—my boy he's run off with the mules, and we don't know whar he is. We 'llow he's gone up in the hills whar we use to live, but we ain't certain."

Susan paused and grasped the gate-post nervously. "Mr. Officer, if you run acrost a little sandy-haired boy with two bay mules and a yaller dog, please be merciful to 'em. My Johnny's little and slim, but he's gritty, and he'll chance it to be shot sooner than give up ary one of them mules."

The squad rode off fifty yards and halted, anxiously watched by the little group at the gate. The commander was inclined to doubt the existence of the small boy. Some one had hidden the mules, it was evident, and where were they more likely to be than in the swamp to the south, the nearest cover offering a chance of successful concealment. With the arrival of this decision the troop wheeled and rode rapidly down the winding lane leading to Bearheaven swamp.

"Shet up!" said Susan to Judith, who on the departure of the soldiers had begun to sob. "Shet right up and go to your ironin'."

With an effort the girl controlled herself and faced her mother.

"I ain't cryin' for nothin',' and I won't be shet up no longer. You think I'm takin' the high-sterics, but I ain't; it's grief. You an' pap 'llow that Johnny's gone to Hickory Hollow, but yer 'llow wrong. Johnny an' them mules are down yonder in Bearheaven, an' them Yanks are on his track to hunt him, like he was a wild beast. But thar ain't no time to talk. I can't stand it to stay here no longer. I'm a-goin' to Johnny."

She darted from the cabin. Bareheaded across the stable-yard she fled. Over the fence, scarcely seeming to touch it, on in a diagonal direction toward a thick growth of young pines she flew. The Raiders had a few moments' start of her, but their course lay along the winding lane, and Judith knew that by taking short cuts through thicket, field, and wood, she could shorten the distance a third. Every foot of ground was as well known to her as to the cotton-tailed rabbit that jumped up before her, or the startled quail that rose whizzing from the broom-sedge. Fortunately she was clad in brown homespun, whose hue was similar to that of the tree-trunks, and her hair to the yellow tint of last year's broom-sedge which surged about her as she ran.

At intervals she saw between the pines and over the sedge the heads of the cavalrymen. They were riding at full speed along the curving road. As she reached a rise in the field a jay-bird flew up, and lit upon a persimmon tree and began to summon his kindred with a shrill note. Fearing discovery, the girl crouched in the sedge, and the downy seed, floating about her, clung to her gown and frosted her hair. Above her thin, flushed cheeks her dark-blue eyes gleamed like bits of polished steel. She had stooped just in time, for at the cry of the bird the men looked toward her. She saw with beating heart that she had escaped their gaze, for the squad rode on.

Judith sprang up and sped down the incline. Before her rose a wood, the southern boundary of the sedge field. Once in this cover her flight could not be seen from the road. She rushed through the blackberry briers, caught the top rail of the fence with both hands, and swung over it like a boy.

The bare feet of the cracker girl were swift, but her brain went faster. She believed that she knew the place where the boy had hidden himself and the mules. About a mile farther to the right of the wood, in the deepest part of the swamp, was a small knoll which rose above the encircling morass like a tiny island. It was thickly fringed with cane, and further concealed from view by the branches of a large tree which had been felled by some opossum-hunter. Johnny and she had discovered the spot while looking for a strayed cow.

Down through the wood she ran like a young doe. The cool gloom was grateful to her heated face, but she did not smell the fragrance of the wild honeysuckles nor of the yellow jasmine bells that brushed her brow. Reaching the morass, overshadowed by great gum and cypress trees and dotted with tufts of water-grass, she leaped from hillock to hillock over the black mud. Here and there on the leaf-strewn pools rose bubbles of marsh gas that broke as her light steps shook the clumps of quaggy grass and cane roots.

She stopped a moment to listen. She heard nothing but the hammering of a log-cock on a dead gum-tree, and the tiny bark of a squirrel. Her feet were covered with mud above the ankles, and her breathing was quick; but the bourne was almost gained.

Continuing her flight she came to one of the creeks which wound through the swamp. Like most swamp streams, though narrow, it was deep. Too wide to be leaped, too full of dead sticks and branches to be swum, crossing seemed well-nigh impossible.

Judith looked in vain along the creek for a fallen tree that might offer a precarious bridge. Upward her despairing glance was met by a muscadine which hung like a great green chandelier over the dark water. Taking a forked stick, she leaned over the creek and drew the vine toward her. Pulling stoutly to test the strength of its attachment to the boughs above, she ran back a few steps to gain momentum, then swung like a pendulum full twenty feet over the water, and dropped lightly on the other side.

If the boy were not there! Her step became unsteady, and her muddy, brier-torn ankles trembled.

"Johnny! Johnny!" she exclaimed, with a husky whisper.

She heard a swishing sound, then the foliage swayed, and Johnny with Tige at his side appeared through the parting reeds.

"Golly, Jude, is that you? Me and Tige took yer for a swamp rabbit or some other wild critter a-lopin' through the swamp. Have the Yanks come to pap's house?"

"Yes, they've been thar a-lookin' for horses and mules, and they've took the road to Bearheaven. I 'llowed you'd be here with them two mules, and I've come to tell yer the Yanks are on yer track."

Johnny's eyes gleamed.

"Let 'em come! Them Raiders can't find us lessern they had hound dogs."

The flexile cane closed behind them, and the mules were discovered, tethered and browsing contentedly on the young cane.

Seated on the stump of the gum-tree which had been the ill-starred opossum's abode, Judith rendered Johnny a terse account of recent events. The boy listened attentively. But Tige, who had greeted Judith with much tail-wagging, began to leap upon her and lick her hands as if he thought Johnny had not greeted her with sufficient enthusiasm. From leaps to barks was a natural canine transition.

"Shet up, Tige!" said Johnny, springing to his feet and seizing the dog by the nape of the neck; but Tige tore loose and circled about Judith with still louder barks. She made an unsuccessful spring at one of his hind legs, which only added to his glee.

"Shet up, you yaller fool!" repeated the boy, clinching his teeth and seizing a stout sassafras switch on which he had been whittling to pass the time away.

Tige easily eluded Johnny's lunges. The dog had not enjoyed himself so much in many a day, and it was not till Judith, armed with another switch, had turned Tige's flank, that Johnny succeeded in giving the dog a smart blow that sent him yelping into the cane-brake.

Tige was finally silenced. But to celebrate the event, the mule Cindy raised her head, turned back her long ears, and gave voice to a sonorous bray that rang through the swamp and floated along the distant river bank in slowly expiring echoes. Johnny seized Cindy by the muzzle to prevent a repetition of the untimely noise, and Judith, fearing the contagion of a bad example, took the other mule in charge.

But the precautions were useless; the mischief was done. From the other bank of the winding creek came a sound of crackling twigs, and horses' feet tramping the mud.

"Johnny, it's the Yanks!" exclaimed Judith, with a look of despair.

In two minutes more the little swamp island would be surrounded and they would be caught like quail in a net.

"Yes," said the boy, gritting his teeth, "but the mules ain't thurn yet."

A loud spashing told that the cavalrymen were crossing the creek, and Tige began again to bark.

"Don't stop to saddle. If Tige shets up maybe we can dodge 'em, and swim the river," said Johnny.

He leaped on Cindy, Judith on Beck.

Just as they broke through the fringe of cane on the south bank of the knoll, a loud "Halt!" rang from the thick undergrowth fifty yards away. They were heard by their pursuers, but not seen. Johnny made for the laurel bush and cane along the winding creek. The mules, though old, were still active and sure-footed, and they were fresher than the Federal horses.

"Halt!" came again from the rear. Still hidden by the cane and laurel, the boy and girl turned a bend in the water-course.

"Fire!" and a shower of bullets whizzed through the shrub, cutting leaves and twigs on every hand. A bit of bark grazed Johnny's ear.

"Are yer hit, Jude?" cried the boy over his shoulder.

"No, are you?"

"No, but I can see blood on Cindy's ear."

Still keeping to cover, they made turn after turn, but sound each time betrayed them, and they failed to increase the distance much from their pursuers. Worse, the men were widening the line of pursuit. The boy's tactics were discovered. He thought of another plan, gave the mule a sharp blow and spurted to the right.

A few hundred yards away was a clearing, a small field formerly cultivated, but now reverting to wilderness. Could ground be gained on the wild ride to this open place, its firmer footing and freedom from trees might enable them to increase the space so greatly that when they re-entered the swamp on the farther side, their flight could not be heard. They were trailed, not by the eye, but by the ear.

"The clearin'!" hissed the boy.

"The clearin'?" gasped Judith.

"Yes, gain on 'em thar; dodge 'em t'other side."

On, on they went with head bent low. A black-jack bough combed Judith's streaming hair, and would have dragged her from the mule, but she grasped its bristling mane. A low beech limb scraped Johnny's back, bursting his "gallus," and tearing his shirt from neck to waist. But the clearing was gained and the pursuers distanced. Half a minute later the squad broke cover, to see pap's mules and their youthful riders dart like arrows into the farther swamp *safe!*

"Halt!" rang the command; this time addressed to the squad.

"Two cracker children and mules! I thought there were ten Rebels well mounted," said the officer, and in deep disgust the troop tracked their own trail back to the road.

*   *   *

The Raid had passed like a summer storm. Three days and nights of sun and dew had broadened the tender leaves above John Cline's cabin, and painted them a deeper green, as a thin woman clothed in brown homespun walked wearily up Blackberry Lane.

The Widow Barbour was tired, but when she drew near Susan's home, the limp folds of her draggled gown grew crisp with curiosity, and her old blue sunbonnet took on an interrogative tilt.

"Things seem 'bout the same as common at Susan's," she said to herself, quickening her pace. "The fence is all thar and the bee-gums is standin'. Nothin's tore down," she sighed, regretfully. "Howsom-ever, I don't hear no hens cacklin'," and her eyes brightened. "But thar's the old black sow sunnin' herself agin the fence fat as ever," she added, sorrowfully.

Lifting the gate latch, Nancy heard a cheerful voice within:

"Bring forth ther raw-yell di-er-dem
And cra-own Him Lor-or-ord of all."

"Thar's Susan a-singin' Coronation, and it's a true word that John-ny's saved his pap's mules," sniffed Nancy, tearfully, and her mind reverted to old Sorrel, miles away, in the hands of the departed Raiders.

Nancy listened to Susan's story with a keen but melancholy interest. Susan was nearing the end.

"When the squad stopped agin on their way back from the swamp and called for some'h'n to eat, I sot in and fried 'em a half side o' bacon, and nigh on to all Speckle's last year's chickens."

"They was fine pullets, Suse."

"Yes, Nance; but when the cap'n told me my boy and gal was safe, I could 'a' slaughtered the whole yard, I was so thankful. I heard the cap'n 'llow to the sarjin, while they sot eatin', that he'd never seed sich bare-back ridin' outsidern a circus."

"Warn't none of 'em teched nowhar?"

"Well, Jude's right smart brier-scratched round the legs, and she left some of her hair in the swamp; but skin and hair ain't like clo'es; they'll grow agin."

"It's told about that one of the mules was hurt."

"A ball bored a hole in Cindy's ear, but Johnny says Cindy had ears to spare; and Jude 'llows to tie a ribbin' in the hole next time she rides to Oakville, for she's got word that Brown's red-headed clerk's laid out to joke her for runnin' from the Yanks. But lan' sakes! Nance, have yer walked all the way from the Hollow?" ended Susan, noting Nancy's bedraggled appearance.

"Yes, Suse," Nancy's thin lips began to quiver, "Sorrel's gone"; and two tears made their way slowly through the wrinkles on her yellow cheeks. She drew a snuff-stained wad from her flat bosom and put it to her eyes.

"Thar—thar, Nance, don't cry," said Susan compassionately, picking up a snuff-box and well-chewed brush which had fallen from Nancy's kerchief. "Sorrel warn't much account."

"She was my onliest critter," replied Nancy, wiping her eyes. "I told the Yanks she was twenty year old, and axed 'em to look in her mouth. But the head robber of 'em all 'llowed that nobody could tell a horse's age by teeth after it was eight year old. Far's he knowed, Sorrel mought be twenty or she mought be only ten. Anyhow, he 'llowed on that horse critters was skace, and Sorrel had pints; which is a true word, for she was an old racer when I got her from Jack Green's daddy. She won many a dollar for old Green when she was young. But I'll never set eyes on Sorrel agin," and the handkerchief went up to her face once more.

Susan offered verbal consolation, but Nancy remained uncomforted. How was she in future to convey her eggs and butter to market? If she were forced to walk, every one at the Hollow would go and come before her. In the midst of her mourning John Cline and Johnny entered.

Noting Nancy's grief-stricken look, John forebore to speak to her, and turned to Susan.

"Thar's great news at Oakville, wife. Word's come that Lee's surrendered, and the war's done."

The handkerchief fell from Nancy's face. In silence she sat and stared at Cline like a sleep-walker.

Johnny's eyes were flashing.

"And Mis' Barbour, what yer reckin? If we didn't find old Sorrel a-wanderin' round the streets! She was so no 'count the Yanks turned her loose; and she's out thar at the gate."

"Do you hear, Nance? Sorrel's come back, and the war's over," said Susan, patting Nancy on the shoulder.

Nancy rallied.

"What d'yer say, Suse?" She clutched Susan's arm. "Sorrel's come back, and the war's done? Don't a human soul know it at the Hollow!"

And Nancy rose to her feet.

Introduction

III. *Alabama Flowering I*

THE early decades of the twentieth century can now be seen as the time of Alabama fiction's true coming of age. Native writers increasingly attracted a large national readership, and in many instances also achieved critical success among the major arbiters of American literary taste. This was the heyday of fiction in the great mass-publication magazines—*Scribners, Atlantic, Harper's, Saturday Review;* and as the record of initial imprints here would reveal, Alabama in the short story was well represented on their pages. In the novel, one Alabamian of the era, T. S. Stribling, also found special achievement and recognition, winning in 1934 the Pulitzer Prize; and a younger contemporary, William March, began what would be a long and distinguished career as a writer of short stories and novels, one that would make him to this day the best-known and best-regarded of all authors associated with the state.

Besides Stribling and March, two other names from the period also immediately strike the eye: Zelda Sayre Fitzgerald and Sara Haardt Mencken. One of the distinct privileges of the anthologist is to return to popular and critical attention the work of these two writers known well as wives of eminent literary figures and not nearly enough as the estimable literary artists that both in their own rights turn out to be. In subject, their work is very much in the spirit of the general flowering of Alabama literature that was taking place; and in craft, if the supreme standard for the fiction-maker, as Henry James once put it, should always be the test of execution, the short stories of these two artists easily set the mark for quality as well.

Also included here are stories by less familiar figures, Edgar Valentine Smith and Howell Vines. It is important that these works, too, be returned to general publication. Like Fitzgerald and Mencken, Smith and Vines prove themselves creators of fictions rich in their rewards in terms of both cultural documentary and artistic achievement. With the writings of others, they surely find their just place once again.

As regards the general character of Alabama fiction of the era, Smith's works provide an appropriate transition from the period just preceding. His historical vision is focused on the state in the early twentieth-century aftermath of Reconstruction; and his literary perspective—involving a rather traditional concern with local custom, gesture, and speech, yet coupled with a distinctively modern interest in the ironic and grotesque—reveals an attempt to extend native realism into new dimensions of creative possibility.

In Smith's " 'Lijah," the last master of Holmacres, the old judge too much a part of history for the new politics, the new law, or even the new agriculture, maintains, for the sake of providing hospitality to visiting Yankee ("Northern," they correct him) land speculators, the fiction of a fabled old house servant, always absent, naturally, when he is most needed. It is the old judge himself, of course, who is doing all the menial work. Amidst poverty and loss, the fabrication is his last hold on a memory of mansions reared up in the wilderness and of an old life of splendor, courage, and gentility. The guests eventually uncover the ruse, and, to their credit, respond as gentlemen themselves, offering the judge fifty thousand dollars for a mica deposit on some ruined land he has considered worthless. Yet neither this happy turn of events, nor the story's humorous ending—the appended notice of a newspaper advertisement placed for an elderly houseservant willing to answer to the name Elijah—serves to obscure a larger historical point. What has been lost here truly can never be at all recovered. Only bought.

In "Miss Ella," Zelda Sayre Fitzgerald gives us another vision of a lost order, this time through a medium of conscious literary experimentation, deriving from her affiliation with the twentieth-century impressionists. Indeed, without this new thrust, the story she tells of lost love would seem by the earlier standards of Southern romance quite predictable: the quaintly formal courtship of the young Miss Ella by Mr. Hendrix; at precisely the crucial moment, the mad rivalry of Andy Bronson and the passion quickly consummated; the murder of Hendrix, come to claim vengeance, by Bronson on the day he and Ella are to be married; the spinster left only to her reddened eyes and bitter memories. What redeems this all from being simply trite is the story's vivid lyricism, the depth of feeling created through the repetition, reminiscent of contemporaries such as Hemingway and Gertrude Stein, of key impressions and images. In bringing the spirit of the expatriate *avant garde* to a traditional subject, and in what we sense must have been her own hard-won knowledge of a woman's heart, Fitzgerald had succeeded in creating her Alabama literary heritage truly anew.

In the selection from *The Store*, one sees that T. S. Stribling's great talents as a writer of fiction, in contrast to those of Smith or Fitzgerald, lay in his mastery of the rather more traditional strategies of literary realism as practiced by Mark Twain, Henry James, or, perhaps here the closest comparison, William Dean Howells. Stribling's overriding concern is social, for presenting the recognizable vision of an everyday environment alive with what Henry James would have called density of "detail," "solidity of specification," "the air of reality." In the plight of Colonel Miltiades Vaiden—his name and title quaint reminders again of an older world never to be regained—we are brought to share the realistic novelist's interest in manners, morals, and above all, money. Vaiden, cast loose in a Reconstruction Alabama where any sense of traditional values has been largely displaced by petty politics and bloodless money-grubbing, seeks his place in the new order only to find his life a series of irksome embarrassments and indignities. There is his shame at his fat wife Ponny; his insult at the hands of drummers who vie for his order of stock for a new store, only to find out that he has no capital; his humiliating complicity in saving the reputation of Handback, the vulgar, drunken hypocrite who has earlier defrauded him of all his future prospects. In the last image of the excerpt—an election poster heralding "The Man from Buffalo—The Hope of Southern Democracy"—we welcome Vaiden to Grover Cleveland's America; and although he will ultimately triumph over his predicament, we can only wonder, along with that other great chronicler of provincial desperations, Sinclair Lewis, at what terrible cost.

As with Stribling, the vision of Alabama life emerging from Mencken's fiction is essentially that of a rather traditional social realism. The main difference between the two approaches lies in Mencken's choice of a closer focus, her concentration on particular concerns of personal emotion. As a result, her work is often invested with the muted, almost confessional quality that we most closely associate with auto-biography. In "Little White Girl," for instance, as in "The Colonel's Predicament," very much at issue is the politics of race; but for the young Susie Tarleton, her idyllic friendship with Pinky, the daughter of her black mammy, undone once and for all by the advent of Alicia Pratt and "her airs and graces," all abstract questioning is completely subsumed in a child's simple attempt to come to terms with growing up white and black in the modern South and with learning to enact and see enacted the studied postures of the difference. In the same moment we sense, to be sure, the fuller implications of the tragedy at a more generalized level of social concern. We do so, however, mainly because of Mencken's ability to treat the matter so acutely in the nearer dimension of the concrete and experiential.

The fiction of Howell Vines, in comparison with that of some other figures here, may seem at first glance oddly dated and even archaic. The writer of the period he perhaps most generally resembles is Edgar Valentine Smith. Like " 'Lijah," "The Ginsing Gatherers" can be best categorized as historical fiction of the local-color variety, the story of Daniel Glaze and his wife Sookie, and of their life in the green wilderness world of the early nineteenth century. Yet in terms of the deeper character of the fictional atmosphere he creates, if Vines resembles any contemporary most closely, it is William March. His fiction, like March's, is the attempt to create a world dense with spells, omens, signs, portents. His vision of life is primal, almost atavistic. The old, half-savage Glaze and his young white girl Sookie, in their wanderings, their wild livelihood, their uninhibited forest lovemaking, seem to pay reverence to all dense, rank creation; and it is just this dark reverence in Vines that makes us recognize his enlistment in the great literary project of the modern, the attempt to recapture a sense of the wholeness of life in all its strange wonder.

This almost sacred sense of the complex mystery of modern life stirs across the whole vast range of William March's fiction; and it is the feature that brings him justly into the company of such well-known contemporaries as Sherwood Anderson, Ernest Hemingway, Sinclair Lewis, Gertrude Stein, F. Scott Fitzgerald, and William Faulkner. We see in him imagings of Anderson's naturalistic grotesques; we find his characters recurrently afoot, like Hemingway's, on a bleak modern landscape of random pain and violence where it is often simply enough to endure; we hear echoed Lewis's indictments of provincial smugness; we feel an intense concern, like Stein's, for the close rendering of spontaneous thought and speech; we recognize an understanding, quite comparable to Fitzgerald's, for the problems of money and class relationship; and we are surely reminded of Faulkner's depictions of a South in transition from a tragic past to a harrowed, uncertain future.

Yet while March does seem to partake in all these ways of the spirit of creative invention that characterized the major writings of the era, he also comes to us always in his works as an author in himself almost inexhaustible in his own range and variety. Indeed, the selection included here can at most serve as but an introduction—and one that an editor can only hope fervently that his readers will follow up—to the remarkably diverse and eclectic vision of ourselves and our century that March left to us.

March's ability to combine traditional Southern subject matter with qualities of arresting modern invention is imaged nowhere more clearly than in "Not Worthy of a Wentworth." The location is the familiar March setting of Reedyville. At issue are his twin great themes: twentieth-century human isolation and the power of social institutions to destroy individual lives. In this case, the problem is an outworn class structure that condemns Caroline Wentworth to a life of loveless solitude. This "unique vessel," as the narrator has heard her described, "in which the most aristocratic blood of Alabama had met and blended," spends all the years of her womanhood in a series of pathetic attempts to marry someone, by her family's standards, not worthy of her.

One would like to imagine that she seeks forbidden romance; but that would be to put a far more exalted face on it than the story permits. The suitors she elects for are themselves hardly a glamorous lot: a young bank clerk, a Jewish watch-repairer, a machinist, a Swiss baker. But it is not all just decadence or perversity. Carrie does truly, in her own poor way, try to marry for love; and therein lies her real tragedy. For it is not so much a matter, we ultimately see, of love to be gotten as love to be given. "Poor Carrie!" remarks Mrs. Kent, the confidante of the young man, an outsider, who supplies the narration. "All she wanted was to marry a man who needed her, one she could love and serve faithfully." Mrs. Kent goes on: "She was the most uncomplicated woman I ever knew." There is the real point. As this is no world for great miracles, so it is neither a place for small ones. There is not room enough among the institutions for the uncomplicated, for those, foolish as they might seem, who would wish only to give simple love. Indeed, it is they who seem to suffer most fully the mad isolation that is the special curse of the modern. So we see in the blighted, scuttling figure who confronts us at the tale's end, old Carrie, that last of her line, the sixty-two-year-old little girl, an insane hag playing in the yard with her dolls and her childish gabble. Here, as in so many of the stories, the curse may be bound up with the special burdens of Southern history. But what is finally important in March is not his provincialism, but his universality. In the harrowed loneliness of his characters, born of their sundry fortunes and estates, we can easily see the modern affliction that has also been too often our own.

'Lijah

Edgar Valentine Smith

FORTUNE had long since ceased to smile on the last master of Holmacres. Then, suddenly, with the advent of the strangers and the coincident creation of 'Lijah, came, too, the visit of the angels.

The two strangers—being strangers—of course, knew nothing of the evil days that had befallen Judge Holmsted, nor were they particularly interested, since their mission concerned not the fortunes, either good or ill, of others but the betterment of their own. What they knew concerning the Judge and Holmacres—other than the fact that the two were intimately connected with the business which was bringing them to the place—was furnished by the aged negro, who, with his ramshackle surrey and ancient nag, eked out a precarious existence driving occasional transients about the countryside. They had found him at the railway station in Wynnesborough, the county seat, and he had driven them along the five miles of deep-rutted road that stretched from the town to Holmacres. Being old, he was naturally garrulous.

For a long time he had sat fidgeting on the front seat of the vehicle, one ancient ear cocked rearward, listening to the unfamiliar accent of the strangers' speech. Finally, during a lull in their conversation, curiosity overpowered him and he half-faced about.

" 'Scuse me, gen'lemens," he observed ingratiatingly, "I don't mean no hahm by astin' it, but—you all is Yankees, ain't you?"

"Northerners—yes," one of them answered smiling. "Why do you ask?"

"Yessuh. I thought so. You jus' don't talk like white folks—I *means* like *us's* white folks, Boss."

The stranger who had answered the query—the younger and less grave-appearing of the two—smiled again. "We'd heard so much of your Southern hospitality that we thought we'd come down and see what it is like."

"Hawspitality? Well, suhs, you is comin' to de place wheah it was invented at—when you comes to see de Judge."

Then the old man—product of a bygone day and still living in the memory of its glories—described the hospitality of Holmacres as it had been and as he still saw it. It was the most fertile plantation in the country, and its owner, Judge Holmsted, by odds the richest man, the most learned lawyer, the noblest gentleman and the most open-handed host who ever breathed. His house was the finest that had ever been built; he set the most sumptuous table in the land; niggers fought for the privilege of working for him, even accepting the humblest tasks merely for the honor of being counted among the Judge's retinue. Judge Holmsted, to sum it up, was real "quality"; not like some of the trash which had sprung up with the last generation.

Thus the strangers were prepared in a measure for the picture which greeted them a few moments later: a grove of broad-topped live oaks, with the house in the near distance, a mansion of cement-walled, slate-roofed dignity, with the huge-columned, two-storied veranda reaching in stately welcome across its entire front. And as they stepped from the conveyance and came up the cape-jasmine-bordered walk, another picture was limned before them: a man well past threescore who had risen from his chair. He had removed his broad-brimmed hat, baring a mane of iron-gray hair, and now stood, despite the dingy frock coat that he wore, a figure as imposing as one of his own Ionic columns, courteously expectant at the visitors' approach.

The younger stranger introduced his companion and himself. They were from the North, as he had explained to the ancient driver, and their business was that of timberland investors. One of their agents had sent reports of hardwood acreage adjacent to the Tombigbee, and they were making a personal trip of inspection. They wished to find a place—a boarding or lodging house, perhaps—closer to the river than the county seat. Did Judge Holmsted know of such a place? They would be in the vicinity for several days.

Masters of Holmacres, since that first one who had erected a mansion in what was at that time a wilderness, had been famed for their hospitality. Nor had they been content with the thought that the neighboring gentry only should be the recipients of their bounty; for that first one, a little strangely perhaps for one of cavalier forbears, had caused to be carved beneath the broad fire mantel in the central hall this inscription:

"Be not forgetful to entertain strangers: for thereby some have entertained angels unawares."

Judge Holmsted was of that breed. "I couldn't think of letting you gentlemen stay anywhere but here." He spoke with a soft slurring of r's and a dropping of final g's which any attempt to put into print serves only to distort and make grotesque. "You must do me the honor of becoming my guests during your stay."

The older stranger demurred. "Why . . . that's awfully kind of you, Judge. But we really couldn't take advantage of your hosp——"

"You'll be taking no advantage at all, sir." There was no hint of subservience in the way the Judge said "sir." It was the courteous form of address toward strangers which had been the custom during his youth. "On the contrary, you'll really be doing me a favor. I'm an old man, gentlemen"—his smile would have won them had they really been hesitant at accepting his hospitality—"a little lonely at times, and I like company. And visitors, nowadays, are rare."

The strangers accepted the invitation with suspicious readiness. They hailed the ancient driver of the surrey, who had remained waiting in the driveway and who now brought in their luggage. For just a moment Judge Holmsted seemed ever so slightly embarrassed, a slight flush mantled his cheeks. And then, without stopping to think what it might mean, he created—'Lijah.

"Be seated, gentlemen," he invited, "while I call some one to bring in your baggage." He took a step toward the broad doorway. " 'Lijah!" he called. There was no answer. He called again, more loudly, " 'Lijah!" and still no one answered. Frowning, he walked to the end of the veranda, and peering about, shouted the name for the third time, with the same result as before.

He turned apologetically to his guests. "That trifling rascal," he explained, "is never about, particularly at this season of the year, when I need him." He glanced about for the driver of the surrey, but the old man had gone. "Come with me, gentlemen." Taking up their luggage, he led them within the house.

Though his welcome to the strangers had been extended in all sincerity (he had not been a Holmsted had it been otherwise) their coming brought a problem—another one—to the Judge. And, somehow, in his declining years life seemed to hold little else save problems, and all of them as yet unsolved.

Time had been when Holmacres threw its doors wide open to the countryside, for its masters had lived in the traditions handed down by its founder. Even now Judge Holmsted, daydreaming at times, permitted his thoughts to stray back to the days when servants swarmed.about the place; when there were stableboys who seemed actually to get underfoot, and house boys who fairly haunted the guests, eager to be of the slightest service. The big stable had contained riding and driving horses, which were not merely to be had for the asking but were almost forced on one. There had been dogs for the fall quail shooting, and master and guests had ridden to hounds. But now . . . it seemed that there remained little of misfortune that could happen. For of the hospitality for which Holmacres had been famous there existed but a shell, a shell so fragile that it might be crushed at any moment. Pity, too, that he, the last of his race, should not maintain the heritage which was his!

Had he belonged to that modern school which placed the mere god of commercialism above neighborliness, he might still have kept himself from actual want. But a friend in financial straits had come to him, and it was a neighborly act to indorse a note for a large sum of money. It was a hideous fate, though, that caused the friend to die, leaving an estate heavily encumbered, and forced the Judge to pay the indebtedness by mortgaging the home of his ancestors.

Even before this, though, the soil of Holmacres, planted for generations exclusively to cotton, had been growing less and less fruitful. Judge Holmsted had seen the yield dwindle year by year. He had divided the plantation into small farms for tenants. Then the northern exodus had begun; one by one the tenants had left, until now, with the few hired "hands" that he could secure, he was cultivating perhaps one-tenth of his tillable lands.

Still, for a time he had not experienced want. His salary as judge of the circuit—which position he had graced for thirty years—while not munificent had enabled him to make a pretense of the hospitality that had brought fame to Holmacres.

Then a new order of things came to pass. Politics was played with the precision—and the heart—of a machine. Those in control of the political destinies of the counties composing the circuit banded themselves together—that is, all of them save Judge Holmsted. Old-fashioned jurist that he was, he refused to lend himself to what he considered certain questionable pre-election machinations. Then the ultimatum went forth: he could submit or take the consequences— political oblivion. He accepted the gage, for he came not only of a hospitable but of a combative breed.

Hitherto his mere announcement that he would be a candidate for nomination at the Democratic primaries had assured his re-election. Now, for the first time in his life, he entered upon a vigorous campaign. He traveled incessantly about the various counties of his circuit, spending, legitimately, of his slender means. He made countless speeches, he met hundreds of friends, and received—promises.

He returned to the practice of law in Wynnesborough, but it seemed that his methods, like himself, had become old-fashioned. Friends insisted that he retained too much conscience to compete with more modern and, in certain instances, as he maintained, less ethical procedures than met his ideals.

"The practice of law," he had said once, when the matter came up, "is an honorable profession. It was never intended that it should degenerate into a display of legal acrobatics."

Clients were few and those who came were not always of the soundest financial standing. But there was always more or less bickering and litigation between the poorer class of hill-farmers, and some of these brought their troubles to Judge Holmsted. They paid their accounts in various ways: some brought small lots of cotton, others poultry and pigs, while one, an aged bachelor recluse of uncertain temper, just before his death had willed to the judge forty acres of land. This, people inclined to be humorous asserted, was in the way of a subtle revenge, for the Judge, suing for the old man, had lost his case; and the hill forty, as it was known, was not considered worth the tax payments.

There had been excessively poor crops. Years, too, when the cotton raised had not paid operating expenses. Twice the Judge had borrowed money—which he still owed—in advance on his crops. And the present outlook, with the late spring rains and cultivation sadly hampered, was now worse than ever.

Even his plainly dwindling income did not cause him to forsake his ideals. These, he insisted, one must cling to, even though he go down with them. Certain other changes, though, had forced themselves on him. Horses and other stock had been sold, since the plantation would not longer support them in numbers. Now all that remained were a few work mules and the Judge's own mount, Grover Cleveland. Servants were dispensed with until all of them save one, had gone. She stayed.

Christened Alabama, she was variously called Miz' 'Bama, Sis 'Bama, and 'Bama, the form of address depending on the degree of intimacy she permitted the speaker, the Judge and those of her race whom she considered her equals using the last named. She had remained at Holmacres after all the others had left, though her wage was more often a mirage than a reality. Latterly, continued urging by certain of her friends that she leave Judge Holmsted's service and go to the city, where her skill as a cook would return her a fabulous income, always met with scornful rebuff.

"But he ain't payin' you nothin'," the tempter would insist.

" 'Sposin' he ain't?" 'Bama, hands on her ample hips, would face the speaker. "You is fergittin' somep'm, ain't you? What 'bout my social p'sition?"

Usually this ended the discussion, for 'Bama, born and reared in the atmosphere of Holmacres, was the recognized leader of her people in the vicinity. No wedding was complete without her in the role of general adviser and master of ceremonies; nor was any funeral fittingly held without her presence to lend due solemnity to the occasion. But sometimes argument failed to convince those who tried to tempt her. Then 'Bama would fall back on flat refusal.

"Go 'way, nigguhs!" she would command. "I wouldn't leave 'is heah plantation foh—foh a *hund'ed dolluhs a yeah!*"

So she remained steadfast at Holmacres as general house factotum for the Judge. It was 'Bama who tactfully reminded him, at those times when the larder became more depleted than usual, that supplies were needed. And it was she who, out of the merest nothing, could serve food fit for a king's banquet. It was 'Bama who attended to the laundry—carefully washing the Judge's shirts to save the frayed cuffs as much as possible—and looked after the scanty supply of household linen. She darned Judge Holmsted's socks, saw that his shiny coat was occasionally brushed, and kept him generally from being out at elbows in the matter of clothing.

Her manifold duties had brought her to the front of the house that afternoon when the Judge summoned the mythical 'Lijah. For a moment she listened in open-mouthed amazement. Then understanding of a sort came to her, as she peeped between the curtains and saw the strangers. For some reason Judge Holmsted wanted it understood that a personage who answered—or should answer—to the name of 'Lijah belonged about the place. And any undertaking that the Judge set on foot was worth seeing to its conclusion. While she lacked the Judge's creative ability, she could, at least, embellish that which he had made. Her first attempt was in evidence that evening when she served a supper that would have tickled the palate of a gourmand.

"Judge," she remarked, taking the privilege of an old servant, "does you know, suh, 'at triflin' 'Lijah ain't got back till yit?"

Judge Holmsted choked momentarily; he seemed to experience sudden difficulty with his food, but he recovered his self-control instantly.

"He hasn't?" he demanded sternly. "Won't he ever learn to come in on time? Tell him that I wish to speak with him the moment he gets in."

"Yessuh. I knows wheah he's at. He's down to 'at river, settin' out catfish lines."

'Bama had cast the die. Judge Holmsted's creation of 'Lijah had been the result of a sudden—and now inexplicable—impulse; probably, upon reflection, he would have made no further reference to him. But 'Bama had given entity to the myth; with a word or two she had made of it an outstanding personality: a house servant who, by implication at least, took whatsoever liberties he chose.

And suddenly the realization came to the Judge that his creation had been nothing short of inspiration. With the present state of affairs at Holmacres, numberless things were sure to happen which might cause embarrassment to one who sought to fill the role of dutiful host; and the lack of a perfect hospitality, in many instances, could be blamed on the erring—though mythical—'Lijah.

"He's one of the older servants about the place," the Judge explained casually to his guests. "Does pretty much as he pleases."

He followed this with a laughing remark about 'Lijah's fondness for fishing. It was almost impossible to keep a negro and a river apart when the catfish were biting.

"I'd like very much to see 'Lijah." It was the younger stranger speaking. "I've read so many stories dealing with Southern plantation life—and especially the old family servants—that I've often wanted to see one of them. And your man, 'Lijah, seems to be typical."

"Oh, he'll be about the place—off and on," the Judge assured carelessly. "And if you're interested in types, sir, you'll probably like 'Lijah."

Thus for the moment he dismissed 'Lijah. But 'Bama, apparently, was determined not to let the errant one off so easily, for, later, as the Judge and his guests entered the high-ceilinged living room, where portraits of earlier Holmsteds gave their greeting from their oval walnut frames, she came to the doorway.

"Judge," she observed meaningly, "I don't 'spect you'll hahdly find no seegars. I seed 'Lijah sof'-footin' it round 'at sec'ta'y whilse I was dustin' 'is mawnin'."

Mechanically, Judge Holmsted's eyes sought the old rosewood secretary in one corner of the room, but before he could speak the younger stranger broke in with:

"Oh, that's all right, Judge." He was laughing heartily as he extended a cigar case. "Take one of these. So, he 'borrows' your cigars, does he? I've simply *got* to see him."

The strangers spoke of their business in the vicinity. The timber which they wished to inspect lay some miles away and, although their actual cruising of it would be done on foot, they would need some kind of conveyance to take them to their starting point. They supposed an automobile could be obtained in Wynnesborough?

Guests beneath Holmacres' roof had never been compelled to hire conveyances. It would have been unthinkable. The Judge explained that the swamp roads were in such condition that an automobile would be impracticable. He had never bought a car himself for this reason. His guests must use one of the numerous horses about the place. He would have 'Lijah hitch one of them to the buggy. It would be the very thing for their trips.

When one of them, giving as an excuse their long railroad journey, suggested retiring, Judge Holmsted, first ascertaining that 'Lijah was nowhere to be found, led them up the broad, winding stairway to their room. He lighted the kerosene lamp. Then, carelessly turning back the bed covering, he stopped in sudden horror. There was only one sheet on the bed!

He turned, his face crimsoning, to his guests. They had seen. "That trifling, worthless—" he began and stopped. "It's 'Lijah—of course, gentlemen—as usual," he said helplessly. "Come with me."

He led them to another room—his own—which for more than forty years no one save himself had occupied. This, he knew, would be in readiness. It always was, for he was fastidious about certain things, among them fresh bed linen. 'Bama attended to that.

"Just leave your shoes outside the door, gentlemen," he said in parting. "'Lijah will polish them."

He found 'Bama in the kitchen. Her answer to his question about the sheets brought home to him dishearteningly the scarcity of household linen.

In the library he picked up the latest issue of the Wynnesborough *Clarion,* a weekly newspaper published in the county seat, but he could not fasten his thoughts on the printed page. There were weightier things to be considered. Plainly, the visit of the strangers—should it prove of some duration—meant a still further drain on the slender resources of Holmacres. Since he had promised his guests the use of a horse, they would have to take Grover Cleveland. The Judge sighed. All of the work-mules were sadly needed, but he must use one of them for his daily trips to his office. By waiting until the strangers had left every morning, though, and remaining at his office till he was sure they had returned, they need never know of the subterfuge he had resorted to for their convenience.

Another matter claimed his attention: the disquieting letter—rather the letter that spelled doom—which had come that morning. The interest payment on the mortgage would be due shortly, and the letter stated brusquely that the mortgage had passed into other hands. Hereafter all payments must be met at maturity. Covetous eyes, Judge Holmsted knew, had long looked toward Holmacres. Once or twice he had succeeded in having his payments extended, but now . . . alien owners—people with no reverence for its traditions—would come into possession of the place. The thought was bitter— unbearable.

Once—more than twoscore years ago—the Judge had hoped that an heir might succeed to his name and estate. But with the passing of the one who could have made this a reality, this hope, too, had died. Better so, he comforted himself now; far better that the odium for failure to live up to Holmacres' heritage be his than that it should have been shifted to a son who would have borne his name.

He mounted the stairs. Just outside the door of his guests' room he found their shoes.

And that night—and for succeeding nights—he slept in the bed that had but one sheet.

But his guests at the breakfast table next morning probably thought that his only solicitude lay in planning for their well-being. He was sorry that, owing to 'Lijah's shiftlessness—the black rascal!—he had been compelled to make such short shift for them on the previous night. He hoped they had rested well.

After breakfast they found Grover Cleveland, freshly curried and rubbed till his coat shone like satin, hitched to the buggy ready for their trip. The vehicle itself bore signs of recent washing; the harness, too, one would have said, had been freshly oiled.

"I wonder how we're going to begin talking business to a man who treats us like members of his family," the older stranger said as he climbed into the vehicle. "We'll have to use a lot of diplomacy."

"We'll just remember," the younger man reminded, "that we've come several hundred miles to secure a property at as favorable terms to ourselves as possible. And that business is business—always."

Judge Holmsted waited only long enough to see his guests off. Then he walked to one of the fields where a negro was plowing.

"Eph," he said, "I'll have to be using the mule for a few days."

"But, Judge, suh!" Eph stared, gaping. "Dis grass! It's plum' rampant since 'em las' rains, suh. Can't you see it's jus' nachelly chokin' de cotton to death?"

The Judge could see, plainly enough. The spindling stalks of cotton were struggling weakly through mazes of Johnson and Bermuda grasses. But he saw something else, too; something that Eph, being a recent comer, could not have seen or, seeing, could not have understood: there were guests beneath Judge Holmsted's roof.

It was the first time that he had ridden a mule since he was a boy. Often then, in a spirit of mischief, he had done so. Things had changed now. Horses . . . dogs . . . servants . . . gone. Everything! Everything save the will to be a hospitable host.

At the little bank in town he was courteously but firmly refused an additional loan. The bank officials liked the Judge—and sympathized with him—but his previous loans were still outstanding. And it was doubtful—exceedingly doubtful—that his crop that year would pay the cost of raising it.

But that evening, as he sat with his guests on the broad veranda, he was solicitous only as to the result of their investigations. Were they finding the hardwood timber of good quality? And was it in sufficient quantity to justify them in purchasing and logging it? He hoped this might be the case; he was looking forward with a great deal of pleasure to welcoming them as permanent neighbors.

He proved himself to be a raconteur of rare ability and charm. The grave-faced stranger seemed fascinated by his stories as he spoke of the days when steamboats from Mobile plied the Tombigbee daily. Now there were only one or two boats weekly. But then many were the gay parties that made the round trip. There was always a negro orchestra on board and stately men and beautiful women, after the dining salon had been cleared, danced the schottische and the polka until the early hours of morning. More than once, too, a steamer had been forced to pull in to the bank while two young blades went ashore and settled their hot-blooded quarrels according to the code. Judge Holmsted sighed reminiscently. Those had been wonderful days.

The air was soft with the softness of Southern nights. There came to them, as they sat there, the odor of cape jasmine and the fainter but more caressing scent of honeysuckle. A light breeze rustled the leaves of the water oaks, shimmering now by the light of the full moon in a mantle of pure silver dust.

The younger stranger lighted a cigar and leaned back in his chair, sighing restfully, "Two weeks of this," he said, "and I shouldn't want to go home. You Southern planters lead an enviable life, Judge."

"It's enchanting," his companion assented.

"We like it, sir—some of us," the Judge admitted. He spoke with a tinge of regret of former neighbors who, one by one, had been lured away by the cities. Many fine old places had been left to the care of tenants and had speedily gone to ruin. But the Holmsteds, being lovers of the land, had always lived close to it. "Maybe we are more firmly rooted in the soil than some of the others were," the Judge said.

"It seems to me, Judge," the grave-faced stranger offered, "that you have a wonderful place here for a stock farm. Aren't these native grasses—I believe you call them Johnson and Bermuda—good for grazing?"

"Excellent, sir."

"That's just what I'd do with this place if I owned it," the younger stranger broke in. He was more outspoken than his elderly companion. "I'd divide it into pastures with good fences, build up-to-date barns and pig houses, and stock it with blooded cattle and hogs. You've your grasses for spring and summer. And I understand that those river canebrakes make fine winter grazing."

"I may try something of the kind next year," the Judge admitted. "I've been thinking for some time of venturing along that line."

Venturing! Blooded cattle and hogs! Fences and barns, when the burning question was one of bare existence! Not that he had never had dreams. Many times he had pictured his broad lands dotted with droves of sleek cattle and herds of swine, with an income assured that would again crown Holmacres with its fair name for hospitality. But the realization of this dream would require money. . . .

It was the next morning that a mocking bird, nesting in a near-by tree, awakened the serious-faced stranger with its early song. Arising, he crept softly to the window and stood listening. And suddenly, as he looked out, he started and stared fixedly. Then a dull, red flush mounted slowly to his cheeks. He withdrew from the window even more softly than he had approached it and lay down again without wakening his companion.

But that morning brought consternation to Judge Holmsted. Modern plumbing had not been installed at Holmacres, and he remembered suddenly that his guests must shave. And there was one item that he had overlooked.

"I suppose, gentlemen," he remarked at the breakfast table, "that 'Lijah—you see I have to keep close check on him—brought you hot water?"

They admitted that he had not.

"He'll be the death of me, yet," the Judge said hopelessly, "if I don't wring his neck soon. He's getting more worthless every day."

The young stranger laughed. "You're more lenient with your servants, Judge, than we'd be in the North. They must attend to their duties there or they're discharged."

"But it's different with us, sir." The Judge smiled. "Take 'Lijah, for example. Been on the place all of his life—going on fifty years. I couldn't get rid of him. If I were to discharge him he'd refuse to stay discharged. He'd simply come sneaking back and I'd have to feed him."

The younger man's interest in 'Lijah was more intrigued than ever. Returning with his companion earlier than usual one evening, he sought out 'Bama. He was eager, he said, to see 'Lijah. But that worthy, as usual, failed to answer even when 'Bama, standing on the kitchen porch, called his name lustily several times.

"When does he sleep?" the stranger asked. "He doesn't seem to be around the place of nights."

"Sleep? Him sleep? You neentuh worry 'bout 'at, Cap'n. All 'Lijah needs is a sof' place on de shady side of a tree when dey's somep'm needs doin' round de house. He'll 'tend to de sleepin'. Dey's jus' two things 'Lijah's good foh: he de sleep-lovin'es' an' de catfish-ketchin'es' nigguh you eveh seed."

"He's typical all right," the stranger laughed. "And I must see him—I've simply *got* to see him before I leave."

Judge Holmsted found himself gradually forming a sneaking fondness for his creation. Maybe it was because he was unconsciously bringing into being an ideal. For 'Lijah was just the shiftless, work-dodging, cigar-pilfering type that the Judge would have loved—the kind that would run rabbits with his bird dogs—provided the Judge could afford the dogs—or slip his pack of fox hounds out on cold autumn nights—if the Judge should ever own a pack—for surreptitious 'coon and 'possum hunting. Yes . . . that would be just like 'Lijah. Indolent, grumbling always, complaining of a mis'ry in his side; absolutely dependent, thoroughly undependable—and utterly likable. In short, he would be perfect. The Judge even caught himself at times murmuring aloud, "The trifling black rascal!"

But such things—oh, well!—they were dreams, visions that an old man was seeing.

As the strangers showed no signs of terminating their visit, 'Bama, with visions of a rapidly depleted larder, began to experience a real concern. With only the Judge and herself to care for, she could have made shift of some sort. Maybe a hint to Judge Holmsted of the real state of affairs might not prove unavailing. So she tried, very diplomatically, one evening at the supper table, to sound a warning.

"Judge, suh," she remarked meaningly, " 'Lijah is been 'mongst de chickens ag'in."

"What of it?" Judge Holmsted smiled on his guests. 'Lijah, he explained, was probably giving a party for some of his friends. "A few chickens, more or less, don't matter, do they, 'Bama?"

"But dese is *fattenin'* chickens, suh; de onlies' ones I had left."

"You don't mind 'Lijah entertaining his friends, do you?" the talkative stranger asked.

"Not gen'ally; no, suh. But he's been gittin' entirely *too* entertainin' lately."

"Doesn't he catch enough fish for his feasts?"

"Yessuh; he ketches plenty fish. But catfish, you knows, is just a nigguh's reg'lar eatin' victuals. Dey uses de chickens kind o' foh dessert."

"You must find his parties something of a drain on your resources."

" 'Tain't no pahty, suh, he's givin' 'is time. It's just a shindig—a plain shindig."

The Judge explained that a shindig was a dance.

"Dance?" The younger stranger seemed amazed. "An old man like 'Lijah?"

"Him dance?" 'Bama gave answer. "Just de thoughts of a fiddle 'll send him shufflin' his feets 'cross de flo—right now! Age ain't purified him none."

'Bama, strictly orthodox in her religious beliefs, was patently outraged by this latest of the hapless 'Lijah's escapades, for as she left the room they heard her muttering:

"An' him wid gran'chillun! I's gwine to have him churched—I *sho'* is!"

Between themselves the strangers discussed the business which had brought them to Holmacres.

"It's showing up even better than the estimate we received," the older man said one evening.

"One of the richest deposits I ever saw," the other admitted.

When they went to their room he complained of not being in the mood for sleeping. The rays of that Southern moon, he said, must have affected him. He felt restless; he'd walk around a bit.

Five minutes later he returned quietly to the house, mounted the stairs softly, undressed silently, and went to bed.

The next morning as they seated themselves at the breakfast table, 'Bama's voice, raised in loud and indignant self-communion, was heard in the kitchen.

"Co'se, *he* don't keer! Out dere diggin' yearthworms to go fishin' wid an' lettin' all 'em cows an' ca'fs git together! Don't make no diffe'nce to him if us *don't* have no milk foh de cawfee."

It was much better, 'Bama reasoned, to blame this lack on 'Lijah than be compelled to admit that their only cow, bitten by a snake two days previously, had died.

But the younger stranger, usually so talkative when reference was made to 'Lijah, was strangely silent now.

Another day, as the visitors were dressing in their room, the more taciturn one spoke of their business. "I wonder," he asked, "if the Judge knows anything about the value of the property?"

"Oh, yes!" The younger man's loquaciousness had returned. "He knows all about it. I was talking to 'Lijah only yesterday—" he made sudden pretense of searching for something in his traveling bag— "and he said the Judge had received several offers for the property, but that he wasn't eager to sell. Saving it as a sort of nest egg, I was given to understand. In fact, 'Lijah said—"

"So, you've seen him?" At the first mention of the name, the serious-faced stranger had seemed surprised—almost startled. Then a look of comprehension—of complete and sympathetic understanding—lighted his grave features. And, as he smiled softly, tiny wrinkles creased the corners of his eyes. "What's 'Lijah like?"

"Just what I expected. Quite a character. Unique. He let me understand how these Southern planters feel about parting with any of their landholdings. From what 'Lijah said, the Judge probably wouldn't even name a figure if we were to approach him on the matter. And don't forget that it would be fatal even to think of trying any haggling or 'jewing down.' He doesn't want for money, with this plantation bringing in a steady income and all the servants he needs. That's not even considering what he gets out of his law practice. Now, I'd suggest—"

"Just a moment!"

At the interruption the voluble young stranger looked up from his traveling bag. Something that he saw—maybe it was the quiet smile in his companion's eyes—sent an answering flash into his own.

"We're partners," the serious-faced man reminded him, "and ought to be frank with each other. Just how long have you known the actual conditions here? That 'Lijah is a myth? That it's the Judge who has been polishing our shoes—"

"And washing that damned old buggy!" The younger man's face was crimson. "And letting us have his saddle horse—the only one on the place—while he rode a mule! Think of it! That hospitable old aristocrat! Poverty-stricken! My God, I—" He stammered and stopped.

"We both understand, I guess." The quiet-spoken man extended his hand, which was grasped in silence.

That evening they announced to Judge Holmsted that, having finished their inspection, they were ready to return home. After thanking the Judge for his hospitality, the younger stranger broached the matter of business. They were not only timberland investors, it appeared, but dealt also in other property. But, as he tried diplomatically to come to the subject uppermost in his mind, he seemed strangely ill at ease for one accustomed to business deals of magnitude.

And finally, instead of the tactful approach which he had planned, he came very bluntly to the point.

"There's a deposit of mica on the hill forty of yours, Judge," he said simply. "Would you care to sell it?"

That old hill forty! Hope blossomed faintly in Judge Holmsted's breast. The strangers might—it was barely possible that they might—pay enough for that rocky, worthless waste to take care of that threatening interest note. If so, he was assured tenancy of his home for another six months. After that . . .

But the stranger was speaking again. "We realize, Judge, that, between gentlemen, there should be no haggling over such a thing as price. We've talked it over, my friend and I, and have decided to offer you just what the property is worth to us."

That faint gleam of hope flickered and died. Evidently the strangers considered the hill forty almost valueless. Foolish! Just an old man dreaming . . . Holmacres . . . home of his ancestors . . . home of hospitality. . . .

He heard the stranger's voice again. He was speaking rapidly. "We can offer you, for all rights to the land, fifty thousand dollars."

Fifty thousand dollars! One watching Judge Holmsted closely might have noticed a sudden throbbing of the blue veins at his temples; might have detected a slight tremor in the hand that went up, trying unconcernedly to stroke his gray goatee; might even have observed his other hand grip tightly for a moment the arm of the chair on which it rested. Maybe, in that brief instant, the Judge saw a dream fulfilled: broad fields fenced to pasture and dotted with sleek cattle and fat swine; bottom lands, yellow with ripening corn; barns and outhouses, as befitted a vast estate; Holmacres, with its doors once more flung wide. . . .

But whatever might have been his emotions, he gave no evidence of them, as he answered with his usual grave courtesy:

"So far as I know, gentlemen, the matter can be arranged on that basis."

When the strangers left next morning he expressed regret that he could not accompany them to town, since urgent matters necessitated his presence on the plantation. They could leave Grover Cleveland and the buggy at the livery stable in Wynnesborough. He would send 'Lijah for them.

After they had gone he seated himself before the old rosewood secretary. Maybe he dreamed again . . . of quail hunting during the crisp months of fall . . . of fox hounds in their kennels . . . of servants. Servants?

Suddenly he drew up a sheet of paper and began writing in a firm, precise script. And when he had finished he scanned what he had written:

WANTED: Negro house servant, male, aged fifty, or thereabouts, for light work in plantation home. Must be willing to answer to the name of Elijah. Apply B. L. H. care *Clarion.*

Miss Ella

Zelda Sayre Fitzgerald

BITTER things dried behind the eyes of Miss Ella like garlic on a string before an open fire. The acrid fumes of sweet memories had gradually reddened their rims until at times they shone like the used places in copper saucepans. Withal she was not a kitchen sort of person, nor even a person whom life had found much use in preserving. She was elegant, looking exactly like one of the ladies in a two-tone print on the top of a fancy glove box. Her red hair stuck out of a choir cap on Sundays in a tentative attempt to color the etching of her personality.

When I was young I loved Miss Ella. Her fine high instep curved into her white canvas shoes in summer with the voluptuous smoothness of a winter snow-bank. She had a lace parasol and was so full of birdlike animation that she teetered on her feet when she spoke to you—sometimes she had meals with us and I remember her twittering about on our hearth after supper, dodging the popping bits of blue flame from our bituminous coal, believing ardently that "one" could keep fit by standing up twenty minutes after eating.

All the people in the world who were not her blood relations were impersonally "one" to Miss Ella. She was severe with the world and had she ordered the universe she would have kept it at runners' tension toeing the chalk starting-mark forever. I don't know which would have upset her equanimity more: the materialization of a race or the realization that there wasn't going to be any. In any case, "one" must keep fit for all problematical developments.

Even her moments of relaxation were arduous, so much so as to provoke her few outbursts of very feminine temper and considerable nervous agitation. She was essentially Victorian. Passing along the sidewalk in the heat of the afternoon and seeing Miss Ella far away in her hammock in the shade of the big elms by the house, her white skirt dusting a white flutter off the snowball bushes as she rocked herself back and forth, you would never have guessed how uncomfortable she was or how intensely she disliked hammocks. It always took at least three tries before she was tolerably ensconced: the first invariably loosened the big silver buckle that held her white-duck skirt in place; the second was wasted because it might result in immodest exposure of her fragile legs, by furling too tightly around her the white canvas lengths. After that she simply climbed into the hammock and did her arranging afterward, which is about as easy as dressing in a Pullman berth. The hammock fanned its red and yellow fringe in a triumphant crescent motion that discomfited Miss Ella. By holding tightly to the strings at one end and desperately straining her foot against the worn patch of clay in the grass underneath, she managed to preserve a more or less static position. With her free hand she opened letters and held her book and brushed away things that fell from the trees and scratched the itchings that always commence when stillness is imperative.

These were Miss Ella's hours of daytime rest. She never allowed herself to be disturbed until the sun had got well to the west and down behind the big house, its last light pulsing through the square hall-ways in the back windows and out the front, vivisected by the cold iron tracery of the upstairs balcony, to fall in shimmering splinters on the banana-shrubs below. At five a decisive old lady rolled up the drive in a delicate carriage, high and springy with a beige parasol top. Her hair was snow-white and her face was white and pink with ante-bellum cosmetics. Even from far away they emanated the pleasant smell of oris root and iris. She held the reins absent-mindedly in one hand, the big diamonds in their old-fashioned settings poking up through her beige silk gloves. Her other arm made a formal, impersonal nest for a powdered spitz. When she called to Miss Ella the words slid along the sun rays with the sound of a softly drawn curtain on brass rings. "Ella! It's time to cool off, my child. The dust is settled by now. And oh, Ella, be a good girl and find Aunt Ella's fan, will you?"

So Miss Ella and Aunt Ella and the white dog went for their afternoon drive leaving the sweet cool of the old garden to the aromatic shrubs, the fireflies and the spiders who made their webs in the box-wood, to the locusts tuning the air for night vibrations and to three romantic children who waited every day for the carriage to roll out of sight before scaling the highest bit of wall that surrounded the grounds.

We loved that garden. Under two mulberry trees where the earth was slippery beneath our bare feet there stood a wooden play-house, relic of Miss Ella's youth. To me it never seemed an actual play-house but to represent the houses associated with childhood in homely stories; it was in my imagination the little red schoolhouse, the farmhouse, the kindly orphan asylum, literary locales that never materialized in my own life. I never went inside but once, because of a horror of the fat summer worms that fell squashing from the mulberry trees. It was dry and dusty, scattered traces of a frieze of apple-blossoms still sticking to the walls where Miss Ella had pasted them long ago.

No one but us ever went near the play-house, not even the grand-nieces of Aunt Ella when they came occasionally to visit. Almost buried in a tangle of jonquils and hyacinths dried brown from the summer heat, its roof strewn with the bruised purple bells of a hibiscus overhanging its tiny gables, the house stood like a forgotten sarcophagus, guarding with the reticent dignity that lies in all abandoned things a paintless, rusty shotgun. Here was a rough oasis apart from the rest of the orderly garden. From out of the delicate concision there foamed and billowed feathery shell-colored bushes that effervesced in the spring like a strawberry soda; there were round beds of elephants-ears with leaves that held the water after a rain and changed it to silver balls of mercury running over the flat surface. There were pink storm-lilies on their rubbery stems, and snowdrops, and shrubs with bottle-green leaves that ripped like stitching when you tore them. Japonicas dropped brown flowers into the damp about the steps of the square, sombre house, and wistaria vines leaned in heavy plaits against the square columns. In the early morning Miss Ella came with a flat Mexican basket and picked the freshest flowers for the church. She said she tended the garden, but it was really Time and a Negro contemporary of his, who did that. In front of the kitchen door, the old black man had a star-shaped bed of giant yellow cannas covered with brown spots and in a crescent were purple pansies. He scolded appallingly when he caught us on the grounds: he was most proprietary about the place and guarded the play-house like some cherished shrine.

That was the atmosphere that enveloped the life of Miss Ella. Nobody knew why she found it sufficient; why she did not follow the path of the doctor's coupé that divided its time between the downtown club and the curb in front of her shadowy lawn. The reason was Miss Ella's story, which like all women's stories was a love story and like most love stories took place in the past. Love is for most people as elusive as the jam in "Alice in Wonderland"—jam yesterday, jam to-morrow, but no jam to-day. Anyhow, that was how it was with Miss Ella, living titularly on the jam of some time ago, skimming over life's emotions like a bird flying low over the water detaching bright sprays into the air with its wings.

In her youth she was as slim and smooth as a figure in blown glass. Compact in long organdies that buoyed themselves out on the bars of a waltz, she stood firm in the angular aloof arm of her fiancé.

He pyramided above her, two deep lines from the corners of his eyes, his mouth closed tight over many unuttered words, a deep triangle about the bridge of his nose. In the autumn he stood for hours up to his knees in the greasy backwash from the river, the long barrel of his gun trained skyward on wide files of green-backed ducks flying south over the marshes. He brought his loot to Miss Ella in bunches and she had them cooked in her white-pine kitchen, steeped in port and bitters and orange peel, til the brown delicious odor warmed the whole house. They sat together over an enormous table, eating shyly in the dim rings of light that splattered the silver and crept softly over the heavy frames of the dark still-lifes that lined the wall. They were formally in love. There was a passive dignity in the currents that passed between them that quieted the air like a summer Sunday morning. The enveloping consideration of him, the luminous fragility of her, they made a harmonious pair.

In those days the town was small, and elegant ladies agitated their rockers with pleasure back of box-wood gardens as Miss Ella and her beau whipped past in his springy carriage, the light pouring over the polished spokes of the wheels like the flowing glint of water over a mill.

He called her "dear"; she never called him anything but Mr. Hendrix. In the soft chasm of the old hall after a late party, he reverently held her hands, hands filled with a dance card, a butterfly pin, a doll in feathers, trinkets of the dance, souvenirs of dreamy rhythms that wavered in her head with the fluctuations of watered silk propelled by the warmth of quiet happiness. They poured the plans for their life together into the moulds of the thick tree shadows and turned them out on the midnight air marked with the delicate tracings of the leaves—modest stable plans of two in love. He told her how things were to be, and she acquiesced, pleased with his quiet voice piling up in mid-air like smoke in an airless room.

They were both religious to a fashionable restrained extent, and it was the church which drew Andy Bronson across the strings of their devotion, to saw them and haggle them and finally leave the broken ends twisting upward, frayed and ruined, dangling loose in tragedy with the resonance of twisted catgut. Miss Ella and Mr. Hendrix planned to be married in the square white church in the spring. Entering from the back where the iron banisters led to the balcony, they planned to walk in solemnity through the misty gusts of face powder, the green smell of lilies, the holiness of candles, to barter with God at the altar; toil and amiability for emotional sanctity. He said that there would be beauty and peace forever after and she said "Yes."

Sorting their dreams absent-mindedly, like putting clean linen in a cupboard, they stood side by side dreaming of that at Christmas time. A church festival was going on and there were eggnog and lemonade and silver cake-baskets filled with sliced fruit cake and bonbonnières of nuts and candy in the Sunday-school room. The church was hot, and young men drifted out and in again, bringing with them the odor of overcoats and cigarettes smoked in the cold, and fumes of Bourbon. There in the smoky feminine confusion stood Andy Bronson, the excitement of Christmas hanging bright wreaths about his cheek bones, a mysterious quiet certitude proclaiming nefarious motives.

Miss Ella was conscious of him in a still world beyond reality, even as she talked with animation of all the years that would churn behind the honeymoon boat that plied between Savannah and New York. From that tremulous duality she shivered into the confusion that followed the bang of the giant firecracker that Andy had lit beneath the steps that led to the balcony. A spark caught in her flimsy Dolly Varden and Ella's dress was in flames. Through the slow split groups laughing, disapproving, explaining, not knowing what had happened, Andy was the first to reach her burning skirts, clapping the blaze between his palms until only a black, charred fringe was left.

The day after Christmas, hid in an enormous box of roses so deep in red and remorse that their petals shone like the purple wings of an insect, he sent her yards and yards of silk from Persia, and then he sent her ivory beads, a fan with Dresden ladies swinging between mother-of-pearl sticks, a Phi Beta Kappa key, an exquisite miniature of himself when his face was smaller than his great soft eyes— treasures. Finally he brought her a star-sapphire (which she tied about her neck in a chamois bag lest Mr. Hendrix should know) and she loved him with desperate suppression. One night he kissed her far into the pink behind her ears and she folded herself in his arms, a flag without a breeze about its staff.

For weeks she could not tell Mr. Hendrix, saving and perfecting dramatically the scene she hopefully dreaded. When she did tell him, his eyes swung back in his head with the distant pendulousness of a sea-captain's. Looking over her small head through far horizons with the infinite sadness of a general surrendering his sword, finding no words or thoughts with which to fill her expectant pathos, he turned and slowly rolled the delicate air of early spring down the gravel path before him and out into the open road. Afterward he came to call one Sunday and sat stiffly in a bulbous mahogany chair, gulping a frosted mint julep. The depression about him made holes in the air, and Miss Ella was glad when he left her free to laugh again.

The southern spring passed, the violets and the yellow white pear trees and the jonquils and cape jasmine gave up their tenderness to the deep green lullaby of early May. Ella and Andy were being married that afternoon in her long living-room framed by the velvet portières and empire mirrors encasing the aroma of lives long past. The house had been cleaned and polished, and shadows and memories each put in their proper place. The bride cake nested on southern smilax in the dining-room and decanters of port studded the long sideboard mirrors with garnets. Between the parlor and the dining-room calla lilies and babies'-breath climbed about a white tulle trellis and came to a flowery end on either side of the improvised altar.

Upstairs, Miss Ella was deep in the cedar and lavender of a new trunk; fine linen night-gowns and drawn-work chemise were lifted preciously into the corners and little silk puffs of sachet perched tentatively over the newness. A Negress enamoured of the confusion stood in the window drinking in the disorder from behind dotted Swiss curtains, looking this way and that, stirring the trees with the excitement of her big black eyes and quieting the room with the peace they stole from the garden.

Miss Ella heard the curtains rip as the strong black hands tore them from the fragile pole. "O Lawd—O Lawd—O Lawd." She lay in a heap of fright. By the time Ella reached the heavy mass, the woman could only gesticulate toward the window and hide her face. Ella rushed to the window in terror.

The bushes swished softly in the warmth. On the left there was nothing remarkable; a carriage crawling away far down the road, and plants growing in quiet now that their flowers were shed. Reassurance of the coming summer pushed her leaping heart back into place. Ella looked across the drive. There on the play-house steps lay Mr. Hendrix, his brains falling over the earth in a bloody mess. His hands were clinched firmly about his old shotgun, and he as dead as a door nail.

Years passed but Miss Ella had no more hope for love. She fixed her hair more lightly about her head and every year her white skirts and peek-a-boo waists were more stiffly starched. She drove with Auntie Ella in the afternoons, took an interest in the tiny church, and all the time the rims about her eyes grew redder and redder, like those of a person leaning over a hot fire, but she was not a kitchen sort of person, withal.

The Colonel's Predicament

T. S. Stribling

I

I N response to his wife's uncertain inquiry about the political speaking, Colonel Miltiades Vaiden called back from his gate that he did not think there would be any ladies at the courthouse that evening.

By laying stress on the word "think" the Colonel not only forecasted a purely masculine attendance in Courthouse Square that summer evening in Florence, Alabama, but at the same time he subtly expressed his own personal disapproval of women appearing at political gatherings at any place or time whatsoever.

The heavy wife in the doorway hesitated at the Colonel's implication. She had wanted to go. She felt the gregarious impulse of fleshy persons to foregather with crowds, to laugh and fraternize with the audience, to propel her large body among her lighter fellows with the voluptuous and genial ruthlessness of a fat person. However, on the other hand, her feminine fear of being the only woman in the audience stood in her path.

But behind these two antagonistic impulses lay another cause of depression which the ponderous wife knew too well but which she never frankly had admitted even to herself. This was that her husband did not want her to go with him to this or to any other public gathering; it was . . . that he was ashamed of her.

This fact wavered in the woman's mind until she expelled it by calling out:

"Oh, Mr. Milt, there'll be a lot of leading men down there, I expect. Maybe some of 'em will offer you a—a better position. . . ."

At this mention of position a disagreeable tickle went through the husband's chest, but he answered in an impassive, corrective tone:

"Not likely such a topic will come up at a political meeting, Ponny."

"Well . . . if it does . . . you . . . you mustn't repulse 'em, Mr. Milt."

"No, I won't, Ponny," he assured her with a solemn face.

He let himself into the street and closed the gate after him. As he did this, the looseness of the hinges, the broken palings, the gaunt outline of his rented house here on this back street in Florence, all combined to give him a twist of repulsion when connected with the thought of a "position."

Because, as a matter of fact, the Colonel had no position. Ever since the Civil War had lost him his place as an overseer on a cotton plantation, he had desired the post and circumstance of a country gentleman. Only nowadays there were no country gentlemen. Nowadays one reached gentility by other methods, but Colonel Vaiden, somehow, had not succeeded in fitting himself into those other methods.

For a long stretch the Colonel's failure had been a kind of standing riddle to persons who had known of his distinguished services during the war and his leadership of the Klan during the Reconstruction. But this riddle gradually lost point with time. So now, as the Colonel glanced back in the twilight and saw in the doorway the bulky outline of his wife, he knew that, besides himself, she was the only human being on earth who believed that upon him, eventually, would fall some great, noble, and extraordinary estate. She was constantly expecting it out of a persistent faith and admiration for her husband's ability.

As the Colonel stepped across a gully in the neglected street he rewarded her loyalty by thinking in a kind of annoyed fashion:

"I should have asked her to go with me . . . damn it . . . Ponny's a good girl. . . ."

Cherry Street, along which Colonel Vaiden moved, was bordered by bare weed-grown lots and an occasional stark frame house with a chicken coop and a privy in the rear. Two or three squares farther on the pedestrian turned westward toward Market Street. Here the neighborhood began to improve: dark masses of magnolias and live oaks screened the houses. Opening on the sidewalks were double gates to admit a horse and carriage, or perhaps a milk cow of mornings and evenings.

These were still ordinary middle-class homes, but this evening they stiffened a determination in Miltiades to reach this stage of luxury. Yes, and, by gravy, he would do even better than that! These frame houses with magnolias and live oaks, he would have something better than that . . . he did not know just what that better ménage would be, but a quiver of impatience went through him to be at it. Whatever he did he must do quickly; whatever he gained he must gain with speed; . . . he was forty-eight years old.

When Miltiades reached Market Street and turned southward toward the courthouse he abandoned his thoughts of future wealth to decide whether or not he should stop by the boarding house and ask his brother, Augustus Vaiden, to go to the speaking with him.

He hesitated over this point, first because he did not approve of Augustus, who did nothing at all. Augustus' wife, Rose Vaiden, ran a boarding house and Augustus puttered about, helping with the cooking, talking to the boarders, walking downtown for letters, and that was all Augustus did. It annoyed Miltiades, such an ambitionless brother!

The second reason Miltiades had for not stopping by was that Rose Vaiden did not like him. He liked Rose all right in an unenthusiastic sort of way, but Rose did not like him in any way whatsoever.

These pros and cons moved through the Colonel's mind with more irony than definition, and now, after he, apparently, had raked together two good reasons for not stopping, the Colonel mentally determined to drop in at the boarding house and take Augustus with him to the speaking.

When this plan developed out of Colonel Vaiden's musings, he had come in sight of the two-storied Vaiden boarding house standing darkly against the sky. A light in the kitchen window reminded Miltiades that Rose and Augustus kept a servant, while his own wife, Ponny, always had had to do her own work. This seemed incongruous. He, Colonel Miltiades Vaiden, without a cook, while Augustus, his younger brother, who had no more ambition than a cottonfield negro, should have one . . .

At this point a movement of surprise, almost of shock, went through the Colonel. In front of the boarding house stood a carriage and horses. For a fantastic moment Miltiades thought that somehow or other Rose had bought them and there they were. Then he knew this could not be.

He walked on curiously, when from inside the half-seen vehicle a man's voice said impersonally:

"Good-evening, Colonel Vaiden. My wife and I stopped by to take Miss Rose and her husband to the speaking. Will you ride down with us?"

Miltiades took off his hat to the woman he could not see in the carriage.

"Thank you, Judge, but the air is so fine tonight I believe I'll continue my walk, if you don't mind?"

The voice in the carriage completely acceded to this request.

"It is a very fine night, Colonel."

And Miltiades went on alone with a vague relief that someone else was taking his brother to the speaking.

Half an hour later, as Colonel Vaiden approached Courthouse Square, a distant burst of cheering told him that the speaking already had begun. As he drew nearer the lilt of the voice of an orator came to his ears. Then he could see the speaker, elevated on the portico of the courthouse in the light of four oil lamps. The man on the platform was Governor Terry O'Shawn, a lawyer of Florence, who had risen to the Governorship of Alabama. That was why Florence had turned out en masse to honor the Governor. He was one of their own townsmen.

Governor O'Shawn stood in the midst of the four lamps shaking a fist over the heads of his audience. He was demanding to know upon whose bosom battened the blood-sucking harpies of Yankee manufacturers!

"Look you, my fellow citizens," he inveighed, "Yankees buy up your cotton at five cents a pound; they manufacture it into shirts, sheets, socks, and what not, and send it back to you.

"But do you get it at five cents a pound? Not by a long chalk! No, they begin with a manufacturer's charge of six cents a yard on calico. The Yankee wholesaler adds two cents more; the Yankee jobber another cent. Yankee railroads tax the South one tenth of a cent per yard. All this is understandable. I agree to it. A manufacturer, even a Yankee manufacturer, must live, although God alone knows what for!"

Here laughter and cheers interrupted the orator. Dignitaries sitting in the shadow on the platform behind the Governor looked at one another in amusement. O'Shawn took a sip of water and then went on full tilt:

"But, ladies and gentlemen, that is not the damnable phase of this premeditated murder of the South. In addition to these onerous and excessive charges of manufacture and transportation, a Republican Congress, sired by Wall Street and dammed by the Yankee manufacturers, has placed a protective tariff of three cents a yard on calico; and today, every time your daughter buys a new dress or your boy gets the goods to make a shirt, some Northern octopus reaches his slimy tentacle into your pocket, Mr. Taxpayer, and mulcts you out of three cents a yard on everything you buy. That's what they call governmental protection!

"But is our raw cotton protected three cents a yard, or a mill a pound, or anything at all? It is not! Our raw products don't need protection! The South, that lovely vestal, whose form was bayoneted by war and ravished by Reconstruction—she doesn't require protection! Such is the even-handed justice of our Republican high protective tariff. What is sauce for the goose is apparently not sauce for the wounded Bird of Paradise. The plight of the South, thrust into the undesired company of the other states of this Union, recalls to my mind, ladies and gentlemen, the apt and searching parable spoken by our Lord and Saviour, Jesus Christ, when He described the fate of that traveler who fell among thieves!"

An uproar of cheers stopped the speaker. Voices shouted:

"Go after 'em, Terry! Give 'em both barrels, Terry!"

Even Miltiades felt a grateful glow at this excoriation of the traditional enemies of his country.

Governor O'Shawn called the crowd to order with an uplifted hand. When the applause stopped, he began again in a soft, round tone:

"Gentlemen, ladies, I can carry the parable even further than that. There was, if I read my Bible aright, a Samaritan, a good Samaritan, who picked up the hapless traveler, poured oil on his wounds, placed him on his donkey, and bore him to an inn.

"I appear before you this evening, ladies and gentlemen, as a forerunner of that good Samaritan. I come as a herald of a great Democrat and a great friend to the South. In counsel he is a Solon; amid the corruptions of our national politics he is a Cato; as a leader of reform against the high tariff embattlements of the Northern plutocrats he is a Richard of the Lion Heart. I refer, ladies and gentlemen, to that peerless leader, that incorruptible patriot, that wise and sagacious statesman, our next President of the United States, Grover Cleveland!"

Shouts, cheers, pandemonium broke out in Courthouse Square.

Hats boiled up between Miltiades and the light. Even the dignitaries on the portico clapped. Governor O'Shawn stood by his table mopping his flushed conical forehead. In the midst of the uproar a rustic voice shouted:

"Say, Terry, who is Grover Cleveland, anyway, an' whar does he come frum?"

This caused laughter, but it stilled the applause to await the answer, because hardly a man had heard the name Cleveland before. The Governor smiled in sympathy with the general amusement.

"Mr. Cleveland is a member of the New York bar."

"Oh, jest another damned Yankee, is he?" drawled the voice.

"He's a nominee of the Democratic party for the Presidency of the United States!" snapped the Governor.

When the orator resumed his discourse, Miltiades Vaiden stopped listening with a restlessness that was natural to him. The Colonel did not enjoy listening to an effective speech from the crowd. If he had been on the platform with the dignitaries, if he were placed so that the speech would pick him out as a man worthy of consideration, a man of position and influence . . .

The mere suggestion of station and power set up a titillation along Miltiades' nerves. He drew a deep breath.

Here a hand touched his shoulder, and a voice behind him said:

"Hey-oh, Colonel, looks like you ort to be up on the stage with the rest of 'em."

Miltiades looked around, balanced between dislike of the hand on his shoulder and the slight gratification of being considered worthy to sit on the platform.

"I don't like to push myself forward," he said gravely.

"You haff to these days, Colonel. Honors used to seek men, but nowadays men seek honors."

"M-m . . . that's true." Then, after a moment, he added, "I was looking for Augustus and Rose, they're in a carriage, have you seen them?" With this Miltiades began moving slowly away from the hand on his shoulder so that its removal would appear unplanned.

The man took down his hand and began to look around.

"There's some buggies yander," he said in the flatted voice of a man whose friendly advances have been declined.

Miltiades walked away in the direction of the buggies on the opposite side of the Square. He was annoyed at himself for treating the countryman in this fashion, but the hand on his shoulder had been even more annoying . . . he put the matter out of his thoughts.

The Colonel had no desire whatever to find Augustus and Rose, but what he had said to the countryman set him going on this errand with some vague idea of keeping his word good. As he drew near the line of shadowy vehicles he began looking for Judge Ashton's carriage, which would contain his brother and his sister-in-law.

The occupants of these carriages usually sat staring fixedly at the speaker. These carriage folk were, in the main, members of the very oldest families in Florence. In the dim illumination from the speaker's table across the Square, Miltiades caught, here and there, the outline of a woman's face. Even half seen, like this, some of them conveyed that odd quality of inherited sensitiveness which is what is meant by breeding.

As Miltiades passed a small single buggy with a pretty bay mare between its shafts, he heard a lover's tiff going on in undertones. A girl's voice was saying tautly:

"Lucius, I—I'll get out!"

A youth's voice replied hastily:

"No, don't get out, Miss Sydna. . . ."

"Then sit on your side and listen to the Governor," advised the girl in annoyance.

"I was listening to him, too," teased her companion.

Colonel Vaiden caught a glimpse of the girl's face, a graceful face filled with the embarrassment of a young girl who had not yet learned to deal with the small improprieties of the admirers whom she attracted.

The Colonel would have walked on past in silence, but the expression of the girl aroused in him a sharp disapproval of the youth in the buggy. Without glancing around he said in a curt undertone:

"Young man, in a lady's presence you should imitate a gentleman, at least temporarily." And with that he walked on.

The faint noises in the runabout hushed. In the silence, Miltiades could hear Governor O'Shawn's peroration:

"And you ladies who have graced this occasion with the bouquet of your faces and the music of your laughter, while you may not sully your fair hands with the ballot, it is yours to see that your husbands and sweethearts march to the polls in November and cast their votes for a white man's party in a white man's land. No true Southern lady would do more; none can do less. I thank you for the inspiration of your presence here tonight."

Here the speaker bowed and turned to men on the platform behind him. This ended his oration.

The usual clapping of hands broke forth. The dignitaries on the portico arose and began congratulating the speaker. The line of carriages near Miltiades started to move. Out of one of the vehicles Miltiades heard the hearty voice of his brother Augustus:

"Milt, wasn't that a speech? Didn't the Governor wade into Wall Street?"

Rose's contralto added something about Marcia . . . Marcia's boy . . . Miltiades did not quite get it. The carriage rolled on out of hearing.

The Colonel moved aimlessly along the street, a little embarrassed to be seen walking in the midst of the moving vehicles. He turned out of their line toward the old Florence Hotel on the corner of the Square.

As he went he thought over the Governor's peroration to the ladies . . . the honor in which Southern men held their women . . . how true were O'Shawn's words. Take, for example, his own action in rebuking the youth in the little hug-me-tight buggy. A Northern man would perhaps have laughed, or have listened and said nothing, but he, a Southern man, had reproved the misdemeanant with a phrase. . . . He continued slowly and aimlessly across the Square with no particular end in view save that, subconsciously, he was putting off as long as possible his return to his fat wife, Ponny.

II

Now that the speaking was over, the crowd flowed away in all directions. The first to get in motion were a small group of negroes who had been listening afar off from the front of the old Florence Hotel. To these negroes the Democratic speaking had been a vague demonstration against their liberty. They had, only a score of years before, been set free from slavery by the Republicans. Now all the group were uneasy lest, if a Democratic President be elected, they should be returned to their bonds. One of their number mumbled:

"We ort to been ovah to Mistuh Landahs' meetin'. He stan' by us; we ort to stan' by he."

"Mistah Landahs is sich a dried-up man," complained a second.

"He is a cu'is man," put in a third.

"All Republicans is cu'is if they's white men," opined the first negro philosophically.

"Not in St. Louis," put in a bullet-headed negro who had worked as roustabout on the steamboats. "In St. Louis, Republicans wears high hats an' smokes big seegars jess lak dey wuz somebody."

"St. Louis ain't Flaunts," put in a cautionary negro.

"Hit sho ain't," agreed the third.

The little group fell silent again, watching the white gathering disperse into the dimly lighted streets. Presently a wizened oldish negro feigned a yawn and said he guessed he'd better be moving off home.

The first negro gave a snort of laughter.

"You do, an' Gracie'll have you movin' back quicker'n you moved off. . . . Dis is Sad'day night."

The smallish gray-wooled old negro turned on his companions and warned them that they had better remember how the she-bears had come and et up forty little children who had mocked Elijah, a servant of God.

At this the other negroes became silent, for the oldish black man was a preacher of sorts. Presently they began to drift away, but the wizened negro who had said he was going home remained where he was on the hotel corner.

He stood for twenty or thirty minutes, then presently sat down on the iron grating which screened the kitchen window of the hotel in the basement. Then he lay down on the grating like a bundle of rags, pillowing his head on his arms. A faint warmth drifted up from the kitchen, alleviating the chill of the summer night. After a while he fell asleep.

Among the vehicles that rattled away from Courthouse Square a large family carriage went north up Market Street, and a block to the west a little runabout turned northward up Pine Street.

In the large carriage Judge Ashton was saying to his guest, Augustus Vaiden:

"Cleveland is a strong man, Augustus, he will carry New York, Pennsylvania, Indiana, Ohio, and, of course, the South."

Augustus, who never gave politics a thought, agreed to this and then added:

"Riding away from the speaking like this reminds me of fox-hunting. It would be almost cold enough to fox-hunt tonight. I wish I was out listening to the old Dalrymple pack."

Judge Ashton laughed a metallic, ringing laugh that was very friendly and pleasant.

"Miss Rose, when your husband gets to heaven, the first thing he's going to inquire about is the fox-hunting."

The two women in the carriage acknowledged this masculine interruption by laughing and reproaching the speaker for impiety; then Mrs. Rose picked up her conversation with Mrs. Polly Ashton where she had left off:

"I don't know whether Marcia will come or not. . . . I hope so."

"I do hope she will. . . . She was such a pretty girl."

"She looks just as she always did," assured Rose; "her eyes are just what they were when she was a girl."

"When is her boy to come down?" inquired Mrs. Ashton.

"In time to start to college this fall."

"What's his name?"

"Jerry. He's named for his father. He calls himself, Jerry Catlin the second."

The elders smiled at this.

"Marcia's boy would be original," opined the Judge, drawing down his horses near the Rose Vaiden boarding house to let his guests out.

"Send young Jerry over to see my Jefferson when he comes," invited the Judge.

"I will," assured Rose. "I've been thinking about some nice boys for him to associate with."

Mrs. Polly Ashton said she knew the boys would have a good time together, and then, as she drove away from the boarding house, she made a mental note that she would keep her son Jeff away from Jerry Catlin the second until she had time to see what sort of a boy *he* was. The amount of time this required was apparently only a few minutes, for presently she decided that Jerry Catlin the second was not the sort of boy she could let her son Jefferson associate with—and that was settled.

In the second buggy, the small rubber-tired runabout which moved up Pine Street, another conversation was struggling along with considerable bitterness.

"I suppose," said the young man driving the bay mare, "the reason the old codger 'tends to everybody else's business is because he hasn't got any of his own to attend to."

The girl compressed into the seat beside him retorted warmly:

"It was his business."

"Was his business?"

To this repetition the girl replied nothing.

The youth went on:

"If he wasn't such an old man I'd show him how to insult me before you, Sydna."

"Yes, I imagine you would, Lucius Handback!" satirized the girl in an access of distaste.

"I would!" declared the youth hotly. "I'd call him to account!"

"Did you know that Colonel Milt Vaiden was the man who led the Klan when they wiped out the Leatherwood gang?" inquired the girl drily.

"What of that? He had men behind him, ready to help him."

The girl pondered a moment and then said in quite a different voice:

"Besides that, Lucius, he had to correct you when you were bothering me back yonder."

The driver turned in the darkness.

"Had to correct me! What's old man Milt Vaiden got to do with me?"

"It isn't with you; it's with me," said the girl in a faraway voice.

"Why, Sydna—what in the world . . . ?" He paused a moment and became jealously speculative. "He—he's not in love with you, Sydna?"

"The idea! Colonel Milt is old enough to be my father . . . and he's a married man. . . . Lucius, you're the awfulest person!" She tried to pull herself away from him in the constricted space.

"Well, you won't tell anything! I ask you a question, and you won't tell me a thing!"

"No, I won't!"

"Then I have to guess," declared Mr. Handback doggedly, "and if you get mad at my guesses I can't help it."

"At least guess something respectable, if you're guessing about me," admonished the girl.

"Look here, what is between you and old man Vaiden, Sydna?" pleaded young Mr. Handback, almost distracted. "Look here—you— you don't love him, do you—or him you?"

At this repeated offense Miss Sydna Crowninshield became permanently silent. She rode on to her mother's home on Pine Street, disregarding as far as possible the pressure of her companion. She alighted without waiting for Lucius to help her to the ground. With a brief good-night she disappeared within her own gate and found her way alone up the fragrant box-lined path.

As the girl walked up this unseen curving path she presently forgot Lucius Handback, and against the darkness there floated a strange, romantic picture of Colonel Miltiades Vaiden and her dead father, whom she had never seen.

It was a battle picture, and it came to her in the likeness of a painting. The painting was all around her in the form of a cyclorama. On the vast canvas she saw regiments of painted soldiers charging across a landscape. The chief figures in this cyclorama were Colonel Vaiden and her dying father. It was, she thought, the battle of Shiloh, where her father had been killed.

All this elaborate mental arrangement had come to her years and years ago, when she was a small child. In Louisville, Kentucky, her mother had taken her to see a cyclorama of the battle of Gettysburg. When she and her mother had seen the picture, her mother had wept. Drusilla's weeping and the battle scene had filled the little girl's heart with pity and terror. And she believed it was a picture of the battle of Shiloh, where her father had been slain. The wounded man nearest her became her father, and a comrade bending above him became Colonel Miltiades Vaiden.

Her father, she imagined, was whispering to Colonel Vaiden, "Take care of my little girl, Sydna," and the comrade bending down was promising that he would.

Now, as Sydna walked up the graveled path to her door tears began trickling down her face that she should have appeared to belittle herself, even through no fault of her own, before her lifelong protector and ideal of chivalry, Colonel Miltiades Vaiden.

While Sydna was feeling these sharp misgivings, Colonel Vaiden himself moved slowly along a diagonal across Courthouse Square toward the old Florence Hotel. The windows of the hotel were alight, and even from his distance the Colonel could hear irregular outbursts of laughter from the lobby.

This laughter, the Colonel divined, came from traveling men who were matching yarns by way of entertainment for the evening. He walked on, listening to the hilarity with the dissympathy of a man harassed by his own affairs and to whom all jests were unpalatable.

A voice behind him calling out, "Mr. Bivins! Oh, Mr. Bivins, just a moment!" caused the Colonel to look around.

A middle-aged man came hurrying up.

"Mr. Bivins, add three rolls of plow lines and a dozen mule collars to my order. . . ."

When the man came closer, Colonel Vaiden saw who it was and felt a sharp impulse to turn and walk on without a word. His dignity, however, forbade that, so he said briefly:

"I am afraid you have made a mistake, Mr. Handback."

Then the merchant discovered his own error and began begging Miltiades' pardon. He explained, with considerable confusion, that in the dark he had mistaken Miltiades for a hardware drummer who was staying at the hotel.

"That's all right, Mr. Handback," interrupted the Colonel with an ancient resentment flatting his tones.

This disconcerted Mr. Handback even more.

"You're about his height. . . . Slim's thinner than you. . . . I oughtn't to holler at folks in the dark, anyway."

"That's all right," repeated Miltiades with distaste.

But Mr. Handback, once involved in conversation, could not disengage himself easily. He followed on to the hotel in the wake of his companion's contempt.

Miltiades presently began enjoying in a sardonic way the confusion into which the merchant had fallen. He thought to himself, "That's what comes of being a thief . . ." And here he was moved by a sharp physical desire to turn and kick J. Handback's rump clear around Courthouse Square . . . the damned apologetic crook!

The Colonel recalled clearly the offense which now reduced the merchant to such an embarrassed favor currier. Handback had accepted twenty-five hundred dollars' worth of the Vaiden cotton in his store on the very day he made an assignment in bankruptcy. It was all the cotton which Miltiades and Augustus and Cassandra and Marcia Vaiden had raised in a season; their whole year's work gone without a penny. That had been twenty years ago.

Now, with this ancient transaction in their thoughts, the two men would probably have walked to the hotel in silence, had not another group of men entering the Square created a diversion.

J. Handback pointed across the dimly lighted plaza.

"Look yonder, won't you? That damned Landers and his nigger meeting just now breaking up!"

Miltiades looked without enthusiasm and said nothing.

J. Handback began again, exaggerating his contempt to cover his own silently arraigned case.

"I swear I wouldn't affiliate with them black monkeys, not to be postmaster all the rest of my life. I wouldn't do it!"

"A man'll do most anything for money," observed Miltiades drily.

"Uh . . . m-m . . . yes, but I wouldn't do that," stammered the merchant. "It cuts a man off from the society of decent men and women. It's social suicide even to vote the Republican ticket here in Florence, much less bob-bashiely with niggers!"

By this time the Colonel really had become interested in the spectacle before him.

"Yes, I've often thought about Landers," he agreed with less animosity toward his companion: "mixes with niggers; attends their stinking political gatherings; preaches social equality by his actions—all to keep a little two by four postmastership here in Florence, Alabama, that pays . . . what does it pay, do you suppose?"

"Oh . . . nine or ten hundred. . . ."

"There you are, nine or ten hundred dollars. . . ."

"And what he can steal out of letters. . . ."

"I never heard anybody accuse Landers of stealing anything."

"No, but I say a man who'll do what Landers does will steal!"

"M-m . . . yes . . . he might. . . ."

"Well, I for one can't stand to rub shoulders with a coon. In my store I keep 'em on the other side of the counter; in my fields I keep 'em at the business end of a plow."

"That's right." Miltiades admitted this reluctantly, because it condoned in a subtle way the merchant's theft of the cotton from his family.

"I just can't stand a nigger," repeated the merchant a little emptily.

At this juncture the two uncongenial companions paused before the hotel door. Bursts of laughter from the traveling men came quite loudly now. J. Handback noticed under his feet a bundle of rags that lay stretched out on the iron grating over the basement window. He gave the object a slight kick. It moved and grunted.

"Hey, what you lying here for?" demanded the merchant stepping back from the bundle.

A negro lifted a blinking face in the dim light of the street lamp on the corner.

"Gittin' a li'l' res'," he grunted.

"Is that you, Lump?" inquired the white man quickly.

"Yessuh," mumbled the negro glumly.

"This is a hell of a place to sleep on. . . . How long you been here?"

"Evah sence de white fo'ks' speakin'," answered the negro resentfully.

"Well . . . don't let me disturb your slumbers," said the merchant with an attempt at humor.

"You mean my slumbahs on dis gratin'?" asked Lump dourly.

"Of course I mean this grating. . . . Look here, nigger, don't get impudent with me!"

"I ain't gittin' impident." The small black man sat up slowly, blinking at the street lamp.

The merchant stood looking down on Lump when a burst of laughter from the hotel lobby seemed to turn his thoughts from the negro. He looked at Miltiades and asked tentatively:

"Colonel Vaiden . . . might I ask you to do me a favor?"

"What is it?" inquired the Colonel dubiously.

"Would you mind stepping in the lobby and telling Slim Bivins to add three rolls of plow lines and a dozen assorted mule collars to my order?"

"No-o. . . . I don't mind. . . . Why don't you do it yourself?"

"Because if I go in Slim'll sell me more collars and rope than I want; then I'll have to drink with him and listen to his jokes. I won't get away till midnight. He can't do you thatta way, because he don't know you."

"Well . . ." agreed the Colonel reluctantly, "what is it you want to order?"

"Three rolls of plow lines and a dozen assorted mule collars."

"We-ell . . . I'll give it in just as you said it to me."

"Thank you very much, Colonel—very much," said the merchant gratefully. "Good-night."

"Good-night," returned Miltiades, wondering a little to hear himself saying good-night to J. Handback. Then he gave an inaudible sniff of laughter through his nose as a man does when he is disgusted with himself.

J. Handback moved off toward Market Street, apparently going to his home in the northern end of town.

The small negro on the grating and the tall man on the step watched him in silence. Once the retreating merchant paused to look back over his shoulder. At last, when he became a dim blur against the walls of the opposite stores, Miltiades saw him change his course in the general direction of East Florence.

A vague speculation floated through the Colonel's mind as to why J. Handback should have turned toward East Florence, but he neither pressed the point, nor did he care. Any unconventionality which the merchant probably had in mind was no more in the Colonel's estimation than where some dog buried a bone. The fellow was a thief. . . .

At another burst of laughter from the lobby Colonel Vaiden turned into the hotel and left the small negro still sitting motionless on the grating, staring up at the street lamp, at a row of gnarled mulberries which began at the corner and extended southward along a line of offices called Intelligence Row, and at the remote indifference of the stars.

Inside the lobby of the Florence Hotel Colonel Vaiden found a group of five commercial travelers with cigars cocked at optimistic angles as they retold bawdy-house yarns and spat at dirty brass cuspidors. On the wall behind the clerk's desk a heroic-sized lithograph of Grover Cleveland stared solemnly down upon the guffawing yarn spinners.

For some minutes Colonel Miltiades Vaiden stood just inside the doorway listening to the lickerish and utterly impossible anecdotes. The Colonel was the sort of man at whom the tale tellers would glance now and then and allow to remain standing where he was. This slight discourtesy did not offend him, but it set him in a mood of ironic musing. Here was he, a man filled with an unavailing certainty of his own ability, and here were these gregarious drummers without a thought of anything beyond cards, whisky, and women; yet he had nothing to do, he was at a social and financial stalemate, while they moved along their grooves like oiled and prosperous automata.

He still thought wryly of this antithesis as he went forward and asked for a Mr. Bivins.

A slender red-headed man arose, introduced himself, and offered his hand with a traveling man's affability. The Colonel explained the extra items which J. Handback wanted to add to his order. Mr. Bivins became businesslike at once. He went to a desk in the lobby, drew out his order book, and poised his pencil.

"What grade plow line does he want?"

The Colonel didn't know.

"Then I'll ship him my second grade. Handback is a man who never buys the best grade of anything, but I understand he sells the best grade of everything."

Laughter broke out in the lobby at this characterization.

"Was there anything else, Mr. Vaiden?" inquired Bivins, laughing with the others at his own jest.

"No, that was all he told me to order," said the Colonel, with half his attention on the drummer's great catalogue.

"No plows, horseshoes, nails, bolts . . . ?"

"No, that was all he said."

"Well, I appreciate your courtesy. Won't you sit down a minute? Andy, bring two glasses of cracked ice. . . . You'll take a snort with me, won't you, Mr. Vaiden?"

Miltiades agreed to the snort and sat down to wait for it. As he did so a faint tentative design began to grow in his thoughts. He began mentally taking stock of every available resource which he possibly might scrape together. He thought over his own family, Rose and Augustus, his sister Cassandra, his other sister Marcia, who lived up in Tennessee. He was considering borrowing some money. The sum he had in mind was five hundred dollars. He wondered if he could start a little business on a capital of five hundred dollars, but then he knew he would never be able to raise that amount among his brothers and sisters, and the notion faded from his thoughts.

His conversation with Bivins had continued in the mechanical fashion of unattended talk. He was asking the drummer how he found business over the country.

"Pretty good now," declared Bivins with a salesman's optimism, "but when we get him seated in the Presidential chair—" he nodded at the lithograph behind the clerk's desk—"you'll see business pick up sure enough. The minute the Democrats get hold of this country the South is bound to boom."

"That's right," put in a drummer with a harelip: "buy ever'thing low, sell ever'thing high, do a rushing trade all the year roun', that's the Democratic platform, Mr. Vaiden."

Miltiades suddenly set aside this irrelevant conversation.

"May I have a talk with you privately for a moment, Mr. Bivins?" he asked.

The drummer's manner changed.

"Certainly." He glanced about, led the way to a door that opened into a hall. He went to a hat tree, rested an elbow on it, and took his cigar from his mouth. "Now, what can I do for you, Mr. Vaiden?"

Miltiades knew almost to a certainty that his request would be refused, but he thought to himself, "It won't make any difference. I'll be as well off refused as I am now." He moistened his lips and said aloud:

"I was thinking of starting a business of my own, Mr. Bivins."

The drummer opened his eyes.

"A whole stock?"

Miltiades nodded.

"Going to run a hardware store, Major?" inquired the salesman, instinctively bestowing some title on his prospect.

"No, general merchandise."

"I see . . . have a hardware department . . . now . . . now, just wait here a moment. . . ."

Bivins went back into the lobby. Miltiades could see him through the open door moving with a kind of springiness in his thin legs to his catalogue on the writing desk.

The harelipped drummer called out in flapping tones:

"Slim, what you goin' to do with that?"

"Select a shotgun. Major Vaiden's ordering it through J. Handback."

The slim man came back alertly with his catalogue.

Militades' confidence was deserting him. He began a tentative:

"Now, Mr. Bivins, as to terms . . ."

"Terms no object," scouted the drummer, "when you hook up with the Black Diamond line, you'll get the goods, and the terms will take care of themselves. All right now . . . adzes, axes, axletrees, ax handles, Axminster carpets, ash trays, ash cans, awls. . . . Oh, Andy," he called to some noise in the lobby, "bring 'em right out here in the hall, will you?"

The lobby door opened, and the negro porter came out with tray and clinking glasses. Mr. Bivins closed his book, handed a whisky to Miltiades, took the other and lifted it to the level of his eyes.

"Here's to love, its joy and fret.
May this bring a solace and help you forget
The woman you want . . . and the woman you get."

Miltiades had no answering cliché. He touched his glass to that of Mr. Bivins, and the two drank solemnly.

The drummer put his glass back on the tray, thumped his catalogue.

"Now, Major, le's start," he urged briskly.

When Miltiades returned to the problem of stocking his store Mr. Bivins proved to be a man of endless memory. He rattled off lists of merchandise almost alphabetically. The Colonel himself had once been an overseer on a cotton plantation, and his memory of the commissary guided his purchases. All the time he was uneasy about really getting these goods from the drummer. Now and then he would interrupt the order in an effort to ascertain the terms on which he was to receive this stock, but Mr. Bivins shooed him down. He would do everything any other house would do.

In the midst of this brisk trading the lobby door opened, and the harelipped man entered the hall. He began, in his jocular voice, saying it took Bivins a hell of a time to sell a shotgun; then he ejaculated,

"How the devil are you selling shotguns with your catalogue opened at slickers?"

Bivins began laughing and admitted that he was selling Mr. Vaiden a complete line of merchandise. The harelipped man was genially outraged.

"Don't you let Slim Bivins stock you up on that Black Diamond trash he sells. What you need is the genuine Bulldog Brand, Mr. Vaiden."

His noise brought other salesmen into the hallway, and for the next two hours Miltiades was deluged with prices and freight rates from Louisville, Cincinnati, St. Louis, and Evansville.

When the night was more than half gone Bivins nodded Miltiades aside and said, "Now, Major, I can ship you my goods in ten, twenty, or thirty days—any time you say."

Miltiades, who had grown dull during this prolonged buying, became alert again at this final adjustment of terms.

"When am I to pay for these things, Mr. Bivins?" he inquired, looking at the salesman.

Bivins came to a halt, a little surprised.

"Why . . . don't you want to pay for them now?"

"Well, no—that wouldn't be convenient," admitted the Colonel a little uneasily.

"Could you . . . pay me half down?" suggested Bivins uncertainly. "My firm would carry the rest for thirty, sixty, and ninety days."

Miltiades came to a halt in his mercantile career.

"Let me see . . . my bill comes to . . ."

"Nine hundred and sixteen dollars," supplied Bivins hopefully.

Miltiades was embarrassed. He thought swiftly that he might borrow two hundred dollars on the proposed stock of goods from his wife's father.

"Suppose I send you two hundred . . . three hundred when I receive the goods?"

"Three hundred?" repeated Bivins in amazement.

"And make payments every thirty days," added the Colonel.

"You can't pay half down now?" pressed Bivins in flatted tones.

"No-o . . ." admitted Miltiades, with a drying mouth, "at present my resources are tied up in a cotton plantation—near BeShears' Crossroads."

Mr. Bivins closed his order book.

"Ed," he said to the dry-goods drummer, who stood awaiting his turn, "Mr. Vaiden here tells me his assets are tied up in a cotton plantation out somewhere near BeShears' Crossroads."

"What's the idyah?" demanded the harelipped man brusquely. "Did he imagine he could buy a stock of general merchandise by giving a mortgage on a cotton crop?"

"I don't know what he thought," said Bivins.

"I told you in the beginning," stated the Colonel with a whitening face, "that we'd better discuss terms first!"

"Hell fire, I thought you wanted to know what discount I'd give for cash!" cried Bivins, and he snapped his rubber band on his order book.

The dry-goods man said querulously:

"Damn it, I've set up here nearly all night! A man never gets ahead by working at night."

The Colonel had a desire to punch their collective heads. A moment ago they were all so polite; now they were sarcastic and insulting. He looked at them inimically:

"Won't a one of you men sell me some goods on time and let me pay for them when I can?"

The dry-goods drummer turned to the porter and told him to lock up the sample room again and not to wake him till ten o'clock next morning.

To this by-play the Colonel made a stiff bow.

"All right, gentlemen. I'm going to do business here in Florence, and one of these days you drummers are going to come begging me to let you open your sample cases in my store. . . . Good-evening."

Colonel Vaiden passed out of the hotel vibrating with anger and chagrin at what had happened. He was not, as he fatuously had forecast, as well off now as he had been before he was refused credit. He had felt all the time that he would be refused, but now that it had come to pass, he was morally wounded and deeply incensed.

He paused on the steps of the hotel damning the drummers to hell. One of these days they would beg him for an order . . . just as he had said.

A late moon had risen and cast a faint glimmer over the courthouse tower and the tops of the gnarled mulberries along Intelligence Row.

Then the Colonel saw the small negro still curled on the basement grating. This annoyed him. He kicked the negro's legs.

"Get up! What do you want to hang around here for all night?" he demanded in brittle temper.

The black figure stirred.

"Got to hang roun' some'r's all night," it mumbled.

"Whyn't you get along home?"

"I git uhlong home I come back fasteh 'n I got."

The white man turned from the negro and started walking along the west side of the Square toward Market Street. Two lights, moonlight and lamplight, lay mingled in faint yellow and white spotulations along the thoroughfare. Miltiades began thinking what he should have said to the salesmen. He should have said:

"Gentlemen, I entered this hotel to do one of your number a slight favor; then I desired to ask him a simple question about the possibility of credit. He wouldn't hear my inquiry until he had run up a long bill of goods; then the group of you insult me about the matter. Do you call yourselves Southern gentlemen?"

Miltiades' lips took on a contemptuous smile as he imagined how the drummers would have stood, quite taken aback at his cold and scathing dignity. Presently this drifted from his mind and left him thinking of the commissary he had run before the war on the old Lacefield plantation down in the Reserve. He had controlled two hundred negroes, fifteen hundred acres of cotton, and the commissary. The commissary itself had been a mere detail in those days, but what he had learned about it would become important when he finally obtained a store of his own.

The Colonel moved up Market Street with the faint moonlight persistently bringing back the old Lacefield plantation days. He remembered old man Carruthers Lacefield and his wife; A. Gray, the son, who was now editor of the Florence paper, and the daughter of the family, Drusilla. . . . Drusilla had been engaged to be married to him, and she had eloped with another man, Emory Crowninshield, on the night before their wedding. . . . Again he recalled very distinctly his return home after the war, how he had engaged himself to Drusilla once more and had seduced and jilted her. That was a long time ago, yet Drusilla's gift of herself to him still stood like a far-away light amid the foggy commonplaces of his succeeding love life.

However, it seemed to Miltiades that after all it was a good thing that he had not married Drusilla. He had not made a success, and their contemplated marriage always tacitly had been founded on his becoming wealthy and successful. He still believed he was going to be successful, but he would not have liked to share with Drusilla this long flat stretch of poverty. For Ponny—for his fat wife Ponny—it was all right, but for Drusilla it would have been impossible.

The sound of footsteps filled the last of the night with a far-reaching, uneven clacking and exorcised the ghost of Drusilla. The Colonel stood looking down the milky blur of Market Street with a faint curiosity as to who could be walking away from town at such an hour. Presently a figure defined itself against the gray pall of the morning, weaving a little from side to side. The man came up within fifteen or twenty yards of Miltiades, then stopped and stood with a hand on the palings, looking at him.

The identity of the befuddled man caused Miltiades not so much surprise as a sort of contemptuous recognition of something he should have guessed. He turned to walk away when the figure came on again as if touched off by a button.

"Why, it's my frien' Colonel Vaiden," it babbled. "Thought for a moment . . . might be somebody . . . wouldn't want to see me out . . . you know . . . late like this . . . but . . . but see I'm in han's of a frien' . . . eh, Colonel? . . . we're frien's, ain't we, Colonel?"

Miltiades stood with military erectness looking at the fellow.

"Well, yes, " he agreed drily, "you might say we're friends, barring the fact that you stole twenty-five hundred dollars from me twenty years ago."

J. Handback came to a pause.

"Still think o' that?"

"Now and then."

"Uh-huh . . . now an' then," agreed the merchant, with wounded gravity, "but . . . but you never conshidered me, I . . . s'pose?"

"I don't know what there is to consider."

"Hol' on," protested the drunken man, "lots to conshider. . . . I . . . I had a big stock merchandise, Colonel . . . trem'lin' . . . trem'lin' on edge of bankrup'cy. I . . . I couldn't say to you that mornin' . . . 'No, can't receive your money, Colonel . . . not solvent.' Immejiately ever'-body would wanted theirs back. . . . They . . . they did . . . few hours later, anyway . . . but . . . but . . . didn't know that then."

Moisture had come out on the face of the merchant in his earnestness.

"Well," said the Colonel after a moment, "we won't stand here on Sunday morning and go into that."

"No . . . no . . . won't go into that. . . ." He stood for a moment or two, ill at ease; then, by way of changing the topic, "Didn't see nothin' more of that damn nigger-lovin' Landers, I s'pose?"

"No, and I hope I won't."

"Amen to that, Colonel. . . . Disgrace . . . 'filiatin' with a lot o' damn dirty niggers . . . ort to be drummed out o' town. . . ." Here he came to another conversational dead end and stood looking around in the graying morning. "Well . . . better be movin' 'long some'r's. . . ."

As the fellow lurched foward, the convention of seeing a drunken acquaintance safely home came upon Miltiades.

"Do you know where you're going, Mr. Handback?" he inquired without enthusiasm.

"Now . . . now, Colonel, I . . . I can't truthfully say I know where I'm goin'."

"Don't you know your way home?"

"Yesh . . . I know my way home, but . . . but I can't go there."

"What's the matter?"

"Muh . . . muh wife not expectin' me." He gave Miltiades a badly done wink. "I'm off . . . seein' 'bout one o' muh farms."

"I see. . . . Then what are you going to do?"

"Well, I . . . I b'lieve I'll jess walk home with you, Colonel . . . set aroun' an' . . . an' talk till church time."

"That's not practical," declared the Colonel at once. "Ponny would see your condition. She might mention it to somebody."

"Don't b'lieve she could tell it on me, Colonel. . . . Don't b'lieve a soul in the worl' have a spishion."

"She might. I wouldn't want to risk it," decided the Colonel.

Miltiades stood considering what was best to do. He disliked the man, but Handback had a very good reputation. He was a deacon in the Methodist church, and the Colonel did not have the petty spite to allow the fellow to waste his good name by wandering around on the streets drunk. So now he took his arm and started thoughtfully back down Market Street toward town.

Handback offered no objection, but began explaining himself more fully.

"Jess been to see a frien' o' mine, Colonel . . . lady frien' . . . sh-she's damn near a lady . . . damn near white, too, even if I do say it."

"M-m," said the Colonel, with the disapproval of one man for another man's unconventionalities.

"Now . . . now . . . man needs a li'l' relaxation," defended the merchant, "relieves business strain. . . . Whicherway we goin'?"

"To the hotel."

"By George . . . good idyah . . . forgot we had a hotel." The merchant's steps depended more and more on the Colonel. "But I should uh stayed out the night at Gracie's . . . ver' nice woman, Colonel . . . kep' her for years . . . Clean . . . discreet, an' . . . an' obligin'. . . ."

They were approaching Courthouse Square again. Some of the lamps, which were gauged to extinguish themselves in the morning, were out. Miltiades angled across the square with his burden.

The single night light burning in the lobby had faded to a small pale tongue of flame in the gray morning. The night clerk dozed with his head on the register. Miltiades did not waken the man but maneuvered his charge up the flight of stairs into the first empty bedroom he found. He stood for a moment breathing deeply from his exertion, then tiptoed down again. The clerk was still asleep. Behind him and above his head was a large lithograph of Cleveland bearing the legend, "The man from Buffalo—the hope of Southern Democracy."

When Miltiades walked out of the door again, the small old negro, Lump Mowbray, had disappeared from the grating over the basement window.

Little White Girl

Sara Haardt Mencken

I

S USIE Tarleton spread out her skirts, sat down on a patch of
Bermuda grass under the big oak tree, and started digging rapidly
in the damp ground in front of her. When she had scooped out
a triangular hole about the size of the piece of broken window glass
she was using as a trowel, she laid the glass down and rested her chin
on her knees. For a moment it came to her, with a twinge of guilt,
that she shouldn't be here digging in the dirt in her fresh afternoon
clothes—she should be out on the front veranda, or stringing four
o'clocks in the garden, like a good little girl. But she hated playing
by herself when there was Pinky to play with.

Pinky was Aunt Hester's little girl, born the month before Susie,
and they had played on the same pallet spread under the big oak tree
when they were babies, for Aunt Hester was Susie's mammy. Now
that she was eight years old Susie didn't need a mammy any more,
except to help her dress in the afternoon, but she hadn't missed a
day playing with Pinky—and she never would!

"Pinky, Pinky," she called in her high treble. "Here I am under the
oak tree!"

There was a scurrying, as of a frantic little animal, along the path
from Aunt Hester's cabin, and with a winged leap Pinky was there.
She wasn't very black—her satiny yellow skin merely looked as if she
had a good tan—and Aunt Hester had trained her stiff black hair to
lie flat to her head. Susie loved the feel of Pinky's skin, and the smell
of the magnolia balm that Aunt Hester greased her hair with, and the
fresh starchy smell of Pinky's calico dresses. She loved everything
about Pinky with all her heart.

"You can pick the roses while I'm finishing the nest for them," she
told Pinky now, and Pinky ran as fast as her skinny legs could carry
her to the garden.

Susie continued digging in the damp ground with the triangular
piece of glass, and when she had finished she leaned her head against

the trunk of the big oak tree. She closed her eyes and sniffed in the sweetly saturated afternoon air. It was nice, she told herself, to play with Pinky.

Even on the hottest day the big oak tree with its mauve cool shade was a wonderful play-house. It was so quiet and far away that no grown-up could intrude upon it without a warning rustle of leaves and boughs. Susie was sure the little white girl who was moving on the next plantation and who was coming to spend the day with her tomorrow, would think it was wonderful too. It was strange to think of a little girl living near her—a little *white* girl named Alice Louise Pratt.

She stood up quickly and curtsied, as she would tomorrow when Alice Louise came to see her. "I am Susie Tarleton," she rehearsed in a small voice. "Who are you?"

"I's hurryin'," Pinky answered her from the garden. "I's comin' fas' as I kin."

Susie dropped her skirts, and stiffened. She hadn't told Pinky about Alice Louise, and for some reason unknown to her, she didn't want to tell Pinky.

She stood there motionless with her hands clasped tightly behind her while Pinky fluttered along the garden path like a gay butterfly with the flowers held high for her to see.

"Here I is!" Pinky called joyously.

Susie parted her lips to answer but her throat was dry, and no sound came. She looked at Pinky's shining face, and reached out her hands for the bouquet.

The next instant both of them dropped on the ground beneath the big oak tree, and Susie forgot all about Alice Louise. Nobody could play penny-poppy show like Pinky! Susie held the bouquet while Pinky patted the sides of the hole in the ground she had made with the glass, leaving a few clods of earth loose to stick the flower stems in. Swiftly yet carefully Pinky lined the hole with camphor leaves; then she selected first one rose and then another.

When she was through, she paused and drew a bunch of lavender from the bosom of her calico dress. "I dunno why I picked *this,* when you said the show was to be onliest of roses, but seem like I couldn't pass it by."

"Oh, it looks *sweet,* Pinky!" Susie cried. The pungent smell of the lavender thrilled her nostrils more than the fragance of the roses. She flashed a warm smile across the gathering dusk: Pinky's taste was perfect; the lavender and the roses looked far lovelier together than the roses ever could have looked by themselves.

Pinky tucked in the last plume of lavender, and started to polish the piece of glass on her plain little ticking underskirt. Then she held up the glass expertly by the very edge so she would not leave any fingerprints on it. The secret of penny-poppy show was to cover the flowers in the ground with the shining glass, then to cover the glass with dirt scraped out of the hole, and to scrape a peep-hole in the dirt to look through; but somehow, this afternoon Susie couldn't bear to see the flowers covered up.

"Wait just a minute!" she cried, and stooping swiftly buried her nose in them as if this were the last time she would ever fill her nostrils with their fragrance.

Pinky waited silently until she sat up; Susie helped her put the glass over the flowers, and, finally, pat the earth over the glass until the ground was as smooth as it had been before. Pinky gathered up the fallen petals, and looked inquiringly at Susie.

According to rule, Susie should scrape back the earth now so they could see the flowers, framed in their nest like a picture, but she sat still, her eyes staring at the ground.

"Dey'll be jes' as fresh tomorrow," Pinky said very softly. "I wuz careful to stick their stems clean th'ugh the wet dirt."

"Let's wait until tomorrow to look at it," Susie answered quickly, before Pinky had got the word out of her mouth.

"Dey'll be jes' as pretty," Pinky promised.

"Tomorrow, then." Susie got up, and walked with Pinky to the far edge of the shadow cast by the big oak tree in the deepening twilight. It was Pinky's suppertime, and she waved a hand to Susie as she disappeared down the path to Aunt Hester's cabin.

Susie stood watching the tall grass on the sides of the path that Pinky's flight had set in motion, then she turned and walked back to the big oak tree. It was quite dark underneath the sheltering branches and invisible insects flew with a humming sound past her ears. A light bloomed in the kitchen of the house. It would soon be *her* supper-time, time for her to go up the trim paths of the garden to the house, yet she lingered in the spooky shadow of the big oak tree.

When, at last, she did go, she ran with all her might and main, staring hard at the bright light in the kitchen, and passing unheeded the white evening flowers that bloomed newly at her feet.

II

In the morning Susie waited on the front veranda behind the Madeira vines for the automobile that would bring Alice Louise. She wore a fresh afternoon dress and her black patent-leather Mary Jane slippers, and her eyes blazed with excitement until they blotted out the rest of her round little face. Impatiently she rehearsed her meeting with Alice Louise.

She stood up and curtsied. "I am Susie Tarleton. Who are you?"

Before Alice Louise had time to reply, "I am Alice Louise Pratt, your new playmate, who has come to see you," a shiny black car turned off the road on to the drive, and stopped at the side of the house.

Susie felt like skipping down the steps to meet Alice Louise, as she skipped down the kitchen steps every morning to meet Pinky, but she stood, motionless, in a breathless hush. Through a hole in the Madeira vine she saw a white man in uniform climb out of the driver's seat, and open the back door of the car. After an incredibly long moment a little girl stepped out sedately; she walked past the man without a word, and the man followed her, carrying a small tan bag with gold letters on it.

They had only a few steps to walk from the car to the veranda steps, yet every detail of the little girl's perfection was imprinted upon Susie's mind. She saw the expensive plainness of the white dress, the pin-tucks and carefully fitted sleeves and rich creamy material. She saw the little girl's slippers, so finely made of dull leather with shaped heels. She saw the little girl's finely woven hat with a blue-velvet ribbon—velvet in summer!—round the crown.

Susie thought of her old sun hat made of plaited grasses, forgotten until now on the landing upstairs, that she wore when she wore any hat at all, and blushed. She was blushing furiously when she faced the little girl at last, and instead of curtsying as she had practised, she backed shyly a few steps.

The little girl bowed to her, and said, "I am Alicia Pratt. Are you Susie Tarleton?"

Susie bowed then, and answered her, "Yes, I am Susie Tarleton. I am glad you have come. But my mother said your name was Alice Louise."

"I changed my name," Alicia announced in a clear, precise voice. "I was named for my Grandmother Pratt but she's dead and I won't be named such a funny name any more."

"Won't you—won't you take off your hat?" gulped Susie. She had never, even in story books, seen anybody as pretty as Alicia. Her skin was really-truly as pale as the petals of a white japonica, her hair, now that her hat was off, was as fine as silk and a beautiful golden color all the way through, not just streaked with golden lights like her own brown mop. And she had what Aunt Hester called "airs and graces."

"You can leave my bag, George," she told the man carelessly. "I'll expect you at five."

Susie was aghast. Perhaps she had better invite Alicia into her mother's drawing-room until Alicia decided what she wanted to play. "Did you want to change your dress first—or anything?" she asked shyly.

"Oh, no," Alicia assured her. "I don't suppose we'll *hurt* anything. I hate rough games."

"Do you know any games?" Susie inquired eagerly.

"I knew about twenty games before I got tired of them," Alicia answered with royal detachment. "I had a playroom all to myself in our house in town and I used to play bagatelle with my governess."

"Bagatelle?" Susie marvelled. She held back the curtains of the drawing-room, and waited uneasily for Alicia's next move.

Alicia smiled. "Tell me about *your* games," she commanded.

For a moment Susie was so rattled she could not speak. She couldn't, she decided swiftly, tell Alicia about the penny-poppy show, or about the corn-silk dolls that she and Pinky played with, or about catching doodles with a broomstraw dabbled in spit. "Well," she hesitated, "I know a *few* games, but I'm afraid you'll hurt your dress."

"Name one," persisted Alicia.

Susie wet her dry lips. "I like to catch doodles," she ventured. "I know a song to sing to them that charms them right out of their holes."

"Ugh!" shivered Alicia. "I wouldn't touch one of the nasty things for a *fortune*."

"We might play greenie," Susie ventured.

"How very silly!" Alicia's soft syllables took away their sting. "It's only a baby game."

"I tell you what," Susie warmly promised. "Let's go out under the big oak tree and call Pinky. I'll take a pillow so you won't hurt your dre·s. Pinky's a million times better at games than I am!"

There fell a strangely chilling silence, broken by Alicia's polite question. "And who is Pinky?"

Susie blushed. "Why, Pinky's my best friend—my playmate," she answered simply, and though she knew Alicia had never had such a wonderful playmate she felt vaguely apologetic and unhappy.

III

The sun was shining brightly but it was cool under the big oak tree. Susie laid the pillow on the ground close to the trunk, and Alicia sat upon it daintily, her delicate little hands in her lap, like a princess upon a throne.

"Pinky, Pinky," called Susie happily, reassured by her familiar outdoors.

Pinky came running along the path from Aunt Hester's cabin like a streak of flame, for she was wearing one of her red calico dresses. She stopped short and bobbed her head with the friendliest of smiles when she reached the shade of the oak tree.

"Hurry up, Pinky," Susie called. "We're waiting for you to play games." Then, with naïve pleasure, she turned to Alicia. "This is my playmate Pinky, Alicia. She's the one I told you about."

Alicia stared at Pinky with her cool gray eyes until Pinky picked at the hem of her dress nervously. "How do you do?" Alicia said at last, icily. "*Miss* Susie said you could play games but I think I'd rather look over her mother's fashion-books. I'd like a glass of water, too, if you please."

Pinky's mouth opened distressedly, and closed. She looked at Susie for help, and Susie gulped. "Please bring us a pitcher of water, Pinky. And all mother's fashion-books on her sewing-table."

Pinky flashed her a bewildered look, and began walking slowly to the house. All the life was gone from her step. Susie felt the blood boiling in her veins as she watched her out of sight: she could have turned upon Alicia and clawed her to pieces. Yet, she didn't. She didn't lift her hand, or say a word.

Alicia stirred on her cushion, and her finely starched dress rustled like tissue paper. "She's a nigger," she declared in her sharp little voice. "The very idea of your playing with a nigger!"

"I like her," Susie said stubbornly, the red burning in her cheeks. "I've always played with her."

"Maybe you did when you were a baby," Alicia's syllables fell silvery cool, "but you're entirely too big to play with her now. Why, you're as grown as I am, and I haven't played with a nigger in ages!"

Susie moved into the darkest spot of the shade, and sat down. She felt, literally, sick inside, as if her stomach were twisting in agony and her heart were too hurt to beat any more. The worst of it was she could not answer Alicia easily, for Alicia's manner *had* made her feel different about Pinky—as though she were siding with Alicia against Pinky whether she wanted to or no.

"Pinky is my mammy's little girl, and we grew up together," she explained again, carefully, despising herself the while.

"Well, you don't have to play with her any more—now," declared Alicia.

Susie nodded and looked up with a half-smile, but her pleasure in Alicia, in the clear golden morning, was gone. She started digging in the earth with a broken twig, to keep from thinking of what she would *say* to Pinky when she came back. I'll say I'd rather play with *her* any day in the week, that's what I'll say, she told herself. I'll say, Alicia or no little white girl will ever make me stop playing with her, that's what I'll say!

Presently Pinky came out of the kitchen door and walked slowly toward them with a pitcher of water and some glasses on a tray. The twig dropped from Susie's hand, and she made a quick motion to Pinky to set the tray beside Alicia.

"*Miss* Alicia would like some water," she said in a flat voice, faintly imitative of Alicia's.

Pinky nodded. Her little yellow face with her sparkling chinquapin eyes had hardened into a mask of sober deference. She set the tray down, and carefully poured a glass of water, without looking at either Susie or Alicia. Susie was amazed. Pinky's manner was as remote, as impersonal, as if they had never met before. In the short space it had taken her to walk into the house and back, Pinky had become a little parlor maid who knew her place. Not even when Susie caught her eye at last and smiled warmly did she blink an eyelid.

"Here are the fashion-books," she said in a flat tone, and put them beside Alicia. Then she did something that caught at Susie's heart like a spasm of pain—she backed away a few steps and curtsied, as the older servants did to Susie's mother, their mistress. The gesture was so admirable that Alicia bowed in acknowledgment.

But Susie closed her eyes to hide the tears swimming in them, and when she looked up again Pinky was gone. In the deepening shade of the big oak tree Alicia seemed paler, more precious, than ever. Like a white japonica, Susie thought with a sharp twinge of jealousy.

Yet she moved over toward her obediently a moment later, when Alicia called to her to come choose paper-dolls.

IV

All during the time she was choosing paper-dolls with Alicia, and even while she was accepting Alicia's invitation to spend the day with *her* tomorrow, Susie was looking forward to the time when Alicia would be gone, and she could call to Pinky to come look at their penny-poppy show under the big oak tree. At last Alicia went home in the shiny black car, and she was alone. It was getting dark but no darker than yesterday, when they had made the penny-poppy show. And Pinky had said the flowers would be as fresh as the day they were picked.

Susie ran to the big oak tree, calling, "Pinky, Pinky," at the top of her lungs. How free she felt as she ran along the path without Alicia tagging her! It was darker under the tree than she had thought, but if Pinky would hurry they would still be able to see the penny-poppy show. "Pinky, Pinky!" she called softly, urgently, and tilted her head sideways so she could hear Pinky's first running steps.

At first she heard only the hum of invisible insects, flying past her ears, and then the humming deepened to the sound of human voices.

She recognized Aunt Hester scolding Pinky, and Aunt Hester's words came clear and hard, like the sound of hickory nuts falling to frozen ground.

"You kin go an' speak to her if it'll ease yo' pain but you tell her you know the diff'ence between a white chile and a black chile, and y'all cain't play together no more. Hit wuz boun' to come. Quit that snifflin' an' go yonder an' tell her lak I tole you."

After a while Pinky came up the path from the cabin. She did not run like a streak of light this time. She came slowly, and she wiped her eyes on the hem of her calico dress.

Susie waited for her under the oak tree near the penny-poppy show, but she knew only too well that they would not look at the penny-poppy show, or ever make another together.

"I heard Aunt Hester," she told Pinky. "I heard what Aunt Hester said." Although her voice sounded calm and grown-up like Alicia's her heart felt as if it would break.

Pinky stood before her in the dim light, rubbing one lovely yellow hand over the other, and it came to Susie that it was really Aunt Hester who had stopped Pinky from playing with her—not Alicia or herself. Susie *had* given in to Alicia while Alicia was her guest, as was proper, but Pinky knew she would come back, Pinky knew Susie loved her better than all the little white girls in the world.

"I can't play with you no more," Pinky said at last. "Mammy says I can't play with you no more."

"I heard her," Susie answered, and in the dim light her face looked as white as Alicia's.

"I have to go back," Pinky whispered, and curtsied as she had before Alicia, "unless—unless you *want* anything."

Susie nodded imperiously as Alicia had nodded before her, as all the little white girls for generations back had nodded to their little black playmates. Only, Susie felt the tears dripping down her throat, and so bitter were they that they tasted like brine in her mouth. "No," she mimicked Alicia completely, "I don't *care* for anything."

For the briefest moment Pinky hesitated; then she turned and walked slowly down the path the way she had come.

The Ginsing Gatherers

Howell Vines

I

THE elderly man and the youngish woman pulled off their shoes and waded the Glaze Shoals in the Little River and came out on the other side not far above the mouth of Glaze Creek. They had left their home across the river on the tip end of the bluff that overlooked the whole Glaze Bend with its rich bottom farm and dense cane brakes. The four o'clocks were open over there in the yard and two powerful and smart dogs were at home to protect the fowls from small varmints and keep the wolves and panthers scared away at night so that the sheep and calves would not be molested in their stables. And in daylight the purple martins or the jaybirds, or both, would keep the hawks scared away from the fowls. The married son would turn out the sheep and calves the next morning and put them up at night.

The "ginsing" season of the year had come and the muscadines were also ripe, and the man and woman were off on a little journey up the length of Glaze Creek and a little beyond to gather ginsing and eat muscadines. The wild fruit and herb hunt would end with a sojourn over the week-end at a neighbor's house about four miles away and near the famous Indian spring where Glaze Creek started. But as for the muscadines, they would eat them just to be doing and for enjoyment, as they could hardly work in the fields, or fish, or walk in the fowl range along the river and below the bluff and hillside without being under a river-muscadine arbor. They were really after ginsing and meant to turn it into gold. Glaze was the man's name and he had given his name to the creek, the bend, and the shoals. Daniel was his given name and Sookie was the woman's given name. Daniel found a girl strange to the country on the bank of the river one day and took her home with him; and that night they started living together as man and wife and had been doing it ever since. She said her name was Sookie and that was all she told him, or so he always said. Daniel was a little stocky, and dark in mien; and Sookie was dark as dusk, and as deep, and built, one could tell, around tendons of great strength and passion.

They were simply out for mutual enjoyment in the woods as had been their custom together for some ten or twelve years. She was a young girl when he got her, for shortly after he had buried his Cherokee wife—the mother of his children—on the bank of the river, Daniel found Sookie and they took up together. Making their something to eat and wear, and spend—on yearly wagon trips to the little capital town of Tuscaloosa about seventy-five miles away—was an easy matter, considering that all this grew in the rich bottom land and in the woods, and in the river, for them while they slept. They followed the creek's course and stopped to fill their sacks whenever they came to the black soil against the coves and foothills where the beeches grew. Wherever Daniel could find beeches standing and dropping mast from which he tolled his mast-fattened hogs there he was almost certain to find ginsing growing. Eating muscadines wherever they found them was only incidental to these pauses for the ginsing roots, as was fondling each other, and it was no great trouble to fill two sacks in the tuber patches splotched up and down the mazy banks of the tiny creek.

And this year they meant sure enough to find a Chinaman somewhere, if possible, and turn these ginsing roots into gold. They might not be able to do it in Tuscaloosa but they ought to in Mobile. If necessary, Daniel would get up a flat-bottomed boat trip to Mobile and try to see a Chinaman. He had in his time helped engineer numerous boat trips to Mobile in the winter time and early spring and he would get up another one if together they failed to see a Chinaman in Tuscaloosa. People said Chinamen had crossed the great water; and he sincerely hoped that at least one had been dribbled in to the new state of Alabama and found himself in the capital town. But failing in Tuscaloosa, there was the thought of Mobile. He could stop at Demopolis on the way down. And he could find out about Montevallo and Huntsville. One thing certain, he meant to get in touch with the first Chinaman to come to Alabama.

Once he could find some Chinamen, fabulous riches were growing in patches as big as his house all around him. And Sookie was with him, if not ahead of him, in all this. Ginsing was about as plentiful as the mast on which his hogs and the squirrels fattened or the beggar lice on which his cows fed. It was as bountiful as poke sallet which they themselves fed on every spring, or sassafras from the roots of which they made tea every winter. When Daniel or Sookie had indigestion, they could chew a ginsing root and get well; and they could trade it to the stores in Tuscaloosa for provisions, but that seemed a small matter when a Chinaman would give you a pound of gold for a pound of ginsing. Pound for pound: that's the way it was. And if they once located a Chinaman or two, the white-flowering ginsing in the spring would become their fallen stars and they would visit them just to look and admire against the time they could pull up the roots in late summer and early fall. Why, already they loved to see the flowers in spring and note how the seed pods increased each bed year by year even as they gathered. And if they would let the roots grow they would get bigger and heavier every year until they would be sights to look at. That new bend up the Little River he had bought back at the land sale, why, he would let the three-leaved and five-leaved herb take the top of all the black ground there. Already it was as thick as heartleaves there. Some of the tubers were as big as his arm, and they would get bigger and bigger in the ground as the catfish and turtles did in the river. Going after a sack of gold would be like going to the beech woods. That was the size of it. He had plenty as it was, but naturally he wanted to be rich. If enough Chinamen would come within reach before he died he would be as rich as doe's cream. That was the problem and all there was to it.

Daniel and Sookie stopped to rest and cool off a little, and compute their ginsing at the spring at the head of Glaze Creek. The little creek and the Cherokees had made the spring famous. The man and woman they were going to see had lived there a little while but had moved out to where they then lived to more cleared ground. Sookie was lying back against the green bank by the spring while Daniel fooled around picking up Indian arrowheads at the old shop place left by the blacksmith who had moved out from the rolling ridge to good open land. He saw a big coachwhip wrapped around a half-grown rabbit, and he teased it to get it to run him. He picked up a white flint rock and chunked at it and the coachwhip looked him over. He made a fuss at the snake and the snake licked out its tongue at him and complied with the worst fuss it could make. Then it uncoiled the rabbit and started for him, and ran him down the bank to the creek, which was called a branch that far up. One had to say, "That's Glaze Creek," or think the thought to recognize it as Glaze Creek there. When Daniel stopped to get something to kill it with, the snake balanced itself on a big embedded rock right over his head, opened its mouth, and made its scariest fuss. That was the climax and Daniel outran the snake to where Sookie sprawled back, looking at the daylight, and did not try to bother the snake any more. He laughed and shivered pleasantly and Sookie joined him.

It took no more than such as this to show Daniel and Sookie a good time and get up a pleasant conversation and a big laugh between them. Anything, just so it thicketed them together more. Daniel had learned to live the thickety life with the Cherokees as tutors and a Cherokee woman as helpmate and partner in daylight and in the dark to such a degree of perfection that he became one of their leaders and their spokesman to the whites. His own farm home and his summer home were filled with Indian utensils, relics, and trinkets such as "tommy hawks," bows and arrows, shawls and blankets. His neighbors could only guess at the Indian secrets he knew, for Daniel played shutmouth along that line. He wouldn't talk, the neighbors said. He had opened up to one person only, his son Daniel—the first white child born in the country—who was then married and raising a family of his own with a white girl, directly across the river from his father. In fact, Little Daniel had sons to whom he was beginning to open up Cherokee secrets. The two Daniel Glazes conversed in the Cherokee tongue as often as in English when off together. There were some important things Daniel had kept from Sookie so that she felt that she hardly knew him. But to compensate for this he never pressed her about her life before he found her, a newcomer in the river country.

Nevertheless, Sookie understood him pretty well and knew the way to his heart. She knew how to enjoy life with him so well that their neighbors said they were as happy as "fee-larks" together. On this day their minds had traveled with them so that they had forgotten the four o'clocks in the yard at home, and the purple martins. When they tried, they could give themselves to the four o'clocks and hold back nothing and virtually be one of the martins; but when they were in the woods, they were in the woods. There their minds traveled like squirrels traveling in the timber, or the Indian hens through it, or the ground-hogs under it. At times their minds sped through the timber like the red deer or to a branch like a mink or a weasel. They had seen so many of all the wild animals while out in the woods together that they could go to sleep of nights counting them up and seeing them again. People said that Daniel had buried himself in the woods. At first a Cherokee woman was buried with him. And some said that later he buried himself deeper with Sookie. Others said that he had buried a white girl with him just as the Cherokee girl had buried him with her. At any rate, Daniel and Sookie played and wallowed and rolled around at the head of the creek, lay down on their all-fours to drink from the spring, and then walked on out the wagon road to Jack Smith's and Alice's house. On the way, there wasn't a step but what they could touch some kind of a tree and keep walking in the road.

II

Alice Smith looked down the spring path and saw them coming. "I see Daniel and Sookie coming," she said. "And they're out gathe'rin' ginsing of course. They've got their sacks full."

"Yes, it's Daniel and Sookie—I might say Daniel and Ginsing," Jack said. "And I just as soon see the old devil and his wife coming as to see them strollops. They'll stay out their welcome. You can bet your bottom dollar on that."

Some of the children and a visiting boy—one of the Waldrops— heard the conversation.

Jack Smith never had known anybody as well fixed as Daniel Glaze who wanted to strollop around so. Neither had Alice. Or anybody else for that matter. Not on the Warrior River or back on the Savannah River in Georgia—and across in South Carolina—where they had come from to the spank-fired new state. Daniel had learned it from the Cherokees and that Cherokee wife of his. They were all gadabouts. They didn't know anything else. That Sookie had made him worse in his old days. An old man had no business taking up with a girl even if he did discover her. That woman couldn't be still at the house like a decent woman was supposed to. They had followed the wild animals so that Daniel was just like one of them, let alone Sookie.

That was the reason the Indians never had anything. They went forth and called on the spirits of spots, or places, and streams as Daniel said. That was their religion. It was a traveling sort of religion. Animals traveled, and so did Daniel and his mate. No other woman would be content to leave the martins and jaybirds in charge of the chickens and guineas and things. But since they bet on the martins that way, they did see to it that the martins stayed with them even after they had raised. Daniel raised a patch of what he called his martin-gourds every year and kept putting up more poles. Somehow or other he charmed them. They had up an understanding it seemed. Daniel said birds could tell when you loved them to the bones. He said he loved the very hearts of the purple martins and made them know it. He made them appreciate him as their friend, he said, but he gave all the credit to the Cherokees. Whenever you saw a martin at your house you could safely say, 'There's one of Daniel's martins."

Daniel and Sookie and deep dusk came to the Smith homestead at one and the same time. "Light, hitch, and come in, as Uncle Cape used to say," Jack said. Alice bade them come in and make themselves at home. It developed that they were all getting along the best kind.

Daniel gave Jack a going-over for not coming across the river and helping him drink rum. He had kept a jug named for Jack Smith from his friends Tommy Lisper and Tommy Prescott and was still looking to some good fellowship over the jug with Jack. He always tried to make it a point to get over a jug of likker with each good friend at least once a year. And Sookie gave them a going-over for not coming over the river and helping them eat watermelons. They had had the *most* of them. The only way to enjoy watermelons to the fullest was to have your friends visit you and help you eat them. Why, watermelons grew like "punkins" for them on the river bank. It was fun to see how much they would grow overnight. Jack and Alice had just not had time to get over; but they would get over there one of these days. "We'll come when you're not expecting us, Daniel," Jack said.

The men folk went to the lot to see about feeding the things while the women folk remained in the kitchen preparing supper. It was a sumptuous meal fit to weight down the revolving table and fill the large family and visitors besides. One thing Daniel had schooled Sookie in to perfection. He had taught her to cook as his Cherokee wife cooked before her. Thus Sookie naturally told Alice again, as she had time before, how she cooked according to the Cherokees. So the two women actually enjoyed themselves telling each other how they cooked.

Sookie's cooking was more like a man's cooking out in the woods or on the river. Say camped out on a wild hog hunt or a midnight supper on a coon hunt at night, or a fish gigging where the fish are cooked on the spot. When she prepared "rosenears" for the table, she roasted them in the shucks in coals. She not only fried fish in the skillet but baked it in a shuck in the coals as well. And she would bake fish on a hot rock. The best way to cook cornbread or flourbread was to bury it in the coals and have roasted hoecakes. Ash cake, she called it. Alice roasted her sweet potatoes in the coals and ashes and that was all. And Sookie had to tell her all about the stews and fixments and messes she made of herbs from the riverbank, fish and turtles from the river, and game from the woods. Daniel's house was noted for its dried fish and dried venison and beef, and Sookie talked a blue streak about that. Alice in turn cooked everything in the old-time white woman's way by boiling, baking, or frying—and sometimes broiling over the log fireheap in the fireplace. The supper consisted of victuals from the garden and field, the bread barrel, and the smoke house prepared in this way, plus milk from the spring served in big goblets and butter served in a huge bowl with much milk still in it. It was a supper the Glazes enjoyed the best kind, and certainly appreciated as a change, but it would have been hard to have eaten a meal at their house without eating fresh eating from the mast or canebrakes, or fish from the river, or dried meat of some kind from the woods. They could not have lived and done well on so many vegetables and field crops all the time as they knew the Smiths mostly did. There was plenty of cured hog meat from the smoke house or the Glazes would have been at a loss even while enjoying the sumptuous change of fare.

III

On the front porch Daniel was explaining how thunder killed turkeys in the egg. He was going into details and speaking from personal experiences. He said that was the reason turkeys do not raise more in the woods than they do. If every close clap of thunder that came did not kill them in the egg they would raise so fast that they would be as plentiful in the woods as partridges or jorees. And that might not be a good thing, for that many turkeys would tear up the ground and take the country.

Daniel and the grown boys were talking of going down in Jack's branch field and catching a coon or two, when, all of a sudden, the wolves came in from the head of Black Creek or the mouth of Wolf Creek and tried to get to the sheep in the stable. This scared the children in bed and got up a general excitement, and a "sicking" on of the dogs. Jack's cur and hound were joined by Bill Glaze's cur and hound who ran over to investigate, and the race was on towards the fork of the creeks. Bill Glaze was Daniel's cousin who had come into the Indian realm on the river with Daniel. It was a moonlight night and there were paths to follow, and Daniel fled after the dogs without looking to see who was going with him. Such as this excited him. He had to get out and follow the dogs regardless. Without saying a word, Sookie and the grown boys followed.

Jack and Alice sat on the porch, thinking about the Glazes and talking. They talked about Daniel and his two brothers and cousin who were the first whites to enter the country. They had respect for Bill Glaze, their near neighbor, who had waited for more whites to come in and married a good white girl. Indeed they had been glad for one of their girls to marry one of Bill's boys. He had helped replenish the new country in the good old Bible way just as they had seen it done back in Georgia and across the river in Carolina. Daniel and Bill were raising up two different races of dogs entirely. Each race had its own kind of sharpness. But the Smiths were all for Bill and his set and against the wild life of Daniel's set. They believed in education and training. People were like animals. They had to be trained. They had to be schooled and not by peckerwoods and soft-shelled "turkles" and wild hogs. This raising children up in the woods to be regular old ground hogs would not do. They spoke with great respect when mentioning Daniel's brother Tom, who traded around with him until he finally hung in at Tuscaloosa and became the first banker there. They knew very little about their brother Bill, who stayed on a while longer with Daniel and finally went to Tom in

Tuscaloosa. They had heard that he followed the Indians into Mississippi.

Daniel was too wild a flower for them. They would not go that deep into the woods. They looked back to the garden flowers the Glaze boys had been back in Charleston. Daniel had thrown himself away and could have done better. He had buried himself in the woods first with a Cherokee woman and then with a strolloping, no 'count, low-down, ignorant white girl. A cultivated, well-educated South Carolinian of Charleston had turned ground hog. He was at first as well prepared for a political career as anybody in Charleston. Daniel had it in him to be somebody. And as long as he was legislator representing the Two-Warriors territory at Cahaba and Tuscaloosa it seemed that he had found himself. But the woods finally closed in on him forever, once the Indian questions had been settled. Now he would be a fit representative for the beavers and otters but not for human beings who believed in progress. He was a good example of what the woods would do to a man if he let himself go. He would go wild and mate with anything that came along just so it was a woman. He had forgotten his A B C's and she never had learned them. It was a sight to see the fine Charleston furniture and stuff Daniel had in his farm home and his summer home and think what he had come to. It was something to study about.

The dogs ran the wolves along Black Creek and on across Dividing Ridge, down Cymbling Branch and into the Short Creek country where Tommy Lisper and his boys lived. All this time Daniel and Sookie kicked around and found themselves in several beds of ginsing and heartleaves against the spots where the beeches grew; and the boys went to the branch field, where the coons had been eating the corn, to see how things looked. Tomorrow ginsing could be gathered there and maybe some roots shaped like a man could be found. If that could be done, it would help out when a Chinaman was found. People said it would make a Chinaman fall all over himself and mumble. Some of these stems had five leaves, too. That would bear investigation the next day. How much a wealthy Chinaman would give to be able to walk in the beech shades and kick around in ginsing and heartleaves! From the way the heartleaves smelled, Chinamen ought to be able to turn them into something valuable. People said these Chinamen believed ginsing would *cure* anything. And a root shaped like a man would *do* anything. If the Chinamen knew about this country they would come over here and settle if they could get permission.

While milling around in this way the Warrior River pair happened upon a doe and some slinks licking salt at a salt lick in a boggy place near a spring. Their hearts beat like bluebirds flitting about in a limb, and in the moonlight night the deer looked white as sheep. Daniel was glad that he had no weapon, not even one of his bows and arrows. It was a picture of heaven to the man and woman with the timber-traveling minds. It took Daniel back to many inspirations such as these encountered with his Cherokee mate out in the woods when their hearts burrowed the earth and drew them down wallowing. Back then they always went out—day or night—and sought such benediction scenes when they wanted to be most intimate with one another. They believed that children should come from such times and that such a child bore a charmed life. Under such circumstances as these he had had the red deer follow him and his mate nearly home. Partly because of such incidents the idea got abroad that the red deer were not afraid of the Cherokees and would even follow them. Daniel told Sookie that the deer mostly followed the Cherokees west—that they had very few deer left compared to what they had when he came to the country. They were afraid of the whites for more reasons than their guns. The red deer were important in the timber-traveling religion Daniel was converted to when he mated with the Cherokee girl.

Following the benevolence of this scene, Daniel and Sookie entered into an intimacy such as Daniel used to enter with his Cherokee wife. Sookie had learned to expect her best times with Daniel upon such occasions and in such spots. He did not believe in the house for such intimacies and neither did Sookie. That's what Daniel liked about Sookie. She had a mind, and a heart, and a body for the woods; and that is what others did not know about her. Daniel had more passion than Jack Smith could appreciate and so did Sookie. No other girl in the country since the native girls had gone west could have matched Daniel even with old age coming upon him. He had wanted to live through such scenes as this with every beautiful grown girl he ever had seen and end up by being buried on the spot. But he considered the Cherokee girls best for such a life except an occasional white girl like Sookie. The Indian girls could best enter into the earthy religion of it all. Oftentimes he wished he could single out these grown girls with the earthy religion in their hearts and experience life with them one by one on the spots all over the river world, and die with them as people said some fish die after such action and be buried in a green bank in the same hole with them. His idea of heaven was to be a young god of the woods, forever living intensely enough to kill and being ever intense enough for an awakened life. That, however, he knew would make a man the equal of the Supreme Being and could not be. In his ordinary moments when he considered this mating business he thought that any man ought to be mighty glad to marry any woman. That was the plan of life. Almost any girl would answer and answer well so that she would be a blessing if taught right. Few if any normal women were at fault if they were not benedictions to their husbands. He believed that almost any normal woman could follow the greatest of men. There were great men and ordinary men and sorry men. But most all women could be great if given the right man.

IV

In the morning it was Saturday. Jack Smith usually spent sweet Saturdays in his blacksmith shop. No matter what the work through the week, he always reserved Saturday for his mendings and creations at the forge and anvil. He was known as a good horse master. All of his boys were talented smiths. People said that it ran in the Smith blood. They could make anything and do anything in a blacksmith shop. They could please themselves and thought they could please God best when in a shop using their heads to invent and their hands to fashion. A man was given a mind to guide the hand in its creations in the blacksmith shop, to farm, to read the Bible, the almanac, and pieces of paper. All of the Smiths believed in knowledge as such and in doing things. But that morning the man from across the river and his mate were there in the way. The Smiths, however, would not have been in the way of the Glazes if they had been across the river that morning. Perhaps the Glazes would have taken them into the woods to show them or tell them something, or down to the river. The

Glazes believed in knowledge that carried feeling with it. Going about the comfortable Glaze home place would in itself have been like being in the woods, for Daniel and Sookie made their home place, which showed beautifully that human beings used there, seem like a part of the green thicket. But the Smith home place was another kind of using place which tallied not at all with the using places of the red deer. Nevertheless, the Glazes enjoyed the change of scene and the contact with other minds. Sookie enjoyed it primarily because Daniel did. They were both fond of the growing Smith girls. Some of the children resented this and some did not. The boys simply enjoyed hearing Daniel talk and did not mind Sookie, for she was Daniel's dough-baker and bed-fellow.

Daniel hung around the shop and kept Jack in a bad humor. Sookie hung around the house and garden and worried Alice a little and interested her some, especially when telling about the Chinaman they hoped to find in town. Jack was a firm and fractious man. He had what was called the Smith fits. That is, he had mad spells, and Daniel brought on these mad spells that morning. Two or three times between watermelon cuttings in the shop and at the house Jack Smith threw his hammer against the shop walls and mildly blasphemed it, the unsatisfactory work he was doing, and all that. Daniel tried to tell him things about the work that made him wall his eyes and want to spit fire.

However, the men got to talking about the Bible and this was a godsend part of the time. Smith was a great Bible reader, although he was not such a terribly religious man. Daniel had read the Bible a good bit in his time but had quit as he had quit other books long before. Like a stroke from this talk on the Scriptures Smith said, "I'm just as glad that there's a devil and a hell as I am that there's a God and heaven." He was known for this idea. The young people thought it was an infidelity or something bordering that but often decided he was right about it when they grew older and knew more about the earth life. Daniel knew enough about the earth life to appreciate the idea and said so. But his idea of hell was not Smith's idea, and he said it was not. The one thought hell was a place of fire and brimstone and the other thought it was a state of being lost and desolate in some place. Hell to Daniel was a place where there were no friendly spirits of spots and none of the earthiness that they congregate to. Smith adduced all this to Daniel's having buried himself in the woods, kept the thought to himself, and got mad at his hammer again.

But the men did agree on the Bible in many places. They agreed on it when it spoke on the man and woman business. Smith never thought of the women and girls as nymphs, and consequently never talked about them from that angle. But he had thought about them in many of the good old Bible ways and could lead any conversation along these lines. Daniel thought there was little difference in the end between the Bible on women and his own thickety ideas on women and he was right there with Smith when he said, "You see, the man that made this world and his legal advisers made a blunder when they made a man without a woman. They seen it wouldn't work. They was experimenting. They seen their mistake when they seen all the man's blunders and mismanagements." The two dark-featured and well-built pioneers got together on this and enjoyed themselves mutually. And Smith went on, "You take me and let me get old and some sixteen or eighteen year old girl come along and I'll want her. If Alice was to be dead, I'd want to marry her. I'd take up with her somehow or other or bust a gut. And if I was to marry the girl, she could ride me a bug hunting to the bluff and make me jump off and think it was fun. A young woman can do to an old man any way under the sun. You take that beautiful young girl who warmed King David's bed. If he'd been left alone with her he'd a give her his kingdom and him a man after God's own heart. The Lord knows we're weak that way and He don't fall out with us for that weakness." They agreed again and Daniel said that Sookie was like the women back in King Solomon's time. She was easy to get along with. Women honored the men folk back then. Solomon had seven hundred wives and three hundred concubines and cooks and house-girls. The women were good women, easy to please and not hard to satisfy. Sookie was like that. Well, Alice was, too.

And about dinner time Jack got to asking Daniel some questions about Charleston, the Cherokees, his Cherokee wife, his terms as a legislator in Tuscaloosa, and Sookie, which Daniel evaded or turned off. Jack did not mind telling all about how he came to the Warrior Rivers with Alice from the Savannah River in Georgia in one of Tommy Thompson's mule wagons in 1820 and first stopped at the great basin in the fork and was outbid on the basin at the land sales. But Daniel knew all about that anyhow. One man had no secrets and the other one had a whole flock of them.

V

Daniel and Sookie went off to the woods for ginsing that afternoon. Daniel, especially, was not out only for ginsing. He was out to strike Cherokee trails where in his day he had had some rolling times. In fact, anywhere he tolled his hogs from the beech mast or acorns, or followed his cattle through the beggar lice or the red deer over their drives to the canebrakes on the riverbank, or the black bear, he could strike these paths. When he went out and killed a wild turkey eating turkey peas, or cut down a tree for a coon, or caught a red horse in the river, he was apt to strike up with the spirits of spots, the ghosts of particular places, still in their old lodgings even with the Cherokees gone. Most of these presences, he thought, had followed the Chero-kees west but some remained. Those who remained kept his religion alive. But there was a wistfulness and a sadness about these that remained not encountered among them in the good old rolling days. Nevertheless, the best that remained hovered over and along these old Indian paths.

That night at Jack Smith's house they had a fine mess of red horses for supper. Daniel and Sookie made the Smiths give way while they prepared the fish and the meal; and the Smiths could not help but enjoy it. They forgot that Daniel and his woman were strollops. While finishing supper Daniel got a fish bone lodged in his throat and couldn't get it out. He tried and tried and followed suggestions, but couldn't make it. The Smiths liked fish as well as the Glazes. Jack had as big a craving for fish in his mouth as Daniel had, but just couldn't take time off to get out and catch them. When he went fishing he had to take off from his work. But Daniel seemed to have no such sacrifices to make in order to get the fish. If Jack had lived right on the river as Daniel did it would have been the same way with him, he declared.

After supper Daniel and the boys were fixing to go to the branch field and catch a coon or two. The coons were eating up the corn. Daniel promised that he would come back over and show them how to catch the last one of them; but in the meantime they would catch one or two and scare the others for awhile. He was also coming back and help them build a wolf pen. Nobody else in the country, he said, knew as well how to catch coons or build wolf pens unless it was Tommy Lisper.

But as they were making preparations to start to the branch field they heard a panther squall. "Listen at that painter," more than one said. "I hear it," more than one replied. Others said, "Yes, it's a painter."

By this time the panther was considerably nearer; in fact, near the house. It was circling and hollering. "It hollers like a woman," Daniel said. Others agreed that it hollered just like a woman. It would jump on a woman if cornered, and it would carry off a child. Woe be unto anything it could seize. Also woe be unto anything it sprung upon. Would the dogs run it? Just then the cur gave his own answer that *he* would. Jack and the grown boys ran out to the stables and by then Bill Glaze's cur had joined Jack's cur and a race was on. Bill Glaze's hound had come over and it joined Jack's hound and together they made a great noise on the trail; but they were afraid and would not *run* it. The panther circled for the Glaze Creek woods and would perhaps go to the river directly across from Daniel's house. Daniel and Sookie halfway decided to get their ginsing and go home. They couldn't carry it all, could they? Yes, they thought so.

While Daniel was out listening and hollering with the boys, the Waldrop boy got a chance alone and told Daniel what Jack Smith said when he saw him coming. Daniel said well, that he was going home anyway and now he certainly would. He found Sookie at the ginsing which she had rounded up and told her that they were going home, that the painter was circling that way. Then he got a chance and asked Jack if he said it. Jack said, "Well, I don't know whether I used exactly them words or not; but I said something like it." Daniel was sorry that he felt that way about it and that was all he said. The ginsing gatherers shouldered their sacks, which bore them down considerably, and lit a shuck after the curs and the panther. All the while Daniel was trying to unlodge the fish bone and Sookie was talking to him about it. He told her what Jack Smith had said. Thank God they could live at home. They didn't have to go see Jack Smith and Alice to get their something to eat.

The panther circled in the Glaze Creek woods a long time and finally struck out for the river at the point directly across from their house. They heard their own dogs join the two curs. They kept to the path, and in spite of a few stops to rest they reached the river as the dogs ran the panther up the river above the field. The dogs were hot in pursuit as they ran over the spot Daniel guessed to be the bank where his Cherokee wife and their child were buried. Daniel and Sookie reached the graves and lay down to rest, and listened to the dogs, wishing all the while that the dogs would tree or catch the panther. In the moonlight night the long blades of grass, the green moss, deer's tongue, ginsing, ferns, the heartleaves, the plantains, wild hyacinths, and the violet plants which covered the bank and its graves—always in the shade—could be told by shape, feel, and smell.

But the dogs did not tree the panther and could not catch it. Finally they quit the chase and came back by the graves where Daniel and Sookie were. There was one thing Daniel had never told a living soul except his son Daniel. Young Daniel later told it to his boys and they in turn told it to an outsider. When Daniel saw the Cherokee girl and wanted her he had to run her down to catch her. He had to run her all over the place on both sides of the river and at last caught her on the bank where she now lay buried. She was willing to be his and became his on that bank. When their child died, she wanted the family graveyard started there. There was where she wanted to be buried. As Daniel prospered, he came to own all the land on both sides of the river where he had to run down the Cherokee maiden. Across the river from where Daniel and Sookie were lying out Daniel had five good houses. In the bend way up the river which he had bought at the land sales was where he and his young wife spent their honeymoon the next day and night. Ever since that day and night up there with her and nothing to interfere but the hum of the great woods, the sounds of the creatures, and the ripples on the rocks, he had been attached to that particular bend. There was where he had so many untouched ginsing beds.

Daniel would be old before he knew it but was still a very strong man so that he did not at the time mind meeting a black bear or a painter out in the woods. Except for Sookie, he would have been a broken man. As it was, much of the time he was a sad man notwithstanding his natural jovial spirits. But he kept it to himself for the most part. He could sit on his porch at home across the river where the four o'clocks were open and the martins asleep and see the clump of beeches and whiteoaks shading the bank where his Cherokee wife and their child lay. He knew that she died of a broken heart brought on when all her people were forced to go west. At least, he attributed it to that. His daughter and her husband and one of his boys had gone west to look for their mother's people and had found some of them. He had labored in Tuscaloosa and Cahaba for more than one term in the interest of the Cherokees. More and more he had become embittered in his heart by the thought of the garden variety of life the whites always tried to advance to as he had experienced it in Charleston. He pitied the whites for their religion. It had come to be almost pointless to him. But he hated the hard hearts among them. But some white men like Tommy Lisper had hearts in them and were good to be with. And best of all, Sookie was like the women back in King Solomon's time.

They lay out together all night enjoying the moonlight night and the river, and the bank, and each other's company, and Daniel thought serious thoughts. The fishbone in his throat bothered him some but less than it had, and they decided it would eventually work out without serious consequences. At the first crack of day they pulled off their shoes and waded the river with half of the ginsing. They would come back for the other later. On their way up the hill path to the house they heard the chickens and guineas fly down out of the cedar trees. Daniel complained about the fish bone in his throat as Sookie started a fire from coals still alive deep in the ashes.

When the fire was blazing hot Sookie said, "Here, pull down your breeches and back up close to the fire."

"Why?"

"It makes no difference why. Do like I tell you."

Daniel obeyed.

Sookie got some tallow and warmed it and went to rubbing Daniel. "If it don't do you no good, it won't do you no harm," she said.

Daniel got to laughing and coughed up the fish bone.

And that day they spent a sweet Sunday together.

Not Worthy of a Wentworth

William March

I HAD fallen into the habit of visiting Mrs. Kent on Wednesday afternoons, and it soon became an established fact that I was expected on that day. She received me on the wide porch which opened onto her garden, and while she fixed my tea and offered me the small, pecan cakes I liked so well, she told me of the town and its people.

On this particular Wednesday I looked idly at the garden while she talked, my eyes fixed on the fig trees banked against the white-washed back fence. She followed my glance and nodded. "Figs will be ripe in another week at most," she said. "The trees are loaded this year." She put sugar in her own tea, then leaned back and said: "I'm glad the crop is going to be good, because Carrie Wentworth and her mother are so fond of them." She paused, then added in explanation, "You see, it's always been understood that the Wentworths have the figs from the branches on their side of the fence."

"The Wentworths?" I asked. "Who are the Wentworths? I don't think you've told me about them yet."

She stared at me with disbelief. "Do you mean to tell me that you've been in Reedyville for two whole months and haven't heard of the Wentworths yet?" She bent forward and patted my cheek gratefully. "You're such a comfort!" she said. "Imagine having somebody all to yourself who doesn't know the first thing about this place!"

"When I think of it," she continued after a moment, "I'm not surprised, after all, that you haven't heard of the Wentworths. They've lost their money and they're gone down a lot since my day. . . . Just ask your mother, when you write her, about old Mrs. Cora Wentworth and her daughter Caroline! She'll remember them all right. . . . When we were girls, your mother and I used to be awed pretty thoroughly at the Wentworth magnificence, and to wonder if we'd ever grow up to be as dainty and accomplished as Carrie." She stopped again, nodded her head and went on with her story, her voice cool and brisk.

The Wentworths, it appeared, had once been a numerous family with their relatives and their connections, but they had died off or moved out of the state until there were left now only the two women next door. Old Mrs. Wentworth before her marriage had been Cora Reedy, so her daughter Caroline was closely related by blood to the Porterfields, the Gowers, and the Claytons. On her father's side there were, beside the powerful Wentworths, the Howards, the Eades, and the Lankesters. It was thus obvious, if I would permit my hostess to be a trifle lush, that Carrie Wentworth was, in a manner of speaking, the unique vessel in which the most aristocratic blood of Alabama met and blended.

This fact was first pointed out by her great-uncle, old Mr. George Gower, during the family celebration which followed Carrie's christening, and the Wentworths, with his words, realized the gravity of their responsibility. When she was old enough to begin her education, Carrie had had a special governess for languages and painting, while her grandmother, old Mrs. Reedy herself, had taught her needlework and deportment. But Carrie had been in no way precocious, in spite of her distinguished ancestry. She learned what was expected of her as well as the average girl, and that was all.

My hostess gave me these preliminary facts with the offhand efficiency of a property manager arranging his set. She was silent for a few moments, recapitulating her facts to determine if anything essential had been left out. "Oh, yes," she said. "Carrie developed a nice soprano voice as a young girl and she took lessons on the harp." It seemed, during these years, that Carrie often played for family guests in the gilded, Wentworth drawing-room, but people were impressed less by her skill as a musician than by the fact that anybody as tiny as Carrie could play an instrument as formidable as the harp at all.

To summarize, Carrie as a young lady had been dainty, pretty and quite accomplished with her music, her water colors, her needlework and her languages, but then so had many of the other girls. It was her laugh more than anything else which made her so attractive. The laugh was clear and tinkling and it differed from the flat laughs of most people in that it leapt upward from note to note with the clear certainty of a coloratura soprano practicing a passage. "Everybody in Reedyville, but her family in particular, took it for granted that Carrie would make a brilliant marriage." said Mrs. Kent. "The only problem was, Where could a man be found who was worthy of her?"

When Carrie was about sixteen she was sent to a finishing school, where she specialized in voice and the harp. She came home that summer and the first thing she did was to fall in love. The boy's name was Herbert Thompson and he worked in a bank. Carrie used to meet him when she could at the old pavilion near James Lake, and Herbert told her all about himself and his plans for the future. He was ambitious, and he didn't expect to be a bookkeeper all his life. He was studying every night at home, and one day he expected to be an accountant or a bank examiner.

It was then Carrie realized that she didn't even know the multiplication tables very accurately, but she went to work at once and before the month was out she was halfway through the arithmetic Herbert had lent her. It was due to Carrie's sudden interest in mathematics that the Wentworths learned about the affair.

When questioned by her family, Carrie admitted that she and Herbert were going to marry just as soon as he was able to support a wife in *any* sort of style; and she thought her interest in arithmetic should be plain enough to anybody with ordinary, common sense. Her future husband was going to be an accountant, and she meant to help him achieve that ambition. It was true his more intricate problems would always be beyond her small, feminine mind, but in time she hoped to become so proficient under his guidance that she could handle most of the lesser, routine matters by herself, thus leaving him free for the important deals when they came up. Naturally they would have little to live on, particularly at first, but, when you came right down to it, who cared?

The Wentworths were shocked at Carrie's attitude, but they were sure nothing would come of the affair, since Carrie and her sweetheart were both so young. Anyway, old Mrs. Wentworth took her daughter abroad in the fall. They returned three years later, when Carrie was about nineteen or twenty. She spoke French, Italian and German fluently now, and she had picked up a working knowledge of Spanish. She made her formal debut in New Orleans that year and she was a great success, but the men she liked didn't come up to the standard the Wentworths had set for themselves, and the one or two that the family regarded as eligible made Carrie, as she expressed it, "sick."

"Carrie and her mother came back to Reedyville the following spring," continued Mrs. Kent. "I'll always remember Carrie sitting in her carriage one April evening about dusk. She was going to a party with one of her admirers from New Orleans who had come to visit her, and, as I gawped, she lifted her dainty, plump shoulders and laughed her famous, tinkling laugh. She had on a white satin gown, and she was wearing a blue velvet evening cloak with a high collar of white fur. I suppose the fur was some sort of fox; at any rate, I'd never seen anything so magnificent before, and it seemed to me that Carrie was exactly like one of the porcelain figurines which my mother kept locked in her parlor."

Mrs. Kent laughed softly. "I must have been about fourteen in those days and I was a big, lummox of a girl. When I got home that night I remember I cried for a solid hour merely because Caroline Wentworth was so dainty and so charming, and I wasn't. I remember Carrie's exact age that way too, because I asked my father to get me a velvet cloak with white fur and he laughed at me. I pointed out that Carrie Wentworth had one, and my mother said, 'Of course she has. She's eight years older than you.'

"What I didn't know at the time," continued Mrs. Kent, "was the fact that the cloak was a present to Carrie for giving up Herbert Thompson the second time. You see, when she got back from her season in New Orleans, she met Herbert at a party and fell in love with him all over again. The family was provoked, but they handled the situation with what most people considered a great deal of common sense. This time they tried to ridicule Carrie out of love."

There hadn't been much the matter with Herbert personally. The greatest objection the family had to him was the unalterable fact that his father openly shaved people in a barbershop at the corner of Magnolia and Broad streets. But Carrie had a mind of her own, and she insisted that she would marry Herbert Thompson and nobody else. She would be very glad to live in a room over the barbershop, among the mugs and old razors, as her family predicted; she would even lather the faces of her father-in-law's customers, as her uncle Ralph Porterfield humorously suggested. She stuck out her firm, Wentworth jaw. She was going to marry Herbert Thompson, she said, and the family might just as well make up its mind now, as later!

She gave in finally, just as everybody knew that she must, and went to visit relatives in Louisville for the season. It looked as though her people were right when they said she would forget Herbert, once she was in different surroundings, because before the year was out she was in love once more, this time with a watch-repairer named Samuel Maneth. The affair had been under way for some weeks before the cousins in Louisville found out about it and wrote back to Reedyville in alarm. Mrs. Wentworth and her mother, old Mrs. Reedy, went immediately to the rescue.

It wasn't that the Wentworths had any prejudice against Jews or anybody else, and it was all right for Mr. Maneth to marry whom he pleased, so long as it wasn't a Wentworth. Then, too, if a Jew did actually marry out of his own faith, it was only reasonable to expect him to have a considerable sum of money. But this little man didn't have a penny to his name beside his wages. He couldn't even hold a job very long.

All the family connections got together that time. The whole thing would be funny, they thought, if it weren't so exasperating, and Carrie's talent for falling in love with the wrong people was really getting to be a problem.

The family feelings weren't helped very much when Carrie attempted to justify herself, to make her position clear. Mr. Maneth was perfectly respectable, she explained, and she had met him when she took her watch to the jeweler's to be repaired. He was so thin and nervous, his hands were so cold and damp, that it was plain to anybody that what he needed was a faithful wife who would cook nourishing meals for him at proper intervals and to see that he dressed himself warmly and took better care of his health. He was not only a watch-repairer, Carrie explained, he was interested in social problems as well, and he was always addressing meetings after his working hours. Carrie had gone to several meetings with him. His mind was so brilliant, she explained, and his theories of right and wrong, particularly with regard to real property, so abstruse, that they were beyond her for the moment, but she could at least read books and learn, and while she never expected to approach him in the intellectual field, she could, at least, give him the sympathetic understanding and companionship which he needed so badly. Certainly she could take care of him, cook for him, wash his clothes if necessary, and raise his children.

At this point Carrie burst into tears, according to Mrs. Kent, and ran out of the room, while her family sat looking at each other in complete bewilderment, wondering from what strain Carrie had inherited her innate commonness. They shook their heads, for Carrie's attitude made it difficult to handle the matter. In the end Mr. Maneth solved the problem for them. Everybody was surprised, as they hadn't thought that he might have his pride, too. He returned Carrie's letters and wrote her a note saying that marriage for them was an impossibility.

Mrs. Kent raised her eyebrows humorously and passed me another pecan cake. "It might have been better all around if Carrie had either been more yielding or independent enough to break away from her family entirely," she said. "At any rate, she didn't do either. She simply drifted along, hoping that things would somehow right themselves. But in the meantime the girls she had known, the girls of her own age, were marrying right and left and starting families of their own, and there sat Carrie with her languages and her skill on the harp waiting for a man to come along who was good enough for her to marry."

The man who suited her family in every particular appeared when Carrie was about twenty-five, and his name, with what Mrs. Kent considered "an unprecedented example of poetic appropriateness" was Rex Ayleshire. He came from Louisiana and he was a distant connection of the Claytons'. He was handsome, witty, intelligent, and he had money; and what was more important, the Wentworth and Reedy families conceded freely that his family was even better than their own.

He was a lawyer who had come to Reedyville to settle the estate of a client, and when the family saw him, they knew that here was Carrie's husband sent to them by a divine providence. They sighed with gratitude when he fell in love with Carrie almost on sight. But Carrie, to their dismay, shook her head, laughed her tinkling laugh and said no. She admitted his obviously superior qualities, but the fact remained that he simply made her "tired."

Then, as if to consolidate her position and to end the family pressure, she fell in love right under Mr. Ayleshire's nose. This time it was a man named Charlie Malloch, a machinist. The whole town was laughing by this time, and they predicted that Carrie would turn up at the machine shop the next Monday morning in overalls, handing Charlie his tools when he needed them.

The family anxiety shifted quickly. It wasn't so much a question now as to whether Carrie could be induced to marry Rex, it was rather how she could be prevented from marrying Charlie. The result was that Rex went back to Louisiana and Carrie and her mother went to London for a visit.

Mrs. Kent lit another cigarette and leaned back in her chair. "Everybody was sure that Carrie would land an earl or a duke or something equally grand. Other American girls, with far less money, family or good looks, had done the same, but when they returned to Reedyville, Mrs. Wentworth told her friends with considerable disgust that Carrie refused to interest herself in her opportunities. She was through with Carrie, she said. She gave her up as hopeless.

"Oh, yes," said Mrs. Kent thoughtfully, "I must tell you this: When Carrie came back from England that time she was wearing exaggerated earrings and she smoked openly and rouged her cheeks and lips. Her clothes were too young for her, so everybody thought. She had taken to dotted swiss dresses, sashes and pink sunshades. She went everywhere in those days and her tinkling, gay laugh was heard a great deal. Her father died about that time, too, and it was found out that while the family was well-off, they didn't have nearly so much as people had thought. . . . Afterwards, with Carrie and her mother living alone, they quarreled more than ever."

But the worst quarrel of all took place when Carrie was in her middle thirties. It seemed that a Swiss baker had come to town and opened a pastry shop. He borrowed money from the bank to get started, and after a time he was doing reasonably well. Carrie, along with the other ladies of the town, used to patronize him. The man's name was Zuckmar, and he was Carrie's age or a little older. It wasn't long after she met him before Carrie began to take up cookery and to comb the town for family recipes, and Mr. Zuckmar started baking little cakes for her with her name outlined in colored icings.

Carrie left off her earrings, her sashes and her organdies and buckled down to the work of helping Mr. Zuckmar make a success of his shop. Before the summer was out he had asked her to marry him, and Carrie had cried for an hour on his shoulder and then consented. But she had learned caution, and she was determined that nobody should thwart her plans this time. She decided to keep their engagement secret until the store was paid for and they were operating free of debt. When this happened, they would simply go to Montgomery or Selma and get married, telling nobody until afterwards.

Indeed, Carrie and Mr. Zuckmar handled their affairs with such discretion that her family had no idea whatever of what was going on, so Mrs. Ralph Porterfield had a shock one Saturday morning when she took a short cut through the alley that ran behind the pastry shop and suddenly heard her niece's coloratura laugh on the other side of the high, board fence. She opened the gate and went in, and the thing she saw took her breath away:

There was Carrie Wentworth with her knees resting on a piece of sacking and her skirt pinned back over her waist. She had a scrubbing brush in her hand, and as she laughed and talked she scoured the kitchen of the pastry shop briskly with lye soap and water. Above her stood Mr. Zuckmar, who was also laughing. He had a spoonful of sticky cake-icing, and he was threatening to pour it down Carrie's back unless she gave him another kiss instantly. They were speaking Italian, so Mrs. Porterfield didn't know what they actually said, but their meaning was obvious enough when Carrie gave in laughingly and lifted her lips upward to his. At that moment Mrs. Porterfield backed out of the gate, not believing, even then, what she had seen.

Naturally the family was shocked at the idea of Carrie married to a pastry cook. Old Mrs. Philip Howard predicted that she would end up clerking in the store or even waiting on the tables, and Carrie forgot her caution for the moment and flared up in her old manner. She said that waiting on tables was precisely what she intended doing, because, after they were married, she and her husband were going to put in tables and sell ice cream and cold drinks. Mr. Zuckmar, she explained later in a more placating voice, was the sweetest, the most honorable and the most marvelous of men, and he was one of the very cleverest, too, once you got to know him, but he was a little helpless, like all men, and she couldn't give him up now, even if she wanted to, because she didn't know what would become of him if she wasn't there to aid him in his difficulties.

The family row that night was the worst in the history of the town, but Carrie refused to budge an inch this time, and Mr. Zuckmar couldn't be moved out of his phlegmatic, even-tempered calm. They might have succeeded, after all, except for two things: Carrie, naturally, didn't have one penny of her own, and Mr. Zuckmar was operating on borrowed money. When the family put the matter before Mr. Palmiller, of the Palmiller State Bank, he saw at once that a girl of Carrie's standing couldn't be permitted to disgrace her family the way she planned. He called his loan and forced the pastry cook out of business. A few days later a committee visited Mr. Zuckmar and suggested that he locate in some town in the West, where business conditions were better. . . . When she got Mr. Zuckmar's farewell note, Carrie began to cry shrilly. "My God!" she screamed over and over. "My God, can't you ever let me alone?"

After that Carrie didn't even bother to quarrel with her mother any more, and for a long time nobody saw her at all. But times were changing rapidly, and after a year or so nobody even thought of her very much, for already she belonged to the past. It was about this time that the Wentworth family had to sell their big house on Reedy Avenue, and move into the cottage whose back garden joined the garden of my hostess.

"And that," said Mrs. Kent, "is the monotonous history of Carrie Wentworth, on your thumbnail! I used to laugh at her, along with the rest of the town, but I don't any more. I understand her too well now." She sighed. "Poor Carrie! All she wanted was to marry a man who needed her, one she could love and serve faithfully. She was the most uncomplicated woman I ever knew." She stopped and laughed softly. "Poor Carrie," she repeated. "If she'd succeeded, she'd probably have bored her husband to death, and he'd have wanted to wring her neck a dozen times a day, but he'd never have given her up. Never as long as he lived. He would have loved her too much."

I sat silent for a moment, watching the shadow of the camphor tree touch the fence slowly and lengthen. Then, all at once, there came a sound of high, tinkling laughter from the Wentworth yard, laughter which leaped upward from note to note and died away. It was almost as if the crystals of a chandelier had been brushed unexpectedly by a passing hand.

"What is she like now?" I asked.

Mrs. Kent said, "Would you like to see her for yourself?" and when I nodded, she got up from her chair, and we walked down the steps and across the lawn. We reached the dividing fence and peered over.

Before us, a withered little girl sat under a pear tree playing with dolls. She was wearing a frock which ended above her knees, and her gray hair hung over her shoulders in thin, exact curls. Her legs were bare except for the pink socks which reached her ankles, and anchored over her ears were old fashioned, steel rimmed spectacles.

Mrs. Kent rapped on the fence to attract her attention and called, "Carrie! Oh, Carrie! Come here a minute."

Carrie looked up with her bright, eager eyes. She picked up an armful of her dolls and skipped to the fence. She stared at me with curiosity.

"How old are you, little girl?" I asked.

"I'm sixty-two," she said, "and my name is Caroline Wentworth." She held up the dolls for me to see.

"We came out to look at the figs," said Mrs. Kent. "They'll soon be ripe again. I know you'll be glad. You and your mother must take all you want."

From inside the house there came a voice surprisingly full and vigorous. "Carrie!" said the voice hoarsely. "Carrie, who are you talking to?"

Carrie said: "I can speak five languages. I can sing quite well. I can do embroidery."

"Carrie!" called the voice in terror. "Carrie! Carrie!"

Carrie said: "Yes, Mamma, I'm coming now." She started away and then came back to the dividing fence, her eyes roguish behind her spectacles.

"My name is Caroline Wentworth," she said gaily. "I can paint in water colors. I can play the harp."

She turned, then, and skipped up the gravel path, her dolls riding before her in her spread skirt, her gray, thin curls tossing up and down to her stride. She reached the door and faced us again. She waved her hand, laughed her high, tinkling laugh and went inside.

When she had gone, we stood quietly beside the whitewashed fence, the late sun touching our hands. It was Mrs. Kent who spoke first.

"I seem to be *bristling* with platitudes this afternoon," she said softly, "and I know how platitudes frighten young intellectuals from the city, but I never heard old Mrs. Wentworth call her daughter, nor see Carrie skip up the walk and into the house, without thinking that the Wentworth back door closes slowly on a whole generation, a period of time, an era which cannot live again." We turned from the fig trees and walked back to the wide, vine-shaded porch. "Yes," I said. "Yes."

Introduction

IV. *Alabama Flowering II*

THE distinguished achievements made in fiction by Alabama writers during the early decades of this century led to a continued flourishing of literary interest and culture in the state. Alabama authors came more discernibly than before to think of themselves as an identifiable group; and in their sense of collective endeavor, coupled often with increasing national visibility, they found encouragement to believe that writing about the distinctive character of Alabama life and history could be of far more than local significance. Indeed, they found that in the very richness and vitality of Southern fiction as social-historical document—a discovery like the one that had taken place during the late 1920s and early 1930s for the Mississippian, William Faulkner—lay the power of its claims upon a modern audience desirous of a fiction still capable of addressing elemental human concerns within some older sense of relation to the world, the sense of a time, a place, and a people.

This air of encouragement was certainly not lost on the new group of talents to appear over the several decades from the mid-1930s onward. Harriett Hassell, Shirley Ann Grau, Harper Lee, Cecil Dawkins, Elise Sanguinetti, and William Cobb continued the successes of those fellow Alabamians who had gone just before. They went on publishing short fiction in the nation's most widely known and prestigious periodicals; they found their works frequently selected for inclusion in various prize collections and other anthologies; and, as was particularly the case for many who came under the tutelage of the University of Alabama's Hudson Strode, they found their longer works and collections passing through the portals of many of the nation's major book publishers.

Perhaps the classic instance of the sort of second-flowering phenomenon I have tried to describe is the case of Harriett Hassell.

Enrolled in Hudson Strode's writing course at the University during the mid-1930s, this shy young woman from Northport had the temerity to ask the master—a man of well-vocalized opinions, whose classroom biases were heavily weighted toward the short story—if she could work on a novel. The result was *Rachel's Children,* a story about a young woman's growing up in the rural South so profound in its sensitivity and so accomplished in its craft that one can barely imagine it the first novel of a literary aspirant.

It is hard not to speak in somewhat the same terms about Harriett Hassell's remarkable short story, "History of the South." To begin with, the title alone, in its intentionally hyperbolic relation to the crabbed, eccentric little drama the story actually plays out, comes close to being a gloss on the treatment of that critical subject across the whole body of Alabama fiction at large. For if it is history that locates the Alabama writer most fully in the world, runs most deeply and most true, it is history of a particular character and definition. It is not history formalized, literalized, intellectualized. Nor is it history become some memorial of grand emotion. Rather, it is a matter of close dramas and quiet recognitions, of things closely experienced and deeply felt, but without bombast or spectacle. In the hands of the Alabama writers most fully attuned to it, it has been a history unlocking its deepest secrets from the lives of everyday people who are its chief inheritors.

In the case of Hassell's story, the momentary opening history provides into itself comes in the gift of a wagonload of family portraits, to the new mistress of Rosedale from, on the day of her death, the old. Apace, the young woman is stirred to childhood memories of her benefactor: the haughty, bitter, self-deluded Annie Laurie Bourne, the governor's daughter left with a husband reduced to clerking in a store and "the poetry of her frustration." The whole story comes flooding back, of the old woman's petty deceits, of her pathetic grapplings, high and low, for social recognition, of a grim, final childhood afternoon on which the narrator, awaiting the birth of a baby sister, has fled from the old woman's spectral presence as she pours out on her kindly, ineffectual husband, a whole lifetime's accumulated rage and pain. "Niggers on white carpets, James Durville," she shrieks, "niggers on white carpets . . . !" Here, in the strange gift, and in the vision of past human mystery it brings back into deepening and informing relation with present human mystery, the younger woman realizes that she has discovered, if not *the* history of the South, at least her own humanly enlarged version of it. Of the portraits, she says at the last, "She sent it all to me. . . ." Yet it takes her husband, a young writer, appropriately, to put this complex drama of consciousness most fully into relief. Even in those rare instances when history promises momentarily to transcend the boundaries of individual lives, it also remains locked enigmatically within, he suggests, heaped up in its queer emblems and images, hoarded even unto death. "Not to you," he says. "But to Rosedale."

More explicitly than "History of the South," the next two selections, "White Girl, Fine Girl," by Shirley Ann Grau, and the chapter I have entitled "Christmas" from Harper Lee's *To Kill a Mockingbird,* concentrate on that particular dimension of Southern history bound up with race. In each—the first focused on a just-released inmate from a black penitentiary, the second on a young white girl whose father has been appointed to defend in court a black sharecropper accused of rape— we see the painful heritage of slavery permeating a whole institutional order. From city to town, prison and saloon to county courthouse and back-country parlor, a modern society struggles against itself as black and white alike undertake the working out of their common bitter legacy.

The deep divisions that endure in that society are exemplified in the opening of Grau's story. There are only two towns significant enough to be worthy of the name, the narrator tells us, in Clayton County: Stanhope and Kilby. The one, bastion of the white class structure, is the state capital. The other, seven miles off, is the seat of the state's black penitentiary. What blacks do penetrate Stanhope go there as chauffeurs or cooks in the great white houses, or as bootleggers quietly supplying upper-class white thirsts. In their own world—on the outskirts of Kilby or in the city's industrial fringes—they subsist, mainly, in a kind of no-man's-land of violence and fearful suspicion. One prison, it would seem, is as good as another. Jayson Paul Evans, released from Kilby after a term for manslaughter, returns in search of the woman for whose love he has killed one friend and bootlegging partner—Mannie, her husband—and has nearly murdered another—his old friend Joe. He finds her, Aggie, at last, living on in defiant isolation, protected from the world of men by her three daughters, including one by Joe and one by himself. Cursing him, and hurling stones and bricks, they drive him from the house, and in numb hysteria, he stumbles away toward a new destination. Down by the mill yards, Joe has told him, there is a white girl, the figure imaged in the title. He finds her, but discovers also that his natural daughter has followed him. He casts the child off, and at the end busies himself with the new woman. It is as Joe had predicted. She looks almost as good, Jayson remembers from somewhere back in the confinement of his lonely confusion, as the girl on the Jax beer sign. White girl, she is, fine girl.

Another view, equally powerful and affecting, of this social-historical dilemma, is presented to us through the eyes of the young white girl, Scout Finch, in the chapter that in many ways stands at the thematic center of *To Kill a Mockingbird*. The first glimmerings of the problem come to her in the taunt of a schoolmate, soon repeated by her cousin Francis, that her father Atticus, a lawyer, defends "niggers." In a child's awakening heart, it is history again, brooding over the state like a dark dream. While Cousin Ike Finch, the county's last Confederate veteran, continues to tell his tales of Chancellorsville and the glorious lost cause, Atticus Finch, man of his century, shoulders the practical burden of dealing in its consequences. Far from Chancellorsville or any last glimmering myth of the fallen South, he will defend Tom Robinson, a poor black wrongfully accused of rape by the daughter of a worthless white tenant farmer. He tells his brother, "Do you think I could face my children otherwise?"

For all the moral beauty of the theme, however, these comments alone would leave the chapter and the book to which it belongs with much an unjustly limited characterization. One must also speak of the larger literary achievement of the narration itself, Scout Finch's retrospective capturing, through the power of regional speech, a sense of the whole felt complexity of experience in her world—and thereby ours as well—in a manner often accurately reminiscent of Mark Twain's genius in *Huckleberry Finn*. Like Huck, Scout can be a master of homegrown hyperbole, and in several instances Atticus is moved to comment on the particular fluency of her cussing. But again like her literary forebear, she plays perhaps best in the mode of naive understatement, her generous and wise perceptions expressing themselves in recurrent deadpan precision. In a lecture on proper dress, her Aunt Alexandra, she observes, has said "I should be a ray of sunshine in my father's life." Scout's retort: "I suggested that one could be a ray of sunshine in pants just as well. . . ." Atticus, she reports at the last, has confirmed the point: "he said there were already enough sunbeams in the family and to go on about my business, he didn't mind me much the way I was."

In sum, it is the achievement of style, rather than any explicit social comment, that gives *To Kill a Mockingbird* its great moral wisdom and authority. Like *Huckleberry Finn,* the book itself is all of a piece with the world it images. Precisely in its unerring fidelity to the concrete and particular, it acquaints us with a vision of things more broadly human and universal.

A similar sense of universality comes to invest what seems, at least in the beginning, the extremely localized vision of Cecil Dawkins's "The Mourner." The story is clearly about Birmingham, here called Galleton. The signs read, "The Magic City—Home of Dixie Steel." On "Bald Mountain" stands the great statue of "The Iron Man." Moreover, the narrative concerns a distinct cultural minority, in this case a community of Italian Americans. Yet even as the relatively simple story begins, a son now returning to his family as they bury his grandfather, it begins to unfold its larger modern implications. Gabriel Orghesi, the artist fled to San Francisco, returns to the past and the ties of place and family, mingling his love with his hope that they may once and for all be cast off. As is so often the case with history here, one embraces the past precisely that it may also significantly be broken with. Outside, the landscape fills with urban dread, the motels thrown up like dayglo Indian camps, and the sulphurous emanations of the orange-glowing furnaces damping the Southern night. Aboard the rushing trains, there is the constant sickness of movement. Still, like Thomas Wolfe's Eugene Gant, Gabriel simply knows that he must be bound away to, if to no other end, simply his own motion. Embracing his mother, who has been indulged in riding with him to one last stop just outside the city, "He allowed them both this sleeping moment; before the rent, the breaking tears, the cry, before this monster he was riding bore him off again to peace and loneliness."

In a lighter vein, but still very much evincing themes and concerns lodged deeply in the native consciousness, is the chapter from Elise

Sanguinetti's *The Last of the Whitfields* that I have here entitled "A Yankee Inquisitor." Once again, we confront the familiar caricature of the starchy, self-righteous Northerner, this time a New York newspaperman named Hopper. His object in coming southward: predictably, to undo overnight a whole legacy of accumulated wrong, in this instance through the writing of an on-the-spot exposé on race. For his homegrown adversary, we get the book's fourteen-year-old narrator, Felicia Whitfield, best described as something of a combination of Scout Finch and Simon Suggs. She regales him with stories of heartbreak over the plight of her "Neeee-gro" friends, as she is at pains to call them, living as she must in what she depicts as an inferno of bigotry. But this is only the beginning. Heartened by these revelations of a kindred spirit, the journalist also shortly invites himself to a black church service ("Why don't he write up something about his own church?" murmurs Velvet, the maid) and later, camera and all, to the home of the minister where he reports getting "some excellent quotes," as well as "a charming picture—of his entire family, in their home. All of them were sitting around their table with their heads bowed."

Once again, the Yankee, hell-bent on rooting out other people's prejudices, becomes the dupe of his own. Meanwhile, the history of the South, for good or ill, goes on in bemused deadpan. If there may not be much black and white can agree on, they can still agree on pious Yankees. Indeed, a final pronouncement on this one, while spoken by a black, nonetheless strikes a telling note of unison:

> Mother asked Isaiah if he liked Mr. Hopper.
> "No'm," he said.
> "Why not?" Arthur asked him.
> "He's hankty."
> "I suppose," was all Mother said.

"Hankty." It is a word that Mr. Hopper no doubt would try to look up in a dictionary. He would not find it, however, for it does not come from a language of books or articles but from a language of place. The legacy of white and black alike, it is a language to be known only by those willing to embrace a whole vision of collective experience.

The final story in this section, William Cobb's "The Stone Soldier," returns to even more traditional ground insofar as the general direction of modern Alabama fiction is concerned. Lyman Sparks, the fat, perspiring, white-suited drummer, arrives in Hammond on his mission of selling the town a commercially produced monument to its Confederate dead. On his way to gain endorsement for the project from the town patriarch, old Major Clayton Hammond, the fast-talking Sparks lingers long enough to ingratiate himself with old Lip, a freed slave, giving him a Bible with its grotesque illustrations crudely drawn in to represent black characters in familiar scriptural scenes; shortly thereafter, he has forced his way into the Hammond parlor, subjecting Miss Iva and later the old, broken Major as well to his bluster and stupid cajolery. Soon the old man has been left behind, however, crying alone with his wounds and memories, and Sparks, having extracted a kind of endorsement from Miss Iva, is departing for home, confident that he has made the sale. Yet his triumph is mixed with a queer, threatening dissatisfaction, somewhere between perplexity and shame. "It's not your fault that you're the way you are, Mr. Sparks," Miss Iva has told him, at the climax of his shabby confrontation with the Major, "any more than it's his fault." Then there has been the framing of the entire episode in the awkward after-scene in which old Lip has given back the Bible. He has one from the Major, he says, in a tone of almost menacing authority, that will do very well.

In historical fiction such as this, we feel as if we are on familiar literary ground. Like his Mississippi cousins, the Snopses, Lyman Sparks is in many ways the new man of the new South: crass, acquisitive, brutish, philistine. What renders him distinctive, however, as in so much Alabama fiction of the modern era, is the element of emotional particularity, of close, subtle concern for the small drama of recognition being played out in this single, benighted soul. In Mobile, the Dixie Monument Company is working full tilt, and in the field, sales are looking right. Yet one ace drummer somehow senses that if that is not all bad, it is not nearly as good as it ought to be; and in his unformed, everyday disquietude with this, he remains, for all his vulgar hustle, disturbingly this side of similar tensions we feel in each of us. As in the other fictions here, a particular encounter with history has been made to speak of modern disturbances and confusions that are basic, and in the fullest sense, common.

History of the South

Harriett Hassell

T HE wagon under my porte-cochère was a bundle of gray boards settling onto the lean mule's tail. I stared at the note on my desk and out the window to the quilt-wrapped portraits in the wagon, and back at the note again. My hands were suddenly cold and sweating, and I did not need to look at the portraits. I had seen them all so long ago, bishops under the Stuarts, royal proprietors, governors of states. I took the cheap paper covered with angular writing in my hands, to feel of it, to make sure of something that had touched me once, and escaped, and touched again.

She had written, "My dear—how nice to know that you are at last settled with that splendid, self-made Martin Hastings whose books make so dreadfully much money!" The pencil had bitten into the paper, hurried by her terrible strength, the tenacious need to say herself out at last in mingled malice and sweetness. "They tell me that you and Martin have restored everything, the house and grounds are exactly as they used to be. How I should love to see it, and how wonderful it is to feel that for you the sun is shining! For me, my dear, since Mr. Durville is gone and I am ill—do you realize that I am eighty-eight, sixty years older than you?—there remains only a last request. I am sending you my portraits, my beloved Bournes and Durvilles. Hang them in the long upper hall, my dear. . . . Forgive an old woman the poverty of their conveyance. . . ."

The starved mule stirred restlessly, so that the portraits slid a little on the wagon-bed. And I kept my eyes turned away from them and wondered why I had ever hated her.

Perhaps of us all my brother Lawrance was the only one who liked her, or maybe it was just that something in him grew fat on what he called "the poetry of her frustration." To please her, while all along Seay Street the verandas rung with talk of Germany at Versailles, he argued about the Civil War.

"The South was never beaten!" she would cry. "Po' white trash, low Northern scum pourin' in over us, burnin' our homes, pressin' our gallant boys back, but they never whipped us, we never gave up. Even at Shiloh, when our blood was drained out to the last drop, we remained undefeated, we fought on!"

"What," Lawrance would loftily inquire, "is the difference between defeat and surrender?"

And she wouldn't say anything in answer, only sit there on our veranda, rocking and staring with her blue eyes fixed on the tumbled leaves in her own yard. Sometimes, with her sitting and staring like that, you could see what defeat had meant to her and to her kind. It would take shape in Lawrance's eyes and communicate itself to the air until it was as if a tapestry unrolled, showing the elegance of that former day and the churchmouse poverty of all the days that followed.

"I know she's tiresome," Lawrance would tell us, half in apology. "But, Heavens, we'd be tiresome too! Never seeing any of her own sort, never anybody that matters to her. Bournes and Durvilles, De Graffenrieds and Pettuses, and all the rest, they're all gone . . . into an obscurity like hers, and she can't follow them. Even the second best, the Stillsons over in Camden and that sort that married money to save themselves, she can't keep up with them, they don't want to look at that old woman reminding them of what they'd be if money hadn't saved their fine blood."

Mamma sniffed. "If we don't matter, she could stay away from here! I feel like I know by heart the whole history of the Bournes and Durvilles and the Civil War, and what do they matter anyway?"

"Look here," Lawrance said, "do you know what ol' man Durville makes clerking in Martin's store? All right, think of it anyway, a Durville clerking. . . . And you know what coal costs. That's why she's always running here. She can't sit on the veranda all day in this weather."

"Oh, Lawrance, is that it?" Mamma stared round at us while we all saw old Mrs. Durville rocking on her veranda in the December cold, her chair pulled into the one sunny spot and her red sweater buttoned tight against the wind.

But it wasn't an hour before mamma said to papa, "She could go to Copper's or Jackson's or even to Horne's. She don't have to come here every day. She does go to Horne's some anyway for all she gabs about Lillian Horne writing books about down-trodden niggers and all; she runs in there every morning, I see her from the window."

Papa laughed a little. "After her morning coffee, I bet. . . . The governor's daughter!" he said.

Mamma nearly screamed, "Well, I can't stand her much longer!" And I knew she was thinking of the baby she was to have soon. I was twelve then, and I knew some things, superstitions, so that I thought the baby might be like old Mrs. Durville. I used to see a little hideous thing with pale blue eyes weeping blood over Shiloh. Mamma said, "If you let her in this house when it happens!" She said, "I bet ol' man Durville does without his coffee!"

When we looked at Mr. Durville in his suit with the shine that came from leaning over Martin's counters, it was hard to believe that he was the son-in-law of a pre-war governor, that once he had owned Rosedale Plantations, or that he had ever been young and danced at Inaugural Balls when Mrs. Durville was fifteen and had just come out. Mr. Durville spoiled the picture. Somehow, we could see Annie Laurie Bourne in pale blue satin with pearls in her high-piled golden hair, but not the dark burnsides of young James Colefax Durville. He was the one the Yankees whipped. He was not feminine enough for the tenacity of remembrance, and because he forgot and she didn't, he was beaten. He was a straw man, neuter. It wasn't possible that he had ever been young and vital, arrogant to take the virginity from her short, stout body. I used to think that this was the reason why she had never had any children; and then I would be ashamed of myself and sorry, not for her, but for the feeling of some barren thing in her, that being barren, yet spawned.

One afternoon, a gawky blond man wearing the khaki uniform of a student in the Veteran's Vocational School, stopped in front of our house and spoke to papa. The next day the Adcrafts moved into two rooms on the first floor. Mrs. Durville was back in the kitchen with mamma when their furniture came, but at the first sounds of activity she was out in front, scraggy hair slipping down and cotton stockings wrinkled over her slipper tops. I remember thinking Mrs. Adcraft looked almost as much like white trash as Mrs. Durville did. She was dressed up and lugging a fat, pasty-white baby the way trash always are. Mrs. Durville emitted thin cries of simulated delight to the baby. She stood a while, holding it, and crooning from her thin mouth, and then she came up to the doorsteps where I was sitting, watching the furniture go into the house, and stuck the baby down under my nose. It looked like a stiff, pallid grubworm, and its flannel clothes, wrapped around it cocoon-fashion, smelled vaguely of talcum powder and dampness.

She said, "Can you believe that you were once this small?"

I felt a long minute go over me while I stared down at the baby and then up at her. My mouth opened slightly as I shook my head "No-o."

Something cruel and sickening came into her eyes. "And can you ever believe that you'll be old and ugly soon . . . wrinkled, my deah? . . . I was pretty once. But just you wait till you marry that fey-eyed Martin Hastings you're always sitting on the backsteps with, talking about books. My deah, Martin Hastings' grandfather was in trade and his grandmother's brother signed with a cross when he was overseer of my husband's niggers! Just you wait, my deah, you'll be old and wrinkled too . . . !" Her voice, pitched high and sweet, with a vileness singing under it, seemed to cut my breastbones open and leave me helpless against the bright malice gleaming in her face. I looked swiftly away.

I hated her then, and this hatred included the Adcrafts with whom, at this time, she seemed somehow identified. Yet I couldn't stay away from them. On Saturdays and in the afternoons when I got home from school, I went across the hall into Mrs. Adcraft's room, and sat on the floor, watching and listening. Mrs. Durville was always there, talking, telling about Rosedale Plantations, the niggers they used to have, and the parties with all the windows hung in satin and velvet and white carpets on the floor. She told Mrs. Adcraft, "Ah, my deah, there's nothing like it now, there was never anything like it!" And once she looked at me with strange eyes. "Can you see it? Those greasy, black bucks, that thing that degraded us, walking over our elegance, those beautiful white carpets?" She shuddered as if she didn't know she shuddered.

Mamma laughed about it rather nastily. "The governor's daughter has come down considerably!" she said. "I wouldn't wipe my feet on Lena Adcraft!" But I heard papa asking Lawrance if there weren't any Bournes or Durvilles left to get a decent job for ol' man Durville. "There ought to be somebody," he said, "some of their people some-where. . . ." Lawrance shrugged angrily. "It's Adcraft's sort that's handing out jobs these days." Papa said, "Yes, and making so infernal much noise doing it."

Mrs. Adcraft was a plump, too-white woman with sandy lashes and pale, bulbous eyes always distended in a look of sensual wonder. Her dress-front lay open over her large, quivering bosom. If Mr. Adcraft came into the room while she was suckling the baby, he bent over and pinched its cheeks, and then straightened up, blaring his eyes, blowing his cheeks out, and booming, "Well, wh' ye reckon happened to ol' Bill Adcraft today?" He strutted, he banged away at his inferiority complex with a hard, tense maleness, jerking at his khaki trousers until Mrs. Durville would cry out, "Oh, Mr. Adcraft! You remind me so much of our Western oil kings, are all our veterans like you? . . . . Ah, my deah, if Jefferson Davis had had your force!"

I suppose their obsequious attention fed her starving vanity, her hunger for an audience, for displaying the sorrowful drama of her nostalgias; and in more material ways, too, they fed her. Through the walls, one Sunday morning, we heard her shrill, half-angry voice. "I do hope I'm not disturbing you, but I did want to ask Mrs. Adcraft if the Herons she was telling me about are related to Captain Heron, Captain Joseph Heron of South Carolina?" There was a succession of more subdued noises, and then Mr. Adcraft's hearty boom, "Well, if you'll make low to eat with Bill Adcraft and his woman, why we'll be right proud to have you!"

Papa's cheeks blew out with his chuckle. "God A'Mighty, when they begin to think Adcrafts know Herons—!" Then he said, "I wonder what ol' man Durville's having for his breakfast?"

Now she hardly went home except to sleep. In the evening, I would find her sitting before the fire in Mrs. Adcraft's room, hemmed in between rows of chairs on which wet diapers hung, steaming offensively in the heat. And always she would be telling about her girlhood, dreaming aloud of the past, of something dark and sweet, the last romanticism. She would ask Mrs. Adcraft to make coffee. "Since you like it so much, my deah. We always had coffee with a little brandy in the evening at Rosedale."

Late in the afternoon, a dark, opulent automobile from Camden stopped in front of her house. A Negro chauffeur in bottle-green livery got down and opened the door for two ladies who stepped daintily forth and minced up the walk between the tumbled spreads of rotting, brown leaves. The ladies were tall and so elegantly slender that their white heads, topped by large velvet hats, seemed to sway perilously like large roses on too-fine stems. Their gait was precise, infinitely lady-like. At every step, long satin slippers gleamed from beneath heavy black silk skirts. They came on and mounted Mrs. Durville's worn doorsteps.

We had been watching from the window, and now mamma exclaimed excitedly, "Is she at home?" and half-turned, ready to call her from Mrs. Adcraft's rooms. Then we heard the side door open, and saw her running across the back lawn and into the rear veranda of her house. In a minute, her front door opened, and there came a series of small, soft cries. One of the ladies said, "My deah Annie Laurie!" in a tone of mingled commiseration and reproach and wrapped her velvet arms about Mrs. Durville's tight red sweater. The door closed on them.

Mamma and I left the window and sat by the fire. A feeling of excitement, of something happening, stirred us. After all, Mrs. Durville had been Annie Laurie Bourne, her father had been governor, and she had danced with members of foreign legations in Washington. A faint, nostalgic glamor touched us with long feathery fingers. Mamma gazed at me with wide, bright eyes. "Well, what do you reckon now! They look like nice people sure enough!" It seemed a long time before the two ladies emerged from Mrs. Durville's house and drove off in their vast automobile and a longer time yet before we heard her running across the lawn to our house.

Mamma and I rushed back to the window, she saw us and waved with triumph. "What do you think, my darlings?" she cried. She was panting, skipping up the doorsteps, her wrinkled face flushed to the glad look of a child. "What do you think? . . . Margaret and Elener Stillson are having a tea for Senator Deacon's wife, their sister, you know. . . . They're sending the car over for me—Friday afternoon, and I'm in the receiving line!"

"Senator Deacon!" We stared at each other with awe-shining eyes that took no account of the Senator's trashy origin. We said, "The Stillson Sisters!" forgetting how one of them had sold her grandfather for money. We heard Mrs. Durville in the Adcraft rooms, clattering away in a high, merry voice.

It was like a fairy story. I wondered if she'd have to run away when the clock struck for midnight. Only, I reminded myself, it wouldn't strike twelve, this was a tea, an afternoon tea with a receiving line and a rich senator for the prince, and anyway, Mrs. Durville was terribly old and already married. All that week we went about smiling a little. We said, "Mrs. Durville's tea party," and when Lillian Horne loaned a gray lace evening gown to her we exclaimed, "Just the thing, just right to wear in the receiving line!" Lawrance sent her a pink rose to wear on one shoulder, and Mrs. Adcraft went with her to the beauty parlor to have her hair waved. It wouldn't be Annie Laurie Bourne, but even the senator, we thought, would know that it had been a Bourne.

Then, it was time, the tea was this afternoon. She came over to our house to let us see how she looked dressed up. We had risen when she came in, and we stood around saying, "You look perfectly beautiful, perfectly lovely!" For some reason, we felt queerly helpless. We gazed at a streak of gold in among her grayish, over-waved hair. Lawrance's face was a still, grinning mask. He leaned against the wall with his hands in his pockets, and said, "Have a good time for me, darling!" The tone was half-cruel, the poet in him deriding some lack in her and in the occasion. She got frightened all of a sudden, the smile wavering on her rouged mouth, and whirled around and through the door like an old, little girl running from a menace of ecstasy.

After she was gone, I kept seeing how she had walked down to the Stillson sisters' waiting automobile, how proudly and with what a flourish she had turned to wave to us when the chauffeur opened the door for her. Mamma said, "She's there by now, Camden's only ten miles off." Hateful words came on my tongue and stopped there, and in a second I was glad I hadn't spoken. Mamma was there in front of me, bent over, staring at me, seeing past me. She tried to get up and fell back into her chair. Rapidly, the breath whistling through her words, she told me, "I knew it'd be too soon . . . your father . . . go call . . . !" I thought I would break in two with fear, but I ran out into the back yard where papa was chopping wood and told him. When he went into the house, I knew suddenly that he and Mamma and everybody but me had forgotten Mrs. Durville's tea party.

Late in the afternoon, I went over to her house and sat on the front porch, rocking in her chair and trying to imagine the party at the Stillson sisters'. I saw her rouged, over-powdered face talking and talking, the long jaws working like scissors. Now she was lifting her hands, gesturing with aristocratic affectation, and now again she was talking to Senator Deacon. She said, "Oh, Senator, and you really think so?" and "My deah Senator, not really?" And all the time she was wishing that Mr. Durville and the Senator's wife were dead so that she could marry the Senator and go to live in Washington where everybody drove around in fine cars and talked Yankee talk and never had to work at all. I could hear her telling the President, "Oh, how like this is to my deah girlhood . . . except, of course, my deah, for the vulgar brogue!"

Behind Lillian Horne's house the sun was setting, throwing great red and orange and purple rhomboids over the eggshell curve of the sky. Something dark and chill moved over the world, stirring the dried brown leaves on the ground. The Stillson sisters' car purred to a slow stop in the street, and Mrs. Durville got out. She came rapidly up the walk, frowning angrily at the stone flags under her feet. Behind her, the car purred luxuriously, going away from her house.

She frowned more sharply, with a look almost of rage, when she saw me. "What are you doing here?" she demanded, and then, remembering, gave a witchlike glance toward my house where the doctor's car sat in the drive.

I got up and stood looking at her. "Mamma's sick," I said, and followed her into the parlor. She switched on the light and told me to sit down; then she went into the next room, closing the door behind her. In a second, I heard the screech of the kitchen door opening and shutting. She had gone out, over to Adcraft's. I got up suddenly, with a dim fear on me, as if some part of me remembered something that the other part could not identify. And then I knew that I was foolish, she could not harm the baby my mother was having.

I waited a long time on the piano stool, staring up at portraits of dead Bournes and Durvilles and down at the faded patterns in the rug, and finally old man Durville came home. He had a greasy paper bag in one hand and a loaf of bread in the other. We went through the hall and back to the kitchen where he sat on the table and began slicing the bread. He smiled at me when I lit the oil stove and toasted a weiner over the blue flame. "We could fry them, you know," he said gently, and washed the breakfast egg from a frying pan. Then he stared at me while I turned the weiners, pressing them against the bottom of the pan to make a sizzling noise in the hot grease. He said, "This is fun, isn't it?" in his even, colorless voice, and smiled slowly. His brown eyes were tired and kind.

He said, "I suppose she's over at Adcraft's." I knew he was talking to himself, but I told him, "She went out the back door, I heard her, she was mad." He said, "Did she leave you here all by yourself, honey?" He took me on his knee and laughed a little, uneasily. "Now you're my little girl," he said.

She came in suddenly. She was still wearing Lillian Horne's evening gown with her own sweater flung over her shoulders. She looked at me first. "You've a little sister, don't you want to go home?" I shook my head, frightened and staring, something in me shouting shrilly, "Is she like you, is she you?" She was gazing at old man Durville with her face squeezed up in its anger.

He said in an oddly low voice, "Sis has been cooking supper for me."

He flinched when she laughed out, stridently and cruelly, striking him with the hard notes of all her envy, garnered and refurbished this afternoon under the Stillson sisters' magnificence. I don't know how I got to my feet, off his lap, but I was standing up, watching them and waiting for an awfulness to come out. Her blue eyes glittered with an abrupt, wild hatred. "If you think I'll drudge for you, James Durville!" she burst out shrilly. She stopped, tears dimming her rage. "I was young and pretty . . . if you think I'll drudge all my days!" she cried brokenly.

The room was suddenly quiet with old man Durville sitting help-lessly by the table with the greasy paper bag in front of him and her weeping with hatred and horror in her eyes. A dark chasm yawned inside of me, turning me sick with a clawing fear of birth, of being alive, of living. A gray terror grew on the room, flags dipped some-where to say that there was no comfort, no remuneration, nothing but old veins running the same poison to a further infliction of wounds. She was moving, her shoulders jerked backward and for-ward, and she was crying in a high, thin voice, like laughter and like screaming, "Niggers on white carpets, James Durville, niggers on white carpets . . . !"

Running across the dark lawn, I heard my new little sister wailing weakly against that sound.

Martin's car stopped in the drive behind the wagon. He got out and came up to the window, and stood there with one hand touching the quilt covering of the topmost portrait, and said to me, "What is it, do we call this 'atmosphere,' or what?"

I looked at him with an empty face. I said, "Look what she sent, she sent all these things. . . . Annie Laurie Bourne. . . ."

His eyelids flickered and something, a shadow, slid over his cheeks before he stopped smiling. He kept his eyes full on me.

"She died this morning. I heard just as I left town."

Maybe I was glad for a minute. The chair I sat in and the desk were real, nothing else was. I pushed at the note, trying to get it out of the way. "She sent them to me—all there were, bishops and king's favorites." It came out of me, flat and senseless. "She sent it all to me. . . ."

Martin turned his head away. "Not to you," he said. "But to Rosedale."

White Girl, Fine Girl

Shirley Ann Grau

T HERE are these two places—Stanhope and Kilby—and there are seven miles between. These are the only two towns that state records list in Clayton County. One of them is the state capital and the liveliest little place in the South: the pine ridges around town, the back yards of outlying houses, hold dozens of stills. And from them come the best corn likker in the state: smooth and the color of good Scotch. The legislators always manage to take a few gallons home with them. (After a man's got used to the doings of the capital, there's nothing so tedious as months spent at his home way out in the counties somewhere.) And for the three months when the two houses or the state supreme court are in session, the price of the likker always rises until it is beyond the reach of the colored people. The wise ones, of course, have laid by a supply, if they have had the money to do that; and those who haven't must sweat out the time sober. The police have learned to be vigilant during this time: extra squad cars circle around the colored part of town, which on these nights hums with a restless aimless anger. The state police come in, too, and their white-painted new shiny cars move up and down the streets. There are more fights this time of year than any other. More knifings. The price of burial insurance goes up. And the warden's desk at Kilby is full of yellow tissue-paper triplicate records of new prisoners.

That's what Kilby—the other place in Clayton—is, the big colored prison. It's a town: just three or four buildings for a grocery; and a railroad platform with the name KILBY painted in white letters on a green board and hung from the edge of the roof, right over the room that has a smaller sign: Post Office; and a few houses around, the biggest one with the yellow clapboard walls and the green shutters for the warden's wife, and the smaller ones painted all yellow for the guards' wives. (The men rarely come down to these houses; they spend most of their time inside the walls; it is as if they have a sentence to serve.) There are other houses for the colored washwomen and the cleaning women and their men and their children. This is the town of Kilby; this is what the county records show. But the real Kilby is half a mile north: the white brick walls and the machine-gun turrets, two on each side, and the men inside: the white guards and the colored prisoners.

You can't see Kilby from any point inside the limits of Stanhope, though if you stood on the capitol steps, on the spot where Jeff Davis took his first oath, you'd be staring in the right direction, and if your eyes were sharp enough, you'd see. But you don't.

But you can see the town from Kilby. On clear days in broad daylight the smoke from the mills comes up plain and still and fans out like a branch in the sky. And the white guards prop their rifles between their knees and the parapet wall and lean on their elbows and watch. And the colored trusties dangle their billies between limp fingers and fold their arms and watch the branch bloom out in the sky.

At night you can see even plainer. During the war, when the mills worked full time on army contracts for tents and sheets and bandages, you could see the smoke come up red against the black sky. After the war, when the mills closed down at night, you could still see a glow— a different one—over where the town was. The lights from the cafés and the clubs: sometimes low under clouds before a storm, sometimes rising straight up, soft like cotton into a clear black sky, sometimes a yellow and small circle under the moonlight. Just lights, from seven miles away over blue pines and fallow patches and little streams that have water in them only during the spring rains; and whole hillsides of hackberries with thorns thick as a rooster's spur; and one river, slow, yellow, and without a bottom; and red dust that any wind— summer or winter—is going to lift and send sliding off down the air. And there is always a wind and the dust moving.

It was a flat hot sun in a powdery white sky when Jayson Paul Evans walked out of Kilby prison. He leaned against the white brick wall and hitched up his belt.

The guard behind him at the gate said: "Waiting for a car to come along and pick you up?"

Jayson moved his mouth in slow chewing circles: "Don't reckon I expect none."

From the top wall another guard called: "Get started there." He was directly overhead looking down.

Jayson stood clear of the wall and bent his head back to see. In the light his wide black eyes turned shiny like the sun.

"Sweet Jesus," the man at the gate said. "Ain't you ever gonna get out of here?"

Jayson stopped looking at the guard directly above him. "I reckon I will," he said to the man behind him. "I reckon I will now."

There was a strip of asphalt to the town, black asphalt with a white painted line down the center. A carefully painted line. He had done some of the work himself a couple of days earlier. That was how he'd cut down his twenty years for manslaughter, working it out in the road gangs.

He did not see a single white person in the town of Kilby; only the colored washwomen hanging out clothes on fences and bushes. The white wives would be inside. He thought of them briefly: in their slips, lying on beds, with shades drawn, fanning themselves slowly, waiting for the evening to come.

Beyond Kilby on the main highway he turned south, the sun beating hot against his left cheek and his eyes beginning to water from the dust. After he had walked nearly a mile, after the white walls were out of sight, he left the road, cutting across the fields, walking in a straight line for Stanhope. These were old fields; the plowed ground had hardened with rain and frost and sun until it was solid as boards, only a little uneven. And it was easy walking.

"I got no cause to hurry," Jayson told a dusty black crow that scratched on the bare red earth. "No cause to hurry." The crow looked at him sideways out of a light yellow eye and hopped into the protection of the barberry bushes.

Jayson laughed and pulled off his shirt. "Scared of me?" He hooked the shirt through his belt and went off at a jogging trot, his heels striking hard against the ground: a big man making long steps. The dust that came up white from the red ground settled on his skin, and sweat ran crisscross lines in it.

There were trees along the low places away to the right; he could have skirted through them. They were pines: no underbrush to make rough going, just a soft floor of needles and a clean smell when his feet crushed them.

He stood and looked at the trees, and wet his lips with his tongue and spit out the dirt taste. But he kept going, the quickest way, right across the old fields that had been plowed wrong first years ago and that nobody would bother with now and that each year got drier and darker and more washed into gullies and more full of powder, so that each time the wind blew across them, summer or winter, their dust would come swinging up on it. Jayson went on, stumbling a little on the sharpest gullies, swinging his arms wide for balance, and singing for company:

"The sun is real hot,
Oh Lord. The sun is real hot
And the wind is hot
And the dust is rolling around,
Oh Lord, Oh Lord, Oh Lord."

The old plowed bare ground went down across two hills like a ribbon trailing and ended on a line of staggering fence posts and dragging wire. Jayson kicked at one post; it crumbled without sound: the center had dried away. Jayson wiped one hand across his bare chest, leaving a black streak in the red-white dust. Then he began to push his way through the bushes. They were elderberry mostly, green and yielding. When his fingers touched the soft round stalks, they bent aside smoothly. From a single laurel he pulled a broad leaf and chewed it slowly, bit by bit, until he had eaten it up the stem.

He was going downhill now. He had to work his way along sideways to keep from falling. The rocks—granite most of them, with sparks of fire in the light—rolled under his feet and he had to hold to the elder stems, pale and smooth. For just a moment he stopped and looked at one and rubbed his thumb up and down its length, from the ground up to as high as he could reach.

The thicket ended as a sharp gully, in its bottom during the summer months just a thin trickle of water, so narrow he could almost straddle its breadth. Jayson scrambled down one of the sharp deep crevices of the side and put his fingers in the water. Then he knelt down and carefully reached in his arm, feeling for bottom; he stretched out his fingers and touched nothing. He drew back his arm and wiped fingers across his lips to taste the water. It was warm from the sun and strong with leaf taste. But he was thirsty and he drank from his cupped hands.

A train whistled to his right. He lifted his head and listened, cocking just a bit to guess the distance. Then he moved off in that direction, following along the bottom of the gully. The tracks, he remembered, were on the far side of the Scantos River, and the whistle had been close, not more than a mile. He had to walk much farther in the twisted gully—two, maybe three miles; but it was easier going than across the fields or the thickets. (You never could tell when you would have to walk miles around a batch of hackberries all tangled together.)

He was beginning to be hungry by the time he reached the river— the broad yellow river moving slowly under the afternoon sun, moving so slowly that you could swear it was solid like ground; moving slowly because it had no bottom.

Jayson tossed a stone out as far as he could, almost to the other bank. "Sweet Jesus," he said, "I reckon you can just rest quiet, you old hungry man inside me. There ain't nothing I can do."

He followed the river south, looking for a way across, looking for a sandbar or a skiff. On the other bank a train went past, a diesel, shining silver in the sun, going all the way to New Orleans.

The heat of the day was beginning to make him sleepy so that he did not see the boys until he could bend over and touch them: squatting on the sands, peeling willows for fishing poles. They turned heads up to him, mouths open with surprise, eyes popping.

"Why," he told them, "if it ain't two nice little boys; two nice little boys my color."

They got to their feet very slowly and began to back away, feeling carefully behind them for each step. The bigger one, light-brown colored, had a hunting knife at his belt. His fingers unsnapped the guard and took hold of the handle.

Jayson laughed. "That a mighty big knife you got there, boy."

The boy held the leather sheath in his left hand; the right loosened the blade.

"You acting like a real man there," Jayson told him. The little one, who had been standing next to him, had disappeared. There wasn't even a sound when he slipped away. "You might could be thinking that you a man."

The knife was out now. The boy held it crosswise in front of him.

"I can see you ain't so foolish to go throwing that thing." Jayson said. He bent down and picked up a brown paper bundle with the grease markings that food leaves. He smelled it briefly. His eyes did not move from the boy, who was on tiptoe now, swaying back and forth, balancing himself for a fight: afraid, but holding his knife steady. And when his lower lip began to tremble, he took it firmly in his teeth.

"I reckon you think you a man," Jayson said. Out of the corner of his eye he had seen the skiff, pulled up on the river sand. He backed toward it, tossing the food package inside, and began pushing it out. Once he stumbled on the uneven bottom, but recovered his balance without taking his eyes from the boy.

The boy shifted his grip on the knife; he held it lightly with two fingers on the blade.

"Ain't no knife gonna stop me," Jayson said, "and I come back and kill you with it."

The muddy yellow water reached his knees. He climbed into the boat and picked up the long pole. He gave two hard shoves and the pole no longer touched solid ground. Then Jayson stood in the boat, the pole held crosswise in his two hands, and looked down at the river and waited until he could drift across the bottomless part and could use the pole again.

On the other side, he left the skiff on the sands and, holding the package of food in his left hand, scrambled up the bluff: the going would be easier along the bed of the railroad. At the top he turned and looked across the yellow river. On the other side the boy had not moved; he was still standing there, the knife ready. And the second boy, the little one, like a black monkey slid down the trunk of the bay tree where he had climbed to be out the way.

Jayson Paul saw the tall twin chimneys of the cotton mill that was on the outskirts of town. "Right over that little bunch of pines." His shoes, which he had tied together by the laces, he swung in circles around his finger. "Right over yonder." He sat down on the ground and crossed his feet under him. A big yellow and black spider dangled from a honeysuckle bush, sliding up and down on its web. Carefully, with one finger, Jayson Paul shifted the thread to another branch. "That ought to mix you up some, Mr. Spider," he said. Then he stretched himself out full along the ground and sang into the heat of the late evening.

"I been in the pen so long,
  Yes, I been in the pen so long,
  I been in the pen so long, baby,
  Baby, that where I been so long."

He drew his knees up close to his chin and wrapped long arms around them.

"I been in the pen so long, baby,
  Too long, baby,
  I gonna stop lying alone, baby,
  Baby, I been away so long."

For a while after he stopped singing he lay there, his eyes closed, thinking how it would be.

Jayson Paul leaned against the tarred black wood of a lamppost

and began to put on his shoes. Smoke from the trash incinerator of
the mill made him shake his head and sneeze.

"Sweet Jesus," he said, "I done forgot how to breathe."

The mills had closed down for the day. There was no one on the
streets; they would be inside eating now. Over the burning the smell
of frying was heavy on the beginning night.

"I be mighty glad to get home," he told himself. "For sure. It be
real fine.

I'm working my way back home,
Oh Baby,
Working my way back home,
Oh Baby
Working my way back home."

He recognized the neighborhood: it hadn't changed. First the scattered houses with stretches of bumpy weedy places between them
and a few cart horses and a cow or two pulling the tops off the longest
grasses. Then houses closer and closer together until at last there was
no space or grass between them, just dirt alleys and dirt streets and
dogs licking the dirt off their paws on front porches and dust lying
over everything; a church, brown-painted with a crooked steeple:
they had had a still in the basement once; he wondered if there was
any there now—he would have to find out. (Once he could have told
you exactly where every batch of brew could be found. It would take
time to learn all the new spots again.)

The street lights went on. He looked up at them, strung out yellow
against a sky that wasn't dark yet. Jayson remembered them looking
that way. He hadn't forgotten anything.

Over to the left was the Pair-a-Dice Bar with its green-painted door
and on each side the full-length posters of white girls drinking Jax
beer. He pushed open the door and went in. There was only one light
burning, a small one without a shade over the bar. The first table was
so near the bar he stumbled into it and stood for a minute blinking.
He saw that they had added more tables but that nothing much had
changed. Behind the bar, the cracked mirror framed in scrolled black
wood; the pin-up pictures stuck into the frame and pasted on the
glass; the three peacock feathers—red and blue and black—dangling
by a cord from the ceiling and turning around and around in each
draft—he had seen all this before.

The man behind the counter leaning on his elbows reading the funny page of last Sunday's paper was coffee-colored and young— too young for Jayson to remember him. And his eyes when he looked up at Jayson were the same color as his skin.

"Man," Jayson told him, "I come looking for somebody."

The light eyes blinked twice. "Who for?"

Jayson pulled out a chair and sat down, backwards so that he could lean his folded arms on the back. "I come looking for somebody but I ain't got no idea where she living at."

"That right?" The young man bent his head toward the funny paper again.

"I ain't seen her in quite a while and now I got to find her."

The years in prison had made him careless. He hadn't noticed Joe standing across the room. Joe, with the red and green baseball cap and the light kinky brown hair that stood up straight in front, almost as high as the snapped-up visor; a short man but very heavy and with the curved baling hook of a warehouseman stuck in his belt. Jayson stood up so quickly that the chair caught against his leg and fell over.

"Hey," the light-colored young man said and lifted his funny paper straight up. "What you doing?"

"I done thought I was seeing wrong but I reckon I ain't," Joe said.

"How you?" Jayson told him quietly. He didn't have a knife or a razor, so he kept his hand on the back of the nearest chair and he bent his knee against the edge of the table, ready to send it over.

"Hey," the young man said, and rubbed his light hairless chin with a quick nervous hand. "What you all doing?"

"You was looking for Aggie." Joe leaned back against the wall, his fingers rubbing the wood cross handle of the hook.

"I might could be doing that." Jayson hunched his back and waited.

"You ain't gonna do no fighting in here," the young man said, and pulled at his fingernails. "You ain't gonna do nothing like that."

Joe turned and looked at him and laughed. "No," he said. "We ain't gonna do nothing like that. Iffen he wants to find Aggie, I reckon I ain't gonna stand in his way."

"You ain't used to talk like that," Jayson said softly.

Joe kept on laughing. "Man, I ain't got no more interest in Aggie. I done had it and finished there."

Jayson stood watching him until he stopped laughing.

Joe said: "I reckon I gonna buy us a couple of beers." He sat down and Jayson took a chair about ten feet away. "Ain't got no cause to be scared of me," Joe said, and rubbed his round black face with his hands. "Ain't carrying no meanness for you for the time you like to kill me."

The young man pulled two bottles out of the rattling ice and brought them over, still dripping, and stuck out his thin yellow hand until Joe paid him.

"Why, Jay, man." Joe turned his head around and pulled off his baseball cap; the base of his skull was crossed by thick white scars. "You like to kill me right. Like you did to Mannie."

"Yes," said Jayson. "I done thought about that time." *He couldn't remember it though. Not very clearly. He had been fighting, but he couldn't swear who he was fighting with. He had killed Mannie and he didn't remember it. Nights in Kilby he had tried to call it back and couldn't. All he could remember was fighting and his mouth open and dry and the taste of dust in it.*

"I done thought about it," he said.

Joe tipped back his head and put the bottle to his lips. When he put it down again, he shook his head and rubbed his hand across his mouth. "I used to could take off a whole bottle one gulp that way."

"I remember," Jayson said. *And he did remember that. His mind was full of pictures of Joe emptying a bottle at one gulp. In some of them there'd be a girl in his lap or hanging around his shoulders. He remembered the feel of their skins, soft and moist.*

"I remember," Jayson said.

"A whole bottle," Joe said. "I used to could do."

"I remember," Jayson said. *He remembered: the stuff they'd made. The best corn likker there was: smooth and sweet on the tongue. They could make their own price for it and find buyers any time.*

It was Mannie who found buyers in the white people from the houses on Capitol Hill, the most important people, who had money and a taste for good corn. Mannie had sold to all of them. That's what he did best— sell. With his broad black face that was always shiny with perspiration even in winter, he had a way with white people; they were always glad to buy from him. He was chauffeur to Senator Winkerston's family, but his money did not come from that job. He only used their car to deliver the likker. It was a plan the police never would have caught on to.

"Never in a million years," Jayson said aloud. They had to go ruin it themselves, the three of them. And because of Aggie.

Mannie spent most of his time up at the Winkerston house. He had a room over the garage. Mrs. Winkerston had had it specially painted for him because he was such a splendid driver. He spent most of his time up there (when he was not actually driving the car or washing it) stretched out on his bed, wearing the silk pajamas he always bought with his share of the likker money.

Jayson had never seen the room, but he had seen the pajamas when they had just come and were still in the box that had the name in fancy Old English letters of the store in New Orleans. And when he saw them he wished for a moment that he had some, too, but just for a moment, because he was wishing for other things.

Mannie had a wife, whom he married in church on Easter Sunday—a tall light-brown woman whose name was Aggie. She lived in the colored section of town because at the Winkerstons' with Mannie there was no room for her and their son.

Jayson remembered: a tall woman, light-colored, a thin face, pinched almost; darkness under the cheekbones; and long eyes set wide apart. A thin woman with full nursing breasts. He saw her sitting on the steps of the house in the colored section that Mannie rented and hardly ever lived in. Mannie preferred his room over the garage with the white family. He knew where his wife was; he could find her when he needed her. When he did, he would take one of the Senator's cars and drive down (the family had no objections to his keeping the car overnight), certain that he would know where to find her. And one time he found Jayson, too.

He was surprised. Even Jayson saw that. His round black face (the smiling affable face that the white people liked) was completely blank with surprise. And he staggered a little bit; he had had a few drinks coming down, the best of the stuff they made.

"I remember," Jayson said. But he did not remember exactly what happened after he looked up and saw Mannie. He had fought and there had been the blood taste in his mouth and there had been the screaming from Aggie somewhere: he heard it far off. His head was swinging from the whisky and the excitement of the fight. And when Mannie's razor slashed along the side of his neck, he felt the blood run but no pain. There wasn't anything but breath coming short and not air enough and dust taste and smell. And from the corner of his eyes he saw the icepick on the table and grabbed for it.

He remembered: after he had finished with Mannie and was straightening up for breath there had been a short jab along his ribs. He had spun aside and brought down a bottle on Joe's neck (Joe, who was Mannie's friend and the third partner, who had driven over with him and stayed out in the car to keep an eye on the stuff they had in the back seat).

Joe held the bottle up to the light. "Used to could take off a whole bottle that way once. Used to once."

"I remember," Jayson said.

"Can't no more. Getting old, maybe. All us getting old."

"Maybe," Jayson said.

"Now you come back looking for Aggie."

"That right." Jayson said.

"She ain't gonna have nothing to do with you."

Jayson grinned. "Just tell me where she at."

Joe shook his head. "She ain't gonna have nothing to do with you." He looked up quickly as Jayson shifted in his chair. "Don't be getting riled up, man. I just telling you what going on."

Jayson put both hands on his knees and bent forward. "What going on?"

"Drink you beer, man."

"What going on?" Jayson said slowly. "You tell me what going on."

"That what I trying to do." Joe sighed and reached for Jayson's bottle. "Iffen you can let me."

"Go head," Jayson said.

"Aggie ain't having nothing to do with no men."

"Go head." Jayson said, staring at him. He ran his tongue briefly over his lips; they tasted dry and dusty.

"She ain't had no luck with them, the three or four. They just give her kids and no money.

"She got three—all of them girls. The boy, the one that was Mannie's, the one that got baptized in the church, he went and drunk some lye water that his ma was washing in and died. The biggest girl, she yours all right. Looks like you.

"And Aggie got plain mad. So she ain't having nothing to do with no men. She don't let anybody come in her house no more. And she got the kids so they don't let their daddies walk down the street. They got to go round the next block or the kids throw rocks at them. And they big enough to hurt." He grinned and poked one finger down the neck of the beer bottle. "You ought to seen what they done to me, walking past. Just walking past. Just coming here, not an hour ago past. Not noticing Aggie. Not even studying on her. Just walking past."

The street was narrow and without sidewalks. On the north side a brick wall began at the edge of the gravel; the late evening sun struck color off the broken glass on the top. Behind the wall and out of sight were the low brick buildings and the vegetable gardens of the white poorhouse. On the south side of the street ran another wall—of houses, mustard color; in front of each, four wooden steps. A solid wall: wood house, alley gate, wood house, and so on for the entire block. Aggie lived in the second one from the corner with her three girls, who were all half sisters.

Evenings it rains in Stanhope. Not hard. Not hard enough to make it any cooler; not hard enough to settle the dust really. The drops mostly stay as they fall and roll around the top layer of dirt in round blobs until they dry away. Althea, who was the second girl and was eleven, walked up and down in the street, breaking the heavy drops with her bare toe. Anna, who was five, sat cross-legged on the top step, the broadest one, the one with the pile of brick fragments. Alice Mary, who was the oldest and Jayson's child, was sitting on the bottom step. She was thirteen, big for her age, with the beginnings of a heavy woman's body. She sat with her head bent into her hands, dozing in the heat of the late evening.

Althea skipped back in from the street with her quick skip and jammed sharp little fingers into Alice Mary's side. "There he come," she said.

The sun was still so bright: Alice Mary blinked and rubbed her eyes. The piece of brick she had fell into her lap. "Who coming?"

"My Daddy Joe." Althea picked up the brick and juggled it in her hand. "I reckon I could hit him way off where he at." She was big for eleven, with the broad shoulders and back of an older boy.

"There he come," little Anna said. "There come Althea's Daddy Joe."

Alice Mary leaned back against the wood steps. "I sure see him now. Come right slam down the middle of the street."

"I can hit him now for sure." Althea did not stand up, but her right hand snapped forward and the piece of brick hit the man squarely in the stomach.

He gave a quick growl of pain and cupped his hands over the sore spot. The three girls laughed.

"Sweet Jesus"—he rubbed his square chin with one hand—"iffen I ever get my hands on you."

Althea stood up, another rock in her hand, and shouted: "Go off, Daddy Joe. You can't walk down our street. You can't walk by our house."

The three girls called: "Go off, Daddy Joe. Go off, Daddy Joe. Go off, Daddy Joe." Then they stood up and, fast as they could, threw the rocks at him. He dodged around the corner at a scuttling run.

Alice Mary stuck her head in the front door and told her mother: "Daddy Joe was coming down the street."

"I reckon I know," Aggie said. She was lying on the bed in the first room, in her slip to be cooler. She worked as a cook in one of the big houses on Madison Street and when she got home she always lay down for a while before she looked for supper. "I reckon I heard all the racket."

While Joe stood around the corner watching them, Alice Mary helped Althea and Anna find other pieces of brick. They always kept a pile on the front top step.

Joe rubbed his hands over his face and stared at Jayson. "That plain what happened."

Jayson grinned and did not answer.

"That it, all right."

"Let kids chase you," Jayson said.

Joe chewed his underlip. "It ain't worth getting you face bashed none. Just to walk down a street."

"I reckon I best visit her for a spell," Jayson said.

"They ain't gonna let you near the house."

Jayson was still grinning when he stood up.

Joe pointed one finger at the Jax beer poster: a girl, a white girl with red hair and green eyes and a mouth open and waiting. "You ought to go looking for one like that."

Jayson hooked thumbs in his belt and studied the poster. "Hell, man," he said. "Where I gonna find something like that?"

Joe grinned.

"You ain't knowing where."

"Sure," said Joe. "I reckon I know where there one looks like that."

"Jesus," Jayson chewed his lower lip. "Why ain't you got her?"

Joe grinned and made crisscross lines on the wet table oilcloth. He was embarrassed. "She won't have nothing to do with me. She says she don't go for nobody little."

"She ain't white."

"Plain near almost," Joe said.

"She ain't like that." Jayson was staring at the poster.

"I done said she is. Hair and all. You plain got to go take a look."

"Where I got to look?"

Joe grinned. "Iffen you went walking through the houses back of Lansford Mill, she come walking up to you."

Sweat tickled down the side of Jayson's neck and he rubbed at it with the back of his hand. "You reckon she would?"

"Iffen she took a liking to you. You wouldn't even need no money."

"You reckon she would?"

"Hell, man," Joe said. "She there almost like she waiting for you."

Jayson swung his leg in wide circles. "I reckon I better see Aggie first."

Joe rubbed his chin and pulled at a stray hair on his cheek. "She's a lot better-looking than Aggie."

"Maybe," Jayson grinned. On the upper left-hand side of his mouth most of the teeth were missing. "But I reckon I will all the same."

"I plain don't study you."

"Man," Jayson said. "I go to Kilby account of Aggie and I sure gonna want her now I out."

"Now you out," Joe said. "What you planning for money?"

"Don't figure trouble getting none, long as people still drinking."

Joe rubbed his hands and grinned. "Like it used to be. Before the fight where Mannie got killed."

"Maybe," Jayson said. "But I got something else I want now."

Joe shook his head and rubbed his teeth with his knuckles. "Aggie ain't young no more."

"Don't reckon I am neither."

"Hell, man," Joe said. "There ain't no use fussing with a woman when she get old."

Jayson grinned. "She was a mighty lot of woman, I remember."

"Okay," Joe said, and tipped back his chair. "You go head. But I'm telling you. She got religion now. She ain't gonna have nothing to do with you."

"Ain't no woman not going to have nothing to do with me," Jayson said. "Now where she living at?"

Over in the direction of the river the chimney sweeps were swinging wide across a sky that was filling with faint summer-night haze. The night wind was beginning to stir the first top dust of the streets.

Inside the mustard-colored wood house Aggie had got up and was beginning to fix supper. The kitchen was two rooms away from the front steps but the noises carried plainly: the banging of pots and the singing, a hymn:

"King Jesus lit the candle by the waterside
To see the little children when they truly baptized.
Honor, honor
Unto the dying Lamb."

In the house where she worked on Madison Street she was very quiet; here she listened to the sounds of pots with pleasure. On Madison Street she was an elaborate cook (to the joy of her employers); here she boiled potatoes and tossed a chunk of bacon in a frying-pan. Then she wiped her face with her hands and went back into the front room to lie down again on the bed with the week-old copy of *Life* she had brought from the house on Madison Street.

Outside, Anna had gone back to sleep, her head pillowed on the step above. Althea was building a little arch of the pieces of rock; whenever it reached a certain height Alice Mary would laugh and poke it with her finger.

The arch of rocks collapsed. "You plain got to stop that," Althea said.

"Why I got to stop?" Alice Mary said "Why I got to stop?"

"You plain got to stop."

"You build it up," Alice Mary said, "and I knock it down." She reached out, but her hand stayed in mid-air. She had seen Jayson coming toward them, coming down the middle of the street, the wood walls of houses on one side and on the other the brick wall with the pieces of glass on top shining faintly under the street lamp.

Jayson stopped in the round circle of light and stood looking at them, his fingers hooked in his belt.

"What you looking for?" Alice Mary called. She had her head turned sideways and she was frowning.

"I come looking for somebody called Aggie," Jayson said.

Anna woke up and reached for the nearest little rock.

"Nobody here called that," Alice Mary said.

Althea tossed a rock from one hand to the other.

Jayson stood still in the circle of light, without moving, and grinning.

"Why you want to find her?" Alice Mary's voice hesitated slightly.

Jayson stretched out one arm to the lamppost and leaned against it. "You got no cause to ask," he said. "You got no cause to ask."

From the lowest step Anna stood up. "Iffen you come up on our sidewalk we're gonna bash you."

Jayson laughed. "Ain't no little rock gonna stop me when I pull you head right off you neck."

Anna threw the rock. It struck Jayson's shoulder and bounced into the street, lifting a little cloud of dust.

"Ain't no little rock gonna stop me," Jayson said, and stood clear of the lamppost, hitching up his pants.

"Pitch him one." Anna pulled at the skirt of Alice Mary's dress. "You pitch him one that'll make his head spin."

"Like I did to my Daddy Joe," Althea said.

Alice Mary did not answer. She was staring at him, and her face was puzzled. A thin face, a girl's face twisted into a woman's.

"Come ahead," they said. "Pitch one. Reckon he you daddy. Pitch him one."

He took one step, grinning.

"Reckon I better," she said.

Her aim was good. He ducked as the rock passed his shoulder. But the second one, the one she threw from her left hand, caught squarely on the head. In dodging one, he had walked squarely into the force of the other.

"Sweet God Almighty." He put his hand to his head and then looked at the blood on his fingers. The ground was shifting under his feet like the trick floors at sideshows.

Another rock hit his shoulder. And another the center of his chest; the pain flashed hot through the length of his body. Objects were passing him, missing him and striking into the ground.

Inside his head was the sound of rocks falling. And all around him dust was heavy in the air, so heavy he couldn't see clearly because of it. But then he saw Aggie.

She was calling to the girls through the front window. "Pitch some more," she kept calling. "Pitch some more."

He decided then. He held his arms in front of his face and started walking toward them. Not running. Not hurrying. But walking. The rocks hurt, but as long as they did not hit his head it was not too bad.

Aggie was screaming. He did not look up but he recognized the sound. He had heard it before, the night Mannie was killed. A door slammed somewhere close. He had heard that sound, too, the same night. She had run away then like she'd be doing now. But there was a difference now. And he could not be sure of it.

He could not see where he was going, with his head covered by his arms. He walked straight into the steps, stumbled and sprawled out full-length on them, one of his hands squarely on the pile of rocks. He wondered what had happened to the kids who had been standing there.

He turned his head slowly, looking up. Alice Mary stood on the porch, her hands raised over her head, and in them a whole brick. He jerked his body aside and the brick gouged a piece out of the wood steps.

He remembered she was his kid when he caught her shoulder and pushed her off the porch. She stumbled backwards and sat down and a little cloud of dry dust rose.

He went through the house. Aggie was not there. In the kitchen a pot of potatoes was boiling on the stove. He knocked it to the floor and then rubbed the side of his hand where the pot had burned it. The potatoes were overcooked. They burst on the floor. He stepped into one; it made it hard for him to walk without slipping.

The bacon was burning. The smoke at the bottom of the pan was so thick he could not see the meat. He knocked that pot off, too, and kicked it into a corner.

He walked all the way through the house, back to the kitchen. He opened the door and stood looking out into the back yard. Behind the shed, through a crack of the boards he caught sight of white cloth. Aggie was out there, hiding and watching him as he was watching her.

And suddenly he began to laugh. The white cloth disappeared. He thought of her running away, dodging along in the alleys between the houses; and he laughed still harder. He stood in the doorway and laughed until he had to hold to the door for support.

He turned and walked back to the front of the house, kicking at whatever came in his way. In the room he yanked the mattress off the bed and the effort made him stagger. He would have liked to smash the house to bits, but suddenly he felt too tired. And he was very hot. He felt the perspiration run down his face and drop with a pulling tickle from his chin. The perspiration ran in his eyes, his vision blurred; he could have sworn that the walls swayed inward, ready to fall on him. He lunged for the door and the safety outside.

He stood on the front steps breathing hard, blinking, until he could see again. Then he remembered the hurting and began to rub the spots on his head and body where the rocks had hit him. He noticed his girl still sitting where she had stumbled on the bare ground of the front yard. She was leaning back on her hands, staring at him. "Don't you know you daddy?" he asked her. It was too dark to see much of her face, but her mouth was open and she was staring up at him. He held on to the porch rail and laughed at her. He let his body swing back and forth as he laughed.

There was a song going through his head. And because he knew Aggie would be close enough to hear, he sang it aloud:

> "*Head is like a coffee pot,*
> *Nose is like a spout,*
> *Mouth is like an old fireplace*
> *With the ashes all raked out.*
> *Oh Aggie, po gal,*
> *Oh Aggie, po gal,*
> *Oh Aggie.*"

The railing was rotten and cracked under his weight. He went down the steps with the tune of the song in his ears.

He stood in the street under the lamp and rubbed his head with both hands; there was a kind of buzzing in it. He could have sworn that the mill was working, but it was all in his head. There was blood on his hand too; he wiped it across the front of his shirt.

He turned so that his heel grated against the asphalt street and looked back at the house where Aggie lived. The two little girls were still gone: they would be hiding under the house. His kid was standing up now, on the steps, her foot raised in mid-air as if she were about to come down and was not sure where the next step was, while it was there, right in front of her. She stood watching him, with her foot out stiff and not too steady. He could hear Aggie calling her: "Alice Mary, you come in here. Alice Mary!"

Alice Mary came down one step as if she hadn't heard. Aggie opened the front door a crack and put her arm through, trying to reach her. "You come in here." Just an arm waving up and down in the air, trying to touch something that wasn't in reach.

He saw that and laughed. He said aloud: "Man, you ain't got no call to be laughing," and shook his head. But he only laughed harder and his voice slid off down the lengths of evening air.

He turned and walked down the street, chuckling and singing.

> "Mouth is like an old fireplace
> With the ashes all raked out.
> Oh Aggie, po gal,
> Oh Aggie."

He stumbled a couple of times and caught himself just before falling. Once his knee brushed the ground. "Man, you ain't got no call to be singing," he said aloud. But he only sang louder so that he could hear himself over the buzzing in his head.

Joe called to him: "You, Jayson!" But he did not stop.

Joe came running alongside. "Christ sake, man," Joe shouted at him, "what you yelling for?"

Jayson stopped singing. His mouth was so heavy that he let it hang open.

"Christ sake, man," Joe said, "the police pick you up sure, with you going around acting like that."

Jayson looked at him, and slowly lifted his left hand and pushed up his lower jaw and closed his mouth. His hand stayed on his chin, rubbing it slightly.

"Man," Joe said, "you sure a mess."

Jayson blinked at him, his vision clearing slowly.

"You got blood all over you face."

Jayson rubbed his sleeve across his face and winced at the soreness.

"Come on inside." Joe took his arm and pointed to the Pair-a-Dice Bar. "And get cleaned up some."

"No," Jayson said, and pulled free. "No."

Joe smiled and tugged at his arm again, persuasively. "You just come on in and have a drink, man."

"No," Jayson said, and swayed on his feet.

There was another man standing beside Joe, a younger man, not much past twenty, tall and thin. Jayson's eyes fastened first on the blue and red print of his sport shirt and then lifted to his face. There was something familiar in it and he stared, trying to remember.

"This here is Al," Joe said. "You remember Al."

Jayson crinkled up his lips with the effort.

"He wasn't nothing but a boy," Joe said. "Before. You remember. Nothing but a little boy."

"I remember," Jayson said. A little boy. Tall even then and skinny. Black legs, running, in short trousers, running up and down, fetching and carrying. And two black eyes, shiny as oil in the light, watching. "I remember," Jayson said.

Al stuck out his hand without a word. Jayson stared at it a moment, then took it.

Joe said: "I been telling him how you come back. I been telling him we going in business again. And get the stuff really flowing."

Al said: "That right?" He was wearing a hat, a brown straw with a red flower-printed band. "You gonna do that?"

Jayson did not answer. He turned away from them. He let his eyes swing in a circle around the street, looking.

"What you looking for?" Joe asked.

Jayson did not answer. He took a deep breath and began to move off. Joe and Al walked with him.

"Where you going?" Joe asked him again.

"That right," Al said. "Where?"

Jayson did not answer. He kept walking slowly.

Suddenly Joe chuckled. "Jesus," he said. "Ain't we plain stupid?" He chuckled again.

"How we stupid?" Al said quickly and, frowning, hunched his shoulders. "What call you got to say we stupid?"

"Don't get riled up, man." Joe was still grinning. He patted Jayson on the back. "We gonna fix you up, man. We sure gonna."

Jayson shook his head and looked at him.

Joe said to Al: "Go tell Nancy what we got for her. You tell her we got somebody here who used to be the biggest fellow around here and he aiming to be it again. That what you tell her."

Al opened his mouth in a quick smile and went off, almost at a run. Jayson stared at his legs, moving like a boy's had, back and forth, on errands.

"Sure," said Joe, and patted him on the back again. "That what you want."

"What?" said Jayson. "What I want?"

He swung his eyes around until they rested on the posters on either side of the bar door, the Jax posters of white girls drinking beer and smiling; girls with long red hair, and mouths open just a little.

"I done told you I know where to find one like that," Joe said. "I done told you that. And now I got to show you."

"Show me," Jayson said.

"That what I fixing to do, man," Joe said. "That what I plain fixing to do."

Jayson remembered the part of town back of the Lansford Mill. It had been a low stretch, marsh almost. He remembered catching frogs there. It was filled with houses now, the yellow painted barracks that the government had built for workers at the cotton mill when they were doing three shifts a day on army orders. The barracks were mostly empty now; a few almost white people had slipped into one of the buildings so quietly that no one had seen them come: three or four families with over a dozen kids and heavy-bellied pregnant women.

Jayson stopped and rubbed his head in both hands. He could see again, almost clearly. But it seemed like the ground was a long way off. His feet scarcely touched it.

"Where I got to look?" Jayson asked.

"Down there," Joe said. "Second one from the end on this here side."

"Ain't no call for you to come," Jayson said. "I reckon I can find it."

Joe grinned. "She know you coming. Al done run all the way to tell her."

"No call for you to come."

"Okay," Joe said. "I'm leaving." He turned around and noticed for the first time that Alice Mary had followed them. "Jay, man," Joe said, "look what we got here."

Jayson turned and noticed his girl for the first time. "You been following me?" he called. She did not answer. Looking at him, her eyes were wide open, so wide open that they did not seem to have any lids. And they weren't brown anymore; they were two flat round pieces of silver.

He walked over and took hold of her shoulder. He shook her so that her body struck into the hardness of his thigh. She was perfectly limp; even her arms flapped.

"You ma say for you to follow me?"

She shook her head but did not answer. The pressure of his arm was steadily increasing. She kicked at his shins sharply and pulled free; he grabbed at her as she slipped back out of reach. He grabbed for her again and his hand brushed her dress, but she was too quick. She stood just beyond his hand, body bent forward slightly, waiting, ready.

"Why you coming after me now, when I ain't want nothing to do with you?"

He studied her for a while between half-closed lids and then turned away. "You quit following me or I fix you good." He walked away and, glancing over his shoulder, saw that she had not moved. He searched with the toe of his shoe in the weeds by the side of the road until he found a rock: a piece of concrete, white, with round brown pebbles in it. Even in the dark he could have hit her easy when he threw the rock, but he did not want to, suddenly. The piece of concrete hit the ground a little to one side of her. She disappeared.

He looked around for Joe, and he was gone, too. Jayson straightened up and took a deep breath: the air was full of night and damp. He rubbed his hands down his sides. His eyes, dark and shiny as oil, moved down the row of barracks on the left side of the street.

He began to walk along slowly, dragging his feet in the dirt road.

It was completely dark now; over the broken stand of a street light, the evening star was tangled in the electric wires. The night wind caught the top layer of dirt from the road and spun it in slow circles.

He walked until he saw her. She was standing in the doorway of one of the barracks, the second from the end. Like Joe said, she was white or nearly white, and she had red hair, bright red hair. It hung over her shoulders in long perfect waves, like water when the wind passes over it. Red hair like a curtain that would draw down like a shade.

She came down the two steps and walked toward him—slowly, putting one foot in front of the other so that her walk was wavy as her hair. The light from the corner shone on the luminous green shadow of her eyelids. She leaned against the gatepost which was all that was left of the fence the government had built. And she waited for him.

Looking at her he began to grin. The skin on his face felt dry and hard and he could imagine it cracking when his mouth moved as wide, bright, he began to grin. "You waiting on me?"

"I might could be," she said.

Christmas

Harper Lee

YOU can just take that back, boy!"

This order, given by me to Cecil Jacobs, was the beginning of a rather thin time for Jem and me. My fists were clenched and I was ready to let fly. Atticus had promised me he would wear me out if he ever heard of me fighting any more; I was far too old and too big for such childish things, and the sooner I learned to hold in, the better off everybody would be. I soon forgot.

Cecil Jacobs made me forget. He had announced in the schoolyard the day before that Scout Finch's daddy defended niggers. I denied it, but told Jem.

"What'd he mean sayin' that?" I asked.

"Nothing," Jem said. "Ask Atticus, he'll tell you."

"Do you defend niggers, Atticus?" I asked him that evening.

"Of course I do. Don't say nigger, Scout. That's common."

" 's what everybody at school says."

"From now on it'll be everybody less one—"

"Well if you don't want me to grow up talkin' that way, why do you send me to school?"

My father looked at me mildly, amusement in his eyes. Despite our compromise, my campaign to avoid school had continued in one form or another since my first day's dose of it: the beginning of last September had brought on sinking spells, dizziness, and mild gastric complaints. I went so far as to pay a nickel for the privilege of rubbing my head against the head of Miss Rachel's cook's son, who was afflicted with a tremendous ringworm. It didn't take.

But I was worrying another bone. "Do all lawyers defend n-Negroes, Atticus?"

"Of course they do, Scout."

"Then why did Cecil say you defended niggers? He made it sound like you were runnin' a still."

Atticus sighed. "I'm simply defending a Negro—his name's Tom Robinson. He lives in that little settlement beyond the town dump. He's a member of Calpurnia's church, and Cal knows his family well. She says they're clean-living folks. Scout, you aren't old enough to understand some things yet, but there's been some high talk around town to the effect that I shouldn't do much about defending this man. It's a peculiar case—it won't come to trial until summer session. John Taylor was kind enough to give us a postponement . . ."

"If you shouldn't be defendin' him, then why are you doin' it?"

"For a number of reasons," said Atticus. "The main one is, if I didn't I couldn't hold up my head in town, I couldn't represent this county in the legislature, I couldn't even tell you or Jem not to do something again."

"You mean if you didn't defend that man, Jem and me wouldn't have to mind you any more?"

"That's about right."

"Why?"

"Because I could never ask you to mind me again. Scout, simply by the nature of the work, every lawyer gets at least one case in his lifetime that affects him personally. This one's mine, I guess. You might hear some ugly talk about it at school, but do one thing for me if you will: you just hold your head high and keep those fists down. No matter what anybody says to you, don't you let 'em get your goat. Try fighting with your head for a change . . . it's a good one, even if it does resist learning."

"Atticus, are we going to win it?"

"No, honey."

"Then why—"

"Simply because we were licked a hundred years before we started is no reason for us not to try to win," Atticus said.

"You sound like Cousin Ike Finch," I said. Cousin Ike Finch was Maycomb County's sole surviving Confederate veteran. He wore a General Hood type beard of which he was inordinately vain. At least once a year Atticus, Jem and I called on him, and I would have to kiss him. It was horrible. Jem and I would listen respectfully to Atticus and Cousin Ike rehash the war. "Tell you, Atticus," Cousin Ike would say, "the Missouri Compromise was what licked us, but if I had to go through it agin I'd walk every step of the way there an' every step back jist like I did before an' furthermore we'd whip 'em this time . . . now in 1864, when Stonewall Jackson came around by—I beg your pardon, young folks. Ol' Blue Light was in heaven then, God rest his saintly brow. . . ."

"Come here, Scout," said Atticus. I crawled into his lap and tucked my head under his chin. He put his arms around me and rocked me gently. "It's different this time," he said. "This time we aren't fighting the Yankees, we're fighting our friends. But remember this, no matter how bitter things get, they're still our friends and this is still our home."

With this in mind, I faced Cecil Jacobs in the schoolyard next day: "You gonna take that back, boy?"

"You gotta make me first!" he yelled. "My folks said your daddy was a disgrace an' that nigger oughta hang from the water-tank!"

I drew a bead on him, remembered what Atticus had said, then dropped my fists and walked away, "Scout's a cow—ward!" ringing in my ears. It was the first time I ever walked away from a fight.

Somehow, if I fought Cecil I would let Atticus down. Atticus so rarely asked Jem and me to do something for him, I could take being called a coward for him. I felt extremely noble for having remembered, and remained noble for three weeks. Then Christmas came and disaster struck.

Jem and I viewed Christmas with mixed feelings. The good side was the tree and Uncle Jack Finch. Every Christmas Eve day we met Uncle Jack at Maycomb Junction, and he would spend a week with us.

A flip of the coin revealed the uncompromising lineaments of Aunt Alexandra and Francis.

I suppose I should include Uncle Jimmy, Aunt Alexandra's husband, but as he never spoke a word to me in my life except to say, "Get off the fence," once, I never saw any reason to take notice of him. Neither did Aunt Alexandra. Long ago, in a burst of friendliness, Aunty and Uncle Jimmy produced a son named Henry, who left home as soon as was humanly possible, married, and produced Francis. Henry and his wife deposited Francis at his grandparents' every Christmas, then pursued their own pleasures.

No amount of sighing could induce Atticus to let us spend Christmas day at home. We went to Finch's Landing every Christmas in my memory. The fact that Aunty was a good cook was some compensation for being forced to spend a religious holiday with Francis Hancock. He was a year older than I, and I avoided him on principle: he enjoyed everything I disapproved of, and disliked my ingenuous diversions.

Aunt Alexandra was Atticus's sister, but when Jem told me about changelings and siblings, I decided that she had been swapped at birth, that my grandparents had perhaps received a Crawford instead of a Finch. Had I ever harbored the mystical notions about mountains that seem to obsess lawyers and judges, Aunt Alexandra would have been analogous to Mount Everest: throughout my early life, she was cold and there.

When Uncle Jack jumped down from the train Christmas Eve day, we had to wait for the porter to hand him two long packages. Jem and I always thought it funny when Uncle Jack pecked Atticus on the cheek; they were the only two men we ever saw kiss each other. Uncle Jack shook hands with Jem and swung me high, but not high enough: Uncle Jack was a head shorter than Atticus; the baby of the family, he was younger than Aunt Alexandra. He and Aunty looked alike, but Uncle Jack made better use of his face: we were never wary of his sharp nose and chin.

He was one of the few men of science who never terrified me, probably because he never behaved like a doctor. Whenever he performed a minor service for Jem and me, as removing a splinter from a foot, he would tell us exactly what he was going to do, give us an estimation of how much it would hurt, and explain the use of any tongs he employed. One Christmas I lurked in corners nursing a twisted splinter in my foot, permitting no one to come near me. When Uncle Jack caught me, he kept me laughing about a preacher who hated going to church so much that every day he stood at his gate in his dressing-grown, smoking a hookah and delivering five-minute sermons to any passers-by who desired spiritual comfort. I interrupted to make Uncle Jack let me know when he would pull it out, but he held up a bloody splinter in a pair of tweezers and said he yanked it while I was laughing, that was what was known as relativity.

"What's in those packages?" I asked him, pointing to the long thin parcels the porter had given him.

"None of your business," he said.

Jem said, "How's Rose Aylmer?"

Rose Aylmer was Uncle Jack's cat. She was a beautiful yellow female Uncle Jack said was one of the few women he could stand permanently. He reached into his coat pocket and brought out some snapshots. We admired them.

"She's gettin' fat," I said.

"I should think so. She eats all the leftover fingers and ears from the hospital."

"Aw, that's a damn story," I said.

"I beg your pardon?"

Atticus said, "Don't pay any attention to her, Jack. She's trying you out. Cal says she's been cussing fluently for a week, now."

Uncle Jack raised his eyebrows and said nothing. I was proceeding on the dim theory, aside from the innate attractiveness of such words, that if Atticus discovered I had picked them up at school he wouldn't make me go.

But at supper that evening when I asked him to pass the damn ham, please, Uncle Jack pointed at me. "See me afterwards, young lady," he said.

When supper was over, Uncle Jack went to the livingroom and sat down. He slapped his thighs for me to come sit on his lap. I liked to smell him: he was like a bottle of alcohol and something pleasantly sweet. He pushed back my bangs and looked at me. "You're more like Atticus than your mother," he said. "You're also growing out of your pants a little."

"I reckon they fit all right."

"You like words like damn and hell now, don't you?"

I said I reckoned so.

"Well I don't," said Uncle Jack, "not unless there's extreme provocation connected with 'em. I'll be here a week, and I don't want to hear any words like that while I'm here. Scout, you'll get in trouble if you go around saying things like that. You want to grow up to be a lady, don't you?"

I said not particularly.

"Of course you do. Now let's get to the tree."

We decorated the tree until bedtime, and that night I dreamed of the two long packages for Jem and me. Next morning Jem and I dived for them: they were from Atticus, who had written Uncle Jack to get them for us, and they were what we had asked for.

"Don't point them in the house," said Atticus, when Jem aimed at a picture on the wall.

"You'll have to teach 'em to shoot," said Uncle Jack.

"That's your job," said Atticus. "I merely bowed to the inevitable."

It took Atticus's courtroom voice to drag us away from the tree. He declined to let us take our air rifles to the Landing (I had already begun to think of shooting Francis) and said if we made one false move he'd take them away from us for good.

Finch's Landing consisted of three hundred and sixty-six steps down a high bluff and ending in a jetty. Farther down stream, beyond the bluff, were traces of an old cotton landing, where Finch Negroes had loaded bales and produce, unloaded blocks of ice, flour and sugar, farm equipment, and feminine apparel. A two-rut road ran from the riverside and vanished among dark trees. At the end of the road was a two-storied white house with porches circling it upstairs and downstairs. In his old age, our ancestor Simon Finch had built it to please his nagging wife; but with the porches all resemblance to ordinary houses of its era ended. The internal arrangements of the Finch house were indicative of Simon's guilelessness and the absolute trust with which he regarded his offspring.

There were six bedrooms upstairs, four for the eight female children, one for Welcome Finch, the sole son, and one for visiting relatives. Simple enough; but the daughters' room could be reached only by one staircase, Welcome's room and the guestroom only by another. The Daughters' Staircase was in the ground-floor bedroom of their parents, so Simon always knew the hours of his daughters' nocturnal comings and goings.

There was a kitchen separate from the rest of the house, tacked onto it by a wooden catwalk; in the back yard was a rusty bell on a pole, used to summon field hands or as a distress signal; a widow's walk was on the roof, but no widows walked there—from it, Simon oversaw his overseer, watched the river-boats, and gazed into the lives of surrounding landholders.

There went with the house the usual legend about the Yankees: one Finch female, recently engaged, donned her complete trousseau to save it from raiders in the neighborhood; she became stuck in the door to the Daughters' Staircase but was doused with water and finally pushed through. When we arrived at the Landing, Aunt Alexandra kissed Uncle Jack, Francis kissed Uncle Jack, Uncle Jimmy shook hands silently with Uncle Jack, Jem and I gave our presents to Francis, who gave us a present. Jem felt his age and gravitated to the adults, leaving me to entertain our cousin. Francis was eight and slicked back his hair.

"What'd you get for Christmas?" I asked politely.

"Just what I asked for," he said. Francis had requested a pair of knee-pants, a red leather booksack, five shirts and an untied bow tie.

"That's nice," I lied. "Jem and me got air-rifles, and Jem got a chemistry set—"

"A toy one, I reckon."

"No, a real one. He's gonna make me some invisible ink, and I'm gonna write to Dill in it."

Francis asked what was the use of that.

"Well, can't you just see his face when he gets a letter from me with nothing in it? It'll drive him nuts."

Talking to Francis gave me the sensation of settling slowly to the bottom of the ocean. He was the most boring child I ever met. As he lived in Mobile, he could not inform on me to school authorities, but he managed to tell everything he knew to Aunt Alexandra, who in turn unburdened herself to Atticus, who either forgot it or gave me hell, whichever struck his fancy. But the only time I ever heard Atticus speak sharply to anyone was when I once heard him say, "Sister, I do the best I can with them!" It had something to do with my going around in overalls.

Aunt Alexandra was fanatical on the subject of my attire. I could not possibly hope to be a lady if I wore breeches; when I said I could do nothing in a dress, she said I wasn't supposed to be doing things that required pants. Aunt Alexandra's vision of my deportment involved playing with small stoves, tea sets, and wearing the Add-A-Pearl necklace she gave me when I was born; furthermore, I should be a ray of sunshine in my father's lonely life. I suggested that one could be a ray of sunshine in pants just as well, but Aunty said that one had to behave like a sunbeam, that I was born good but had grown progressively worse every year. She hurt my feelings and set my teeth permanently on edge, but when I asked Atticus about it, he said there were already enough sunbeams in the family and to go on about my business, he didn't mind me much the way I was.

At Christmas dinner, I sat at the little table in the diningroom; Jem and Francis sat with the adults at the dining table. Aunty had continued to isolate me long after Jem and Francis graduated to the big table. I often wondered what she thought I'd do, get up and throw something? I sometimes thought of asking her if she would let me sit at the big table with the rest of them just once, I would prove to her how civilized I could be; after all, I ate at home every day with no major mishaps. When I begged Atticus to use his influence, he said he had none—we were guests, and we sat where she told us to sit. He also said Aunt Alexandra didn't understand girls much, she'd never had one.

But her cooking made up for everything: three kinds of meat, summer vegetables from her pantry shelves; peach pickles, two kinds of cake and ambrosia constituted a modest Christmas dinner. Afterwards, the adults made for the livingroom and sat around in a dazed condition. Jem lay on the floor, and I went to the back yard. "Put on your coat," said Atticus dreamily, so I didn't hear him.

Francis sat beside me on the back steps. "That was the best yet," I said.

"Grandma's a wonderful cook," said Francis. "She's gonna teach me how."

"Boys don't cook." I giggled at the thought of Jem in an apron.

"Grandma says all men should learn to cook, that men oughta be careful with their wives and wait on 'em when they don't feel good," said my cousin.

"I don't want Dill waitin' on me," I said. "I'd rather wait on him."

"Dill?"

"Yeah. Don't say anything about it yet, but we're gonna get married as soon as we're big enough. He asked me last summer."

Francis hooted.

"What's the matter with him?" I asked. "Ain't anything the matter with him."

"You mean that little runt Grandma says stays with Miss Rachel every summer?"

"That's exactly who I mean."

"I know all about him," said Francis.

"What about him?"

"Grandma says he hasn't got a home—"

"Has too, he lives in Meridian."

"—he just gets passed around from relative to relative, and Miss Rachel keeps him every summer."

"Francis, that's not so!"

Francis grinned at me. "You're mighty dumb sometimes, Jean Louise. Guess you don't know any better, though."

"What do you mean?"

"If Uncle Atticus lets you run around with stray dogs, that's his own business, like Grandma says, so it ain't your fault. I guess it ain't your fault if Uncle Atticus is a nigger-lover besides, but I'm here to tell you it certainly does mortify the rest of the family—"

"Francis, what the hell do you mean?"

"Just what I said. Grandma says it's bad enough he lets you all run wild, but now he's turned out a nigger-lover we'll never be able to walk the streets of Maycomb agin. He's ruinin' the family, that's what he's doin'."

Francis rose and sprinted down the catwalk to the old kitchen. At a safe distance he called, "He's nothin' but a nigger-lover!"

"He is not!" I roared. "I don't know what you're talkin' about, but you better cut it out this red hot minute!"

I leaped off the steps and ran down the catwalk. It was easy to collar Francis. I said take it back quick.

Francis jerked loose and sped into the old kitchen. "Nigger-lover!" he yelled.

When stalking one's prey, it is best to take one's time. Say nothing, and as sure as eggs he will become curious and emerge. Francis appeared at the kitchen door. "You still mad, Jean Louise?" he asked tentatively.

"Nothing to speak of," I said.

Francis came out on the catwalk.

"You gonna take it back, Fra—ancis?" But I was too quick on the draw. Francis shot back into the kitchen, so I retired to the steps. I could wait patiently. I had sat there perhaps five minutes when I heard Aunt Alexandra speak: "Where's Francis?"

"He's out yonder in the kitchen."

"He knows he's not supposed to play in there."

Francis came to the door and yelled, "Grandma, she's got me in here and she won't let me out!"

"What is all this, Jean Louise?"

I looked up at Aunt Alexandra. "I haven't got him in there, Aunty, I ain't holdin' him."

"Yes she is," shouted Francis, "she won't let me out!"

"Have you all been fussing?"

"Jean Louise got mad at me, Grandma," called Francis.

"Francis, came out of there! Jean Louise, if I hear another word out of you I'll tell your father. Did I hear you say hell a while ago?"

"Nome."

"I thought I did. I'd better not hear it again."

Aunt Alexandra was a back-porch listener. The moment she was out of sight Francis came out head up and grinning. "Don't you fool with me," he said.

He jumped into the yard and kept his distance, kicking tufts of grass, turning around occasionally to smile at me. Jem appeared on the porch, looked at us, and went away. Francis climbed the mimosa tree, came down, put his hands in his pockets and strolled around the yard. "Hah!" he said. I asked him who he thought he was, Uncle Jack? Francis said he reckoned I got told, for me to just sit there and leave him alone.

"I ain't botherin' you," I said.

Francis looked at me carefully, concluded that I had been sufficiently subdued, and crooned softly, "Nigger-lover . . ."

This time, I split my knuckle to the bone on his front teeth. My left impaired, I sailed in with my right, but not for long. Uncle Jack pinned my arms to my sides and said, "Stand still!"

Aunt Alexandra ministered to Francis, wiping his tears away with her handkerchief, rubbing his hair, patting his cheek. Atticus, Jem, and Uncle Jimmy had come to the back porch when Francis started yelling.

"Who started this?" said Uncle Jack.

Francis and I pointed at each other. "Grandma," he bawled, "she called me a whore-lady and jumped on me!"

"Is that true, Scout?" said Uncle Jack.

"I reckon so."

When Uncle Jack looked down at me, his features were like Aunt Alexandra's. "You know I told you you'd get in trouble if you used words like that? I told you, didn't I?"

"Yes sir, but—"

"Well, you're in trouble now. Stay there."

I was debating whether to stand there or run, and tarried in indecision a moment too long: I turned to flee but Uncle Jack was quicker. I found myself suddenly looking at a tiny ant struggling with a bread crumb in the grass.

"I'll never speak to you again as long as I live! I hate you an' despise you an' hope you die tomorrow!" A statement that seemed to encourage Uncle Jack, more than anything. I ran to Atticus for comfort, but he said I had it coming and it was high time we went home. I climbed into the back seat of the car without saying goodbye to anyone, and at home I ran to my room and slammed the door. Jem tried to say something nice, but I wouldn't let him.

When I surveyed the damage there were only seven or eight red marks, and I was reflecting upon relativity when someone knocked on the door. I asked who it was; Uncle Jack answered.

"Go away!"

Uncle Jack said if I talked like that he'd lick me again, so I was quiet. When he entered the room I retreated to a corner and turned my back on him. "Scout," he said, "do you still hate me?"

"Go on, please sir."

"Why, I didn't think you'd hold it against me," he said. "I'm disappointed in you—you had that coming and you know it."

"Didn't either."

"Honey, you can't go around calling people—"

"You ain't fair," I said, "you ain't fair."

Uncle Jack's eyebrows went up. "Not fair? How not?"

"You're real nice, Uncle Jack, an' I reckon I love you even after what you did, but you don't understand children much."

Uncle Jack put his hands on his hips and looked down at me. "And why do I not understand children, Miss Jean Louise? Such conduct as yours required little understanding. It was obstreperous, disorderly, and abusive—"

"You gonna give me a chance to tell you? I don't mean to sass you, I'm just tryin' to tell you."

Uncle Jack sat down on the bed. His eyebrows came together, and he peered up at me from under them. "Proceed," he said.

I took a deep breath. "Well, in the first place you never stopped to gimme a chance to tell you my side of it—you just lit right into me. When Jem an' I fuss Atticus doesn't ever just listen to Jem's side of it, he hears mine too, an' in the second place you told me never to use words like that except in ex-extreme provocation, and Francis provocated me enough to knock his block off—"

Uncle Jack scratched his head. "What was your side of it, Scout?"

"Francis called Atticus somethin', an' I wasn't about to take it off him."

"What did Francis call him?"

"A nigger-lover. I ain't very sure what it means, but the way Francis said it—tell you one thing right now, Uncle Jack, I'll be—I swear before God if I'll sit there and let him say somethin' about Atticus."

"He called Atticus that?"

"Yes sir, he did, an' a lot more. Said Atticus'd be the ruination of the family an' he let Jem an' me run wild. . . ."

From the look on Uncle Jack's face, I thought I was in for it again.

When he said, "We'll see about this," I knew Francis was in for it. "I've a good mind to go out there tonight."

"Please sir, just let it go. Please."

"I've no intention of letting it go," he said. "Alexandra should know about this. The idea of—wait'll I get my hands on that boy. . . ."

"Uncle Jack, please promise me somethin', please sir. Promise you won't tell Atticus about this. He—he asked me one time not to let anything I heard about him make me mad, an' I'd ruther him think we were fightin' about somethin' else instead. Please promise . . ."

"But I don't like Francis getting away with something like that—"

"He didn't. You reckon you could tie up my hand? It's still bleedin' some."

"Of course I will, baby. I know of no hand I would be more delighted to tie up. Will you come this way?"

Uncle Jack gallantly bowed me to the bathroom. While he cleaned and bandaged my knuckles, he entertained me with a tale about a funny nearsighted old gentleman who had a cat named Hodge, and who counted all the cracks in the sidewalk when he went to town. "There now," he said. "You'll have a very unladylike scar on your wedding-ring finger."

"Thank you sir. Uncle Jack?"

"Ma'am?"

"What's a whore-lady?"

Uncle Jack plunged into another long tale about an old Prime Minister who sat in the House of Commons and blew feathers in the air and tried to keep them there when all about him men were losing their heads. I guess he was trying to answer my question, but he made no sense whatsoever.

Later, when I was supposed to be in bed, I went down the hall for a drink of water and heard Atticus and Uncle Jack in the livingroom:

"I shall never marry, Atticus."

"Why?"

"I might have children."

Atticus said, "You've a lot to learn, Jack."

"I know. Your daughter gave me my first lessons this afternoon. She said I didn't understand children much and told me why. She was quite right. Atticus, she told me how I should have treated her— oh dear, I'm so sorry I romped on her."

Atticus chuckled. "She earned it, so don't feel too remorseful."

I waited, on tenterhooks, for Uncle Jack to tell Atticus my side of it. But he didn't. He simply murmured, "Her use of bathroom invective leaves nothing to the imagination. But she doesn't know the meaning of half she says—she asked me what a whore-lady was . . ."

"Did you tell her?"

"No, I told her about Lord Melbourne."

"Jack! When a child asks you something, answer him, for goodness' sake. But don't make a production of it. Children are children, but they can spot an evasion quicker than adults, and evasion simply muddles 'em. No," my father mused, "you had the right answer this afternoon, but the wrong reasons. Bad language is a stage all children go through, and it dies with time when they learn they're not attracting attention with it. Hotheadedness isn't. Scout's got to learn to keep her head and learn soon, with what's in store for her these next few months. She's coming along, though. Jem's getting older and she follows his example a good bit now. All she needs is assistance sometimes."

"Atticus, you've never laid a hand on her."

"I admit that. So far I've been able to get by with threats. Jack, she minds me as well as she can. Doesn't come up to scratch half the time, but she tries."

"That's not the answer," said Uncle Jack.

"No, the answer is she knows I know she tries. That's what makes the difference. What bothers me is that she and Jem will have to absorb some ugly things pretty soon. I'm not worried about Jem keeping his head, but Scout'd just as soon jump on someone as look at him if her pride's at stake. . . ."

I waited for Uncle Jack to break his promise. He still didn't.

"Atticus, how bad is this going to be? You haven't had too much chance to discuss it."

"It couldn't be worse, Jack. The only thing we've got is a black man's word against the Ewells'. The evidence boils down to you-did—I-didn't. The jury couldn't possibly be expected to take Tom Robinson's word against the Ewells'—are you acquainted with the Ewells?"

Uncle Jack said yes, he remembered them. He described them to Atticus, but Atticus said, "You're a generation off. The present ones are the same, though."

"What are you going to do, then?"

"Before I'm through, I intend to jar the jury a bit—I think we'll have a reasonable chance on appeal, though. I really can't tell at this stage, Jack. You know, I'd hoped to get through life without a case of this kind, but John Taylor pointed at me and said, 'You're It.' "

"Let this cup pass from you, eh?"

"Right. But do you think I could face my children otherwise? You know what's going to happen as well as I do, Jack, and I hope and pray I can get Jem and Scout through it without bitterness, and most of all, without catching Maycomb's usual disease. Why reasonable people go stark raving mad when anything involving a Negro comes up, is something I don't pretend to understand . . . I just hope that Jem and Scout come to me for their answers instead of listening to the town. I hope they trust me enough. . . . Jean Louise?"

My scalp jumped. I stuck my head around the corner. "Sir?"

"Go to bed."

I scurried to my room and went to bed. Uncle Jack was a prince of a fellow not to let me down. But I never figured out how Atticus knew I was listening, and it was not until many years later that I realized he wanted me to hear every word he said.

The Mourner

Cecil Dawkins

THE tracks coming into Galleton wind down the mountain walls that hold the valley in a giant vortex, the town at its center. Once on the valley floor, the skein is lost in a web of swirling bands and innumerable junctions that converge, at last, upon the yard and then the shed, a great steel-ribbed maw, hollow, echoing, a skin-covered skeleton without muscle or viscera, no heart, and an empty womb.

Gabriel sat with his cheek against the train window, one foot on his suitcase. It was dusk and the lights outside were coming on. When the conductor opened the door, the smell of the diner in the car ahead sweetened the conditioned air. His stomach muscles grabbed,

[From a collection of short stories by Cecil Dawkins, *The Quiet Enemy*, published by Penguin Books.]

sore and knotted from motion sickness in spite of the bitter pills he'd swallowed. He turned his face to the window and saw his reflection, saw it and through it to vague moving masses and figures in the yard. His face in the window was a smear of black eyebrows unbroken over his nose, and a long oval jaw and cheekline that might have hung from hoops on his ears like false whiskers, an easy face to caricature. The noise of the clacking wheels thundered for an instant before the conductor closed the door. The little boy across the aisle got up again for water. He'd kept on his hat all the way down from St. Louis, an imitation pith helmet, straw painted white, with Lion Tamer stenciled across the crown.

The other passengers began to stir, to stand and stretch and reach down luggage from the overhead racks. One old woman got her bundles together and trudged up the aisle to stand at the door. Then the aisle filled before the train stopped. He watched the boy's helmet topple as, outside, his father lifted him. He'd traveled alone, the lion tamer, now he was home again, a child. His face pouted and posed. Gabriel waited for the car to empty before rising and gathering his things.

A porter came toward him when he stepped down onto the platform. He shook his head and muttered, following the stragglers down the concrete stair and into the dank tunnel that led under the tracks to the terminal. He climbed the ramp. The station was bright after the tunnel and the train. The people, the booths, the benches like pews in a church were small under the domed ceiling three or four lost stories high. On the street outside, he set his suitcase down and waited for a taxi. Before him the long avenue pointed toward the heart of the city. Across the mouth of the viaduct that spanned the railroad yard the neon sign bubbled—GALLETON, THE MAGIC CITY. And in smaller lights, HOME OF DIXIE STEEL. Beyond, the downtown lights blinked like afflicted eyes. Stars sparked the surrounding hills. Atop Bald Mountain the Iron Man held his torch. And away off across the valley the glow from the furnaces scorched the sky.

He hailed a cruising cab, climbed in, and gave the address. The driver grunted, reached back and slammed the door. 'First time in Galleton, son?'

The muscles of his stomach braced as the cab lurched forward. 'No.'

The cab entered downtown traffic. The tires caught the streetcar tracks, hummed a moment, and jumped aside. What's his hurry? Gabriel wondered. It used to take half an hour. A half hour. He wanted to sleep. Last night at this time . . . let's see . . . the night before, Salt Lake City. Last week . . . . He backed away. He saw himself, a figure grown pin-size in distance. When he was a kid on his way to the dentist he'd thought, a half hour from now I'll be through it, tomorrow at this time . . . Or confession. It was the same when the nuns herded him with the rest across the schoolyard to the church, to confession.

They were through the city. The cab took all the shortcuts. He thought: for once, an honest cabby, prides himself on his honesty, a simple measure of worth, a matter of short cuts.

He watched the signboards and drugstores. The laundry: WE WASH EVERYTHING BUT THE KIDS. The parts shop with its yard of wrecks. We salvage everything but the . . . He let it go. There was the motel like an Indian village. Teepeetown. Heap big deal. He leaned forward and began to direct the driver. They were getting close now. In the fairgrounds the stockcar races were on. Gutted mufflers roared, rubber screamed. The circle of track was hidden behind a white board fence. Floodlights looked down on the race he couldn't see. The speakers blared, 'Round and round they go, where they stop . . .'

The cab turned off the avenue and climbed the hill. Now it crawled. Gabriel watched the houses pass. Now he could call the names of the people who lived in them—Mancini, Amendola, Vlato, Morello. And under the noise of the speedway, voices called across the street. It was good dark now, and behind the hilltop the blare of the furnaces sat like a sunburst on the head of a saint.

'It's up there,' he said.

The house was lighted from top to bottom, but there weren't any cars out front. When they stopped, he paid the driver and then stood looking up at the house while the cab drove off.

All there but the lightning rods and porcelain baubles. All there— turrets, bay windows, the round towers and coconut frosting. As real as Disneyland. Up they moved, Morello—Giardini—Vlato—Virciglio, up from the banks of the mill to the iced and frosted summit of the hill, out at last from the shadow of the railroad sheds, away from the giant furnaces, they moved. And with them, moving also into the many-storied ghosts of a dead time, the keepers of homes for the aged, and the Greek morticians.

The skinny figure of a woman tripped toward him down the sidewalk. He recognized her. Mrs. Ricardi. The name played in his head. Mrs. Ricardi. *Misericordia.*

He turned. *Misericordiam tuam. Miserere nobis.* Before she could recognize him, he climbed the bank and started up the path in the shadow of the trees. *In nomine Patris, et Filii . . .* He mounted the steps and crossed the porch and stood a moment looking through the screen door into the lighted hall before he pressed the bell. And whoever said you can't go home again? Home is where the heart is, cold and pickled in a bottle like the embryo of a freak. Home is where you hang yourself. Home sweet *homo sapiens,* conglomerate polygot *in nomine . . .*

The chimes of the doorbell sounded. *Sanctus, sanctus, sanctus,* blessed is he who comes . . .

A priest came toward him down the hall. His brother.

'Gabriel!'

'Hello, Vincent.'

'Thank God you've come. The funeral should have been yesterday, but Mamma wouldn't hear—not till you'd come. I didn't think——
If you wired, we didn't get it.'

'Where is she?'

'At the undertaker's. They'll be back soon. People keep coming.'

Gabriel set his suitcase down in the hall and walked into the living room. It was smaller and the wainscoting darker than he'd remembered. Vincent came behind him and took up his pipe from the smoking stand.

'I gave him the last sacrament myself,' he said.

Gabriel nodded.

'He lived a long life, and—' there was a shrug in his voice—'a good one.'

Gabriel turned and looked at him.

'A good life as he saw it,' Vincent said.

Gabriel yawned. 'Anything to eat?'

Vincent led the way back to the kitchen. The round oak table was laden with dishes that made a mountainous landscape under the white cover cloth. Gabriel lifted a corner and drew out a chicken leg. Vincent poured milk from a flowered pitcher and handed it to him.

Leaning against the door, he looked at the room while he ate. The linoleum was bright and new, but the naked light bulb hung yet from its knotted cord. He stripped off the last meat from the drumstick and washed it down with milk.

'What now, Vince?' he asked.

Vincent shrugged. 'They haven't much. The house—a little insurance.'

'Teena has a job.'

'She doesn't make a lot. This is a big house, expensive to keep.'

'They'll have to get rid of it,' Gabriel said. They looked at each other.

Vincent shrugged. 'Time enough to talk about all that later.'

Gabriel felt the nausea from the train returning. 'I'm all in,' he said.

'They won't be long now.'

He wandered through the rooms, Vincent strolling behind him, his hands in his pockets, his face behind its chimney of pipe smoke. He looked into the doorway of the dining room that had for years been his grandfather's bedroom. The old man had feared the stairs. He'd hoarded life, that old man who'd talked so much of heaven. Well, he was gone now. The bed was made. Not a crease or rumple marked where he'd been. Gabriel looked over his shoulder at his brother. 'A good life,' he snorted.

'Why don't you lie down?' Vincent said. 'I'll call you when they come. Go on, you look worn out.'

Gabriel went into the room and dropped across the bed. The light from the hall silhouetted Vincent in the door.

'Two kinds of people, Vince,' Gabriel said. 'Parasites and hosts.'

'Only one host, Gaby. One host for all of us.'

Gabriel grunted. 'Don't talk shop to me, Vince.'

'All right. Two kinds of people. So if you're not a host, then you're a parasite.'

'They teach you logic in the seminary, Vince?'

'Logic and ethics,' Vincent said. 'Be good to Mamma, Gaby. She's been beside herself.'

'Go away. Let me sleep.' He rolled on his side and waited to hear Vincent's footsteps down the hall before he closed his eyes.

The smell of the old man was in the room. It was in the pillows and mattress, the smell of stale tobacco and that sour smell common to old men and babies. Gabriel fell asleep. He dreamed of the forbidden cave he and Vincent had explored as children. The entrance was like a big groundhog's burrow, a hole under the hillside too steep for houses, where a little wood still grew. The place was called McFarland's Spring because at the foot of the hill, in the McFarlands' vacant lot, springs bubbled out of the ground, almost hidden by fern and lined with the soft limestone called soapstone. You could rub the smooth surfaces with wet hands and stir up a gritty lather.

To enter the cave, you had to slide on the seat of your pants. The hard-packed earth was always slick and moist. At the bottom you crawled under a rock and came out into a little room where the floor was always muddy. It was dark and dank, smelling of urine, for tramps used the place. There, they always whispered.

The bed sagged and Gabriel struck out, grasping for balance at the covers. He opened his eyes. His mother sat beside him, and for an instant he felt the old fear, the guilt, of being discovered with muddy trousers.

'Mamma,' he whispered. 'Mamma *mia*—'

She put her hand on his forehead, brushing back his hair. 'My Gabriello, my boy.'

Her eyes were a little wild, and her black hair stood high and wild on her forehead. She whispered wordlessly, her hands touching him as they might feel a child for broken bones.

He put his arms around her and tried to rise, but she fell over him, sobbing. He could see the glow of Vincent's pipe in the dim room and the picture of Vincent the child came tunneling back to him, Vincent out of the light, Vincent watching with hunger in his eyes while his hands found something to occupy themselves, a piece of string, a rubber band, something to twist while he watched there from the darkness the two of them together in the light. Gabriel let his breath escape slowly, forced out of him by the weight of her on his chest. When it was gone, he couldn't breathe again. He put his arms around her and raised up.

'How are you, Mamma? All right?'

'My boy—my Gahbee.'

Then Vincent switched on the light. Gabriel stood up, drawing her to her feet.

'Come in the parlor, Gahbee,' she said, taking his hand and leading him. 'Teena! Tony! Eva Marie! Your brother he's home. Come look at him.'

In the parlor she stood him under the light, holding on to his arm. 'Why you're so pale, Gahbee? You don't drink! You wouldn't do that to me.'

'I had a beard, Mamma. I shaved it off.'

'Oh, no beard, Gahbee. Let it show, your face. Why you hide your face?'

He led her to the big square couch with a walnut slatted back and eased her down. She caught his hand and he stood awkwardly before her.

'Gaby!'

He turned. His sister, Eva Marie, rolled toward him, looking, in her pregnancy, like a pyramid of bright-colored balloons. He stared at her. She'd been slim and beautiful when he saw her last, this gross woman. She hugged and kissed him, and he felt like a pole in her arms. Her husband Antony came behind her.

'Hallo, Gabriello. Long time no see. Your sister, she eat me outa house and home. Some woman. Whatta woman.' He shook his head at the wonder of her and pinched her bottom proudly. He was a small man, a grocer and keeper of fancy fruits.

They shook hands. 'Hello, Tony.'

'You oughta see our boys, Gabriello. We got big boys—like their mamma. Whatta girl!'

'Our last one, our Vincent, he's mean as you were, Gaby.' She giggled and shook. 'We wanted you to be Godpoppa to him.'

'Leavim alone, leavim alone. Tellim all that later,' his mother said.

Then he saw his aunt Teena standing in the door, miffed at having been so long overlooked.

'Have you eaten, Gabriello?' She'd show them who held this house together.

He nodded. 'Yes, Teena. How are you?' He bent and kissed her lips, which she compressed tightly to hold her lipstick intact.

'Where's your bag? Your things oughta be got out and hung up. All the company we had, you'll need your clothes. I'll hang the wrinkles out.' She was a tiny thing, getting dumpy now, and she wore her skirts short to show off her little feet, of which she was very proud.

'It's too late, Teena. They've been too long in the suitcase.'

'You never know,' she said. 'Let me at 'em, no telling what I might do.' She winked. 'Save you a pressing bill.' She had seen his suitcase and now she went to pick it up. He moved to take it from her, but his mother grabbed his sleeve.

'Is she your mamma? Who's your mamma? Come here, sit by me.'

Teena struggled off with the weight of his canvas bag, mincing in her little shoes. He let himself be pulled down. They all settled in the circle of chairs that made the room look as if it were arranged for a meeting of some kind.

His mother put her hand over his, plucked his fingers, traced his knuckles, patted. 'Poppa's gone now, Gahbee.'

'I'm sorry, Mamma.'

'Are you, my boy? Yes, we must all of us grieve. He was such a strong man. Never did he miss a day's work in his life, Gahbee. Think of it! Not a day. We can all be thankful for that. He had his health to the end.'

Teena called from the kitchen where she'd hauled out the ironing board. 'A fine constitution. All the doctors said it, Gabriello. A constitution unheard of in a man his age.'

'And Gahbee's like him. They were like as two peas. That's why,' his mother nodded, 'that's why they never got on together. Too much alike.' She leaned toward him with her wild eyes. 'He said, Gabriel, Poppa said every day, "Tell that boy to come home where he belongs. Get him back here. If he's so set on painting, let him paint houses, all the houses on this hill. There's good money in that."' She laughed. 'He'd be tickled to know he was the one brought you back, Gahbee. He was always one to have his way.'

'Fine figure of a man till the day he died,' Teena called in. 'And he laid out beautiful too.'

His mother was plucking his fingers again. 'Like as two peas. I tell 'em all. Gahbee's the one like his Grampa. All my children handsome and beautiful. But Gahbee's the one. Now Vincent, he's a fine fellow. But a priest got no business to be handsome. It's more against him. Turns the girls' heads and makes their mammas sick in church at the loss.' She laughed. Gabriel looked across the room at Vincent grinning in the doorway.

'Tell me where you live out there, Gahbee.'

'You got a car?' Tony wanted to know.

'I live upstairs at this lady's house, Mamma, like I wrote you.'

'Ahah!' Tony said. 'A lady!'

'How she feed, that lady?'

'She doesn't feed me. I just room there. I eat out.'

'At's no good, eat out! A growing boy needsa be fed at home.'

'Mamma,' he laughed. 'I quit growing.'

'Hah! Vincent, he grows still.'

Tony clapped his knee. 'In the belly.'

Gabriel looked again at Vincent, but he could not see his face clearly behind the smokescreen his pipe put out.

'Let *me* tell you about growing boys,' Eva Marie said, waving her hand. 'I got three and I know all about 'em. You only seen just the one, Gaby, my Andrew. The middle one, he's got them black brows with light hair, like you. Teena she says that hair, it comes from our father.'

Thump! His mother's fist came down on the walnut arm of the sofa. 'Don't speak of that tenor your father here in this house where Poppa passed. Oh, Poppa, he told me. But I wouldn't listen. Weak, he said, useless. More woman that one couldn't find nowhere than me, your mamma! Too much woman for that singer.' She laughed a short hoot of laughter. 'I give him children, fine children, all in a row. Vincent, Eva Marie, Gahbee. Beautiful children! And off he goes, Gahbee nothing but a child. And all my other children, them I never had . . .' Her shoulders shook, and her voice pierced. Gabriel felt somewhere deep under his ribs the long-forgotten but instantly familiar tremor, like the tremor set up in the house by the Frigidaire motor starting at night in the darkness under the cellar stairs, remembered from his childhood. Vincent crossed the room to sit beside her and take up both her hands.

'Mamma, now Mamma.' But she snatched her hands away from him.

'Let us pray, Vincent. Lead a prayer. The mysteries, the sorrowful mysteries, for Poppa.' She took Gabriel's hand and drew him closer. 'And the joyful ones too, Vincent, for my Gabriel come home.'

Antony heaved himself out of his chair and onto his knees. Gabriel heard the thud as Teena knelt beside the ironing board out in the kitchen. Vincent took out his rosary and helped his mother down. Only Eva Marie, solemn now in her pregnancy, tugged her skirts toward her knees and remained enthroned in the big wing chair. They waited. Gabriel plucked at the sofa cushion.

'On your knees,' his mother said. 'You will get down on your knees, Gabriello.'

He looked at her wild eyes, watched her hands grasp for him. The others did not look up.

'Kneel!' she shouted. 'You will this once be like us. Kneel to your God, Gabriello Orghesi. Kneel!'

Trembling suddenly to his scalp, Gabriel slid to his knees.

And quickly Vincent began.

Finally, in the car going to the undertaker's, Vincent asked him, 'You're going back?'

He didn't answer at once. He knew his brother's mind. Why did you come at all? Then, angry at the words that, though unspoken, nevertheless lay palpable between them, he mouthed, 'The sooner the quicker,' and immediately despised his own facetiousness.

They rode in silence, Vincent too big for the car, a big dark giant whose hands on the wheel looked like a man's hands driving a child's push-pedal car. He hunched down to see out of the windshield.

Gabriel laid his head back and looked up at the sudden sun that leaped against the hill as steel was poured, like fire from a cauldron tipped in hell. And then came the roar. The city seemed then to him like a gigantic prostrate functioning body, pillowed on the hills. Eyes and arteries, now the bowels. The smell of sulfur seeped around the windows and rose up through the floorboards.

'God,' Gabriel said, 'I'd forgotten.'

The undertaker's establishment was the only building lighted now on the littered street. It was a one-story brick building that might have housed a grocery in this long-dying suburb under the plant, and it opened directly onto the sidewalk. No awning-covered walk, no tended grass, unnaturally green, no muted lights spotted on colonial false front, no euphemistic legend under glass like a church announcement of next Sunday's sermon attempted to call the place a 'funeral home'. It was simply, almost brutally, what it was, the undertaker's place of business. Inside, the walls, dirty from the mill, were watermarked in pale patterns, distortions by Dali. And against the smell of sulfur, no flower could have breathed. Lights blazed from naked ceiling hangings. Nothing here was indirect.

In the parlors old men lined against the walls, speaking in gruff whispers, a people consecrated to death, rededicating themselves each

Sunday, and now in the middle of the week. It walked to meet them in familiar forms, diseased or crippled, seldom peaceful, and one had seen a brother drop from catwalk to cauldron of molten steel that blazed like an incandescent pool on the sun, had seen his brother drop and try to run across that viscous fire while his legs melted under him and, poised, startled on his shrinking stumps, he slowly sank, his mouth gaped open at whatever it was he contemplated. They lined the walls in awe, timid, speaking now and then in low tones the language that, like a wall, kept them isolated and safe in this world where their children walked away but where they would always stay, uneasy.

They stared respectfully at Vincent, the priest. They nodded when spoken to, suddenly bestirring themselves, pushing upright from the walls, smiling uncertainly, bobbing heads and twisting caps like wheels in their gnarled and scaly hands. And it would take a while for them to unwind and relax again against the walls. Gabriel felt their eyes on his back as he passed and they tried to place his familiar face.

He followed Vincent into the 'chapel' from which the body would be moved in the morning to the church. He tried to examine his feelings as he walked down the uncarpeted aisle where his footsteps clacked. He found no feelings to examine.

Vincent stepped aside into one of the pews to kneel, and Gabriel walked ahead. The body revealed itself to him in pieces, first the nose, unnaturally powdered, and then the shock of hair that had sprung loose from where they'd tried to paste it down. The unnatural darkness of the hair over that aged face, powdered and rouged, made the old man look strangely alive, like a young actor playing an aged corpse. And then he saw the fist and he thought: he died like that, clenching that fist, and they couldn't pry it loose. Someone had drawn a black rosary through the clamped fingers. The old man's hand gripped it like the collar of a thief he did not mean to get away. The rouge could not hide that burnt black mottling under the skin where the furnaces had left their brand. The fist, the mottled face, the springing hair would have mocked death had it not been for the undertaker's crude art that sought to make him 'natural.'

'I've come to bury you,' he said silently to the corpse.

The flared nostrils seemed to breathe and the stiff black hairs protruding seemed to quiver. Gabriel might have trembled like the boy he used to be had there not been the ludicrous art of the undertaker to reassure him.

He could hear the old man's voice shake with rage, scream, 'Not you. Death!' turning it to a privilege. Hearing the voice, Gabriel felt the old man standing there at his elbow, looking critically down into the bright pink tufted box. He drew his shoulders in, shrugged, to rid himself of the phantom and to try to place the old man where he'd had him so he could speak without being interrupted. 'I forgive you,' he said. But again he heard from somewhere behind him, 'Who the devil do you think you are?'

He turned quickly and, without waiting for Vincent, went out past the pairs of shifting boots with high, creased tops and humped and rounded toes scarred by ends of pipe and corners of sheet and rails. A voice said *'Scuse.'* He waited on the sidewalk for Vincent to come out, and as they drove home again he closed his eyes, pretending sleep.

But he could not sleep, not even when, in his old bed, hard and narrow as the cot of a monk, he wrapped himself in darkness. He lay on his side and looked out the window and down across the street to where Mrs. Ricardi sat in her porch swing, silhouetted against the yellow light in her lace-curtained windows. How many nights had he gone to sleep watching her there? Mrs. Ricardi. The Wanderer. Living alone, spending her days over the neighborhood, from kitchen to kitchen, drumming her fingers, finishing sentences other people started——

'It's going to be ——'

'A pretty day—a pretty day——'

'Fall——'

'Late—late this year—oh late——'

——impatient to be off again, Mrs. Ricardi. He knew he would see her there, if he woke early, waiting for signs of life, sipping her lemonade—for her bowels, she said, and she attributed to it not only her regularity, but her longevity as well. Then she would wander again, across yards, through gardens, down alleys, from house to house, her arms crossed and held tight to her flat slab of breast, her thin body driven by some wind that only she could feel. And eventually she would tell you how, when she was a girl, the sewing-machine people voted her Miss Twinkle Treadle and put her picture on their directions booklet and gave her a sewing machine free.

Across the valley he could see the television towers on the mountaintop. He thought of San Francisco, the lights on the hillsides, like luminous honey in a giant comb. Cassidy, Bowles and the others would be at the wharf now, cracking crab and drinking beer and talking. Cassidy would be doing most of the talking, the Right Reverend G. B. Shaw Cassidy. That big Irishman. 'You're a dreamer, Gabe,' he'd say. 'Me, I'm a realist.' And he drew a picture of the world exploding—all very detailed in the dismembered bodies and blood in the manner of a medieval rendering of hell, and in the corner a serene little figure with a beard painted children's blocks on a Mondrianesque canvas. 'That's you, Gabe,' Cassidy said.

'Take up writing, Cassidy,' he answered. 'You're good at anecdote.'

Composition, architecture—Cassidy said a painting must have those things. The painter's duty to mankind—and, more important, mankind's duty to the painter. The painter, in Cassidy's philosophy, deserved to be kept and coddled like a concubine. Modern art was irresponsible because it was 'Rarefied, escapist.' Cassidy liked words. But Cassidy was a realist. He painted things—tables and apples and chairs and cats.

In the beginning Gabriel had talked too. 'What is real?' he asked. 'You think this table—that cat—they are reality? They are things. Put them before you they become a wall. Things are walls to go through.'

'Then go through them,' Cassidy would shout. 'Don't for God's sake deny they are there.' And he would try to persuade him he must go to the University (where he could take classes from Cassidy). An artist cannot be illiterate, he would say.

And Gabriel would wave a blessing in the air before Cassidy's face, intoning 'Universitas Californiensis.'

Whereupon Cassidy, incensed, would grumble off, and he and Bowles would sit until the fish houses closed and then move up to Chinatown, and be caught by morning in a Settlement basement watching those strange young men and women who spoke a language more foreign than the Chinaman, who claimed the city as theirs and reduced art and God and the sidereal universe by the most common denominator, who loved their fellow man (so long as he was filthy, diseased, destitute, or mad), who sometimes turned on him and Bowles and said, 'Speak, man, speak.'

And sometimes Bowles would speak to them while they listened intently, 'Gone, man, gone.' And Gabriel would compose his face while Bowles reveled in nonsense to see how long they'd listen before recognizing it. Bowles had three degrees. He knew it all. But he only believed one thing—that there were no answers for Bowles. And, poor fellow, he was a good painter, better by far than Cassidy, good enough to know how mediocre good can be.

'Now you, Gabe, maybe you've got it.' He attributed it all to a Southern-Italian-Catholic background. 'You've got plenty driving you away. Maybe if they drive you far enough you'll get there. Maybe you'll do it, you're ignorant enough, you've never learned the horror of tolerance,' he would say toward morning when he was, mercifully, drunk at last.

It was only when he was very sleepy that he let himself think again of the old man lying ill at ease in death on the tufted pink in a dark and unfamiliar place, locked up, a commodity in a box, alone for this long night. He saw again the fist that had not meant to clutch a rosary. He asked, When did it come, this anger like a yoke we wore, binding us and holding us apart? I am my father's son, he said to the presence listening, angry, inarticulate. Whoever he was, that singer of Italian arias, I'm his, however bad you hated. For I saw early that simple truth in your fierce and vengeful eyes when you looked at me, at the brush in my hand, at the wobbling homemade easel, and asked if I didn't want to sing. He said, The anger came the day you cut my hair and, shorn and grim, I yet refused to bawl; it came when at the age of twelve I was by your commandment circumcised; it came when I, sixteen, crept in from being with a girl and you and your razor strop preached chastity and virtue. You're dead, he said to the presence, go lie down.

When he slept, he was riding again, across the luminous wastes of the salt flats at night, lost in that northern desert the color of leprous flesh. And over and over he dreamed those words he'd prayed as a boy here in this place from which he'd never hoped to escape: Oh God, grant me one grain of the salt of Thy wisdom—one grain—and I will carry the sacrament of it to the altar of my own fashioning on the peak of this earth where it may illumine mankind forever and ever, amen. Your servant, Gabriello Orghesi. And P. S. Oh my Father, deliver me.

In nomine Patris, et Filii. Before the altar, black-vestmented, the priest, his brother, raises hands. And in the aisle, the bier. *Oramus te, Domine.* Bows down to kiss the stone.

Credo in unum Deum . . . Suscipe . . . Pater Noster, qui es in coelis . . . Libera nos, Domine . . . Per omnia saecula saeculorum . . . Dominus vobiscum . . . Benedicat vos omnipotens Deus Pater et Filius, et Spiritus Sanctus . . . Deo gratias.

Through it, Gabriel sat, knelt, stood, the responses on his tongue, before the museum, the shrine, the tabernacle opening to gape. 'I forgive you,' he said. And the old man thundered.

Later, beside the open grave, he stood long after all the prayers and holy-water sprinkling. His mother plucked his arm. 'Gabriello, come.'

He pulled himself free and finally was left alone under the tent, hearing the caravan of cars, feeling the black-robed presence of Vincent up the green slope, waiting. The gravediggers, sullen at his interfering presence, began their tasks. Up came the rails, the canvas straps, away the paper grass. And there the earth—naked raw red gash exposed. He took up a shovel and onto the dull glow of the coffin the fresh dirt spattered. But while he leaned on the shovel and watched, the old man stood beside him, at his elbow, watching too. Defeated, he flung down the shovel and turned.

Vincent slid behind the wheel and there between them the old man sat.

At home he gathered up his things in the canvas bag and zipped the zipper while she wailed beside him and his stomach, knotting, felt like the stomach of a bilious child. Impatient, he waited in the kitchen while she packed a shoe-box lunch for him to take along, fussing Teena, miffed acolyte, out of her way. Hysteria sat like a mask on her face. Silent in the front room with lingering friends, Eva Marie and her frightened boys.

'I'll send you money every month,' he said, able to speak now it was so close. Later he could think of how.

'Money!' she cried.

He stood at the door of the old man's room, smelling the aged smell of him, seeing the imprint of a body on the spread.

He shivered, then remembered it was his own.

Then through the city again, two cars to the station. Himself and Vincent, their mother, *the old man,* in one. Behind them, Eva Marie and the boys in the furious chariot Teena hurled against the traffic, her little foot determined on the gas, her neck craned so she could see out at all.

On the noisy platform they huddled around him, all but Vincent, who held himself apart, puffing too vigorously upon the pipe in his clenched teeth. The boys shouted shrilly over exploding steam, listing what they wanted of the West. Horses. Guns. Real hats and leather chaps. A tumbleweed. One Indian (they were being reasonable). Some ropes.

His mother, gesturing with her hands, was suddenly quite gay. If she breaks, he prayed, let it be after. She told him to eat and say his prayers. He reached for the shoe box under her arm, but she turned aside.

'Anh-anh, not yet, Gabriello. I got a surprise.'

'She's going too!' one of the boys shrilled over the conductor's 'All aborrrt.'

Gabriel whirled, sought the faces that smiled their sly secret, all but the closed up face of Vincent behind his formidable pipe.

'That's right, Gabriello,' she said, hugging the shoe box, moving to the step a porter flung down below the high door of the coach. 'Why you think I pack so big a lunch, hah?'

He backed into the shadow of the train, facing them. But he knew it was a joke and he had to help them with it. He turned to laugh with her, but she was gone. He saw the shoe box disappear into the train, helped aboard by the conductor who looked at him and shouted again, 'All aborrrt!'

They piled upon him, the boys and Eva Marie, kissing, while Spartan Teena stood aside, a tableau of courage under fire. And Vincent took his pipe out of his mouth and stepped up to shake his hand and grasp his arm. Gabriel wrenched free.

'No. Look here, Vince, what's the meaning——'

But Vincent took his arm again. 'Hurry.'

'Vince, what's she doing, Vince! Vincent!'

But he was standing on the steps, hoisted up by his brother, who stood on the bottom step, barring his way. 'Go along with it,' Vincent hissed into his face.

'Get her off of here!'

'You can do this one thing.'

'No. Not with me. She can't go. Not with me.'

'You are a fool,' Vincent said, his face straining red while he clung there and the train began to move. The others waved and shouted. He glimpsed tears on Teena's face as the edge of the car cut off his view of her. The others, fat Eva Marie and the shouting boys, ran alongside. 'Jump, Vincent! Jump down!'

'You've tricked me,' Gabriel shouted into his brother's close face.

'We have us a time, hah?' Now she laughed. 'We have us picnics out there?'

'Lots of picnics.'

'I can pose for a picture, Gahbee. Remember that time? You made you that—whatcha callit?'

'Easel.'

'Yes. And I sit down and let my dinner burn. Remember?'

'I remember.'

'And you call it Madonna. Is sacrilegious.' She laughed. 'You was just a boy.'

Then, recalling his infirmity, she took a pill from her large black pocketbook. 'Here, right this minute, swallow.'

He took the yellow pill on his tongue and washed it down while she followed the movement of his throat.

'You don't look like Poppa,' she said. 'You look like that singer.' And she lapsed back into silence, staring at the wall of clay outside and close to the window, passing in a blur, dizzying.

Five minutes more and they'd emerge upon the summit. Five minutes after that and Tony's face would grin up at them, pleased at his part in the conspiracy.

'We got us a long trip ahead,' she said sadly.

He laid his head back and gave in to weariness. He had accomplished it. He had returned and now he left again. *Libera nos, Domine. Gratia.* He heard her spring and felt her at his side.

'Sick already!'

He shook his head, feeling the surge of the curving cars and her kneading fingers on his hands. She pulled his head to her shoulder and stroked his hair.

'Gabriello—Gahbee—my boy,' she crooned.

He allowed himself the pillow of her, for soon they would emerge from that steep place onto a plain and he would be alone. The clacking wheels turned and churned and birth is not a thing of ones, one spasm, one swelling, one hour of pain, one cry. Between the wombs of woman and the grave, upon this belly earth, the fetus re-enacts itself a thousand times; breath tears and struggles in its caul; the shroud awaits; the angel of despair spreads wings like nets to catch the risers; bear your birth, the angel said. He allowed them both this sleeping moment before the rent, the breaking tears, the cry, before this monster he was riding bore him off again to peace and loneliness.

A Yankee Inquisitor

Elise Sanguinetti

WELL, everybody in town found out Mr. Hopper was visiting us. I guess it was Mrs. Foster that went around telling it. Father says if you tell Mrs. Foster anything it's just like publishing it in the *Reader's Digest*. She must have gotten on the phone early, because the next day at Sunday school Melissa Stewart (she's the one with four telephones in her house) said, "Hear you got a nigger lover in your house! Everybody in town's talking about it."

That made me perfectly furious and we'd just got through renouncing the pomp and the devil, too. The pomp and devil is part of the Episcopal catechism and we have to memorize the whole thing.

"You're not suppose to use that expression," I said. "It's common."

"What's common?"

"You're supposed to say Neeee—gro lover," I said, and just walked on off down the street.

I guess I shouldn't have walked away like that because then I knew I wouldn't get a ride home. Melissa and them's mothers always come in the car to get them, but Mother makes me walk. She thinks it's foolish to ride everywhere. Even if a blizzard or something would suddenly hit Georgia, there I'd be, all alone, struggling to get somewhere.

Anyway, I'm glad I left Melissa. She's my best friend, but she simply hates it if something good happens to you. Nobody famous ever visits the Stewarts; they never have any out-of-town guests at all. I guess Mrs. Foster had told everybody what Mr. Hopper thought about the South. They don't like Neeeegro lovers in Ashton. They like Neeegroes better than they do the lovers. It's most peculiar.

I got to thinking about all that while I was walking home and, too, I was wondering how was I going to get a chance to present my intellect to Mr. Hopper. Mother and Father occupied him practically all the time, and even after breakfast I didn't get a chance to see him alone. Also, I was pretty scared at the idea of talking to him. Isn't it funny that in the nighttime when you think up doing something, it seems a whole lot easier than when the morning comes. But one thing is if you get your mind up on something, like saving your brother or something, you can pretty well do it. Besides, as I say, I have a tremendous faculty for being untruthful sometimes.

Anyway, I came dragging on up the driveway to our house and right away I saw Mother and Mr. Hopper out in the garden. Mother wasn't going to church. When we have unspiritual guests in the house she doesn't usually go. She gets furious, not going, but I guess it's nicer being considerate of the guest.

Mother and Mr. Hopper were bending over looking at the Christmas roses. Mother simply adores the Christmas rose. She planted them about three years ago and they've bloomed every year just at the right time.

"Yeeeees," said Mr. Hopper. "Stunning." He straightened up. "Oh hello, Felicia."

"Hello, Mr. Hopper." Right away my heart started pounding away. I was wondering if I really dared to discuss anything with him or not. I knew I couldn't with Mother there, of course.

He walked over to our largest camellia bush. "I never realized they bloomed this time of year," he said. "Wait until I tell my friends in New York." He kind of waved his hand. "Camellias instead of snow."

It was a very nice day. There wasn't a cloud in the sky and it was almost like spring. I guess up in New York it was storming with snow.

"I love the camellias, too," Mother said, "but my favorite, of course, are the jonquils. We don't see them until March. Let me show you." We walked over to the side of the hill. "By March, the entire hillside is covered with jonquils."

"Stunning," Mr. Hopper said.

"Yes, it means spring to me," Mother said. "I love to see them when they're first pushing through the ground." She smiled at Mr. Hopper. "There's a poem I love, by Sara Henderson Hay, the poet. It's so lovely."

"Oh?" said Mr. Hopper.

"If I can remember—There's two lines I especially love:

> And bladed jonquils, pricking through,
> Can split my very soul in two.

"Yessssss, beautiful!" said Mr. Hopper.

Mother pushed back a strand of hair and sort of laughed into the breeze. "It reminds me of my two youngsters—just now at the age they are now. They're kind of pricking through."

They both looked at me. Embarrassing! I'm not like any bladed jonquil. I wish Mother wouldn't say things like that. I kind of started whistling off around the holly tree. I didn't want them to stand there smiling at me like I was a weed or something.

"It's a beau-ti-ful, beau-ti-ful garden," Mr. Hopper said.

"Thank you. Both Allison and I enjoy gardening." She turned to him. "I wish you had time to see the farm."

"That would be—"

But then Velvet called for Mother; somebody wanted her on the telephone. I could have cried with joy.

She hurried toward the house and Mr. Hopper and I were alone. *Now* was the time, I thought. My heart really started banging away.

Mr. Hopper was looking up into the holly tree. "This tree must be fifty years old, at least."

"Uh huh," I said and started yawning. "Ohhhh me."

"Sleepy?"

"Me? Oh, no. I just *do* wish my Neeeegro friends were coming over this afternoon."

I yawned very loudly again and Mr. Hopper looked at me pretty sharply. "Do you have Neeegro friends?"

"Of course! Most of my friends are Neeee-gro." I tried to look exceedingly bored. "I've got hundreds of them."

"Do they come *here?*" he asked. "To your home?"

"Occasionally. Not very often. Mother and Father seem more partial to my white friends. I have one Neeeegro friend, Melissa Stewart." (She'd die!) "She used to come quite frequently, but Mother and Father put a stop to it."

"Why did they do that?"

I wished he'd stop staring at me. I didn't dare look at him, so I just kind of casually started pulling a few berries off the tree. "I don't know *why* they don't like them to come. I guess it's because of Mr. and Mrs. Ewing and them."

"What do *they* have to do about it?"

"Oh, I guess they didn't think I should be seen with just colored people all the time. I think they spoke to Mother or something." Gosh, my heart was about to pop right out of me. I looked up at him. "But I forgot, you met the Ewings last night. Didn't you?"

"Yessss, I met them all right." He had this kind of peculiar frown on his face and started looking at his fingernails. "Wouldn't you like it, actually, wouldn't you, if your Neeegro friends could go to school with you?"

I remembered he'd asked me that before, when he first came. "Yes," I said, "now that I think about it. I'd adore it if Melissa Stewart could go to school with me. People in the North go to school with Neeeegroes all the time, don't they?"

"Some do."

"How I *do* wish it were the same here! You know, I don't think I'd mind it even if I were the only white person in the room."

He didn't seem to be listening. "Perhaps *your* generation—you and your friends can do something about all this. The Neeegro just isn't treated right down here. Is he?"

"No, he's not." I started digging my heel in the ground. "And *poor* Velvet! She suffers so. So does Isaiah. They've told me so many things."

"What have they told you?"

"Ohhhh—" I started yawning again—"Velvet says she goes home lots of times and just crieeeees because she's Neeee-gro."

"She shouldn't do that."

"No, she shouldn't. I usually try to cheer her up about it—also Isaiah. It's very pathetic."

"You're a nice girl, Felicia."

I kind of turned the corners of my mouth down. "Thank you," I said. "Thank you."

There was this kind of silence, but then Mr. Hopper started beaming around all over the place. "How would you like for me to take your picture, Felicia?"

I nearly collapsed. "Me!? For your magazine?"

"Maybe," he said. "We'll see how it turns out."

I started kind of smoothing my hair back. I knew I looked a wreck, but I had on my black and white plaid dress. "Well, sure!" I said.

"Good then. Let's see—"

"Are you going to put what I *said* in the magazine?"

"What you *said?*" His eyes kind of bulged.

"Uh huh. You know, about me and colored people and all?"

"I might. Yes, I might!"

"Well, surely you can take my picture!" I nearly floated away with delight.

"I'd like to show the Northern girls what a fine Southern girl looks like."

I couldn't help smiling, but then I had this other thought. "Do you think that—uh—" I kind of looked away for a second—"Uh—don't tell Mother or anything. She's quite peculiar. She—uh—"

"Oh, do you think she would mind?"

"Oh, no! She—uh—sometimes she thinks it's kind of vulgar being in newspapers and magazines and things. It's really quite peculiar."

"Haven't you ever had your picture in the newspaper?"

I started rolling my eyes upward. "Oh, I've had chances! But, you know, Mr. Hopper?" I kind of laughed. "I've been so silly. I used to think it was vulgar, too, being in newspapers and things. I got over it, though."

"Most young girls in the North *like* to have their pictures in the paper."

"So do *I!* Now, I mean. I'd just as soon have my picture plastered all over the place. It's nice to be public like that, I think."

"Well, let's see." He started looking around. "Where would a good place be? What about on the front veranda? By one of the pillars."

"All right. You don't have your camera, though!"

"I'll get it."

"Don't let mother or anybody see you," I called after him. I was so excited I could scarcely talk.

Well, Mr. Hopper took a stunning picture. I was smiling extremely broadly and sort of had my hand touching one of the pillars. The only thing was I kept thinking about my legs. See, I'd started growing pretty fiercely and my legs are very, very thin. They don't touch in the middle where they're supposed to. I did everything to try to make them touch but I don't think they did.

Mr. Hopper said he thought he'd gotten a "fine shot." He liked the front of our house and he was sure I'd added great measures to it. He didn't know exactly when his article would appear. Probably not until late summer or fall. But when we were going in the house he told me he was certainly glad he'd come to Ashton. "It's been a gold mine. Those people last night and now my little talk with you." He smiled down at me very nicely. "Amazing," he said. "Simply a-mazing!"

During lunch I didn't say much while we were eating. I was thinking too hard about all the lies I'd told. Still, what I told Mr. Hopper wasn't all lies. I really *do* love many colored people. If, say, I saw Velvet somewhere and she was writhing away in a gutter or something, I'd just about die myself. Velvet can make me terribly mad, like out at the farm that time when she told on me, but I'd do anything for her. I really would, and if she died I'd never get over it. I'd go and put violets on her grave every Sunday. I might even do it if Freedonia died.

You don't know Freedonia, but she's Velvet's niece. She's my age and she used to wear red ribbons in her hair all the time. When we were children Velvet used to bring her by the house. We'd play, but the only thing is Freedonia and I are different. What she wanted to do was play Swinging Hips all the time. What you do is you stand by the elm tree, put your hands on your hips and then walk real crazy and fast with your hips swinging all over the place. I thought that was very boring, but Freedonia nearly killed herself laughing over it. What I wanted to do was jump the boxwoods. Do you know that to this day I can clear a five-foot boxwood without even touching it. Freedonia couldn't stand to do that. She'd try, but almost every time she'd land smack in the middle. Mother got kind of furious because Freedonia had broken about six of her best boxwoods. I don't know what ever happened to Freedonia. She moved to Detroit when we were six. Sometimes I wonder what became of her.

The only thing is I don't like mean niggers and that isn't bad to say. Velvet says it herself. I told her it wasn't cultivated to say "nigger," but she said it was all right if they were mean. "Ain't no other word for 'em," she said. "That's what they is—mean niggers!" You'd die over them and I don't think even Mr. Hopper would like them. They hate white people, mean niggers do. Velvet said so.

Anyway, after lunch Mr. Hopper said he wanted to go around and see something of the people of Ashton. He wanted to make a call on the head of the N.A.A.A.A.C.P. and he wanted to visit with Velvet's preacher. Velvet's preacher is widely known in Ashton and just about everybody in town has contributed money for this new church he wants to build. People have contributed for centuries. You'd think it ought to be built by now.

"Why don't you let Isaiah drive you?" Mother said.

"That would be nice. *Thank* you," Mr. Hopper said.

I knew Isaiah would flip over that. Sunday is his day off. One thing, though, I knew Isaiah was counting on a pretty big tip from Mr. Hopper. Tips are the only thing Isaiah likes about guests. He can always tell whether somebody's gonna tip pretty good or not.

"He ain't no count," he says about some people. "He jes a one-dollar man." What Isaiah likes is a "fi-dollah" man. I kind of think he thought Mr. Hopper was a "fi-dollah" man; he was being so nice to Isaiah and everything.

Mother went into the kitchen to tell Velvet about Mr. Hopper wanting to go to her church that afternoon.

"What for?" she asked with this down-in-the-mouth look she gets sometimes.

"Because he wants to meet your minister and because he's interested in all things American," Mother said.

"Why don't he write up something about his own church," Velvet mumbled to me after Mother had gone.

"Maybe he doesn't have one," I said. "He's divorced." My uncle that is divorced has simply left the church. He never goes. It worries the family no end.

"Pshaw," Velvet said. That's what she always says when she's thinking somebody's white trash.

"Will you be there, Velvet, in church?"

"If I kin ever get outta here, I will."

"You've got time," I said. Velvet's church doesn't begin until two in the afternoon. "Be sure and tell me about it!"

Mr. Hopper had his camera slung around his neck which was a very unspiritual way to go to church, I thought. Isaiah had on his driver's cap, too, the one Mother gave him for Christmas. He's only supposed to wear it when he's driving, but he wears it practically all the time. He's simply wild about it.

"I won't be gone very long," Mr. Hopper said. "I just want to have a chat with a few of these people."

"Fine," Mother said.

"See you later," Arthur said, and he followed Mr. Hopper out the back door!

I nearly fainted. I didn't know *he* was going with Mr. Hopper.

"Ar-thur!" Mother called to him. "Where are you going?"

"I'm just going with Mr. Hopper."

"It's all right," Mr. Hopper said.

"No, I don't believe so," Mother said.

"No, Arthur," Father said. "Not this time."

Arthur came dragging on back to the house. "Goooo-ud night, you act like I'm a child or something. You can't do anything around here."

"Mr. Hopper would rather be alone, I'm sure, " Mother said. "He can speak more freely to the people."

"He *asked* me to go," Arthur said.

"I don't want us to have any part in any of Mr. Hopper's investigations," Father said.

My face started getting red. I wonder what he'd say if he knew Mr. Hopper had taken my picture and was also going to quote my intellect in his article. I decided then and there I wouldn't tell anybody about it, not even Velvet or Isaiah. After it came out, they'd all collapse with surprise.

"What time does his bus leave?" Mother asked. She looked very exhausted.

"Five," Father said. "He has an eight-o'clock plane out of Atlanta."

"Is he going back to New York?" I asked.

"No, Florida, I think."

Northerners are always going to Florida in the wintertime. We're always having visitors come by to see us on their way to Florida. Most Southerners wouldn't think of going there then because of all the cheap rich people there then. Besides, Southerners know the weather down there, and they laugh at all the Northerners that think they're going to swim and stuff when all they do is freeze to death and sit around looking cheap and brassy. Not all Northerners are like that, I guess, just most of them. They're very loud, as you know.

"Pretty difficult man, wouldn't you say?" Father asked.

Mother just flipped her hand. "Now, Allison, this is the last. I'm just tired to death of having people here like that—people we'll *never* see again."

Father just kind of laughed.

Mr. Hopper and Isaiah didn't come back until just about bus-time. Both of them were bustling around, trying to get all his junk together.

"Fascinating. Ab-so-lute-ly fascinating," Mr. Hopper said about Velvet's preacher. "He gave me some excellent quotes and I took a charming picture—of his entire family, in their home. All of them were sitting around their table with their heads bowed."

I almost died. Me and Velvet's preacher would be in the magazine together! Just us. I kept thinking what everybody in Ashton would say. Mother would collapse. My face started getting scarlet. I shouldn't have let him take my picture. I know I shouldn't've.

"You've been simply charming," Mr. Hopper said to Mother. "Don't know when I've enjoyed anything so much. Bless you. Come to New York sometime."

"We will!" Arthur said, and I couldn't even open my mouth.

Isaiah was struggling through the door with Mr. Hopper's typewriter and stuff.

Mr. Hopper shook hands with Father. "I'll remember the quails," he said. "You'll hear from me next year."

"Good!" Father said.

"Have a good trip," Mother called after him.

Mr. Hopper grinned back at her and hustled on out to the car and Isaiah.

"Well," Mother said after he was gone. She gave out a huge sigh. "That is that!"

"I wonder what sort of information he got this afternoon," Father said.

"The Lord only knows," Mother said. "But, Allison, I certainly hope he doesn't include us in anything."

"He won't. At least he won't use our names. He assured me of that."

But the *picture,* I thought. I shouldn't have done it! I shouldn't have. I *know* I shouldn't've. And I had all the way to the fall to worry about it.

At six Isaiah came back with the car. The bus had been late. He came dragging on in and I knew he was in a horrible mood because of working on Sunday. I don't blame him much; Sunday's a day of rest.

He came on in the living room to give the keys to Father. He really looked beat up. I decided to try to cheer him up.

"How much tip did he give you, Isaiah? Was he a fi-dollah man?"

"Nothin'," was all he said.

"Whaaaat?" Mother said. "You mean he didn't even *tip* you? Did he leave anything for Velvet?"

"No'm."

Mother looked at Father. "Well, now, *really,* Allison. That makes me pretty sore. After all his high-sounding talk, too!"

Father didn't say anything. He just got up and gave Isaiah three dollars. "Give this to Velvet when you go home," he said. He gave him another three dollars.

"Goooo-ud night!" Arthur said. Even Arthur knows how to tip.

Mother asked Isaiah if he liked Mr. Hopper.

"No'm," he said.

"Why not?" Arthur asked him.

"He's hankty."

"I suppose," was all Mother said.

But I didn't say anything. I was wondering if Mother and Father could actually kill me. They could try, I know. And they probably would when the picture and article came out.

The Stone Soldier

William Cobb

I

I T was nine-thirty in the morning when he stepped off the train, and the first thing he did was to pull the wrinkled, big, red bandana out of his hip pocket and slowly wipe his face. He grunted under the heat and stood looking around—at the deserted platform with only one old Negro standing in the two-foot strip of shade next to the yellow wall, under the sign that said, in peeling whitish letters, HAMMOND; at the dusty street that ran away from the station, toward the east and toward the new sun; at the small frame buildings lining the street and the few brick ones; and halfway up the street, at the sign that said MADISON HOTEL, and under that, *Dining Room,* in smaller letters. He grunted again and looked at the Negro.

"Mornin, Uncle," he said. His white suit was stained under his armpits and wrinkled up the back; it was tight across his bulging belly, and the pants hugged his legs and made his thighs look like fat sausages under his belly. There was an early-morning stubble on his fleshy jowls, and he exuded an odor that was part sweat, part cheap bourbon, and part that universal smell of the fat person emerging from close quarters. His hat was pushed back to reveal a matted, yellow widow's peak over his squinting eyes as he looked at the small straw suitcase beside him, and then at the Negro, who hadn't answered him.

"I said mornin, Uncle," he said.

"I said mornin," the Negro answered. His face was in shadow, and the fat man couldn't tell by his tone of voice if he were trying to be smart with him. He paused a moment, looking around.

"The Lord doth send heat and make white and nigger alike sweat under it, don't he?" the fat man said. "Lord if he don't."

"Yes sir," the Negro said.

"But Goddam if a man got to stay out in it, has he? I'll just be gettin on up to the Madison Hotel for a bath and a shave, and then I'll be tendin to my business and be gettin on my way. But Lord if it ain't hot as the fires of almighty hell." The Negro said nothing, and the fat man widened his eyes and peered into the shadows at his face. The fat man's eyes bulged in their sockets; they looked as though they were loose inside his head. They kept moving back and forth, just slightly, a slight wiggle as if they might have been too well greased and he couldn't quite control them; it made him tilt his face slightly to the side and peer like an old woman trying to thread a needle. He stood there looking at the Negro for a minute, and he couldn't say anything. Because the Negro's lower lip was stretched; it hung down over his chin, glistening wetly, startlingly red against the dull, brown skin like the meat of a dog, torn open by buzzards, looks red against the bloated brown belly. The Negro moved his head, and the lip flapped, and his eyes bored into the fat man's with an incomprehensible message. The fat man felt the heat of the sun against the side of his sweating neck.

"It's open for business," the Negro said.

"What?"

"Madison Hotel," he said, and the lip flapped.

"My name is Lyman Sparks," the fat man said. He pulled out the bandana and swiped it around his neck; he reached into the folds of fat over his belly, into a pocket of his vest, and pulled out a small card and handed it to the Negro. The Negro didn't look at it; he just held it in his hand, at his side. "I do quite a bit of business with colored folks," the man said. "Not that that's what I'm here for, but you just well kill two birds with one stone, I always say." He looked slyly at the Negro, and a grin revealed blackened, twisted teeth. "And that's what the boss says too. Got to please the boss, ain't that right?"

The Negro moved out of the shadow. He was much taller than Sparks, with a high, slanting forehead and tight black hair sticking closely to his head; his arms hung loosely at his sides, and his legs were thin under the coarse cloth of his breeches. Sparks found himself looking at the soft, moist underlip, which was even more red when the sun hid it.

"Now," Sparks said, "what is your name?"

"Lip," the Negro said. His eyes bored into Sparks.

"Well now," Sparks said. "Well now. I reckon you're a freed man?"

"That's right," Lip said.

"Well then, I reckon I can talk to you man to man, or salesman, with somethin you need and want, to buyer who'd gointa be eternally grateful that I happened along. Ain't that right? Like, now that you your own boss, ain't no reason why you can't decide what you want to buy and what you don't, now is it?"

"It ain't much I want to buy," Lip said. Sparks grinned slyly at him again.

"Well now, suppose I was to take you in with me on the sellin side? Suppose I didn't want you to buy anything. Suppose I wanted you to sell with me?"

Lip didn't answer him. He just stood there, his dark eyes level on Sparks.

"Course when I show you what I got, ain't no doubt in my mind that you gointa want one, too. And ain't no reason why I can't just give you one, long as we gone be partners, now is it?" He tilted his head to the side, as though he couldn't quite get Lip into focus. "Well now," he said, and he grunted as he knelt to open up the straw suitcase and began to rummage around among papers and pieces of clothing until he found what he was looking for, a small black book that was unmistakably a Bible.

"Now, I know you go to church, am I right? Sho you do, I know that by just lookin at you. And I can see you know what this here is I'm holdin in my hand. But reckon you do? Now just reckon you do?" He opened it and shoved it under Lip's nose, and the Negro took it and looked at the picture in front of him.

It was a well-known picture; Lip had seen it in the Episcopal church, made out of glass in a window; he had seen it when he helped Johnny Pope clean up down there. It was the one of Jesus, holding a little sheep in his arms and with other lambs around his feet rubbing up against his legs like cats will do. Only one thing was different. Jesus' face was dark, and his lips were thick, and his hair was darker, only still long and soft looking, and his hands holding the little sheep were dark, too.

Lip stood there looking down at it; he could hear Sparks breathing heavily beside him as he let the pages flip through his fingers, and it opened to the picture of the boy Jesus in the temple, when he was twelve years old. Here, too, he was a young colored boy, with some sand stuck to the paper that reflected the sunlight and made it look like a bright halo over the boy's head. The book seemed light and flimsy in Lip's hand; the pages were not slick like the ones in the Bible he had at home, but rough and coarse, and the printing was, in places, light and faded looking.

"Well?" Sparks said. And when the Negro didn't answer, he said, "Well, what do you think of it?"

"I reckon I already got a Bible," Lip said.

"But not like this one, I bet," Sparks said. He laughed, then. "Go on. Take it. I'm givin it to you, ain't gone charge you a cent for it. I do like that sometimes, good business, I always say. So you can just take it, and it don't obligate you in any way whatsoever. No sir." He looked slyly at Lip again and grinned. "Only thing is, I sho do think you ought to show it around. You know, show it to all your good friends, cause they gone sho want one, too, don't you reckon? After all, they freed men now too; ain't nobody to tell em what they can't have and what they can, and that's just what my company felt like after the war. Figured you colored folks ought to have products of your own, that's all."

"I don't know," Lip said.

"Hell, ahhh, Lip, I ain't askin you to sell for me. Nothing like that. Just let folks know that I got em, and where they can get em. That's all. You gone be doin them a favor."

Lip didn't answer. He just stood there, looking at the fat man with those deep eyes, large and red-rimmed, but steady.

"You understand that ain't my business. Hell no. That's just a little sideline. A little service, you might say. A public service. I don't charge but a quarter for em, and that's some fine worksmanship goes into that artwork, you can see that. And hell, the quarter don't hardly pay for totin em around. No, I got other business round here, big business—but I figured I just might kill two birds with one stone."

He grinned again and tilted his head.

"Well, you just take that one, anyhow, hear? I want you to have it, free of charge. Let's just say, as a gift from a stranger who ain't never been in Hammond before. Maybe that'll bring me some luck on my other deal, my big deal." He winked at Lip and wiped his neck with the balled-up bandana. "I didn't come here just to sell no Bibles. No sir. But you just keep it, and you know where I'll be. The Madison Hotel. Ask for Mr. Sparks." He closed the straw suitcase and glanced up the sun-bright street to the hotel. A cotton wagon was coming slowly down the street, and the mule's hooves made little clouds of dust rise out of the motionless air. "Good to seen you, Lip. And that's Sparks, Lyman Sparks from Mobile." He pulled at his crotch, set his hat low over his eyes, and headed up the street on his sausage legs.

From where Dale Spivey was sitting, on the porch of the hotel, he could see Sparks leave the platform and start up the street. He had been watching while Sparks and the Negro were talking, his cane-bottom chair leaning back against a post at the edge of the porch. He was holding a pipe on his lap, and his eyes were half closed like the eyes of an old cow standing in the shade. He watched Sparks, lugging the straw suitcase, pass the wagon and tip his hat to the old Negro on the seat, and wipe at his neck with the red bandana.

"Walks straddle-legged like he scared some of the fat on his legs gone rub off his privates," Dale Spivey said.

He was speaking to Mr. Downey, who had been sitting in exactly the same position as Dale Spivey, only with his chair leaning back against the wall of the hotel.

"Who?" Mr. Downey said.

"That drummer."

Mr. Downey let his chair fall with a dull thump, and he leaned forward to look up the street at Sparks. Sparks came on slowly, already out of breath, bent at the waist and craning his short neck toward the two men on the porch. They watched him come up and stand in the street until he got his breath, wiping at his sweating face; then he came up the steps onto the porch.

"Mornin." His breath wheezed out around the word. "Lord if it ain't hot."

"Mornin," the two men said at the same time.

"My name is Sparks, Lyman Sparks," he said. "And I would assume you to be Mr. J. P. Downey, owner and proprietor of the Madison Hotel."

"That's right," Downey said.

"Well, I'm pleased to meet you," Sparks said. Then he looked at Dale, still leaning back in the cane-bottom chair, his eyes half closed and the cold pipe clenched between his teeth.

"That's Dale Spivey," Mr. Downey said.

"I'm happy to make your acquaintance, Mr. Spivey," Sparks said.

Dale just nodded, and Mr. Sparks tilted his head to the side, and his eyes shifted; then he looked off up the street and at the buildings giving away to a few houses as the road ran down a hill. In the distance he could see the river, pale and shimmering under the sun, and the white-limerock ditches at the side of the street reflected the sun back at him. "Lord, it's gointa be another one, ain't it?" he said.

"It's September," Dale said.

"And rightly so. Rightly so," Sparks said. "But it sho nuff makes it uncomfortable for heavy folks." He sat in an empty chair and placed the straw suitcase carefully against the wall. The chair creaked under him as he pulled at and straightened his crotch. "Well now, Mr. Downey, I'll be wantin to put up with you for a while, but it's sho no hurry about it. I trust you do have room for me." Mr. Downey nodded. "I'll be transactin some business from here, but it's a mite early in the day to be talkin business deals, so I'll just set here for awhile with you all if you don't mind."

"Fine," Mr. Downey said.

They sat quietly for a while, and Sparks watched the heat waves rising off the road. An occasional wagon would go by, loaded with cotton, and the driver would raise his hand in greeting, and the men on the porch would do the same. Mr. Downey was a small man, with a thick, rough-looking shirt and a string tie, and a graying moustache; his face was sun-spotted and deeply tanned, and his eyes were small and bright and quick. Dale hardly moved at all; his heavy boots rested on the heels, and his breeches were drawn up his legs for the occasional slight breeze. His chin rested on his chest and his drooping eyes kept closing and opening and he kept taking the pipe from his mouth and putting it back. When he spoke suddenly, Sparks thought that someone else had come onto the porch.

"You had some business with John Thomas?" Dale said, and Sparks' eyes shifted to Dale.

"Who's that?" he said.

"John Thomas, the nigger down there at the station."

"Oh yes. Well, not business, I don't guess you'd say." He paused a minute. "That nigger told me his name was Lip."

"It is," Mr. Downey said. "John Thomas Lip."

"Oh," Sparks said. Then, after a minute, "Wonder what make his lip hang down like that?"

"He come right from Africa like that," Dale said. "One of them tribes in Africa, that he come from. They lips growed like that."

"Well, I declare," Sparks said. "Now don't that beat all? I never seen one of them before. I reckon you learn somethin ever day, don't you?"

"His mammy was like that too," Dale said. "Both of em belonged to Major Hammond. The old woman died before the war." Then his eyes closed.

"Well, I declare," Sparks said. "Beats all, don't it?"

Sparks watched Mr. Downey take a plug of tobacco from his pocket, pick a few pieces of lint off of it, cut a neat plug, and put it into his mouth. He waited until the hotel proprietor had chewed it a while, and he could see that Mr. Downey could talk.

"How is Major Hammond?" he asked, looking at Mr. Downey.

"Not good, I don't think," Mr. Downey said.

"Sick?"

"Well, he don't ever leave the house anymore. Miss Iva, she takes care of him, but he just sets there in the house and rocks."

"Well now, that's a pity," Sparks said. "That's sho bad. Man like that."

"You know the Major?" Dale asked, and his eyes opened a little. His chin came up off his chest a fraction.

"Well, no, not really. But Lord if I don't feel like I do. I heard enough about him." He wiped at his face. "Sho bad. Hear he lost ever thing he had. Sho bad."

Dale laughed. It was a low, muffled rumbling from out of his chest. "He could still write you a check for ten thousand dollars."

"Well now, I could too. I could write you a check for a million dollars, but that don't mean it'd be any good."

Sparks knew right then that he had moved too fast, and his eyes wiggled as he looked at Dale and then at Mr. Downey. They looked straight ahead, and he couldn't read their eyes. "But Lord, what does it matter?" he said. Mr. Downey let his chair fall again with a thump, and he leaned forward and spat a yellow stream over the edge of the porch. "Yes sir, I always say, what does it matter?" Sparks repeated.

But they didn't answer him. Sparks wiped at his face and neck and stood up. "Well, I just might get inta that room and get me a clean shirt on befo dinner, yes sir," he said. He picked up the suitcase and looked at Mr. Downey.

"Just tell the nigger," Mr. Downey said, hooking his thumb over his shoulder at the door. "He'll show you."

"Fine," said Sparks. He moved toward the door. "I hope you gentlemen will take dinner with me," he said. "In any case, I'll be down after a while. And it was certainly nice to've met cha." After he heaved through the door and into the gloom of the hotel, the two men sat without speaking for a while.

Then Dale said, "That son-of-a-bitch has got shifty eyes." And Mr. Downey just nodded and reached for his plug.

II

Sparks could feel the sweat running down the insides of his legs and down his collar as he walked through the town and he took out the fresh bandana, his third for the day, to mop his face. And then, at last, he was standing at the gate, looking up the sandy walk to the house and at the hint of lace curtains at the darkened windows and at the dusty verbena and smilax shading the veranda. The iron plowshare rattled on its chain as he pushed through the gate and puffed up the path to the porch. He knocked and then looked through the colored glass at the side of the door, cocking his head like a man trying to look at another man's woman without his knowing it, but when he saw the Negro woman coming up the hall, he snatched his hat from his head and stood, holding it over his belly, and waited for the door to open.

"Good afternoon," he said before the Negress could speak. "I was wonderin if I might have a audience with the Major. With Major Hammond."

The Negro woman was as big as he was; she stood blocking the door, looking levelly at him. Her broad face was bright yellow, and her skin was as moist and looked as soft as fresh baked bread; it shone dully over her broad nose, and her biceps bulged under the sleeves of a white house dress. She looked him up and down, at his dusty shoes and wrinkled suit, at his sweating face and matted hair.

"What?" she said.

"See him," he said. "See Major Hammond."

"The Major don't see nobody," she said and made a step back as though to close the door in his face.

"Well then," he said, "I'd like to see Miss Iva Ward Hammond, then, if you don't mind."

"Miss Ida restin," she said.

"Well now, this is a matter of great importance, Auntie, and I'd be glad to wait," he said and moved toward the door.

"You wait here," she said and pushed the door gently to. After a minute she reappeared and opened the door widely for him to enter.

"Miss Ida say for you to wait in the parlor," she said; "she be downstairs in a minute." She disappeared into the damp gloom of the hall toward the back of the house. Sparks realized with a sudden sense of pleasure that the house was much larger than it had looked from the outside; he went into the parlor and put his hat carefully on a deep-crimson sofa, slightly worn at the corners, and walked over to the window. He could see all the way down to the river from the window, to where the dusty road wound down to the landing and the big, stone storage barn that the young Negro at the hotel had told him was haunted because the walls ran water. But Dale Spivey had told him that the walls sweated because they had stored salt in it during the war. Then he looked around the room, at the two oil portraits over the mantel, in peeling gilt frames, the man looking stiff and staring, with steel-gray eyes and hair, and the woman looking stiff and rosy-cheeked, with a mountain of black curls piled over her head. He noticed the framed Stars and Bars on one wall, with black-edged holes in it, and brownish stains in one corner, and the bookcase crammed with leather-bound volumes between the windows. He took one of the books out and looked at the flyleaf, it was spotted and brown, and in faded ink was scrawled across the page: "Winslow Hammond, Rose Hill, 1834."

"My brother, Winslow, the oldest," he heard a voice say, and it startled him. He turned to see her standing just inside the parlor. "He was the only one of us that liked books and literature," she said. "Really liked them."

She came into the room and stood across from him, and his eyes flicked over her, from the dark dress, black or navy blue, down to the floor where he could hardly see the tiny shoes beneath, back to where her blouse gathered around her neck with white lace, to the face with the high white forehead that might have been chiseled from the limerock river bluff at the edge of town. Her gray-black hair was pulled back sharply to a knot at the back of her head. Her eyes were wide, but not staring, and were a clear, deep brown, steady on him as she came across the parlor. The thought that he had seen them before flickered into his consciousness and out again as she stopped and looked at him.

"I'm Iva Hammond," she said, and her lips were just a thin line over the strong, jutting chin. "Carla says that you'd like to see me, Mr. ——"

"Sparks. Lyman Sparks," he said. He looked at her eyes again, and there was the same question, the same look. He cleared his throat.

"I was hoping to see the Major, Miss Hammond," he said, "but I think you can help me."

"Won't you sit down, Mr. Sparks?" she said and sat herself on the slightly worn, red sofa. He took the rocker across from her, put his bulging legs out before him, and smiled his twisted smile at her. She looked steadily back at him, and he could read nothing in her face.

"Would you like a cool glass of water, Mr. Sparks?" she said. Before he could answer she called Carla, who came with a tray and a pitcher and two tall glasses and poured him a glass. He tasted it and smacked his lips.

"Ahhhh, that's good," he said. "I don't know when it's been so hot."

"It's the lime," she said.

"I beg your pardon, mam?" he said.

"The lime, in the water. Makes it so good. My father always used to say that that was one of the best advantages of this river bend, the lime water."

"It is good," Sparks said. He tilted the glass and had another swallow, and smiled at her, and said Ahhhh again. They sat quietly, and he could hear a clock ticking somewhere, and he heard Carla moving around in the back of the house.

"Well, Mr. Sparks, what was it you wanted to talk with me about?" she said.

"Well now," he said. He reached into his vest, pulled out a card, and leaning forward with effort, passed it to her. "Miss Iva—" He paused and grinned, "Miss Hammond, is your name Iva or Ida?"

A slight smile flickered at her thin lips, and she said, "It's Iva, Mr. Sparks. Though most of the Negroes call me Miss Ida. They have as long as I can remember."

"Well, Miss Iva," he said, grinning, "as you can see by my card, I represent the Dixie Monument Company, Mobile branch."

"Yes," she said.

"And I'm in this area, what you might call, solicitin for future buildin of monuments and callin on the most prominent citizens in each town to discuss it. Naturally, the first folks I'd call on in Hammond would be the Hammonds theirselves," he said, and he grinned and nodded to her.

"What sort of monuments would these be, sir?" she said.

"Why, Confederate monuments, Miss Iva, of course." Her expression didn't change, and the brown, deep eyes seemed even deeper. "Now we've sold one over at Livingston; it's possible that you've seen that one, and well, most of the towns are gointa be puttin em up sooner or later, and well, Miss Iva, we just feel like we got the best product for the people. Yes mam, ours is guaranteed to be standin long after a hundred years is up."

Miss Iva got up from the sofa and went to the window. His eyes followed her, and then turned inward as if he were examining what he would say next, or making it up, or trying to figure whether he has been too quick as he had been with Spivey and Mr. Downey. Then he fished into his coat and pulled out several pieces of paper, with drawings. They were slightly damp, and he brushed at the lint and bits of tobacco stuck on them, and heaved himself up from the rocker.

"You might like to look these over, Miss Ida. Of course, you'd want to see the real thing. But I can tell you, it's some fine art work goes into these statues, yes mam. And, too, right now we got cannons from about ever major battle in the war. Any one you want, you just name it and we'll supply. And it'll be the real thing, yes mam, the real thing. We don't believe in pushing off cannons made up there in some factory after the war like some of the companies are doin. Why, they's a company in Georgia claimed they had all the cannons from Chancellorsville for sale with their statues, and by God, they wasn't a one of em the real thing." He couldn't tell what she was thinking, or even if she was listening to him.

Then she turned from the window, and the dark eyes bored into him as she came back to the sofa and sat down.

"Mr. Sparks," she said, "I don't think you understand how scarce money is in Hammond right now. I don't think you know about our situation here."

He quickly arranged a sorrowful expression on his face. "Of course I do, Miss Ida. My company does, I mean. Why, we've taken that into consideration. Let me tell you, mam, that we've got a plan, yes mam, a plan for your whole town. Why, you can take up to fifty years to pay for it. We can arrange just about anything you want."

"Why?"

"I beg your pardon, mam?"

"I only asked why, Mr. Sparks," she said.

His eyes seemed to be jumping from one side of her face to the other.

"Never mind," she said. And then, "But why do you come to me?"

He grinned. "Why, well now, Miss Ida, you ought to know that. A man like me wants to do business with the right kind of people. And you know that if you, or the Major, said to the people of this town that they ought to buy one a these statues, which they sho ought, ain't no doubt about that, then they'd buy one. Now that's my business. I know what the people need, but I can't always get it over to em what they need. But the right kind of folks, you ain't got to sell, now ain't that right?"

"Well, I don't think that this is the time."

"Well, now, Miss Ida, you just ought to think about that. Now is the time to," and here he paused, "honor your dead. Our dead. Folks need to be reminded of those young boys that gave they lives for they country. Now, you sho believe that, now don't you?"

She glanced quickly at him, and he could detect that question in her eyes, that question that he'd seen before, and she said, "Mr. Sparks, I don't need to be reminded of the tragedy of the war."

"You don't, Miss Ida, now don't you think I know that? But what about all them folks that're gointa come after you? What about them? What about—"

He stopped, and his eyes were on the door to the parlor, and she knew even before she turned that her brother was standing there, and she knew what he looked like. Sparks' mouth was standing open and his eyes were active, and the beads of sweat were standing out on his face. And she thought about the Bible that Carla had told her about, the one the man had given Lip, and that Lip had brought to the kitchen door when he came to eat and had shown Carla, and that Carla had laughed at with the still strong laugh that echoed all over the house. And she disliked Mr. Sparks even more than she had before, because her brother was in the room now; she turned and looked at him.

He was leaning on the carved walking stick, in the old robe, his bad foot trailing behind him. He was small and frail, and his pale-blue eyes were so light as to look all white, except for the red rims and the tiny red veins. He had a high forehead, but his hair was thin and short and stuck out from his head in a mad tangle; his mouth hung open, and his head nodded forward and jerked. His hands on the cane were thin and wrinkled and the veins stood up on the backs. He hobbled slowly into the room and squinted at Sparks.

"This is my brother, Clayton Hammond, Mr. Sparks," she said. "He's not well," she added.

Sparks went forward toward her brother. "Why Major, I'm indeed happy to make your acquaintance. Why, I've heard so much about you, and well, it's a honor to meet a great officer like you."

The Major stood there like a weak sapling, his head moving slowly back and forth as he looked at Sparks. "What's your business, sir?" he said, and his voice grated like the bottom of a skiff when it's pulled out of the river onto sand.

"Mr. Sparks was just—" and she was going to say leaving.

But Sparks, moving with surprising quickness, was across the room in front of her brother, saying, "Sparks, Lyman Sparks, Major Hammond, and I'm happy to make your acquaintance. Yes, indeed, I really come to Hammond just to see you, and it woulda been a disappointment sho nuff if I hadn't got to talk with you."

The Major looked at him with his pale-blue eyes, and Sparks grinned. The Major's lips were thin and quivering, and sparse, gray whiskers clung to his wrinkled chin.

"Well now," Sparks said, rocking back on his heels to pat his bulging belly with both palms. "Well now, I reckon we can talk business now." And he glanced over at Miss Iva.

"No, I don't think we will, Mr. Sparks," she said.

"But, Miss Ida——"

"I've already told you, Mr. Sparks," she said. "We can't help you. It's not us that you ought to be talking to."

"Well now, Miss Ida," Sparks said, "I reckon the Major just ought to hear what I've got to say."

Miss Iva stood looking at him, one hand on the back of the rocker in front of her, her lips in a straight line and so tightly drawn as to be almost invisible. Sparks turned away from her smoldering eyes to the Major, who stood hunched over his cane.

"State your business, sir," the Major said.

And so Sparks told him about it, his eyes shifting from one to the other while Miss Iva stood watching him, watching him show the drawings to the Major, or rather, holding them in front of his face. He had begun to sweat with the effort and had pulled out a wrinkled, red bandana to pass it over his face from time to time. When he finished the whole spiel, he stood waiting, tilting his head at the Major.

"Chancellorsville," the Major said. "Chancellorsville."

"Yes, those fellers claimed they had the cannons from that battle, and Lord if they wasn't ever one a fake," Sparks chuckled.

Miss Iva crossed the room and stood beside her brother. "Mr. Sparks, I think my brother is tired now, so if you don't mind, I'll take him back."

But the old man stood rooted to the spot, looking at Sparks, and a gleam came into the dull eyes, a glimmer of understanding, and his old lips moved slowly.

"A soldier," he said. "A stone soldier?"

"Why that's right, Major Hammond," Sparks boomed. "That's right. A stone soldier, standin there guardin the town." And his finger pounded the drawings in his other hand. "Never thought of it like that, no sir."

And then the old man was crying, dry rasping sobs coming from deep down inside his body, so that his head shook, and two tiny tears made a path across his leathery cheek. Sparks straightened up, and Miss Iva put her arm across the withered shoulders.

"Why, Miss. Ida," Sparks said. "Why, what did I say?"

"It was nothing you said, Mr. Sparks," she said. "He's just old, you understand."

The old man's head was down, and he was mumbling, something about Chancellorsville and a river, and Sparks backed up against the wall, suddenly afraid again, afraid for his deal, and he quickly wiped his face.

"Well now," he said, "I reckon I'm sorry."

Her eyes were on him for a moment before she spoke, and he looked away. She spoke quietly, "It's not your fault." She paused, and then she said, "It's not your fault that you're the way you are, Mr. Sparks, anymore than it's his fault." She stopped speaking, and he hung his head, felt the clammy, wrinkled suit sticking to him. Carla had come to the door, and Miss Iva walked the old man over to her, and the servant disappeared down the hall with him; then Miss Iva crossed the room to the window, walking slowly, as though she had suddenly grown very tired, and Sparks, as quietly as he could, walked over to the sofa and picked up his hat and twisted it in his hands. Then she turned from the window and came toward him.

"Mr. Sparks," she said, "what you've brought here is no concern to me. If this town wants a monument, then it's all right with me, but it's not up to me to make the arrangements with you, do you understand?"

"Some great art work goes into these statues, Miss Ida," he said, a hint of a whine in his voice.

She was still standing across from him, a hand on the rocker. "You go to see George Mayhew, at the *Hammond Express*," she said. "Talk to him. Tell him I sent you, if you want to."

He tilted his head to the side and saw her sharply and clearly, standing in the dim parlor as her eyes bore into him. And there was the question, the burning question; but he thought only of leaving, of fleeing, because he had what he had come for. There was nothing else for him in that house, the house that held the Major and his sister; he wanted only to get away, to complete his deal and get away. She had thrown open the door for him, but he couldn't understand why. He had only to walk out and put her behind him, to get on the train and walk into his boss's office and be patted on the back, and start getting his commission checks; but he stood looking at her. Instead of elation, there was a hollow, cold lump in the pit of his stomach, and he felt ugly and fat and sweating; he twisted his hat in his hands.

"Miss Ida," he began and stopped. After a long, hollow minute, he said, "Well now, it was a pleasure meeting you, Miss Ida," and he walked quickly across the room and down the hall and out the door. Once in the street he could see the Madison Hotel sign in the distance, through the rising waves of late afternoon heat. He began the long haul up the hill, in the dust, the sky red with sunset behind him. There was a tightness in his chest that was not caused by breathlessness; and he felt it again, stronger, when he passed a small frame building where some Negroes were sitting, and heard the low, ringing laugh. He looked at the faces; at the large, white eyes with the dark pupils and the shining white teeth; and at the one face that was not smiling, but was twisted grotesquely by the bulging, bulbous, red lip that hung down over his chin. Sparks turned his face toward the hotel and moved on, the sweat on his neck moving, unchecked, down over his collar and down the wrinkled back of the grayish suit, orange-tinted now in the dying sun.

III

He was standing on the platform, and he had just heard the 11:15 blowing before it crossed the trestle upriver, the trestle that Dale Spivey told him had been built by Bedford Forrest just a month before he was captured up at Gainesville. It would be a matter of minutes before Sparks would be away from Hammond, speeding toward Mobile. He stood squinting in the sun, his eyes red-rimmed from the bottle of corn whiskey that he'd drunk in his room in the hotel last night. He had been plagued by a sense of guilt that he could not understand, and he'd drunk the whiskey and had passed out, fully clothed, across the bed about daylight. George Mayhew had his ad for the *Hammond Express,* the one drawn up by his company in Mobile; he had the sanction of the leading citizen of Hammond (a fact that he had wasted no time in spreading around), and there was no doubt in his mind that he had made a sale. Once Hammond put up a statue, a stone soldier (that's what he thought of it as, now, because of the Major; and every time he thought about the stone soldier the image of Major Hammond leaning on the cane, sobbing quietly, would flash across his mind, but he would manage to put it quickly away, out of sight), he knew that the other towns across the state would soon follow suit and they would be his. Of course, the deal wasn't closed, but it would be. He allowed himself to smile, and he glanced around the platform and up the street toward the hotel, where he could make out Dale Spivey, tilted back in the chair on the porch; then he heard footsteps beside him and he looked around, and up, into the dark eyes, and his own eyes flickered over the lip and the white shirt with the sleeves torn out and with the collar missing.

"Well now, mornin, John Thomas," he said, squinting up in the near-noon sunlight. The Negro nodded to him, and after a moment held out his hand; Sparks looked, and there was the Bible. He'd almost forgotten about it, and it was a moment before he realized that the Negro wanted him to take it back.

"Why, that's all right, boy, you can keep it," he said, grinning. "You understand, I didn't come here for that, and well, I'm too busy for it anyway, and it don't matter that I didn't sell any. That one is yours to keep. I give it to you, and it's yours."

The Negro lowered his arm for a moment, and then held out the book to him again. "I don't want it, Mr. Sparks," he said. "I got a Bible give to me by Major Hammond a long time ago."

"But not like this'n," Sparks said.

He avoided looking into the Negro's eyes.

"I thank you," John Thomas said, "but I reckon I want you to take it back. I don't want it."

The train, with a roar, was approaching the platform now, and Sparks picked up the straw suitcase and wiped at his face.

"Well, Goddam, if a man don't take somethin give to him free, he don't deserve it, I don't reckon," and he took the Bible. "Well I see you, Lip," he said, and he moved toward the train.

From his seat he could look out onto the platform and the yellow station and the dusty street leading up the middle of the town. The train moved away, and the scene got smaller, and Sparks could see the Negro standing on the platform, moving back into the shadow against the wall. He was leaving, and the image of the Major and of Miss Iva standing in the dim parlor welled up in him, and he swallowed them down. The train was cool after the sun of the dusty street, and he looked down at the Bible in his hand. Then he opened the straw suitcase and put it back with the others, among the dirty shirts and wrinkled underwear and damp bandanas. He settled again in the seat, tugging at his crotch and pulling his breeches legs down so that they did not cut into his thighs. He placed the wrinkled hat in the other seat and relaxed, looking out at the rolling pastures and clumps of trees in the distance.

"I'll just never understand some folks," he said. And a sense of relief swept over him when he closed his eyes, for he realized, now that he was on his way back to Mobile, that he did not have to understand.

Introduction

v. *Alabama Fiction Today*

THE three selections in this final portion of the anthology reveal the continuing vitality of the tradition of native realism established by Alabama writers from the 1840s onward. They also suggest its ever-increasing range of vision and interest. The first, from Charles Gaines's novel, *Stay Hungry,* focuses on contemporary urban Alabama, in this case Birmingham. Moreover, it is urban Alabama depicted across a cultural spectrum extending from gymnasiums, cheap cafeterias, and roadside honky-tonks to exclusive country clubs and the mansions of the new industrial aristocracy. The second excerpt is an introductory portion of another novel, Albert Murray's *Train Whistle Guitar.* Here, the subject is the contemporary experience of growing up black in Alabama, and the location the railroad yards and industrial parks by the Gulf near Mobile. The third selection, from one more novel, Howell Raines's *Whiskey Man,* returns us at the last to the familiar fictional terrain of the countryside and small town. The particular location is north Alabama, and the topic of contemplation what the narrator calls the "Historical Mistake," the division of cultural perspective continuing to this day to separate the people of the mountain north from those of the agricultural south. Yet as in so many selections before, whatever the specific instance of historical inquiry, again the matter truly at issue is the burden of Southern history at large.

The title of the selection from Gaines has been chosen to suggest the ambitious range of the author's attempt to capture the broad complexities of contemporary urban life. "Three O'Clock" is the name of the Five Points club where Craig Blake, wealthy ne'er-do-well, sportsman, and at present, apprentice body-builder, is taken by his new friend Joe Santo. There, he meets also Mary Tate Farnsworth, from Opp, Alabama, currently Santo's girlfriend and soon to be

Blake's. The Three O'Clock, the narrator tells us, is "like a thousand other southern bars, heavy with bad air and waiting on something violent to happen." The wait is not long. For his efforts in the ensuing melee—ignited by Blake's flippant identification of himself and his cohorts as Auburn football players—the Birmingham playboy finds himself bloodied, halfway in love, and as alive, he realizes, in the presence of Joe Santo and Mary Tate Farnsworth, as he is ever likely to feel again.

"Woodstream," the second half of the title, denotes the country club, named for the posh area over which it presides, the oldest and best in the city, where Blake sits the next morning nursing his injury, his hangover, and his new realization of a world outside his familiar one of luxurious complacency and rich-boy dabbling. In the club, his old friends and schoolmates talk of debutantes, golf scores, and cotillion parties, and twit him for "chasing down weirdos." Meanwhile, his thoughts drift back to the night before, when Santo, standing in Blake's great, ghostly house on the mountain, has named kinds of crystal in the cabinet like a lover. At the club, the talk goes on about the search for an "awthintic" to entertain at a celebrated annual party. To his friends' queries, Blake responds that he may know just such a person as they have in mind. For now it is just another word, a frivolity. He will have a long way to go in the book to his prize of wisdom. It will be the realization, his gift from Santo and Mary Tate, that "awthintic" may be the only word in the language that matters.

In "Gasoline Point, Alabama," the focal figure is an authentic of particularly vivid order, the black Luzana Cholly. For the narrator, recalling his boyhood, it has been nothing but Luzana Cholly, the gambler, the singer, the blues guitar player, Luzana Cholly with his holler and his walk. "Whitefolks used to say he was a crazy nigger," the narrator recalls, "but what they really meant or should have meant was that he was confusing to them." He goes on: "Somehow or other it was as if they respected him precisely because he didn't seem to care about them one way or the other. They certainly respected the fact he wasn't going to take any foolishness off them." The blacks, the Gasoline Point people, the narrator realizes, knew him much better. They called him "crazy" and in it the narrator sees they talk of "something like poetic madness." What made him Luzana Cholly was "that he was forever doing something unheard of if not downright outrageous, doing the hell out of it, and not only getting away with whatever it was, but making you like it to boot."

The true magic of Luzana Cholly, however, imaged here in the sweet, sad music of the narrative prose, is in his music. There is the song of his voice, "which was as blue-smoke sounding as the Phila-mayork-skyline-blue most beyond blue steel railroad bridges," and the memory of "how he was forever turning guitar strings into train whistles which were not only once-upon-a-time voices of storytellers but of all the voices saying what was said in the stories as well." Here is the music indeed. It is nothing less than the whole long black song of life itself.

The narrator's perspective in the final section falls between the extremes of vision imaged in the first two. Brantley Laster comes from that great middle range of experience familiar to most natives of the state: small-town, rural, middle-class. The descendant of a grandfather from the northern counties who has served as a reluctant Confederate conscript at the behest of the powers to the slaveholding South, he has stood on the boulevard in Tuscaloosa in front of the fraternities, listening to the whiskey voices of rich boys and imagining the ghosts of their ineffable girls. He has felt the loss of the girl he has loved since childhood, gone to Agnes Scott and fallen to yet another fraternity boy, this one from Georgia Tech. He has heard his professors from Selma and Mobile and Montgomery drive home the aristocratic fraud about the perfidy of the mountain north; and he knows further that it will go on, this thing he calls "The Historical Mistake," that the perpetrators of the lie will go on sending their sons "to Sewanee or Davidson or Washington and Lee, where the sons can learn to tell the lie in all its high Episcopal splendor, so that conceivably the lie can get better and deeper and more like truth with each generation, until finally even the niggers and the hillbillies will believe it, and perhaps the gentlemen-scholars themselves can forget how their people had started a war too big for them and had to make other men fight it for them and lost it anyway and finally were reduced to begging our help to make the free slaves keep on picking cotton for nothing." At issue here, beyond class or race, beyond love even or growing up, is the old theme. In one more version, it is History; and in this case, as in all the others, it should remind us finally that there has never been just one Alabama, but really any number of Alabamas, with each, in its odd, stubborn way, having a good deal to tell us about the larger entity.

There remains to be said here something not about what might also have been chosen from recent writing by Alabamians about the state, but rather about what is being written at this very moment. Creative writing in Alabama has never been stronger, nor its products more abundant and excellent. Continuing the tradition of Hudson Strode, there is the flourishing program in creative writing at the University in Tuscaloosa. There is similar interest and energetic commitment as well at the University in Birmingham, the University in Huntsville, and at South Alabama in Mobile. Distinguished authors teach and write fiction around the state, at Auburn, Montevallo, Springhill, Troy, Livingston, Birmingham-Southern. There are numerous literary publications and various local productions of councils on the arts. At the state and local level, various support groups offer handsome annual awards, and there are often impressive collections of prize publications. The state's cultural and educational centers offer frequent colloquia and major literary festivals. Numerous outreach programs have been developed to encourage writing in the schools. In places large and small around the state, students write about their homes and lives and produce handsome books that commit their work to permanent literary memory.

As this anthology should attest, Alabama fiction has had a long and colorful life in its past. On the basis of current activity and prospects, one can say with confidence that it promises to have an equally long and colorful one to come.

Three O'Clock and Woodstream

Charles Gaines

I

ALL THEY ATE were vegetables. Each of them picked four or five from the cafeteria line of squash, corn, baby limas, turnip greens, black-eyed peas, carrots, spinach, okra and stewed tomatoes, poured them together on a plate and took the others in dishes. They each filled two trays with vegetables and glasses of water and it took three waiters to carry the garden of food to a table.

At the table Santo mixed Tiger's Milk into everybody's water, including Craig's. It was crowded stuff, he said: every thirty grams has nine vitamins, five minerals and eighteen amino acids. Craig watched his, waiting for it to fizz.

They ate and drank the way they lifted weight—loudly, greedily, ignoring everything else. Santo stopped them once to discourse on lima beans, studying one at nose level on the prongs of his fork. They were, he said, the most satisfying vegetable of all—full of carbohydrates; a fat, natural shape that was more interesting than a pea's, and a good green, a green you could trust. Franklin, Wall Street and Johnson (who was named Walter but called Hump for his curved, beefy back) stopped chewing and listened as though they had waited months for a lecture on lima beans. Their attentions never got far from Santo; they checked constantly on his reactions and their own seemed to be described and enlarged by his, as if he were a kind of lens that made everything look bigger and more important. Craig had never seen anyone as hungrily aware as Santo. His thin eyes sopped up whatever was around him and his face reflected everything he saw, heard or felt. He would stare at, even touch a forkful of peas or corn or okra before swallowing it, and do it so naturally that doing it seemed normal.

They ate for over an hour, and then rode together in Wall Street's car to Five Points, to a bar near Santo's apartment that he said had good music and good pigs' feet. To avoid closing at midnight it was called a club—the Three O'Clock Club. But it was really just an upstairs, noisy room with a bandstand and dance floor in the center and weak-legged little tables ringing them. The band was on a break when they got there. A too-loud jukebox was playing and a few couples were dancing to it. The place disappointed Craig in Santo—it looked like a thousand other southern bars, heavy with bad air and a waiting on something violent to happen—and for the first time since he had left it he thought about getting back to his car.

A tall man met them at the door. He had one white eye and was thin and mean-looking as a knife blade. He nodded at Santo, who seemed pleased to see him. "Mary Tate's in the back," he said. "Y'all want a table?"

"Please, Hayes," Santo grabbed Craig's arm. "Hayes, this is a friend of mine—Mr. Blake." Hayes and Craig nodded. "You know the others."

"Uh huh. I know 'em. Franklin you stay offa people tonight, you hear." Franklin just stared at him.

Hayes gave them a table in the front of the room near the bar. Wall and Johnson each bought a pitcher of beer and a plate of pigs' feet and Franklin got a glass of muscatel. Santo ordered water for his Tiger's Milk and left the table. In a few minutes he was back with the receptionist from the studio and another girl. Craig had had a whiskey sour and was beginning to feel better about the place.

The receptionist's name was Mary Tate Farnsworth. She was from Opp, Alabama, was a champion water skier, and was Santo's woman—all this Craig got from Franklin in the first two minutes that she was at the table.

He didn't need Franklin to tell him she was mad at Santo, but Franklin told him anyway. She had been waiting an hour on Joe and had not expected him to be with all these people. She sat bent at the waist to him, her legs crossed and one little foot flicking up and down as she fussed. She was not exactly beautiful—her jaws were too square and her eyes too big for the rest of her face—but she was very exciting to look at. She was small with a straight back and lovely arms and legs. Her movements were clean and functional, as though they had developed on ice or roller skates, someplace where balance was important. But the thing that made you stare at her was a flickering vitality, an energy that throbbed like a pulse under her expressions. It was a very sexy thing. She almost seemed to glow.

The other girl's name was Terry and she looked like she had seen about anything the Three O'Clock Club had to offer. She gazed indifferently over the dance floor and popped her gum and occasionally put her hands on the small of her back and threw out her chest.

In a little while the band came back and they were good in a loud, country way. The club was full. With the return of the band the noise got more cheerful.

Franklin sat next to Craig drinking muscatels as fast as he could order them and talking. He had gotten into weights, he said, after high school. He was working in a car wash as a backseat man and doing a little bodybuilding when he heard Erickson had fired an instructor. He went up and told how his mama was a dietician and got the job. Erickson was a prick, he said, but he knew his stuff and Franklin owed him for taking him off backseats. Craig asked him if he went in for the contests too and he shrugged and said naw, not too much. He finished his wine. The calves, he said; the goddamn calves had held him back. He had worked them so hard he thought they would pop off, but the mothers wouldn't grow. He got sullen after that and ordered another drink.

Gorging on platters of pigs' feet and pitchers of beer, Johnson and Street were in boisterous tempers and they wanted Santo to sing.

"Hayes *wawnts* you to, Joe. Cause all the pelts lak it so much." Hump grinned and the grin ran hundreds of laughter creases up his face.

"I don't want to sing," said Santo. "They got a singer up there." He grabbed Johnson by the shirt and pulled him closer to him. "But I'll tell you what, Hump old buddy, I'll tell you a story instead." Hump nodded. "It's a sad story about the failure of love. But you've got to *listen*." His eye glittered and Hump nodded again.

"Well, one day this guy was banging around in the woods, you dig, when he comes on a Rary. The Rary was just lying there curled up by a tree. So the guy takes it home and feeds it milk, and the Rary starts to grow. It was small at first like a ping-pong ball, but it grew fast and pretty soon it was big as a basketball and still growing and the guy was giving it four gallons of milk a day. Then the Rary started getting tired of milk and wouldn't eat anything but calf liver—he'd eat maybe ten, twelve pounds of that a day. He got so big he was taking up most of the guy's living room, his hair was shedding all over everything and he was eating the guy out of house and home, so the guy, whose name was Walter like you, Hump, decided he had to get rid of it. He tried giving it to his friends but none of them wanted it, and the zoo didn't want it . . ."

"Why didn't he put him back where he got him at?" asked Wall. He looked thoughtful, like he was trying to decide whether to believe all this or not.

"Because man, he couldn't let the Rary starve. Whenever the Rary got hungry he made little screams and the guy couldn't handle that." Santo was hunched over the table, fingering his glass. His hands were very quick and active despite their size; they were always picking up things, twirling things. "So the guy decided to have a talk with the Rary. He went into what was left of his living room and said, 'Listen, Rary, you're taking up my whole room here, shedding hair all over the place and eating me out of house and home. Nobody else'll take you so I've got to get rid of you.'

"Well the Rary was upset, but he said, 'OK, Walt, just do it the quickest way you can.' So the guy pried the Rary out of his house and tried to shoot it but the bullets just bounced off, then he rolled it down to the lake and tried to drown it but the Rary just floated like a big cork. He tried some other things and they didn't work either so finally he rents a huge dump truck, see, puts the Rary on and drives out to the highest cliff he can find. He backs up to the edge of the cliff and yells back, 'Well, so long Rary. This is it,' and starts raising the bed of the truck."

Santo looked up to gather their attention. Mary Tate and Terry were talking to each other and listening to the band. "The guy raises it and raises it and raises it but the Rary won't fall off. Finally the bed is vertical and the Rary is just stuck up there in one corner, so the guy gets out and walks around to the back and says. 'What the hell is this?'

" 'Let's go home, Walt,' says the Rary.

" 'Home, hell,' the guy says. 'Why don't you fall off?'

" 'Well, Walt,' says the Rary, '. . . it's a long, long way to tip-pa-Rary.' "

Santo looked around, his face holding in his own laughter, waiting for the others. But nobody was ready for him. There was an embarrassing minute of silence, then Mary Tate tore away from watching the band and jumped beautifully into the breach. Her face forgot everything but that Santo needed her. She shot a hand over to take his on the glass, said, "Oh Christ, baby, that's great," and roared laughing. Santo followed her and they rocked back and forth at each other, mouths wide, her laugh rising high and raunchy over his. Then all of them were laughing, looking refreshed as if they had just fallen into cold water.

It was the first time Craig saw them do that to people and the picture stayed the clearest he had of them: Mr. Alabama and his woman, joined at the hands around a glass of potent milk, laughing like hell, by themselves.

After four drinks the Three O'Clock Club looked much better to Craig. He felt like he had known the other people at the table all his life. There was a pool table near the bar. In graduate school he had killed a lot of Iowa nights fingering felt, developing an impatient, flashy game. He asked Franklin if he wanted to play. Franklin didn't, particularly, but played anyway and they shot a game of straight to fifty. Franklin played like a farmer, resting the cue on his knuckles and closing one eye as he shot, but he took a long time between balls and sank a few.

"You're pretty good," he told Craig after an easy combination bank.

"I'm pretty good at most things," Craig said and immediately regretted it. The whiskey had loosened up like a cough his feeling of having been absurdly outmatched and beaten earlier that evening. Franklin looked over at him and he covered up. "I used to play a lot in college."

"Uh huh," Franklin said. And after a while, "Joe went to college."

"Did he?"

"No shit. He invents things too . . . collects glasses."

"He's quite a guy," Craig said and bent over a shot.

"Joe? You goddamn right he is." Franklin's voice got louder. "Lemme tell you something, buddy, when he takes Mr. America, the big one, he'll have done it *all*. And he don't even care about it. Sheeat. If it wadn't for Thor he wouldn't even be messing with this crap. He don't *need* it, man; he's done it all. You know they ast him on the Edward Sullivan show to sing Indian songs? And that he was American white water champion in a one-man open canoe? And that he woulda made the U.S. Olympic team as a downhill skier except he broke his leg . . ."

Craig put down his cue and stared dumbly at Franklin, stunned at Santo's resourcefulness or sense of humor or at Franklin's gullibility, or at all three. Did he *really,* for God's sake, tell people . . .

Franklin was ending with a flourish. ". . . Mrs. Mamie Eisenhower wrote and ast him to make her one of his Indian necklaces."

"Oh."

That was all Craig could think of to say. He finished off the last five balls as quickly as he could.

There was a group of men between the bar and their table. As Craig walked past, following Franklin's broad back through the room, one of them stopped him.

"Hey buddy," the man said. "What are y'all?" He looked up curious and impressed like somebody asking for an autograph. "Y'all are the biggest bunch of men I ever saw. Y'all play football or what?"

"Yeah. We play for Auburn," Craig said. The man squinted over at their table. "Those big ones are defensive linemen and the redheaded one, that's Franklin Coates, the all-Conference end."

"What are you?"

"I'm a scatback."

"Oh. Yeah," the man said. "I figured y'all was something like that. Thanks buddy—hey, what's your name?"

"Blake. Buck Blake."

"Yeah. Well thanks, Blake. War Eagle." He waved and gave Craig that diminished little smile that people use on athletes.

Craig walked like a scatback back to the table.

Somebody had gotten him another drink. Wall and Terry were dancing and Santo was talking to Hump and Franklin, so he took the drink and sat down by Mary Tate.

"Hi," she said. "You know you look like a swamp."

"Like a what?"

"A swamp. With all that brown hair and eyes and stuff. I really like the way you look. I been wanting to tell you that."

Craig glanced over at Santo, then said, "Thanks. I like the way you look too."

They talked for the next hour, together at first, then as Craig kept drinking she only listened and he kept talking, getting louder, bragging. He told her about the trip he had made to the Keys in May for tarpon, the one in February to Acapulco for sailfish, the one in September to shoot dove in Texas. He explained to her, with a diagram, the principle of lead in wing shooting. She smiled him on and he talked until finally he ran down and just sat there, quiet and shamed.

"Do you want to dance?" she asked after a while and again he checked across the table. "Joe don't like to. He won't care."

He followed her out to the dance floor watching her walk, shoulders thrown back, moving so cleanly and economically she didn't seem to touch her clothes. She danced the same way—began and ended each movement at exactly the right place as he stumbled around following her.

After two dances he got dizzy and was guiding her messily back to the table when someone pushed him. He turned around into a furious little man in a striped tee shirt who said, "Watch where you're going feller."

When Craig turned back to Mary Tate the man stepped between them. "Hey. Djew tell my friend you play ball at Auburn?"

Craig said yes, politely. Then the man put both hands on Craig's chest and pushed him backward.

"Well, you're a lie," he said. He was trembling with anger and Craig wondered how in the hell he could have gotten so mad so fast. The man pushed again, gently as a gust of wind, and stepped after him. "You're a lie, eggsucker, cause I watch every game they play. They ain't *got* no Blake and they don't even *play* no scatback." Another push.

Craig had quit hoping he could walk out of this and was looking around wildly for a bottle or a chair when Franklin appeared like a genie next to him and shoved the man four feet back across the floor. Franklin crouched beside Craig, his rage blooming like a flower, up all at once with the other on a high complicated anger. Graceful and remote, they stared at each other across the dance floor, frozen right on the edge of moving to the real music of the Three O'Clock Club.

"You want to push, catfucker, push me." Franklin said. He did his little shuffle that was like putting out cigarettes with both feet.

"I'm gonna tell you *once*," the man said. "I gotta black belt in karate."

"I've got a black belt too, babe, and it ain't in no karate." Franklin told him this with relish.

Craig saw Hayes come flailing at them through the crowd and at the same instant saw the striped tee shirt charge and disappear as if it had been swallowed in the blur of Franklin's arms. Within the four or five seconds it took Hayes to reach them, Franklin shoved the man to the floor, pulled the tee shirt over his head and began hitting the place where his face was with full steady swings like chopping wood. Hayes and two of the man's friends got to Franklin at the same time and started dragging him off what looked like a runover dog underneath. At that point Craig stepped mindlessly back in and was pelting the back of one of the friends with unnoticed little punches when he heard more than felt something go ca-thunk across his ear . . . and then nothing else but a loud buzz and the sound of himself throwing up.

"You got hit with a beer bottle," Santo said. Craig was sitting with Santo, Mary Tate and Terry at a quiet table in the back of the room. There was vomit on his shirt the color of whiskey sours, his ear felt sticky and hot and his right forearm and hand were bloody. People were still scrambling around on the dance floor.

"How you feel, old buddy?"

"Me? I feel fine, how's Franklin?"

"I sent Wall and Hump over there, he'll be all right. Franklin loves to fight. He'd rather fight than eat."

"Oh," Craig said.

"What do you like to do most?"

His head was buzzing and he was having a hard time concentrating. He tried to laugh but when he looked up he saw Santo really wanted to know. He sat there hulking and shadowy, ignoring all the wild commotion behind them, his tough face looking curious and eager and amused as a hunting dog's, waiting for Craig to tell him what he liked to do—as though they were two barebacked ten-year-olds, chewing straws and shooting the breeze on some sunny hillside. And all of a sudden Craig felt tremendously happy. It was a lightheaded, full sensation, like taking a deep breath of sunlight and cold air. Santo sat there looking like his downtown portrait wanting to know what he liked to *do*. Craig thought maybe he had grown up with that face . . . every line looked so familiar. It had been a long time since lunch and Foss—and for some reason he could barely remember Foss. He felt overwhelmingly content.

"I like best, maybe . . . to fish dry flies over big brown trout . . . with a bamboo rod." "Where?" "In rivers." His mind was smoky, drifting like a fog on water. Mary Tate was smiling. "What kind of rivers?" "Big clear . . . dark rivers."

"We'll do it!" he heard Santo say, and heard himself laughing. "We'll do it, then. You know Mary Tate here really likes you. We'll all go do it together."

"Look, were you really"—he wanted to know this—"a white water canoe champion?"

"We can talk about that," Santo said, bending over him. "Sure. We can talk about that too."

II

NESTLED IN THE red hills above Birmingham are three country clubs. The one called Woodstream is the most beautiful, the hardest to get into and the oldest. It is old enough to seem ageless. If you stand on the terrace behind the club on a late afternoon, everything around you—the caddy house, the wooden bridges crossing the stream, the big trees and shrubs—can seem to have been there forever just as they are now. Not even the club's members seem to change. They are still rich. They still hum *I Could Have Danced All Night* and stay at the Plaza when they go to New York. They still have their dinners served to them on silver by still-smiling blacks in high-ceilinged dining rooms. The Woodstream Country Club is theirs; its big, handsome rooms are full of their Elizabethan syllables and refined scents.

The clubhouse is an elegantly bright, columned building with the private look of a home. It is surrounded by thirty pastoral, tended acres that are absolutely free of annoyances: the land either sweeps broadly like a lawn or rises and falls gently between tender little hummocks. Lying around in here at pleasing intervals and in places where you can neither see nor hear them from the club, are a swimming pool, built so carefully into the landscape it looks like a lake, an easy eighteen-hole golf course, and six excellent Rubico tennis courts.

The tennis courts are fenced-in and staggered up a hillside like terraces. They are green with bright white stripes. In the early morning you park above them and walk down through the big pine trees that are all around and that make the courts seem like a gay, comfortable glade, hearing the comely thwock of tennis balls on gut, smelling the antique smell of boxwood and the courts themselves that have just been sprayed and rolled.

From his car Craig could see Foss, sparkling in his pressed white Lacostes, waiting in a lawn chair in front of the pro shop. On the number three court was a game of doubles, nobody else. It was nine o'clock and the sky was hard as blue enamel. As he walked down the needled path, the soft resinous air, with its formal quiet and almost palpable feel of healthful leisure and good spirits, touched and satisfied him as it always did. He felt bad, but at home.

Foss looked hearty and cheerful, like he had just eaten three bowls of Wheaties and brushed his teeth. "How was your date?" Craig asked him.

"Educational. Somebody hit you with a barbell?"

There was no missing the ear; it was swollen like a blood sausage. "Beer bottle."

"No kidding? In that health place or what?" Foss looked interested.

"In a place called the Three O'Clock Club. In Five Points. Do you want to play tennis or not?"

"Nice company," said Foss.

They took the first court and started warming up. Foss had a pretty game, with the long backcourt strokes you get only from about a thousand dollars' worth of lessons. He hit the ball flat and hard and bounced around stylishly near the base line. Craig hurried him into playing before the heat got to his hangover. He enjoyed the first set—fresh gritty crunch of his shoes on the court and the soft, dry, early air. His serve was coming in and he won it, but Foss took the second and the third and by then Craig wasn't enjoying it any more.

They drank a Coke on the porch of the pro shop. There were people on all the courts now and it was seriously hot. Foss was chewing on a piece of ice and talking about his debutante for this season.

"She knows a lot but she doesn't enjoy anything. She's not interested in anything but talking." At a party the night before she had kept Foss in a back room away from everyone else talking about J. R. R. Tolkien for God's sake.

"She sounds fun."

"Yeah." Foss shook his head and chomped down on another piece of ice. "Well, it beats the hell out of Mr. Alabama and his friends."

"They enjoy themselves, Foss. You're really a snob, buddy, you know that?"

Foss snorted. "You are too, but a worse kind. This . . . *experience* thing of yours, digging into how different people live and all. That's a very selfish, snobbish thing. Turgenev calls it putting on a peasant's blouse. It's slumming is all it is."

Foss had a nasal tutorial sound in his voice and Craig suspected he had made up the stuff about Turgenev. "You're full of shit," he said and let it go at that.

They played one more set and a little after noon they walked down the hill to the club. In the basement of the clubhouse, along with the locker rooms and golf shop, was a big oval dining room called the grille. It was an airy, wood-paneled, comfortable place with heavy furniture and a tile floor. You could enter it directly from outside in tennis or golf clothes without going through the formal upstairs of the building. It was crowded and they waited for a table at the long bar and shot poker dice for the lunch. Craig took eight horses straight, then lost one and took two more—a week's worth of lunches.

"Them bullets is sho comin for you, Mr. Blake," Chub said and chuckled. He leaned on his counter, polishing a glass and wanting a game, probably the best poker dice roller in the state.

"They're not coming good enough to roll you, Chub."

He chuckled again. "Nawsir, I guess not."

Chub had been behind that bar forever, polishing glasses, chuckling, beating people at poker dice. On at least half the days of every summer between grammar school and college Craig had joked and shot dice with him at noon—between tennis in the morning and golf in the afternoon. Like everything else at Woodstream, that was a tradition.

They finally got a table and ordered club sandwiches and iced tea, the traditional lunch.

"Someday I'm going to order hash," Craig said.

Foss shook his head. "You can't; wouldn't work. They wouldn't even give it to you."

Two golfers came in, their cleats snapping on the old tiles. They stood at the bar talking to Chub, sweat towels dangling like tails from their belts.

"There's Halsey and Packman," said Foss.

"I see them. How about letting me finish my sandwich before you start your goddamn socializing." But Foss was already waving and they came snapping over, bringing their beers and the dice cup.

"Yes *suh, yes suh,*" said Halsey. For some reason that was how he greeted people. "Hello, my men."

He was a tall, freckled lawyer with a lot of inherited, blue-chip money, a big family and a whiney voice that sounded like wind in a louvred door. George Packman had been Craig's roommate for a year in prep school. He was sturdy, athletic and quiet.

Halsey looked at Craig. "Foss hit you with his rocket serve or what?"

"I ran into a door. How's the golf course?"

"It's *absud.* The grass on the greens is three inches high and you damn near have to putt with a wedge." He craned around the room. "I want to talk to somebody on the maintenance committee."

"Pete just means he's five strokes down," said Packman. "How was your trip to Mexico?" he asked Craig.

"It was all right. We saw a lot of sails and wahoo."

"Why don't you get a job, Blake?" said Halsey.

"I ask him that too from time to time," said Foss. "He's too busy chasing down weirdos."

Packman was smiling. "You all wouldn't know what to do with his time if you had it."

"Getting hard to say he spends it elegantly," said Foss.

Halsey ordered four beers and they rolled for the tab. "Are we going to play golf, or not?" Craig asked Foss. He was through with his lunch and was already tired of the sitting, the conversation and the steady drone from the roomful of perfumed, chattering ladies. Foss was in no hurry.

"In the heat of the day, my man?" said Halsey, and went into one of his bad imitations of W. C. Fields. "Why don't you forgooo. We'll have some gentlemanly conversation, and exchange of vieww s, good lager and a roll of the diiice. Forgo today and we can play a foursome in the morning."

Packman was agreeable and so was Foss, who was always delighted by Halsey, and Craig felt the afternoon slip completely out from under him. Time did that often and usually pleasantly here, where built in as secretly and solidly as the plumbing was the comfortable sensation that any part of a day was as leisurely insignificant as any other. You might as well play gin as tennis, you thought. Might as *well* drink this bloody mary as drive back downtown to work. Usually limp enough to enjoy this, Craig was too restless for it today. He was in love again and that always made him antsy.

Since he was about seven years old he had been falling into complicated frequent love, less often with people than with ways of doing things, whole life styles, as they were suggested to him by little gestures and postures and sounds. When he was nine he had watched a man in a donut shop stretching and shaping dough and for years after was in love with being a baker. A big part of his long affection for salt-water fishing had to do with the way charter-boat mates, with a motion like turning a key, can wire shut a baitfish's mouth. At various times recently he had been in love with rodeoing (from having watched a man in a plaster cast from chin to waist being helped onto a bull), sky diving (a professional packer on his knees making precise pleats in a big orange chute), trapshooting (the gracefully mitered joint between man and gun and the sound of the shout to pull) and a score of women, because of the way they crossed their legs or fingered their hair or knitted their brows or held animals or threw footballs.

He had always gone around with his nose down like a truffle hound sniffing out fresh experiences to get excited about, to explore for their mysteries and ticks, and for their closeness to the heart of things. Yesterday he had stumbled into a whole grove of them—lifting, posing, vegetable feasts, bar fights. He was crazy about all that now, and about Santo and Franklin and Mary Tate (her straight back, her flicking foot as she scolded Santo, her rush to his story and her poise).

At two that morning in the living room of his house after they had brought him home, she sat in a spindly Chippendale armchair his grandmother had used, as quietly, with as elegant a purchase as that old lady herself, while Santo looked in the back for ice for Craig's ear and Franklin wandered around saying dazed things like, "sonofabich." She sat on the edge of the chair, hands in her lap, looking delighted and possessed by the room.

"God, y'all are great," he had mumbled to her, staring and still drunk. "I just think y'all are . . . great."

"Wudga pay for this goddamn place?" Franklin asked him, rubbing his hand over the crushed velvet arm of a couch.

"Not mine," Craig said, and Franklin looked at him like he thought he might have stolen it from a department store. "It's my parents' house."

"Where are they?"

"Dead."

"Oh. Then it's yours."

"No. It's theirs."

"Shut up, asshole," Mary Tate told Franklin.

Santo brought back the ice in a towel, holding in his other hand a bottle of crème de menthe and four small pressed glass goblets. "This is fabulous. It's fabulous," he said, his eyes jumping around the living room, handling everything in sight. He held up one of the goblets to a light and turned it on its stem.

"Teasel. There's some bellflower back there, and some twisted grape . . . Look at this, Mary," he said, squinting up at the tiny colored glass. "That's some of the best darned teasel I ever saw."

They drank a crème de menthe to that. Santo hummed *Your Cheatin' Heart.* The old house soughed around them out of its old unuse, and Craig had found himself wide-eyed in love again.

Halsey was talking about a party, his long freckled face cocked for sarcasm. "They're having everybody in the city as usual. A black tie dinner dance with quail . . . for the multitudes. It's ridiculous. The thing is, discrimination has gotten to be a dirty word with all this Supreme Court crap and everything. I'll keep these four jacks in two."

"That's the thing all right," said Craig. "What are you talking about?"

"The Walterson's party in August. And they're having Guy Lombardo again in the ballroom for Christ's sake."

"Are you going, Craig?" Packman asked him.

"Nope. That's my vacation, I'll be in Montana."

"Why don't you get a job, Blake?" Halsey whined again. "Anyway she called me last week, Amy did, and wanted to know if I knew a singer. Said she wants her 'awthintic' this year to be a folk singer who can sing *Greensleeves*. Cause that's her favorite song."

"Did you know one?" asked Packman.

"How would I know somebody like that?"

"Craig's been hanging with some 'awthintics' lately," said Foss.

They all looked up at Craig.

"Can you put her on a singer, Blake?" Halsey was grinning, dice cup in hand. Looking into his long soft, wolfish face, Craig suddenly had a beautiful idea, one he could see like a snapshot.

"Maybe so," he said and laughed at the thought. "Yeah, I might know somebody for her, Halsey."

Gasoline Point, Alabama

Albert Murray

THERE was a chinaberry tree in the front yard of that house in those days, and in early spring the showers outside that window always used to become pale green again. Then before long there would be chinaberry blossoms. Then it would be maytime and then junebugtime and no more school bell mornings until next September, and when you came out onto the front porch and it was fair there were chinaberry shadows on the swing and the rocking chair, and chinaberry shade all the way from the steps to the gate.

When you climbed up to the best place in the chinaberry tree and looked out across Gins Alley during that time of the year the kite pasture, through which you took the short cut to the post office, would be a meadow of dog fennels again. So there would also be jimson weeds as well as ragworts and rabbit tobacco along the curving roadside from the sweet gum corner to the pump shed, and poke-salad from there to the AT & N.

You couldn't see the post office flag from the chinaberry tree because it was down in Buckshaw Flat at the L & N whistlestop. You couldn't see the switch sidings for the sawmills along that part of Mobile River either, because all that was on the other side of the tank yard of the Gulf Refining Company. All you could see beyond the kite pasture were the telegraph poles and the sky above the pine ridge overlooking Chickasabogue Creek and Hog Bayou.

You couldn't see the blackberry slopes near the L & N Section Gang Quarters because first there were the honeysuckle thickets and then Skin Game Jungle where the best muscadine vines were and in which there were also some of the same owl tree holes you knew about from fireside ghost stories about treasures buried by the pirates and the Confederates.

Southeast of all of that was the L & N clearing, across which you could see the trains and beyond which you could also see that part of the river. Next on the horizon due south was Three Mile Crest, which blocked off Dodge Mill Bottom and that part of Three Mile Creek. So you couldn't see the waterfront either, nor any part of the downtown Mobile, Alabama skyline, not even with real binoculars.

Nor could you see One Mile Bridge beyond the treeline to the southwest. Nor the pecan orchard which you knew was due west looking out over the gate and the sunflowers and across the AT & N cut, which you couldn't see either. Nor African Baptist Hill. But between that neighborhood and the Chickasaw Highway was the Southern Railroad, whose night whistles you could sometimes hear as sometimes after midnight you could also hear the M & O, the GM & O and the GM & N en route to St. Louis, Missouri and Kansas City by way of Meridian, Mississippi.

All you could see due north up Dodge Mill Road beyond Buckshaw Corner and the crawfish pond that was once part of a Civil War artillery embankment was the sky above Bay Poplar Woods fading away into the marco polo blue horizon mist on the other side of which were such express train destinations as Birmingham, Alabama and Nashville, Tennessee, and Cincinnati, Ohio, and Detroit, Michigan, plus the snowbound Klondike of Canada plus the icebound tundras of Alaska plus the North Pole.

The Official name of that place (which is perhaps even more of a location in time than an intersection on a map) was Gasoline Point, Alabama, because that was what our post office address was, and it was also the name on the L & N timetable and the road map. But once upon a time it was also the briarpatch, which is why my nickname was then Scooter, and is also why the chinaberry tree (that was ever as tall as any fairy tale beanstalk) was, among other things, my spyglass tree.

I used to say My name is also Jack the Rabbit because my home is in the briarpatch, and Little Buddy (than whom there was never a better riddle buddy) used to say Me my name is Jack the Rabbit also because my home is also in the also and also of the briarpatch because that is also where I was also bred and also born. And when I also used to say My name is also Jack the Bear he always used to say My home is also nowhere and also anywhere and also everywhere.

Because the also and also of all of that was also the also plus also of so many of the twelve-bar twelve-string guitar riddles you got whether in idiomatic iambics or otherwise mostly from Luzana Cholly who was the one who used to walk his trochaic-sporty stomping-ground limp-walk picking and plucking and knuckle knocking and strumming (like an anapestic locomotive) while singsongsaying Anywhere I hang my hat anywhere I prop my feet. Who could drink muddy water who could sleep in a hollow log.

The color you almost always remember when you remember Little Buddy Marshall is sky-blue. Because that shimmering summer sunshine blueness in which neighborhood hens used to cackle while distant yard dogs used to bark and mosquito hawks use to flit and float along nearby barbwire fences, was a boy's color. Because such blueness also meant that it was whistling time and rambling time. And also baseball time. Because that silver bright midafternoon sky above outfields was the main thing Little Buddy Marshall and I were almost always most likely to be wishing for back in those days when we used to make up our own dirty verses for that old song about it ain't gonna rain no more no more.

But the shade of blue and blueness you always remember whenever and for whatever reason you remember Luzana Cholly is steel blue, which is also the clean, oil-smelling color of gunmetal and the gray-purple patina of freight train engines and railroad slag. Because in those days, that was a man's color (even as tobacco plus black coffee was a man's smell), and Luzana Cholly also carried a blue steel .32-20 on a .44 frame in his underarm holster. His face and hands were leather brown like dark rawhide. But blue steel is the color you always remember when you remember how his guitar used to sound.

Sometimes he used to smell like coffee plus Prince Albert cigarettes, which he rolled himself, and sometimes it was a White Owl Cigar, and sometimes it was Brown's Mule Chewing Tobacco. But when he was wearing slick starched wash-faded blue denim overalls plus tucked in jumper plus his black and white houndstooth-checked cap plus high top, glove-soft banker-style Stacey Adams, which was what he almost always traveled in, he also smelled like green oak steam. And when he was dressed up in his tailor-made black broadcloth boxback plus pegtop hickory-striped pants plus either a silk candy-striped or silk pongee shirt plus knitted tie and diamond stickpin plus an always brand new gingerly blocked black John B. Stetson hat because he was on his way somewhere either to gamble or to play his guitar, what he smelled like was barbershop talcum and crisp new folding money.

I can remember being aware of Luzana Cholly all the way back there in the blue meshes of that wee winking blinking and nod web of bedtime story time when I couldn't yet follow the thread of the yarns I was to realize later on that somebody was forever spinning about something he had done, back when all of that was mainly grown folks talking among themselves by the fireside or on the swing-porch as if you were not even there: saying Luzana and old Luzana and old Luze, and I didn't know what, to say nothing of where Louisiana was.

But I already knew who he himself was even then, and I could see him very clearly whenever they said his name because I still can't remember any point in time when I had not already seen him coming up that road from around the bend and down in the L & N railroad bottom. Nor can I remember when I had not yet heard him playing the blues on his guitar as if he were also an engineer telling tall tales on a train whistle, his left hand doing most of the talking including the laughing and signifying as well as the moaning and crying and even the whining, while his right hand thumped the wheels going somewhere.

Then there was also his notorious holler, the sound of which was always far away and long coming as if from somewhere way down under. Most of the time (but not always) it started low like it was going to be a moan or even a song, and then it jumped all the way to the very top of his voice and suddenly broke off. Then it came back, and this time it was already at the top. Then as often as not he would make three or four, or sometimes three followed by four, bark-like squalls and let it die away in the darkness (you remember it mostly as a nighttime sound); and Mama always used to say he was whooping and hollering like somebody back on the old plantations and back in the old turpentine woods, and one time Papa said maybe so but it was more like one of them old Luzana swamp hollers the Cajuns did in the shrimp bayous. But I myself always thought of it as being something else that was like a train, a bad express train saying Look out this me and here I come and I'm coming through one more time.

I knew that much about Luzana Cholly even before I was big enough to climb the chinaberry tree. Then finally I could climb all the way to the top, and I also knew how to box the compass; so I also knew what Louisiana was as well as where, or at least which way, it was from where I was.

At first he was somebody I used to see and hear playing the guitar when he was back in town once more. I hadn't yet found out very much about him. Nor was I ever to find out very much that can actually be documented. But it is as if I have always known that he was as rough and ready as rawhide and as hard and weather worthy as blue steel, and that he was always either going somewhere or coming back from somewhere and that he had the best walk in the world, barring none (until Stagolee Dupas (*fils*) came to town).

Anyway I had already learned to do my version of that walk and was doing the stew out of it long before Little Buddy Marshall first saw it, because he probably saw me doing it and asked me about it before he saw Luzana Cholly himself and that is probably how he found out about Luzana Cholly and rawhide and blue steel in the first place.

During that time before Little Buddy came was also when I was first called Mister. Miss Tee, who was the one I had always regarded as being without doubt the best of all Big Auntees, had always called me My Mister; and Mama had always called me Little Man and My Little Man and Mama's Little Man; but some time after Little Buddy Marshall came she used to drop the *Little* part off and that is how they started calling me Mister Man before my nickname became Scooter. But long before Little Buddy Marshall came I had been telling myself that Luzana Cholly was the Man I wanted to be like.

Then Little Buddy Marshall was there and it was as if time itself were sky-blue; and every day was for whistling secret signals and going somewhere to do something you had to have nerves as strong as rawhide to get away with. Luzana Cholly was the one we always used to try to do everything like in those days. Even when you were about to do something that had nothing whatsoever to do with anything you had ever heard about him, as often as not when your turn came you said Watch old Luze. Here come old Luze. This old Luze. If Luze can't ain't nobody can.

*

And then not only had we come to know as much as we did about what he was like when he was there in the flesh and blood, we also knew how to talk to him, because by that time he also knew who we were. Sometimes we would come upon him sitting somewhere by himself tuning and strumming his guitar and he would let us stay and listen as long as we wanted to, and sometimes he would sneak our names into some very well known ballad just to signify at us about something, and sometimes he would make up new ballads right on the spot just to tell us stories.

We found out that the best time to signify at him because you needed some spending change was when he was on his way to the Skin Game Jungles. (Also: as far as you could tell, gambling and playing the guitar and riding the rails to and from far away places were the only steady things he ever had done or ever would do, except during the time he was in the Army and the times he had been in jail—and not only had he been to jail and the county farm, he had done time in the penitentiary!)

We were supposed to bring him good luck by woofing at him when he was headed for a skin game. So most of the time we used to try to catch him late Saturday afternoon as he came across the oil road from Gins Alley coming from Miss Pauline Anderson's Cookshop. Sometimes he would have his guitar slung across his back even then, and that he was wearing his .32-20 in his underarm holster goes without saying.

Say now hey now Mister Luzana Cholly.

Mister Luzana Cholly one time.

(Watch out because here come old Luzana goddamn Cholly one more goddamn time and one goddamn time more and don't give a goddamn who the hell knows it.)

Mister Luzana Cholly all night long.

Yeah me, ain't nobody else but.

The one and only Mister Luzana Cholly from Bogaluzana bolly.

(Not because he was born and raised in Bogalusa, Louisiana; because he once told us he was bred and born in Alabama, and was brought up here and there to root hog or die poor. Somebody had started calling him Luzana because that was where he had just come back in town from when he made his first reputation as a twelve-string guitar player second to none, including Leadbelly. Then it also kept people from confusing him with Choctaw Cholly, who was part Indian and Chastang Cholly the Cajun.)

Got the world in a jug.

And the stopper in your hand.

Y'all tell em, 'cause I ain't got the heart.

A man among men.

And Lord God among women!

Well tell the dy ya.

He would be standing wide legged and laughing and holding a wad of Brown's Mule Chewing Tobacco in with his tongue at the same time. Then he skeet a spat of amber juice to one side like some clutch hitters do when they step up to the plate, and then he would wipe the back of his leathery hand across his mouth and squint his eyes the way some batters sight out at the pitcher's mound.

Tell the goddamn dyyyy ya! He leveled and aimed his finger and then jerked it up like a pistol firing and recoiling.

Can't tell no more though.

How come, little sooner, how the goddamn hell come?

B'cause money talks.

Well shut my mouth. Shut my big wide mouth and call me suitcase. Ain't nobody can do that.

Not nobody that got to eat and sleep.

I knowed y'all could tell em. I always did know good and damn well y'all could tell em. And y'all done just told em.

But we ain't go'n tell no more.

We sure ain't.

Talk don't mean a thing in the world if you ain't got nothing to back it up with.

He would laugh again then and we would stand waiting because we knew he was going to run his hand deep down into his pocket and come up not with the two customary nickels but two quarters between his fingers. He would flick them into the air as if they were jacks and catch them again, one in each hand; and then he would close and cross his hand, making as if to look elsewhere, flip one to me and one to Little Buddy Marshall.

Now talk. But don't talk too loud and don't tell too much, and handle your money like the whitefolks does.

Mama used to say he was don't-carified, and Little Buddy Marshall used to call him hellfied Mister Goddamn hellfied Luzana ass-kicking Cholly; and he didn't mean hell-defying, or hell-fired either. Because you couldn't say he was hell-defying because you couldn't even say he ever really went for bad, not even when he was whooping that holler he was so notorious for. Perhaps that was *somewhat* hell-defying to some folks, but even so what it really meant as much as anything else was I don't give a goddamn if I am hell-defying, which is something nobody driven by hell fire ever had time to say.

As for going for bad, that was the last thing he needed to do, since everybody, black or white, who knew anything at all about him already knew that when he made a promise he meant if it's the last thing I do, if it's the last thing I'm able to do on this earth. Which everybody also knew meant if you cross me I'll kill you and pay for you, as much as it meant anything else. Because the idea of going to jail didn't scare him at all, and the idea of getting lynch-mobbed didn't faze him either. All I can remember him ever saying about that was: If they shoot at me they sure better not miss me they sure better get me that first time. Whitefolks used to say he was a crazy nigger, but what they really meant or should have meant was that he was confusing to them. Because if they knew him well enough to call him crazy they also had to know enough about him to realize that he wasn't foolhardy, or even careless, not even what they wanted to mean when they used to call somebody biggity. Somehow or other it was as if they respected him precisely because he didn't seem to care anything about them one way or the other. They certainly respected the fact that he wasn't going to take any foolishness off of them.

Gasoline Point folks also said he was crazy. But they meant their own meaning. Because when they said crazy they really meant something else, they meant exactly the same thing as when they called him a fool. At some point some time ago (probably when my favorite teacher was Miss Lexine Metcalf) I decided that what they were talking about was something like poetic madness, and that was their way of saying that he was forever doing something unheard of if not downright outrageous, doing the hell out of it, and not only getting away with whatever it was, but making you like it to boot. You could tell that was the way they felt by the way they almost always shook their heads laughing even as they said it, and sometimes even before they said it: Old crazy Luzana Cholly can sure play the fool out of that guitar. Old crazy Luzana Cholly is a guitar playing fool and a card playing fool and a pistol packing fool and a freight train snagging fool, and don't care who knows it.

I still cannot remember ever having heard anybody saying anything about Luzana Cholly's mother and father. Most of the time you forgot all about that part of his existence just as most people had probably long since forgotten whether they had ever heard his family name. Nobody I know ever heard him use it, and no sooner had you thought about it than you suddenly realized that he didn't seem ever to have had or to have needed any family at all. Nor did he seem to need a wife or steady woman either. But that was because he was not yet ready to quit the trail and settle down. Because he had lived with more women from time to time and place to place than the average man could or would even try to shake a stick at.

The more I think about all of that the more I realize that you never could tell which part of what you heard about something he had done had actually happened and which part somebody else had probably made up. Nor did it ever really matter which was which.

Not to anybody I ever knew in Gasoline Point, Alabama, in any case, to most of whom all you had to do was mention his name and they were ready to believe any claim you made for him, the more outrageously improbable the better. All you had to do was say Luzana Cholly old Luzana Cholly old Luze. All you had to do was see that sporty limp walk. Not to mention his voice, which was as smoke-blue sounding as the Philamayork-skyline-blue mist beyond blue steel railroad bridges. Not to mention how he was forever turning guitar strings into train whistles which were not only the once-upon-a-time voices of storytellers but of all the voices saying what was being said in the stories as well.

The Historical Mistake

Howell Raines

At 7:30 that evening, people had these positions: Franklin D. Roosevelt was in Georgia; Bluenose Trogdon was in the Sipsey River gorge; B. B. Laster was in his house on the Crane Hill Road; Blake King was in her father's house on the Fever Springs Road; I was above my grandfather who was sleeping in Jesus. I was taking some whiskey and thinking:

—That future historians will not want to overlook the cemeteries of America, least of all that of Milo, Alabama. In it is buried Elroy Laster, my cousin, a Pover County farmer who got a job helping build the bridge over the Sipsey gorge and, being unused to work in high places, fell off. He was one of seven so killed, according to a plaque at the bridge. I never saw him. In it is buried my mother, who died young. I did see her, but not for long. In it is buried my grandfather, a reluctant soldier who was drafted into the Confederate Army at gunpoint by conscription patrols from the slaveholding counties to the south. My grandfather, who turned fifteen in the last year of the war, was not alone in his reluctance. The Peace Society was strong in the hill counties because no one owned any slaves to fight a war over. Winston County, just north of us, seceded from Alabama when

Alabama went into the Confederacy. This was not wise. The patrols did a lot of hanging and burning in Winston County. In the other free counties, most people did what my grandfather did, which was to go on to the war and surrender the first chance he got. I always counted his action most admirable, an adjustment to things as they were. Since he survived it, the war was an adventure for my grandfather and I think it made him a man.

—That the chief adventure he had was the dog in the road. When the war ended, my grandfather started walking home from Virginia. In South Carolina, there was a dog in the road. Nearby was a plantation house of the type built by people who had a reason to fight the war. There were people watching from the portico of the house, and my grandfather asked them to give him food and also to speak to their dog on his behalf. They did neither. The dog had its head down and was growling. It was a big dog and meant to kill him, my grandfather judged. The people meant to let it. He was afraid that if he killed their dog, they would kill him. On the other hand, his options were limited. He stunned the dog with the first lick of his staff, popped its head like a watermelon with the second. The people watching from the big house never said a mumbling word.

—That this was a family legend. I never saw my grandfather. He was buried under the long, elevated granite slab upon which I sat as if on a park bench, drinking whiskey. The slab's inscription said:

BRANTLEY LASTER

1849–1890

ASLEEP IN JESUS

—That my grandfather was part of what I called the Historical Mistake and what one of my history professors used to call "the perfidy of the mountain north." For a while, this professor was a very important man in my life. He was from Montgomery, and he claimed he was very close to the family of the girl who had married the writer F. Scott Fitzgerald—an "honorary cousin" he called himself. He said that people like Fitzgerald's wife would guarantee the perpetuation of the "Confederate nobiliary tradition" in American letters. There was a time at the University when I believed such shit, when I could have slit my throat for not being from that rich and gracious, mist-shiny country where Scott Fitzgerald got his wife.

—That my enlightenment began the day the honorary cousin of

Fitzgerald's wife lectured about "the hillbilly-nigger alliance" in the Reconstruction. He made us copy down a quotation from a Montgomery *Advertiser* editorial from 1870. He held up the fragile, yellowed old paper, said it had been in his family for years. It moved him very much to read it:

> South Alabama raises her manacled hands in mute appeal to the mountain counties. The chains on the wrists of her sons and the midnight shrieks of her women sound continually in their ears. Is there a white man in North Alabama so lost to all his finer feelings of human nature to slight her appeal?

Had they heard my grandfather when he asked for help?

—That I figured out the lie for myself, which is the only way you can learn about it at the University. You will not be told by the professors from Montgomery and Mobile and Selma, who have decided to spend their lives teaching the lie of their fathers, that they were the sinned-against rather than the sinners, that men like my grandfather were history's villains and its fools. No, they will stay there until they are old men, telling the lie; and they will send their sons to Sewanee or Davidson or Washington and Lee, where the sons can learn to tell the lie in all its high Episcopal splendor, so that conceivably the lie can get better and deeper and more like truth with each generation, until finally even the niggers and sons of hillbillies will believe it, and perhaps the gentlemen-scholars themselves can forget how their people had started a war too big for them and had to make other men fight it for them and lost it anyway and finally were reduced to begging our help to make the free slaves keep on picking cotton for nothing. Of course, they got their way in the end. Even the Reconstruction, for all their wailing about manacles and nigger-rape, was not more than an inconvenience. In the end they had had to suck up to the new Yankee money in Birmingham, but they came out of it running the state the way they ran the University, which was why the last road cut, the last river bridged, the last school built was always in the hills, the land of the nigger-dumb white slaves. The gentlemen-scholars taught none of that, but I learned it anyway and kept it to myself. When you do not believe the prevailing lie, it is best to keep silent, lest you get something like Winston County got, something that will not please you.

—That losing Blake was part of my education in regard to the true meaning of the Historical Mistake and how it reached across the years to dictate the direction of all things trivial and grand, who would win and who would lose. I remembered walking in the darkness down University Boulevard, listening to the whiskey dances going on in the fraternity houses. I remembered dry October nights and the rich boys' laughter drifting down with the music from the verandas where their women moved like clouds. I knew then that if I ever lost Blake it would be to that other South, their world of ease and twilight laughter.

—That the best times I ever had were during my freshman year at Alabama, the year before the letters started coming. The train bringing me from Tuscaloosa would pass on through Atlanta and before long it would be pulling slowly into the little Decatur station, long, curling clouds of steam whipping back past the windows on the winter air. I would look out and see the red-brick buildings of the college set back in the oaks, and Blake would be waiting there on the platform, hugging herself in the frigid afternoon light. Then she would spy me through the coach window and run to meet me, her long coat flying.

The flask was half empty, and I had taken just the right amount of whiskey—enough to help, but not enough to show.

I got up from my grandfather's grave, left the cemetery and walked on out the Fever Springs Road to Blake's house. It was the only house around Milo that had a lawn of grass rather than swept dirt. Riley King was something of a gardener. In fact, he was an educated and civilized man and for that reason lonely, a man out of place, living testimony to the fact that staying in Milo was a habit you needed to break early and for good. I knelt down to pet the King's old dog, one of those long-haired curs we called shepherds on the theory that a dog of that type could be trained to herd sheep in a country that had sheep.

Blake's voice came out of the darkness of the porch.

"Daddy wants you to come in," she said.

I heard the porch swing squeak as she got up and came to the top of the steps to meet me. Her silhouette moved in front of the yellow window; light from the window spilled across the yard beside me. The dog stood in the light.

Riley King just wanted to tell me how proud he was of us. In all the years he had been principal at Pover County High, he said, this was the first time that two people from the same class had finished college. He said Blake was going to teach for him in the coming year and that he wished he had an opening for me.

I thanked him and said I didn't think teaching was in my line anyway. Standing there in Riley King's house with his daughter made me feel guilty about reviving the old poaching joke with Ozro, guilty but a little powerful, also. Riley King was a widower. He had raised Blake from an infant by himself. She meant the world to him, and I had spent a lot of years worrying that he would find out about Blake and me. Blake, with that damnable boldness of hers, had never feared getting caught as much as I had. Yet, once it started between us at so young an age, there was never any question of stopping. Having Blake became as necessary as breathing. All the time we were growing up, I couldn't escape the feeling that I was doing Riley King some deep and cutting harm. But I knew this, too. I could have set him on fire and watched him burn rather than give up his daughter.

"Thanks for being so nice to him," Blake said later, as we strolled down the road toward Milo.

"It was nothing. I'm nice to everyone. It's just the way I am."

"I know," she said softly.

"For god's sake, Blake, I was being sarcastic."

I looked over at her walking beside me. Her face was indistinct in the darkness.

"I know that, too," she said, "but it's still true. You were always the kindest, most gentle person in everything we did."

There, she had done it, touched the first tentative finger to the stinging nettle of our old physical familiarity. For years I had been her gentle lover, more led than leading. Losing her had changed that. I had learned that the secret to getting laid in Tuscaloosa was to be exactly the kind of man the gentlemen-scholars professed to despise—to be brutal, a liar, a man of faint honor, to be exactly what their old fathers, by the proof of history, had been. I say I learned it, but the learning was not altogether in my control. A certain rage was involved and that, too, had to do with Blake.

"Are you still nice?" she said, not without a mild, elusive sarcasm of her own. "Is Brantley Laster still a nice boy to know?"

"Don't be coy," I said.

"Why do you make this so difficult? I just came back to see how you are. Aren't you glad to see me at all?"

"Surprised," I said, "more surprised than anything."

"You're not giving an inch, are you?"

"You broke me of that, two years ago."

We walked on down the deserted road toward Milo, walked without touching, as if the first brush of arm against arm could obligate us back into all the old intimacies. It had been more than two years, in fact. Late in my second year at the University, I began getting letters from Blake that were not like all the other letters she had written.

"You broke me of that when I started getting those wonderful letters saying how you were no longer the most homesick girl at Agnes Scott. I won't lie to you, Blake. I quit loving you in self-defense. That was what I learned at the University, and I learned it better than anything else."

Which was a lie. I had never learned it so well at all. But there was no mistake about what the letters had done to me. They had burned themselves into my memory, until I could think of nothing else. I had thought about the letters until I knew I would be headed for Tuscaloosa's other famous institution if I did not teach myself to stop. The letters. At first, there had been only the casual mention that she had decided to go to some parties as a cure for the pain of being away from me. I should do the same, she wrote; it would be good for both of us; she was making good friends, but it was nothing serious. Then, came the letters about the special good friend, patiently explaining how it might be something serious in a way she didn't quite understand yet, but we should keep in touch. That summer I went home for my last trip until I graduated, but Blake was not there. She was on holiday, Riley King told me, with good friends from college.

"It didn't have to be that way," she said. "You chose the way it would be, that we wouldn't stay in touch."

"You gave me a wonderful hell of a choice," I said. "You were going to belong to somebody else, but I could keep writing you letters if I wanted, and I would get back letters from you saying how wonderful it all was. It didn't seem a very promising way to live."

"It wouldn't have been like that," she said.

"How would it have been?"

We had reached the Y, which was vacant now of the mule wagons, Hoover wagons, the few cars and trucks that had brought the people in from the sticks to see Franklin D. Roosevelt. Blake and I stopped walking and paused for a moment to look out across the broad, hard-packed dirt expanse where the three roads met. Milo, our home-town—two stores, a constable's shack, the post office in the crotch of the Y, the railroad shed down by the T&G crossing—in the wake of Roosevelt's passage had settled back already into its high and hopeless isolation. Off across the Y in front of us I could see against the night sky the tall false front of the Good Neighbor Mercantile. I felt in my pocket for the key to the heavy iron padlock on its front door.

"Oh, Brant," Blake said softly, "I don't know, I just don't know."

It took me a moment to realize that she was answering the question I had asked some time earlier. I had not expected an answer. It was not that sort of question.

"Come on," I said. "Let's go open the store and get a Coke."

We drank them in the back, leaning against the cash register counter, burning only a single kerosene lamp. It threw a circle of amber light, steady and dim like the illumination in an old painting. As I stood beside her in that mellow light, I thought of Blake's body, trim and familiar under her light dress, and regret washed through me like a tide.

"I don't believe what you say about choices," she said, watching the Coke bottle as she twirled it in her fingers, tracing lines in its skin of moisture. "Life isn't like that. We were together for a long time, then we had to be apart, and now we are together again. You live each time as it comes. No one can change the past for you. You must live as if it didn't exist."

"That's the way you lived in Atlanta," I said, "—as if I never existed. It's a talent I don't have, Blake, ignoring the past. Not to know everything that's happened is like being kept from some great secret. You not only don't know the secret, but you don't know if others think you a fool."

Blake listened with her head lowered, her hair swinging forward along each side of her face in curving brown curtains. I knew I could put my hands in her hair, lift her face, kiss her if I wanted to, have her right there if I wanted, and that if I did that, all my resolve would be gone and, if I had learned anything, my survival, too.

"Can't you see you want to be treated like a child, Brant, wanting someone to make everything perfect for you? You have to take the rough with the smooth."

"Don't condescend to me," I snapped.

"I'm sorry, Brant, but I want you to see how crazy it is. Who cares about us? Who is it that is supposed to know this great secret, to think you a fool?"

"You know the answers," I said.

"I just don't see how it matters."

"Maybe you really don't," I said. "I've thought about it so long and have it so straight that maybe I assume you have it figured out, too. Maybe it never crossed your mind the way I would feel or maybe you didn't want to think about it. Look, I know you, Blake. I know the way you are in love, how you don't hold anything back. So now you've been with someone else and what can you tell me except the truth about the way you were with him? And the truth doesn't leave us anything, because when I know that, I can't go on."

I stopped. Just to talk about the way she might have been in other cities, with other lovers, stirred that old lust for vengeance, those old self-defeating obsessions it had taken me so long to conquer. I had spent a lot of time learning how not to think of things; I didn't want to go back.

"Maybe you don't know everything you think you know," she said.

She looked at me, fixed me with a faint, innocent smile, holding out the promise that although she might have loved legions after me, she had never gone with them where we had gone. It might have worked, too—hell, would have worked; I'd have taken her back right then, fulfilled all Miss Sarahgrace's predictions in a minute—but for one piece of knowledge that scratched around inside my brain like the single grain of sand that makes the oyster build its pearl.

"I know enough," I said. "I know plenty of things that might surprise you."

"Surprise me," she said, holding the same confident, patronizing look. And I wanted to surprise her, but to tell Blake what I knew and how I had come to know it would cost more than it was worth. Even if I could never have her, I wanted her to think of me in a way she could not if she knew everything I had done to find out about her.

"What could I say to surprise you?" I said. "You know everything you did. I only know a little."

Blake put her Coke bottle down on the counter and moved in closer to me, putting herself within my reach. I felt myself buffeted by the power she had when she was turning her whole attention on you, making you feel like the only person in her universe.

"You talk like a detective," she said, "always going on about what you know. Maybe you should pay more attention to what you feel. That's why I came back here, Brant, because here with you I always felt like a whole person. I wanted to feel that way again, that oneness I had when I was with you. When I didn't have you, there was always something missing. Doesn't it mean anything to you that I came back?"

"Yes, it means something," I said. "It means you got ditched. Your wonderful Georgia Tech man dropped you like a bad habit."

"We just don't see each other any more," she said.

"I thought that would never happen," I said. "In your last letter, you said you were feeling so sure you were going to marry him it was unfair not to tell me. You were very considerate. You said I had a right to know."

"I was wrong," she said. "I didn't love him that much."

"And him?"

"I don't know. Maybe he didn't love me all that much, either."

"After all you did for him," I said.

"You bastard," she said softly, backing away from me a little. "Don't you realize I could have had any of them, kept them I mean, anybody over there I wanted. You just don't know what it was like over there."

"I know more than I want to," I said. "I know you got ditched by your fine blond-haired fraternity boy."

And I realized suddenly that I had gone in further than I had intended, said more than I should have said. I had given the actual physical description of a man I was supposed never to have seen. Yet Blake just stood there, looking puzzled, and I thought it surely must be an act. I might have saved us both a lot of grief if I had told all I knew right then. For I thought I knew a great deal, and as it would turn out, I did not know the main things at all. What I knew was no more than one thread of the hangman's rope.

"Is that supposed to be a joke, the thing about the blond-haired boy?"

"Yes," I said, "a joke, a little riddle." Thinking she was still lying, I added: "Don't pretend you don't know what I'm talking about."

"I swear I don't," she said.

"You're really getting quite good at this," I said. "Would you like a drink?"

I took out the half-empty whiskey flask and held it out to her, but she had withdrawn into her own fierce and puzzled beauty, into that damnable strength she had. She folded in upon herself, became a rock, beyond me, beyond curiosity about anything I could say.

"I think I'm ready to go home," she said.

So I closed down the store, left it in darkness, and walked her in silence back out the Fever Springs Road, past the cemetery, past the high school where she would teach, back to her home, where we stood in the black shadows of the porch.

"I don't understand why you treat me like this," Blake said at her door.

"You try," I said. "It's not hard to figure out. You might say I know the truth and the truth has made me free. I have adjusted to things as they are."

"Don't talk that way," she said. "It's just a way of making yourself distant from me. You know that you were as free of me as I was of you."

"Yes, I accept that. We both made our choices."

"I hope your choice will make you happy, Brant. Will you be happy being free of me?"

"Maybe I will."

Then she went inside and I went out in the night thinking I had done what I had to do, ripped it with her for fair and all and ever.

Free of Blake is another lie, of course, a way I never was. Even after I became good at not thinking of her, I always had the dream I had gotten on my last trip to Atlanta. I had caught the train without warning Blake that I was on my way, believing like a fool that I could change her mind if only I could see her one more time. The trip had remained my secret; I never let Blake see me. But after that I always had the dream with its images of blasted landscapes flickering past the train window—first the dead steel mills of Birmingham, then the linthead factories of Georgia where the Scotts piled up the money to build their fine college for ladies, next the dreary sprawl at Atlanta, and finally the college itself, the fine buildings, their bright windows shining down through the trees at dusk. Whenever it came, the dream brought back the foolish feeling of finding myself in the darkness outside Blake's dormitory, my only baggage the packet of farewell letters from her, and only then realizing what a fool's mission had brought me there unannounced, unwanted, a reminder of an accident which had happened a long time ago in her life. Everything was in the dream, every detail of how I found her free and happy with the blond-haired young man in the fine clothes; seeing Blake again revived the dream in all its power, and the memory of it cut like a new razor falling through flesh as easily as through air, cutting to the bone. The dream was enough of itself, but it was also the symbol of much more, for if there had been me and then another in my place, there was the possibility of an infinity of betrayals I had never dreamt of. I had had the dream long enough to know it had no cure, but I went to find the medicine man anyway.

Biographical Sketches

The Old Southwest

Johnson Jones Hooper

Perhaps the best known of early Alabama authors, Johnson J. Hooper was born in Wilmington, North Carolina, in 1815. The son of a failed newspaperman, Hooper went to Lafayette, Alabama, in 1835, to study law in his brother George's office and was subsequently admitted to the Alabama bar. He married Mary Brantly in 1842 and then embarked on a career as a journalist, becoming editor of the Layfayette *East Alabamian,* where he published his first short story, "Taking Census in Alabama," in August of 1843. The story was read and reprinted by William Porter in his *New York Spirit of the Times* in September. In 1845, Hooper published his most famous work, *Some Adventures of Captain Suggs,* a series of sketches, written in part to parody certain popular campaign literature of the era, but also establishing the titular character as one of the most vivid and interesting figures in all of Southwestern Humor. Hooper's interest in politics and political writing shortly led him to Wetumpka, Alabama, to edit the *Alabama Whig,* and later to the state capital, Montgomery, to write for the *Alabama Journal.* Poor health forced him to abandon this endeavor, and he returned to Lafayette to practice law. Though he published two other books, *A Ride With Old Kit Kunker* (1849) and *The Widow Rugby's Husband* (1851), Hooper began to resent his reputation as a humorist, wishing to be considered a "serious" journalist and politician. He moved to Richmond, Virginia, where he died in 1862.

Joseph G. Baldwin

Born at Winchester, in the Shenandoah Valley of Virginia, in 1815, Joseph Glover Baldwin moved around the South before coming to Gainesville, in Sumter County, in 1839. A lawyer by profession, as were many of the literary practitioners of Southwestern humor, he served in 1844 as a representative in the state legislature, and in 1849 he made an unsuccessful run for Congress. It was also during these years that Baldwin wrote his famous work, *Flush Times in Alabama and Mississippi*, an extended set of sketches whose rascally heroes were often considered an affront to various polite sensibilities. To criticism, he would generally reply, "Who ever heard of a tolerable hero?" During his writing career, Baldwin produced two other works, *Party Leaders* and *S.S. Prentiss;* but he also remained heavily engaged in the law. He moved briefly to Mobile in 1853, and then a year later left Alabama for good, moving to California, where he recorded a distinguished career as a lawyer and ultimately served as Chief Justice of the California Supreme Court. His death came in 1864.

John Gorman Barr

John Barr, the true prodigy of early Alabama literature, was born in 1823 in Milton, North Carolina. In 1826, his family moved to Raleigh, where his father died. Then, in 1835, he moved with his mother to Tuscaloosa, where she too died. The orphaned Barr did well on his own, however. He apprenticed himself to a printer and was sent to the University by a local merchant who admired his mind and ambition, entering at age fourteen and taking his master's degree at eighteen. He studied law and was admitted to the bar in 1843 at age twenty. After service in the Mexican War, Barr returned to Tuscaloosa to practice law and help edit the Tuscaloosa *Observer*. His first short story, "Salted Him or An Auctioneer Dooin All the Bidding," was published under the pen name of "Omega" in William Porter's *New York Spirit of the Times*. He later published other stories there, but then quit writing in 1857 to pursue a career in politics, seeking nomination for a congressional seat but ultimately withdrawing his name to avoid a convention deadlock. This gesture earned him the consulship to Australia from James Buchanan. But he never arrived. Barr died at sea of sunstroke two days out of Brisbane in 1858.

Alabama Baroque

Caroline Lee Hentz

Caroline Lee Hentz was born in Massachusetts, but after marrying Nicholas M. Hentz in 1824, she spent most of her adult life in the South, including eighteen years in Alabama at Florence, Tuscaloosa, and Tuskegee. While she had done some writing during this time, including an early work, *Aunt Patty's Scrap Bag*, it was only after she moved again, in 1848, to Columbus, Georgia, that she committed herself fully to a literary career. Of her later life there, and in Marianna, Florida, came several more books, including *Linda; Rena, or the Snow Bird; Ernest Lynwood;* and, probably her most famous production, *The Planter's Northern Bride*.

Augusta Evans Wilson

Born in Columbus, Georgia, in 1835, Augusta Evans Wilson spent her early childhood in Texas, and then in 1851 moved with her family to Mobile, where she remained for the rest of her life and became surely the best-known Alabama writer of the nineteenth century. Her literary career began prodigiously early and went on for a long time: her first novel, *Inez, a Tale of the Alamo*, was completed when she was fifteen; her last, *Devota*, was published in 1907, two years before her death. In between, becoming along the way the wife of Col. L. M. Wilson and the lady of "Ashland Place," she published a string of immensely popular novels including *Beulah, Infelice, Macaria, St. Elmo, 'Vashti, At the Mercy of Tiberius*, and, after a fifteen year hiatus, *The Speckled Bird*. Although derided at times for her ornate style and sentimental didacticism, Mrs. Wilson enjoyed throughout her life great public celebrity; and her writing also produced for her one of the first major incomes to be made by any woman author in America, with lifetime earnings of more than $100,000.

Samuel Minturn Peck

Known chiefly as a poet, Samuel Peck was born in Tuscaloosa in 1854, the youngest of nine children. He grew up there and attended the University, taking an A.M. degree in 1876. He then went to New York City to study medicine at Bellevue Medical College and duly received his M.D. in 1879; but he declared that he had "no taste for medicine" and never practiced, turning instead to writing. In 1886, his first volume of poetry, *Caps and Bells,* was published to moderate popular acclaim. He published six more volumes of poetry before 1925, including *Rings and Love Knots* (1892), *Rhymes and Roses* (1895), *Maybloom and Myrtle* (1910), and *The Autumn Trail* (1925). The culmination of his long career came in 1931, when the Alabama legislature established the State Laureateship in his honor, a post he held until his death in 1938.

Alabama Flowering I

Edgar Valentine Smith

Edgar Valentine Smith was born in 1875 in Jemison, Chilton County, and spent the major part of his adult life in Birmingham, where he was one of the most celebrated figures in a literary circle called "The Loafers," other members of which included Octavus Roy Cohen and James Saxon Childers. In 1923, Smith gained national attention with "Prelude," which was judged the best short story written in the country and winner of the O. Henry Prize. Other O. Henry awards followed for the stories " 'Lijah" and "Cock-a-Doodle-Done." Despite this measure of fame, however, Smith continued to work throughout his most productive years at what he considered his primary occupation of journalism with the *Birmingham News.*

Zelda Sayre Fitzgerald

Wife of F. Scott Fitzgerald and herself a major figure of the Jazz Age, Zelda Sayre was born in Montgomery in 1900. After a rebellious teen age that included her being enshrined as a legendary partygoer at the University of Alabama, she married Fitzgerald in 1920 as the finale of a tempestuous, long-distance courtship that began while Scott was in the army stationed near Montgomery. The famous couple traveled about Europe and America leaving a trail of anecdotes behind them. They settled for a while in Hollywood, but returned East a short time later. In this period Zelda published several short stories, including "Southern Girl" and "The Ice Palace," and various essays and sketches. About 1927, her mental health began to deteriorate severely, and from 1930 until her death she was in and out of various institutions. She did publish a novel in 1932, *Save Me the Waltz,* and a play in 1933, *Scandalabra*. Her last years were spent between her mother's house in Montgomery and the Highland mental hospital in Asheville, North Carolina, where she died in a fire in 1948.

T. S. Stribling

T. S. Stribling, along with William March one of the better-known Alabama writers of the first part of this century, was born in 1881 in Clifton, Tennessee. He spent nearly all of his life, however, in north Alabama, studying at the Normal College of Florence (now the University of North Alabama), and, after taking a law degree at the University of Alabama, returning there in 1905 to begin a career. He found the work unrewarding, however, and in 1921 turned to literature. In the years following, he published a considerable number of novels, the best known of which, *The Forge* (1931), *The Store* (1932), and *Unfinished Cathedral* (1938), may be thought of as forming a north Alabama trilogy. *The Store* also brought Stribling the Pulitzer Prize. He continued his long and productive career in Florence, with two brief intervals of teaching novel writing at Columbia University in 1946 and 1950, until his death in 1965.

Sara Haardt Mencken

Sara Haardt was born in Montgomery in 1899 and began her outstanding intellectual career at the Margaret Booth School there, from which she graduated in 1916. She then went to Baltimore and Goucher College, where she graduated Phi Beta Kappa in History in 1920. It was at Goucher that she published her first short story, "The Rattlesnake," in 1917. She subsequently taught at both Goucher and Booth. In 1922, she wrote a series of sketches for the Richmond *Reviewer* entitled "Strictly Southern," and in 1923 she published "Joe Moore and Callie Blasingame" in *Smart Set,* which was edited by H. L. Mencken. Thus began a seven-year courtship which ended in their marriage in 1930. Meanwhile, she continued to publish, and even after the marriage always under her original name. "Miss Rebecca" ran in the Richmond *Reviewer* in July 1924, and later that year the Baltimore *Evening Sun* published a series of her editorials. The author fell ill, however, in 1925, and took some time away from writing to recover, and while she became well enough to travel to

Hollywood for some screenplay work in 1927, she never regained full health. Nonetheless, she continued to write essays and stories, including "A Little Girl Grows Up," and "Dear Life," as well as a novel, *The Making of a Lady*. A final collection of stories, *Southern Album*, was published by Mencken after her death from meningitis in 1935.

Howell Vines

Howell Vines was born at Short Creek, Alabama, in 1899. He grew up and went to school in Jefferson County. He attended the University of Alabama, and later, Harvard. Vines's career included the teaching of literature at Shorter College, Rice University, and the University of Richmond. He published two novels, *A River Goes With Heaven* (1930), and *This Green Thicket World* (1934). He also published short stories in the *Atlantic Monthly* and the *Saturday Review*.

William March

The celebrated Alabama author William March was born William Edward Campbell in Mobile in 1893. He attended the University of Valparaiso in Indiana and studied law at the University of Alabama, working afterward as a law clerk in New York City until joining the U.S. Marines to fight in World War I. Returning from the war to Mobile, he undertook a successful career in business, becoming eventually vice-president of the Waterman Steamship Company. Close to a decade later, during an incapacitating illness, he developed much of the narrative that would become his first novel, the immensely vivid and innovative *Company K*. Afterward, although traveling widely in Europe and America and remaining heavily involved in business pursuits, March continued to concentrate on his writing. *Company K* was published in 1933; *Come In at the Door* in 1934; *The Tallons* in 1936; *October Island* in 1952; and *The Bad Seed* in 1954. He also became an immensely gifted and prolific writer of short fiction, publishing widely in leading periodicals and prize story anthologies, as well as in individual book-length collections such as *The Little Wife and Other Stories, Some Like Them Short,* and *Trial Balance: The Collected Short Stories*. While returning to Mobile throughout his adult life for several periods of residence, he moved finally to New Orleans, where his death came in 1954.

Alabama Flowering II

Harriett Hassell

Harriett Hassell was born on a farm near Northport, in Tuscaloosa County, in 1911. At age fifteen, she entered the University, but within a brief time began a seven-year absence, during which she published several stories and articles. Returning to the University to study with Hudson Strode, she quickly produced "History of the South," published in the October 1937 issue of *Story* magazine, and judged winner of that year's National College Short Story Contest. More national celebrity followed with the publication by Harper's in 1938 of *Rachel's Children,* considered to this day one of the most sensitive and acute depictions ever rendered by a young novelist of family life in the early twentieth-century South.

Shirley Ann Grau

Shirley Ann Grau was born in New Orleans in 1930, but she spent most of her years of growing up in Montgomery. Her first book, *The Black Prince and Other Stories* (1955), established a literary reputation quickly enhanced by the publication of novels such as *The Hard Blue Sky* (1958), *The House on Coliseum Street* (1961), *The Keepers of the House* (1964), *The Condor Passes* (1973), and *Evidence of Love,* and a further collection of stories, *The Wind Shifting West* (1973). She has also been a prolific writer for periodicals, with work appearing in *The New Yorker, Mademoiselle, Saturday Evening Post,* and *Atlantic Monthly.* Her greatest public honor has come with *The Keepers of the House,* for which she won the 1964 Pulitzer Prize.

Harper Lee

Harper Lee grew up in Monroeville, Alabama, where she was born Nelle Harper Lee in 1926. She attended the University of Alabama in the mid-1950s, and then moved to New York where she worked for a brief time at a desk job, but shortly thereafter began to concentrate full time on *To Kill a Mockingbird.* This novel, her only one to date, was published in 1960 to immense praise and was the next year awarded the Pulitzer Prize.

Cecil Dawkins

Cecil Dawkins was born in Birmingham in 1927 and received her undergraduate degree in 1949 from the University in Tuscaloosa, where she studied creative writing with Hudson Strode. She went on to Stanford University on a creative writing fellowship, completing a master's degree in 1953, and then taught at Stephens College in Missouri until 1958. Her short fiction has appeared in the *Paris Review*, the *Sewanee Review*, the *Georgia Review*, and the *Saturday Evening Post*. Her book-length publications include a collection of short stories, *The Quiet Enemy*, and *The Live Goat*, a novel.

Elise Sanguinetti

Elise Sanguinetti was born in 1926 in Anniston, where her father was Harry M. Ayers, the well-known publisher of *The Anniston Star*. Receiving her early education in private schools in the South, she went on to study at St. Olaf's College in Northfield, Minnesota, and also at the University of Oslo, Norway. Then, returning to Alabama, she attended the University in Tuscaloosa, where she became a creative writing student of Hudson Strode. Her first novel, *The Last of the Whitfields*, was published in 1962 and received great critical praise, with frequent comparisons to the work of J. D. Salinger and Harper Lee. During her subsequent career, she has continued to place well-received novels with major publishers, including *The New Girl* (1964), *The Dowager* (1968), and *McBee's Station* (1971). With her husband, Philip Sanguinetti, she now lives in Anniston, where she continues to write and also to contribute generously in time and effort to the promotion of various cultural activities in the state and region.

William Cobb

William Cobb was born in 1938 in Greene County and was educated in the public schools of Demopolis. He received his B.A. from Livingston University and his M.A. from Vanderbilt, where he studied with Donald Davidson. "The Stone Soldier" was the title entry and Reader's Digest Foundation first-prize winner in *Prize College Stories of 1964*, published by the editors of *Story* magazine. Mr. Cobb continues to write and teach at the University of Montevallo.

Alabama Fiction Today

Charles Gaines

Charles Gaines was born in Birmingham in 1942 and grew up there. A graduate of Birmingham-Southern, he also attended the University in the early 1960s and then worked for a time as an administrator for the federal government in Green Bay. His first novel, *Stay Hungry,* was published in 1972. In addition, he has written short stories and articles for magazines such as *Harper's* and *Sports Illustrated,* as well as documentary works on sports including *Pumping Iron* and *Staying Hard.* His latest fiction is an adventure novel, *Dangler.*

Albert Murray

Albert Murray, a distinguished teacher and lecturer as well as an author, was born in Nokomis, Alabama. He grew up in Mobile and later attended school at Tuskegee Institute, where he also taught literature for a time. He then began a career in the air force, from which he retired with the rank of major. He has since taught at Colgate University and the University of Massachusetts, and has delivered the Brick lectures at the University of Missouri. Besides many short stories and critical essays, Murray has published *The Omni-Americans* (1970), *South to a Very Old Place* (1972), *Train Whistle Guitar* (1974), and the lecture series, *The Hero and the Blues.*

Howell Raines

Raines was born in Birmingham in 1943 and grew up in the hill country of northern Alabama. After graduating from Birmingham-Southern, in the early 1960s he worked as a reporter for the Birmingham *News* and *Post-Herald.* He then moved to Atlanta, where he was political editor for the *Constitution* and where he is currently employed by the New York *Times.* He was nominated for a Pulitzer Prize in National Reporting for his coverage of Jimmy Carter's 1976 presidential campaign. Raines also contributed to the collection of political essays, *Campaign Money,* in 1976. He has published two books, the novel, *Whiskey Man,* and *My Soul is Rested,* a chronicle of the Southern civil-rights movement, both in 1977.

About the Editor

Philip D. Beidler is Assistant Dean of the Graduate School and Professor of English at The University of Alabama. He received his B.A. degree from Davidson College and his M.A. and Ph.D. from the University of Virginia. He is author of *American Literature and the Experience of Vietnam* (University of Georgia Press, 1982) and is co-editor of *The Mythologizing of Mark Twain* (University of Alabama Press, 1984).